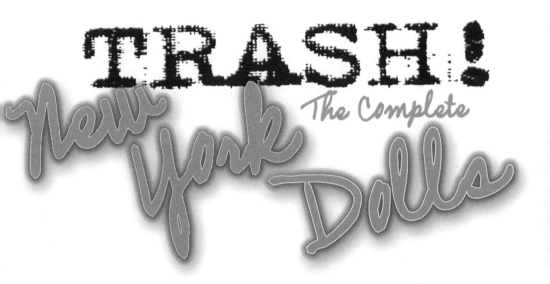

TRASH! The Complete New York Dolls

KRIS NEEDS & DICK PORTER

Plexus, London

For Michelle and Donna.

Dedicated to the memory of
Arthur Kane, Jerry Nolan, Johnny Thunders and Billy Murcia.

'The New York Dolls were a great attitude. If nothing else, they
were a great attitude.' – *Johnny Thunders*

All rights reserved including the right of
reproduction in whole or in part in any form
Copyright © 2006 by Kris Needs and Dick Porter
Published by Plexus Publishing Limited
25 Mallinson Road
London SW11 1BW
www.plexusbooks.com

British Library Cataloguing In Publication Data

Needs, Kris
  Trash! : the complete New York Dolls
  1. New York Dolls (Musical Group) 2. Rock musicians -
  States - Biography
  I. Title II.Porter, Dick
  782.4'2166'0922

ISBN 10: 0-85965-369-2
ISBN 13: 978-0-85965-369-5

Printed and bound in Great Britain
Book and cover design by Rebecca Martin

Contents

Acknowledgements

Special thanks to Rick Rivets for his ceaseless assistance throughout the writing of *Trash*! Also to, Stu Wylder, Steve Conte, Joey K, Roberta Bayley, Suzi Quatro, Diana Bailey, Adrian Perkins, and Craig McIntosh, who either provided some excellent interview material, answered thorny questions or otherwise oiled wheels.

For helping with photographs at the eleventh hour, I would like to give special thanks to Chris Ridpath for his own and Michael Geary's photographs of the Dolls at the Mercer Arts Centre; also special thanks for helping with photographs to Brian Young, Chris Duda, Dennis Recla and Joseph Donnelly. Additional thanks to Amelia Pearson and Christabel Olech for the provision of essential assistance and materials, and the largest of shouts to Donna Greene for putting up with it all.

Dick Porter

Special thanks also go to those whose input, past and present, played an essential part in this story: Sylvain Sylvain – 'the heart and soul of the New York Dolls' – for his blessing on this project and his war diaries. David Johansen for doing it again and the time in New York. Mariann Bracken, for looking after her little brother Johnny. Pete Frame, for his priceless interviews with David, Johnny and Jerry. Jayne County and Leee Black Childers, for being on form over 30 years later. Nina Antonia, for her support and relentless flying of the Dolls flag. Brian Young, for his archival goldmine and pure fan perspective. Simon Trakmarx, for keeping the faith and hooking us up. Carlton P. Sandecock, for the Syl connection. Alan Hauser, for Thunders anecdotes and records. Joseph and David Stopps/ FML, for technical assistance. Parker DuLany, the New York connection, for contagious inspiration. Phil Alexander, Nicky Denuth and Andrew Male at *Mojo* for letting me see the Dolls in New York. Michelle, my puss'n'boots, for being there again.

Honorary mentions, past and present: Gail Higgins Smith, Patti Palladin, Cherry Vanilla, Bob Gruen, Morrissey, Mick Jones, Keith Richards, Robin Banks, Deborah Harry and Chris Stein, Colin Keinch, Suicide, Mott the Hoople, Iggy, Lenny Kaye, Pat Gilbert, Simon and James Mattocks, Marty Thau, Walter Lure, Topper Headon, Johnny Green and family, Keith Smith, Tony James, Primal Scream, Clinton Heylin, Michelle Kerr and Dave Bason at Roadrunner Records, the Ramones, Gary Powell, Jonas Stone, my son Daniel Lee Needs, and the kids: Abbey, Chloe, Jamie and Ellie.

Kris Needs

Foreword

The Dolls were only supposed to last for a week or so. It wasn't meant to be a career. It was like a school musical project gone wild!

We were so far ahead of our time, we didn't even realise it. We never sat down around a big table and worked out a master plan to dress up as girls and shit. It all just happened between us. We didn't even realise what we were doing.

Everybody else took notes and took it to the bank, but we broke our legs because we were running so damn fast. We were actually inventing it all. We were young and screaming our generation's next move.

That's why I feel that kids are still picking up on it. As far as I'm concerned, every generation at one point or another finds something intriguing about the Dolls, whatever it is.

But you've got to make it on your own. It's kinda hard, but you've got to find your own way. Take your influences and love your influences. Live your own life. You can't live my life, or David's life, or Johnny's life. This is your time.

The only thing that we ever pass down: it is what it is and that's what it's gonna be.

Sylvain Sylvain, New York, 2006

A Place Where
They Don't
Expect Nothing

'To me, Ronnie Spector and Elvis Presley were the
first king and queen of punk.' *Sylvain Sylvain*

Think of any of the major players in the five-decade pantheon of rock'n'roll history, and it's likely their geographical backgrounds will also come to mind. Elvis Presley radiated the down-home politeness of a God-fearing hick from Southern-fried Memphis. The Beatles were quickly assimilated into the global consciousness as loveable Liverpudlian scallywags, establishing an archetype for Northern roguishness that remains an enduring feature of the British rock landscape. Similarly, the Beach Boys exuded blinding rays of wholesome sunshine, direct from sunny California.

Such positive associations were fitting for the fifties and sixties – decades that encompassed much that was progressive in terms of societal, techno-logical and creative advancement. However, as the 1970s got underway, a global financial squeeze began to bite. The optimism and energy that suf-fused the summer of love and put men on the moon was crushed on the wheel of harsh economic reality. Blasting astronauts at a sterile hunk of rock a quarter of a million miles away was deemed an expensive indulgence, and anyone hoping to drop out and put flowers in their hair was likely to become cold and hungry pretty quickly.

New York City was overspending its way to near-bankruptcy as a means of propping up its creaking public services. As the federal deficit rose to unprecedented levels, traumatised veterans began pouring home from Vietnam. These unfortunate volunteers and conscripts were an embarrass-ment to an administration that saw the ongoing conflict as a political liabili-ty, and significant numbers of the returning servicemen joined the hustlers, beggars and junkies on New York's sidewalks. The city still had glamour – but it was the desperate, fading allure of a diva in decline.

Right on cue, the New York Dolls emerged from the city's outer bor-oughs. They were a band that embodied all the ersatz glitz, excess, and deca-dence of the city from which they took their name. Just as much as Elvis, the Beatles or the Rolling Stones before them, the Dolls would represent a geo-graphic and cultural *zeitgeist*.

Back in the 1950s, as the hardships of World War II began to fade, young men and women on both sides of the Atlantic had looked to put their privations behind them and blow off some steam. Cash was still short, so cheap fun became the order of the day. A trip to the local dancehall provided an affordable night out, and a fuck afterwards was usually – more or less – free. Thus, we got the birth of rock'n'roll and a baby boom.

This population spike led to an increased demand for housing, which drove construction in the areas surrounding major cities. Behind the twitching curtains, suburbia rocked. The Rolling Stones became London's ambassadors to the world – except that they hailed from the suburban 'satellites' Johnny Rotten would decry a decade and a half later. At the time this hardly mattered, as their impact ensured they could represent the capital with surly ease. And anyhow, nobody in Des Moines lost any sleep worrying whether the Kings Road stretched as far as Dartford.

As those who could afford it escaped the crumbling inner cities for nicer, whiter neighbourhoods, bridge clubs and ghettos sprang forth in equal measure. London and New York became the economic, social and cultural hubs of vast outlying areas, populated by economic migrants who still identified themselves as 'Londoners' or 'New Yorkers'.

In New York, the outer boroughs developed distinct identities while remaining umbilically connected to the urban mothership. As Pulitzer Prize winning journalist Jimmy Breslin observed, the first-generation children of the new suburbs quickly developed their own attitudes: 'People born in Queens, raised to say that each morning they get on the subway and "go to the city", have a resentment of Manhattan, of the swiftness of its life and success of the people who live there.'

As rock'n'roll established its own constantly shifting tableau of style and fashion, being where it was at became very important indeed. In a milieu where coolness was the prime directive, it helped to be hip to the 24 hour buzz of the metropolis. An aspirant rocker could achieve far greater credibility by hanging out in (or professing to hail from) Greenwich Village than if he had remained in Yonkers.

The offspring of those who migrated to the suburbs took the reverse journey in search of rock'n'roll Babylon. In the anonymous, densely populated heart of the city, it was far easier to see bands, score drugs and get laid. Such hedonistic commuting gave rise to diverse scenes, among which those who hailed from the hinterlands identified with the big city just as readily as if they came from its urban nucleus.

The New York Dolls exemplified this pattern – suburban rockers drawn to the core of the Big Apple like glamour hungry maggots. They didn't just identify with New York; they seized ownership of the city's very name, crashed the party in Manhattan, and claimed for themselves the role of Times Square's hippest guttersnipes. The Dolls were like some supernova caricature, in which all of rock'n'roll's defining characteristics, its excess and sleaze, were distilled into one perfect, shambolic whole.

The classic Dolls line up of vocalist David Johansen, guitarists Johnny Thunders and Sylvain Sylvain, bassist Arthur Kane and drummer Jerry Nolan played some incendiary gigs and made two albums which – while suffused with beautifully chaotic energy – didn't do their teen anthems full justice. More than anything, the quintet left behind a legacy that would later be claimed by the punk rockers. The Dolls have been called the missing link between the Rolling Stones and the Sex Pistols, but have never received their rightful acclaim as one of the greatest and most influential rock'n'roll bands.

The Dolls' musical makeup and haphazardly glamorous image was a twisted projection of their influences, through a lens caked in semen and glitter. They simultaneously parodied and paid homage to the Stones, adopted the street sass and doomed romantic air of girl groups the Ronettes and the Shangri-Las, and tapped into the louche, sexually-ambiguous scene that thrived in New York during the heyday of Andy Warhol's Factory to produce a glorious collision of sound and image. But their attitude was gleaned from the street gangs they'd observed, and sometimes hung out with in their teens. They may have worn drag, but their pouts were shot through with testosterised vitriol.

To understand the essence of the New York Dolls and what made them such a unique, perfectly flawed group, it is necessary to gain some understanding of New York City itself. The Dolls could only have been spawned from the coruscating energy that coursed through its neon-lit streets during the late 1960s. It was a period of extremes and opposites – the violent unity and ruthless survival tactics of the city's gangs, juxtaposed against the unadulterated hedonism and preening of the ultra-hip scene that had found an unlikely but innovative emperor in Andy Warhol. Like a dishevelled colossus, the Dolls were rooted in both worlds.

In the immediate post-war decades, New York was synonymous with relentless, brutal violence to the point of stereotype. One of the city's main paradoxes has always been how appalling deprivation and poverty co-exist alongside ostentatious glamour. The city has always been a birthing chamber of fearsome creativity but the polar harshness of New York's day-to-day life is unlike anywhere else. Success and its attendant glamour are extreme, but the cold reality of life and death is always nearby – unforgiving and immediate.

New York carries a myth and mystique all of its own. One glimpse of the spectacular skyline and you can fall in love with the place. After all, you've seen it a thousand times before in books and movies. Even by the early 1800s, the overstuffed, bustling streets had forced the city to expand upwards, creating the skyscraping vistas and urban chasms that would epitomise its topography 200 years hence.

Since the seventeenth century, the city's growth has been punctuated by extreme poverty, violence and lawlessness. It also created a perennial pleasure industry, particularly in the bars and brothels that sprang up on the Bowery – that lower Manhattan stretch that starts below Houston Street, the northern border of the Lower East Side, and leads into Little Italy and Chinatown. By the 1830s, the yawning gulf between rich and poor resulted in the disenfranchised underclass striking, rioting and pillaging. This established a template for unrest in the city that, in turn, fed a desperate hunger to escape the misery of grinding poverty. As those trapped beneath the breadline yearned for a way out, a desire for escapism grew which would fuel the entertainment industry and criminal excesses in equal measure.

During the 1900s, many aspirant immigrants passed through the big iron gates of Ellis Island, off the coast of New Jersey and opposite Liberty Island. Their futures were often decided in a two-minute examination from an immigration officer. Once admitted, these new Americans found that establishing a new life could be a hard, degrading process that left them open to exploitation. (It still takes guts to make any kind of dent in New York, even today.) By the beginning of the twentieth century the flow of huddled masses had become a deluge.

None of the New York Dolls could be called 'all-American boys' in the white bread sense of the phrase, all being products of an immigrant or refugee lineage that settled in New York's outer boroughs. Johnny Thunders' grandparents passed through Ellis Island *en route* from Naples and Sicily. Sylvain Sylvain's family had escaped from Cairo via Paris. The family of the band's original drummer, Billy Murcia, had fled from the criminally violent streets of Bogota, Colombia. Arthur Kane was of Irish descent, like many of his Bronx neighbours, while David Johansen's background intertwined strands of Irish and Scandinavian ancestry. In a city where everybody was an immigrant, the Dolls were the consummate New Yorkers.

Like any major city, New York has its own distinctive musical identity. During the 1950s and early 1960s, the individual Dolls' childhood and adolescent soundtracks were provided by radio stations where they heard the latest hits direct from hub central. George Fedorcik – who would later become one of the founding Dolls, in his guise as guitarist Rick Rivets – was one of millions of eager young listeners captivated by the tinny sounds coming from their cheap transistor radios: 'We had radio stations that would play all this great music, and if you didn't have a transistor radio you were either a geek or a real square,' he recalls. 'All my friends would go to bed with a radio under their pillow listening to the WMCA Good Guys, or the stations that played R&B, and fall asleep with their radios on. We took them everywhere, and would tape the wires to frames of phoney glasses so we could listen in school. They would have these great shows like you see in the movies, with Murray the K, and have ten different acts, and they would do their hit and then the next act would come on and it would be great.'

The seeds of the New York Dolls were sown in Queens. Even among the madly exaggerated multicultural melange that is New York, the borough exemplifies the city's diverse cross-pollination. You can walk the length of one avenue and pass through neighbourhoods where the shop fronts switch from Jamaican to South American to Greek to Korean in the space of a twenty-minute stroll. There are larger communities heavily populated by Irish and Italians, as well as the project blocks that have billeted black and Puerto Rican families into hells stacked higher than the ghettos of previous generations. Sometimes just crossing the road can take you to another continent.

At the turn of the twentieth century, Queens was a loose association of villages with broad, airy streets. It took the building of the subway to hook it up with the city and open it up to the overspill of migrants from Gotham. Some neighbourhoods continued to exemplify all-American suburbia, as if itching to join up with Long Island on the adjacent eastern side. Today, however, although most of Queens is pleasant enough, it contains areas that bear more resemblance to some of the rundown parts of Brooklyn.

Although the Dolls would become synonymous with Queens' thoroughly seamy underbelly, Johnny Thunders was the only member of the group to be born within the borough. He came into the world as John Anthony Genzale, on 15 July 1952. His mother and father – Josephine and Emil – were first generation Italian-Amercians whose own parents had made the pilgrimage to the new world in the aftermath of World War I.

However, Johnny would have little to do with his father, who opted for wine, women and song over parenthood and walked out when he was a baby. 'I knew him more than Johnny did,' recalls Mariann Bracken, Johnny's older sister. 'He was never around. There was only the three of us – it wasn't easy, it was tough. There were a lot of struggles, but it was good. I brought Johnny up because my mom worked.' Irrespective of Emil's desertion, Josephine and Mariann doted on the new arrival and ensured that he wanted for little.

Johnny spent his early childhood in East Elmhurst, an area of Queens where large numbers of Italian-Americans had settled. Until about 1900, the area had been known as Newtown, but had been renamed at the behest of property developers to distinguish it from Newtown Creek – a waterway polluted by local industry, which used the tributary as a dumping ground. East Elmhurst was adjacent to Corona, originally another predominantly Italian neighbourhood, which became famous during the 1940s as the home to such jazz greats as Louis Armstrong, Dizzy Gillespie and Clark Terry.

According to Mariann, Johnny 'was a [typical] little boy – he could be quite bad. He'd play cowboys and Indians and all that stuff.' He was duly packed off along 80th Street in the direction of nearby Jackson Heights to attend Our Lady of Fatima School, where he proved resistant to the strictures of a staunchly Catholic elementary education. 'Johnny hated school,' remembers Mariann. 'My mom was called to the school a lot because Johnny was acting up or not doing his homework.'

In addition to a regular flow of bad behaviour reports, he developed a passion for baseball inspired by the achievements of Mickey Mantle – the charismatic hero of the all-conquering New York Yankees, who won seven World Series between 1951 and 1962. Former schoolmate Rich Scarpetta recalls Johnny being an all-round athlete: 'We played on the same baseball team. He was the second baseman and I was the shortstop. He was a spray hitter and very fast. He also ran on the Our Lady of Fatima track team. I raced him in the 220 – he shot out to an early lead but then faded in the final turn. I burned him with my blazing speed!'

Johnny played for his school and neighbourhood teams, as well as taking part in numerous pick-up games in nearby Meadow Corona Park. The family lived close enough to Shea Stadium – home to the New York Mets – for his dreams of playing there to be fuelled on a daily basis. However, Johnny's nascent sports career was to be rudely derailed by the Little League rules, which insisted that the fathers of all boys should be present. 'He loved baseball,' recalled Mariann, 'but, because our father didn't participate, he couldn't play.'

This regulation prevented Johnny progressing into the Junior League, where he might have been picked up by one of the professional teams that scouted him when he was twelve years old. Johnny would subsequently claim that his refusal to have a haircut brought about the end of his brief baseball career. Either way, with his dreams of emulating Mickey Mantle over, he switched his focus to music and swapped his bat for a guitar.

Aside from gritting his teeth through some less than enthusiastic gigs as an altar boy – which pleased Josephine – Johnny had nothing in the way of formal musical training. Like millions of other children of the 1950s, young Johnny's first exposure to rock'n'roll came courtesy of the television, and Elvis Presley. The rays of cathode rebellion emanating from the screen sparked a passion that would come to dominate Johnny's life. 'Johnny used to sing,' Mariann recalls. 'When he was in the hospital having his tonsils out he was singing for the nurses and he was only three years old. Johnny loved the guitar since he was three.'

The next stage in Johnny's education came courtesy of Mariann. 'I was into rock'n'roll. He would listen to it with me,' she remembers. 'He loved Elvis Presley. He used to imitate Elvis all the time.' She was also heavily into girl groups like the Shangri-Las, Angels and Crystals, who enjoyed a brief golden age for the first half of the sixties.

This era is defined by several records subsequently hailed as classics – which, when they appeared, were as startling and groundbreaking to American kids as the Stones and Beatles were in the UK. The New York Dolls' subsequent fixation on teenage angst and doomed romance came directly from these groups – themselves a sexy descendant of the fifties adolescent soundtrack created by street corner finger-poppers like Dion Di Mucci and the Four Seasons. This was also the music favoured by the local street gangs, who turned to rock'n'roll in moments away from their eternal turf battles.

Mariann would play her records constantly, providing the soundtrack to Johnny's childhood. 'It was good living with a sister who was older than me,' Johnny told *Zigzag* in 1980. 'I got to listen to all of Mariann's records . . . lots of the sixties girl bands . . . I liked music ever since I was a little kid . . . Eddie Cochran and Gene Vincent . . . music's always been important.'

In 1973, Dolls vocalist David Johansen would explain to *Record Mirror*'s Martin Kirkup, 'The New York girl groups were really our biggest influence . . . We saw the Shangri-Las many, many times. I used to see them every chance I had, they were our local band, on local TV a lot. Really, they're my favourite band from the sixties, and all the other chick bands from then . . . The Jellybeans doing, "I Wanna Love him So Bad", the Dixie Cups, the Cookies, "I Want A Boy For My Birthday".'

There were a lot of girl groups, mainly puppets in the hands of avaricious producers who used them to realise their own musical vision (and make pots of money in the process). The subject matter of their songs had a narrow constituency, being rooted in pure teenage angst, lust and love. Mariann loved to play the Angels, whose biggest hit came in 1963 with 'My Boyfriend's Back'. Handclaps, glamour and sass gave otherwise vapid post-rock'n'roll pop an injection of sexy street smarts. Records like 'He's So Fine' by the Chiffons were simple perfection and struck a potent chord with young lovers everywhere – particularly in the big cities, where daily life could be spectacularly unromantic.

The most famous stable of such groups belonged to Phil Spector – who built his legendary Wall of Sound through the overdubbing of legions of musicians all playing the same part. Prone to bouts of creative and personal lunacy that would ultimately lead to a murder rap in 2004, Spector gained much of his early experience working unaccredited on arrangements and production with R&B-influenced fifties songsmiths Mike Leiber and Jerry Stoller. He co-wrote the deliriously lush street anthems 'Spanish Harlem' and Ben E. King's 'Stand By Me', which he also produced.

In November 1961, Spector set up his own label, Philles Records. With assistance from successful songwriters such as Jerry Goffin, Carole King and Jeff Barry, he set his sights on cracking the charts. The label's first number one came in 1962 with 'He's A Rebel' by the Crystals, and was quickly followed by a string of similarly luminescent ghetto love songs like the sublime 'Uptown'. The Crystals ruled the Philles roost at first, while 'He's A Rebel' set a blueprint for the black-clad anti-hero later celebrated by the Shangri-Las.

The following year, Spector turned his attention to the Ronettes, a gorgeous trio from Spanish Harlem who swept to chart success with shimmering hits like 'Be My Baby', 'Baby I Love You', 'Walking In The Rain' and 'Do I Love You'. Their coolness would be reinforced the following year when they toured with the Rolling Stones. (Stones guitarist Keith Richards has hinted that he had a brief fling with Ronettes frontwoman Ronnie – much to future husband Phil Spector's chagrin.)

To the young Johnny, such juicy titbits peppered the trail of discovery that lays outstretched before all passionate music fans. A visit to the 1964 World's Fair also left him greatly impressed by instrumental band the Ventures – who had recently had a top-five hit with an updated version of Chet Atkins' 'Walk Don't Run'.

The radio brought Johnny into rapt contact with the primitive R&B of the Stones. Their guitarist, Keith Richard (spelled without the 's' back then), might also have laid the blueprint for Johnny's behaviour and pharmaceutical consumption – except that Keith had the money and contacts for the best drugs, and top facilities when it came to rehab time; while Johnny would later struggle to elevate himself above the hand-to-mouth existence of the street junkie, with all the danger it carries.

But, before the drugs arrived in the late sixties, an adolescent Johnny was smitten by the Stones' high-octane take on the blues and rock'n'roll. And, crucially, by the sound of their guitars.

The anti-authoritarian stance of the Stones infused Johnny's streetwise bearing. He assimilated, and never lost, their proto-punk 'we piss anywhere, man' defiance. When he finally got to meet his hero at a Fifth Avenue bar late in the 1960s, he would pocket Keith's empty cigarette packet as if it were a blessed relic.

Another huge influence on all the future Dolls members rose out of the girl group scene – the Shangri-Las.

Leiber and Stoller had already provided a string of seminal rock'n'roll and R&B classics for Atlantic Records. In the early sixties the duo decided to branch out on their own, and started their Red Bird label, which, through the release of around a hundred singles during the period 1963-66, came to epitomise the 'girl group sound'. The unlikely consequence was that they unwittingly supplied the group that would subsequently be credited with kick starting punk rock with their most enduring inspiration.

At first, most of the label's output came from the songwriting-production team of Ellie Greenwich and Jeff Barry who, working with Phil Spector, furnished the Dixie Cups with their massive hit 'Chapel Of Love' and provided the ultimate Big Apple anthem with the Ad Libs' 'The Boy From New York City'. Then, one day in mid-1964, a kid called George 'Shadow' Morton walked into the Brill Building – New York's 'home of the hits' – and, in true punk style, blagged himself a job as in-house producer.

Morton came from the streets, having grown up in Brooklyn's notoriously tough Bedford-Stuyvesant section, and had known Ellie Greenwich years earlier. He boasted he could make a hit record in a few days, although he was yet to put himself to the test. Under pressure to come up with a song, he called up some female acquaintances who had a part-time group he called the Shangri-Las, and overnight wrote 'Remember (Walking In The Sand)' for them. The label bosses were impressed enough to take him on permanently. The song sounded like nothing else around at that time. Morton used seagulls and crashing waves to create a desolate, dramatic effect. It immediately established his signature sound, which would carry the Shangri-Las through some of the most remarkable records ever made.

This most legendary girl group of all broadened the scope of what was possible on a seven-inch single by imbuing their songs with unprecedented levels of drama. Morton's use of dramatic backing and sound effects produced something akin to the musical version of teen romance comics.

Initially, the Shangri-Las were a quartet, all hailing from Queens – lead singer Betty Weiss, with her sixteen-year-old sister Mary, plus Marge and Maryann Ganser on backing vocals. Their breakthrough single, 'Remember' went to number five in the US and also made the top ten in Britain, where their early version of the moody pop video featured on *Top of the Pops*. For two short years, the Shangri-Las were the most lustrous, fantasy-stoking exemplars of teen yearnings, and sold millions of records in the process.

Morton continued to shape the girls' startlingly innovative studio sound. For the follow-up he invented what became known as the 'death disc' – a three-minute aural tragedy, where the love interest meets his, or her, maker. According to the sleeve notes of the group's eponymous 1965 debut album, 'Shadow hired a pack of local boys in black leather jackets and motorcycle boots to drive through the studio at timed intervals, gunning their motors and squealing their brakes. The Shangri-Las squinted through the gas fumes at the leader of the pack, and out-sang his screeching tires.'

'He's good/bad – but not evil', one Shangri-La assured another of the most charismatic biker boy.

One of Morton's signature devices involved employing spoken word passages that created a disarming sense of intimacy, heightening the sense of dramatic narrative within the songs. Some have passed into the vernacular of rock'n'roll, like the 'Is she really going out with him?' intro to 'Leader of the Pack' – later recycled by the Damned to herald the start of 'New Rose' and consequently, British punk on vinyl.

Written by Morton, Greenwich and Barry, 'Leader' became the most feted teen-tragedy bubblegum epic produced, reaching number one in the US at the end of November 1964, and number eleven in the UK the following February. (It would be reissued twice in the UK during the seventies, on each occasion attaining a higher chart position than on its original release.)

The Shangri-Las' 1964 trash anthem, 'Give Him A Great Big Kiss', so captivated the young Dolls that they turned it into a highlight of their stage show, reworded in the masculine. They also hijacked the opening declaration – 'When I say I'm in love, you best believe I'm in love, L-U-V' – for their own 'Looking For A Kiss'.

By the time the Shangri-Las recorded 'Out In The Streets' (later covered by the Dolls) in April 1965, their boy protagonist was growing out of hoodlum culture – 'He don't hang around with the gang no more.' Their next single, 'I Can Never Go Home Any More', upped the tragedy stakes as the girl left home, only for her poor mom to die of loneliness. In 'Give Us Your Blessing', the young couple elope in the wake of their parents' disapproval of their marriage – and die in a car crash. On a sunnier note, 'Sophisticated Boom Boom' saw the girls let loose in an upmarket club where 'the girls were wearing formals and the boys were wearing ties'.

Most of these songs concerned the innocent girl hooking up with the kind of boy her parents wasted their breath in warning her about. He usually wore shades and a leather jacket, as in 'Dressed In Black'. It was magnificent stuff that had far greater resonance than the normal fluffy pop of the period.

'It can honestly be said that they don't make records like this any more,' wrote *Melody Maker*'s Richard Williams on the sleeve notes to the group's greatest hits collection. 'The art of compressing action and emotion into a seven-inch, three-minute disc is almost dead but with Shadow Morton and the Shangri-Las it reached a particular peak of perfection.'

While Johnny grew up on the doomed sugar rush of the girl groups, he was also getting off on the same thing that all those rebels in the Chiffons and Shangri-Las songs were hopped up on – rock'n'roll.

Whereas the girl groups provided Johnny's palette of influences with its anima, Eddie Cochran and Gene Vincent – swathed in black leather and testosterone – supplied its animus, its corresponding balance. 'I picked up all my writing and knowledge from Eddie Cochran, he was my biggest inspiraton,' Johnny later told Brian Young on a Belfast radio show.

Eddie was born on October 3 1938, in Oklahoma City, and was eleven when his family moved to Los Angeles. Even at that young age he had achieved a rudimentary mastery of the guitar and, by the time he was fifteen, found himself being touted as something unusual back then – a good looking white teenager who could play the guitar with energy and passion.

Cochran's life was changed in 1955 when his band supported Elvis Presley at a gig in Dallas. He underwent a rock'n'roll epiphany, and became desperate to bust out of the hillbilly market he was mired in. His first big break was scoring a part in Frank Tashlin's spoof rock movie *The Girl Can't Help It*, where Eddie sung his new song 'Twenty Flight Rock'. The performance was enough for one of Gene Vincent's backing band, the Blue Caps, to comment, 'He was Presley plus he played terrific lead guitar.' There was certainly a touch of Elvis in Eddie's attitude, quiff and provocative on-stage gyrations, which also incorporated the wildness of black artists like Bo Diddley and Little Richard.

Cochran started recording rock'n'roll in earnest during the summer of 1957 and – after a few false starts – arrived at 'C'mon Everybody' in October of the following year. After hitching up with producer Tommy 'Snuff' Garrett – the head of A&R at Liberty Records, who had initially signed Phil Spector – Cochran recorded a string of energetic hits, including 'Three Steps To Heaven' and 'Cut Across Shorty'.

Eddie visited the UK to tour and make some TV and radio appearances during the early months of 1960. On Easter Sunday, at the end of the highly successful trip, he was in a car bound for the airport when a tyre blew out, causing a crash that killed Eddie and injured the other passengers. Eddie Cochran, with the world at his feet, was dead at the age of 21. Tragically, he enjoyed more success and hit singles after he died than during his brief life.

Among the injured passengers aboard Cochran's death trip was Johnny's other rebel rock hero, Gene Vincent. Whereas Eddie's death would preserve his eternal image of a spread-legged, angelic wildcat hammering out magnificent teen anthems like 'Summertime Blues', Vincent survived the crash but saw his career slide, as he drowned the pain that the crash left in his leg by guzzling booze and pills.

Gene Vincent was rock'n'roll's dark delinquent. He patented the classic black leather, draped-over-the-microphone-stand stance later adopted by the likes of Jim Morrison. He was the street corner hustler, a sleazy guttersnake capable of the most incendiary performances.

Born Vincent Craddock in Norfolk, Virginia, in 1935, Gene started his musical career when he emerged from the merchant navy aged 21. Smashing his leg in a motorcycle crash meant he had to wear a leg-brace for the rest of his life, but he used the disability as a prop. He changed his name to Gene Vincent and entered one of the talent shows organised by Capitol Records to find the new Elvis. No contest. Gene won a record contract and delivered the first of a stream of hits with 'Be-Bop-A-Lula', closely followed by two more million sellers in 'Wear My Ring' and 'Blue Jean Bop'.

If the Shangri-Las had sown the seeds of teen rebellion in young Johnny Genzale, with their mythical men in black leather, then Gene Vincent and the Blue Caps provided the mythos made flesh. Gene continued to make albums studded with wild rockabilly belters like 'Say Mama' and 'Who Slapped John', but his refusal to meet and greet radio DJs meant he got little airplay – which sharply diminished his prospects of national success. By 1959, Vincent's drinking, tax problems and lack of success forced him to seek work outside of the USA.

The car crash that killed Cochran scarred Vincent for life – mentally and physically – increasing his need for self-medication while he orbited the heliosheath of the European gig circuit. Gene never lost his rabid following in the UK, but stuck out like elephant's ears sheathed in black leather on the perky TV pop showcases of the early sixties.

Regardless of the changing trends, Vincent maintained his relentless rock-'n'roll furrow and even signed to influential British DJ John Peel's Dandelion label in the late sixties, releasing an album called *I'm Back And I'm Proud*. But alcohol eventually took its toll, and Gene died in California in October 1971. He left behind a formidable legend, and those volcanic tunes of the fifties had captivated many young rebels – providing a behavioural role model for the New York Dolls.

As the beat boom of the mid-1960s gathered momentum, Johnny's fascination with the Rolling Stones also led him to uncover their influences – just as thousands of punks would look beyond the Ramones and the Pistols to seek out the Dolls, the Stooges and the MC5 more than a decade later. Among the roots of the Stones' R&B antecedents, he discovered such illustrious performers as Bo Diddley and Howlin' Wolf – whose amazing guitarist, Hubert Sumlin, became a particular favourite.

By the time Johnny left Our Lady of Fatima to take up his place at New Town High School, in Jamaica, Queens, he had spent many hours exploring the sonic topography of rock'n'roll and was looking to make his own dent on the landscape. His first guitar came courtesy of his mother's hard-earned savings. 'His mom got him one when he was eleven or twelve,' recounts Mariann. 'He'd just sit in his bedroom all the time and play it. He taught himself the guitar – he never had any lessons.' But he knew he wasn't a one-man band, and high school was just the place to meet some kids who had the same ideas.

Sylvain Sylvain was to prove exactly the sort of cohort that Johnny was looking for. Born Ronald Mizrahi on 14 February 1953, he spent his early childhood in his native Cairo before his family fled Egypt for Paris, as a result of the anti-Semitic policies of President Gamel Abdel Nasser. Like many other Egyptian Jews, the Mizrahi family became increasingly marginalised as the 1950s wore on. After Syl's father lost his job as a banker and the family were stripped of their possessions by the state, it became clear that any hope of a tolerable life lay outside of their ancestral homeland. 'We were thrown out after the Suez Canal crisis,' explains Syl. 'We were actually exiled and we moved to France . . . everything that my father had was nationalised.'

The family (parents, Syl, and his older brother) travelled by Greek merchant ship to France, ending up in a Paris hotel. 'We were in Paris for a few years and then we filed for immigration to the United States,' he recalls. The family applied to emigrate via a Jewish resettlement scheme, and sailed across the Atlantic in 1961. As their ship sailed toward their new home, the Mizrahi family was greeted by the cinematic sight of the Statue of Liberty looming through the mist. 'To me the whole image of the United States was tall buildings, like New York,' recalled Syl. 'I was really taken in by the commercials of the time. I thought that every girl would look like Marilyn Monroe and that for breakfast you'd have Bazooka bubblegum and then Coca-Cola for dinner!'

Initially, the family was housed in Buffalo, upstate New York (where you go if you want to take in Niagara Falls *en route* to Canada). But they failed to settle and, after a brief relocation to Brooklyn, arrived in Jamaica, Queens.

Jamaica had been redeveloped during the early 1960s to provide low-cost housing affordable to migrants from all corners of the globe. Subsequent to the 1965 National Immigration Act, the area became home to black, Jewish, Asian, Puerto Rican, South American and Latino communities. The poverty and overcrowding ensured that the crime rate was high, and the area became notorious as a place where it was unwise for strangers to stray.

Close to the west of Jamaica is East New York, one of the most dangerous and desolate areas of Brooklyn. On the east is Hollis, a more prosperous neighbourhood that would later produce rap titans Run DMC. To the south is the sprawl of JFK airport.

Although the young Syl was disappointed not to be enjoying the bubblegum and Coca-Cola diet he'd dreamt of, he was immediately transfixed by his visual introduction to rock'n'roll – courtesy of the Beatles' 1964 appearance on *The Ed Sullivan Show*. Syl demonstrated what would become an abiding – and ultimately lucrative – interest in fashion by adopting the Beatle look, complete with mop-top and stack-heeled boots. He recalls, 'My mother never wanted me to wear my hair down because that meant that I was gay. I used to hide my Beatle boots in the basement of my building. I would walk out of the house in the morning with my hair all combed back and then I would go down to the laundry room, put on my Beatle boots and mess up my hair and try to look Beatle-ish. I found out that girls really liked that.'

Like Johnny, Syl was a fan of the girl groups, as well as some of Britain's more visceral acts such as The Who. 'They had those "ooohs" that reminded me of girl-groups, but it was guys doing it,' he later explained to *Toronto Sun* journalist Kieran Grant.

As a small child, Syl's father had bought him a small oud – a Middle Eastern stringed instrument that looks like a cross between a lute and a mandolin. Once in the States, he extended his fascination with music by moving up to a $13 Spanish guitar from Macy's department store. 'The biggest way I learned to play guitar was with the Ventures,' he recalls. 'They used to make those albums, *Learn How To Play Guitar With The Ventures I, II* and *III* – I'm sure I had *Volume I*, which taught you "Pipeline". That was a song I taught Johnny, which he made a career out of.'

Sylvain was sent to the local Robert A. Van Wyck Junior High School, on 144th Street, Jamaica. Like many immigrant kids, he was the subject of ridicule on account of his limited knowledge of the English language, and also his mass of black corkscrew hair. 'The first words I ever learned in English was, "Fuck you." The other kids would come up to me and say, "You speak English?" and I would say, "No." They would go, "Fuck you."'

Fortunately, there were plenty of other kids in the same boat, who banded together for what Syl describes as 'survival reasons'. One of his first friends was Billy Murcia, whose family had been forced to flee their native Bogota, Colombia after his property developer father became entangled with local gangsters during the construction of an ice-skating rink. When this venture failed, Murcia senior took the safe option and left town with his wife and three children, before the local hoods could take their losses out on him. The Murcias subsequently took up residence in a large house in Jamaica, Queens.

Billy's older brother, Alphonso, introduced him to Syl by insisting that the two younger boys fight for his edification. But, according to Sylvain, it was 'more like a cartoon than a fight', and they ended up as best friends. The Murcias' house had a reasonably sized basement where Syl and Billy held their first band practices. Their friendship endured as the pair graduated to New Town High School, where they first noticed a quiet, longhaired Italian-American kid called Johnny Genzale.

Johnny preferred to keep to himself but had acquired a reputation as a troublemaker, which ensured that the two parties eyed one another from a distance rather than hung out together. 'My first impression of Johnny was that he was a real cool looking cat,' recalls Syl.

Aside from shared experiences of coming to the US from abroad, the common ground between Syl and Billy was their love of music. 'We were like neighbourhood kids who would learn everything from every other guitar player that was anything,' says Syl. 'Especially black blues kids who had their dads and their grandfathers and their uncles teaching them how to play the blues. I gravitated to them like crazy. There were only five or six kids in the whole school that were black anyway and three of them played guitar. Two of them I knew and I said, "Please teach me."

'Basically, I was self-taught – so I learned how to go see somebody then come home and mirror what they're playing and be able to do the same thing. I did that with BB King, I did that with Albert King. In 1967, the first time I ever saw John Mayall he had Mick Taylor, who was a motherfucker on blues guitar.

'Me and Billy would go to all the clubs. Back then they would be only serving Coca Cola. We used to go to the Cafe Au-Go Go, Cafe Wha' and see the Blues Magoos and stuff like that. Me and Billy would fucking get out of school and hang out. It was really funny, it was kind of cute, we'd wear matching bellbottoms and shit and go to Greenwich Village and hang out on the corner of West Fourth Street and Bleecker Street. The window of the Night Owl would be blocked off by a curtain but they'd leave about four inches open. We couldn't get in there because we were too young but we'd see groups like the Blues Magoos that way.'

In July 1967, the regular summer concerts in Central Park provided Sylvain and Billy with a rock'n'roll epiphany, courtesy of Jimi Hendrix playing his first major New York gig, supporting blue-eyed soulsters the Young Rascals. 'We'd never seen amplifiers quite that tall,' marvels Syl. 'These were like Marshall stacks. They only had one each, a Marshall stack with two cabinets. They came out and looked outrageous and they were doing songs that we already knew about. These were like staple Top Forty Greenwich Village songs for bands. Like, if you don't know these songs you really couldn't get a gig and we were trying to learn these songs. One of them was "Hey Joe", and of course, "Wild Thing" . . . We couldn't believe it – Jimi came out and played all this stuff and the whole thing changed in one fucking half-hour. The Young Rascals came out and we fucking booed them! And they were our favourite band! But we fucking booed them because everything had changed. I got on a whole different platform, at first we were so swallowed up we just said, "Shit!"'

In addition to being dumbstruck by the extreme volume and energy of the Experience's live set, Syl and Billy were influenced by the trio's unique look. Later when they had set up their clothing enterprise, Truth & Soul, they would ask their seamstress to approximate these styles for their own outfits. 'We would buy the material then tell her like, "Hey, copy this jacket,"' remembers Syl. 'So we're in these flowered kind of jackets that were basically inspired by the whole Jimi Hendrix Experience thing anyway. One day, we were walking down Seventh Avenue, going to the subway to go back to Queens and we passed by the Wellington Hotel. Who comes out but Noel Redding and Mitch Mitchell? They noticed our jackets and they stop us. They were going, "Where d'you get the clothes?" And we go, "Wow, we love you guys!" And they started ragging on Jimi Hendrix because he's staying at the Plaza and he's having them staying at the Wellington.'

Unlike the gregarious Syl and Billy, Johnny was something of a loner. Mariann remembers him being 'very private'. His hatred of formal education resulted in him dropping out of school between the ages of fourteen and fifteen. 'See, school in America is very. . very . . . social, I guess,' he told *Zigzag*, adding, 'and I never really joined a gang . . . I useta have more fun just hangin' out in the neighbourhood parks.'

Jamaica is peppered with small public spaces like Tilly, Kings and Liberty – the usual meeting place for neighbourhood gangs. Johnny's local Italian-American gang was the 90th Street Fast Boys, and, although it later suited his image to claim membership, he was no more than peripheral to any petty crime, street fighting or general misbehaviour involving the Fast Boys. For a kid who, despite his baseball prowess, was by no means a jock, and who looked decidedly odd with his long raven-black hair and sharp clothes, it was necessary for his survival to have friends among the local teenage thugs.

Former Jackson Heights resident Lynn Paul remembers Johnny as a smart, almost collegiate looking teenager: 'He always wore a nice shirt with a nice pair of pants or jeans. His hair was longish for the time, but when you compare it to his Johnny Thunders days, it was quite short. He seemed more filled out too. When I look at the photos of him in the New York Dolls, I always think that he looked too thin in his face.'

The Genzales remained in their tiny East Elmhurst apartment until Johnny was in his early teens, then moved in with his grandmother when her husband died. He stayed there until he was fifteen, but left home when his mother remarried. Around this time, he took the stage name of Johnny Volume and formed a band called Johnny and the Jaywalkers, who played rock'n'roll standards in suits at weddings and birthday parties. 'He had a little band who used to play bar mitzvahs in a little hall,' remembers his sister Mariann.

Marty G, a former baseball team mate of Johnny's from the Silksox Boys Club, remembers some of these early performances: 'Back in those days it seemed like the only thing he could play or had the confidence he could play was "Wipe Out". I remember he played it on more then one occasion at the Junior High School 145 talent show. He craved the attention of girls and I must say he seemed to always get the attention he looked for.' In order to support Johnny and his band, Mariann took a job with a small catering firm, which helped get them gigs.

It was during this period that the hippie movement gained prominence, supplanting the straightforward rock'n'roll of the mid-1960s beat combos, garage bands and girl groups with patchouli-scented peace and love and mesmeric, acid-fuelled flights of whimsy. For the dapper Johnny, who'd been weaned on the visceral assault of Gene Vincent and the doomed romanticism of the Shangri-Las, this simply wouldn't wash. He would shortly gravitate toward the darker alternatives that sprang up, in the shape of high-energy guitar groups like Detroit's Stooges and the politically-charged MC5.

Johnny also took to travelling into the city to check out visiting British bands such as The Who and the Small Faces, who continued to tread a rock-'n'roll path far removed from the interminable ragas beloved of the hippies. At these shows, Johnny attracted a good deal of attention on account of his appearance, his 'Keef'-style exploding birds-nest coiffure neatly complimented by tailored women's velvet suits customised by his mother and sister.

One of those confident enough to talk to Johnny was Janis Cafasso, a teenager from Long Island who regularly made the trek into town with her cousin Gail Higgins Smith. After meeting at a gig in 1967, Johnny and Janis became an item. The couple were soon inseparable. 'Him and Janis really stood out,' Syl explains. 'They were like club kids are today, but this was in our neighbourhoods when we were growing up.'

The couple would regularly hang out in Central Park on Sunday afternoons, which was where Johnny first caught the eye of Arthur Kane – a gangling, softly spoken teenager from the Bronx, who was made even more noticeable by an unruly mass of blonde hair.

Born on 3 February 1951, Arthur Harold Kane Junior was a model student – attentive, naturally clever, with a bright future. His mother was a staunch Presbyterian, and instilled a quiet sense of spirituality within her son that would endure for the rest of his days. He attended Martin Van Buren High School, 'which was one of the top schools back then,' recalls George Fedorcik. 'I met Arthur in an English class I was taking. He sat behind me and was really quiet and straight looking so we didn't really hit it off at first. I played trumpet and he played clarinet in the school orchestra so we did see each other around, and we also had gym together, but he was always hanging at the handball courts while I was on the baseball field. I often wondered why he would always hang around the handball courts until I went there one day and saw the lot of them smoking joints and playing a radio. From then on it was the handball courts for me.'

As is often the case with precociously tall youngsters, Arthur was rather withdrawn, which earned him the ironic nickname that would stay with him for life. 'He was called "Killer" because he was just the opposite. He was a gentle giant who would never harm anyone,' recalls George. 'He was athletic in school and was very good at gymnastics, which is pretty difficult for a guy of six foot two. The name "Killer" just didn't fit the way he behaved – he was far from a killer.'

Like Johnny, both Arthur and George prided themselves on looking different and nurtured separate ambitions of forming a band. 'A classmate of mine – Ted Fodera – played a mean guitar and I asked him if he could come around some Saturday and show me a few things on the guitar,' explained George. 'The first time he came over he had Arthur with him. I wasn't too keen on him then as he was kinda straight and very smart so I didn't think we had anything in common.

'It turned out that Arthur played guitar also, so Ted wound up showing us both a few songs and pretty soon we had put a group together with Ted, Arthur, Danny Lorenzo on drums and myself. We never really got to play any gigs as we were pretty bad, but Ted and I did get a gig as a duo at a church dance for the older folks. We were too loud and the power was cut during the first song, so we sheepishly went back to work in the coatroom and were paid – but it wasn't for our musical ability, it was because we didn't lose anyone's coat.

'After that me and Arthur got a proper band with a bass player, Ken Finger, and a drummer-vocalist, Stu Feinholtz Wylder, who would join us years later in the Corpse Grinders.'

In addition to providing him with a practical grounding in rock'n'roll, Arthur's mid-teens were notable for the startling change in his normally reserved character. It all began with the tragic early death of his mother from what was suspected to have been cancer. Like many naturally smart youngsters, Arthur's intelligence tended to make him more aware, more sensitive, than many of his peers. It was hardly surprising that the unexpected loss of a parent hit him hard.

This situation was exacerbated when his father started a new relationship. 'His father's girlfriend – who became his stepmother – didn't like him for some reason and did her best to make sure that his father got him out of the house,' explains George. 'It must have been really hard on him to first lose a mother and then have your father turn on you because of some bitch girlfriend. She basically had the father disown Arthur so he had no family and it must have been killing him. He put on a good front but inside he must have been hurting bad. His father would have nothing to do with him after he married this woman, so Arthur was alone.'

Arthur lost interest in his schoolwork, developing an enthusiasm for drinking and pill popping as a means of negating his emotions. Despite these traumas, his innate abilities allowed him to graduate from Van Buerk in spite of a noticeable decline in his grades. Arthur had little interest in further education or getting a job. Aside from getting wasted, the focal point of his young life was rock'n'roll. 'There wasn't much aside from music that interested me and Arthur,' recollects George. 'We went through our surfing phase when we would get up at five every morning and go to the beach to catch a few waves, but as our hair got longer and our clothes got crazier the beach wasn't that appealing – especially when you've been out all night playing some club or coming back from some party.

'We were interested in our guitars and we would go through them like crazy. We decided that we needed Gretsch guitars one day, so me and Artie took a few hundred out of the band and bought the *Buy & Sell* and found a couple of used guitars that sounded just great. We went to see mine first and it was an orange double cutaway like John Lennon used for a short time, and then we went to see Artie's. His turned out to be a Green Double Anniversary just like the one Brian Jones had played at one time or another.

'We felt so good driving back to Artie's house so we could try them out. What a rush when we plugged in and heard the sound of feedback, just like on the beginning of "I Feel Fine" by the Beatles. Then we found out that the Velvets used Gretsch's also – so we were cool man, real cool. Ken, our bass player, even went out and bought a brand new Fender Jazz Bass. Now we were pros.'

Emboldened by their new status, Arthur and George took their new band – which they came around to calling the London Fogg – to the city, in search of where it was at. 'We would take the subway to the Village and go to the Cafe Wha' – which we wound up playing several times, along with all the clubs that were springing up in the Village,' explains George. 'I remember when the Velvets were playing at the Dom for weeks and we would try to get in using phoney ID's and the music was just so out there. That's when we really started to get better and get a lot more gigs at strip clubs and frat parties. Just the whole vibe of the city at that point in time was great. The sounds and the smells of the city were just so overwhelming when you were a kid on the loose – wild in the streets. It was like anything goes.'

Their choice of 'the London Fogg' highlighted Arthur and George's love of sixties garage rock, drawing upon the anglophile vibe that epitomised many *Nuggets*-era bands.

'The Fogg covered songs by the Stones, Yardbirds, Kinks and American garage bands like Count Five, Beau Brummels, and the Music Machine,' explains George. The attachment of a geographical reference point was a big hit with Arthur, foreshadowing his subsequent enthusiasm for the 'New York' prefix placed before 'Dolls'.

'"London Fogg" was the brand name of a rain jacket that Stu used to wear,' recalls George. 'One day when thinking of names somebody picked up his jacket and read the label and there it was – "London Fogg" – so from that day on we were the London Fogg, but then – for whatever reason – we shortened it to just "the Fogg". Before that we were the Poor Boys because we used to wear those Poor Boy sweaters, so there were the Vagrants and the Vagabonds and the Tramps, so why not the Poor Boys?'

In addition to places to play and bands to check out, the hip centre of town opened the young suburbanite duo's eyes to the latest fashions. 'When we started hanging in the city we came across all these second-hand shops in the East Village, and we would buy stuff that we would see the British groups wearing and try to come as close as possible to copying them,' reminisces George. 'When the Yardbirds came to New York, we went to see them at this club we used to go to called the Action House.

'Me and Artie go to see the band and wind up hanging out with them the whole night and the next night. We looked them over very carefully and checked out what kind of shoes they wore and their shirts and jackets. Then we hit the thrift shops, buying used leather motorcycle jackets *a la* Jimmy Page, shirts with lots of frilly ruffles, silk scarves and red boots.

'We got very heavy into velvet and satin. I had the Brian Jones-Jack Flash hairstyle while Art, on the other hand, went the other way and got a really short mod-style haircut that really was out there. Very Twiggy-Julie Driscoll looking. I think that we both had a sense of fashion very early on in life.

When the movie of *West Side Story* came out, we all wanted to look like Bernardo – the leader of the Puerto Rican gang. Him and Tony Curtis had the coolest hairstyles. Plus with the tight black jeans and purple shirts and garrison belts, what could be cooler?

'The sneakers had to be black PF Flyers that look just like the Converse sneakers that the Ramones later wore. Then they came out with these shoes called Seatbelts, because the inside of the shoe looked like the rolled and tucked seats of the hot rods that were big in California then. And you always had a pair of PRFCs (Puerto Rican Fence Climbers) that had to be as pointed as a shoe can get. They were great if you were being chased, because they were so pointy that you could climb a fence faster then the guy or guys that were chasing you.'

Deciding that having a drummer who also sang was too reminiscent of mid-sixties chart toppers Gary Lewis and the Playboys, Stu Wylder was ejected from the Fogg's drum stool so that he could 'concentrate on singing and creating general mayhem'.

'We recruited Gerard Dinces because he was really loud and had a great set of Ludwig drums,' says George. 'On the other hand the guy was a number one asshole who was not only obnoxious but rude and crude and smelled really bad. So we used him for a few months until we started college.'

The Fogg's line-up was finalised with the addition of a new drummer, Kenneth 'Sparky' Donovan, who would subsequently rejoin George in the Brats during the late seventies.

George had first encountered Sparky while enrolling for college. 'I had just graduated from high school and was about to enter college, not having a clue what I wanted to do in life except play music. I had gone to register that day with Gerard Dinces, who was also clueless about what his life's calling was.

'We were sitting in some room, filling out our entrance papers, when we saw this tall blonde with a red suede jacket standing at the doorway, looking as confused as we were. Dinces (who had a very bad vision problem) says to me, "Check out the hot blonde at the door." So I stop what I'm doing – as any seventeen-year-old would – to check out this hot blonde. To my surprise, "she" turned out to be a male and he's walking straight to our table.'

Like George, Sparky had little idea of which courses to take. The trio chewed over their options, and decided that communication arts was the best. 'This sounded cool to us,' recalls George. 'After all, we could be DJ's or cameramen or news reporters or maybe even janitors at a TV station.' It quickly transpired that Sparky shared similar musical tastes to George and Arthur, and was also a useful drummer without any apparent hygiene issues. To facilitate Sparky's incorporation into the Fogg, Dinces was dropped.

Although the individual members of the Fogg had little genuine enthusiasm for their studies, further education was a necessity for any high school graduate who didn't fancy ending as a bloody smear in Uncle Sam's South East Asian folly. 'This was the time of Vietnam,' explains George. 'The guy with the longest hair in our school and a double for Dave Davies [lead guitarist of the Kinks] graduated – and wham, next stop Nam. We read in the paper that he had been hit by a grenade and was almost killed. He spent almost a year in hospital healing and then they wanted to send him back.

Now we were stuck, what to do.' College provided the solution – 'as long as you were in some sort of school they wouldn't draft you.'

Nearby, Syl and Billy were treading a similar path. After quitting New Town High they made serious efforts to get a band together. After a few false starts with various personnel, including future Doll Jerry Nolan, they recruited a more musically proficient bass player called Mike Turby – who had been in a fairly well known Queens rock'n'roll group called the Orphans. The trio called themselves the Pox and, in 1968, got as far as signing a management contract with Harry Lookofsky (the father of Mike Brown, who'd been in the Left Banke of 'Walk Away Renee' fame).

However, as the trio began treading water in the shallow of backroom bars, Turby lost patience and departed for San Francisco. 'We were gonna go in and make a record,' explained Syl, 'but our lead singer freaked out on a girl and left for California. That was the end of our big career.'

Although they weren't full US citizens and thus had no need to beat the draft, Syl and Billy enrolled at Quintanos – a well-known *Fame*-style school located behind Carnegie Hall that groomed students for careers in the performing arts. 'It was sort of like a school for young professionals,' explains Syl, 'a lot of cool people came out.' (One of whom was Mary Weiss of the Shangri-Las.)

The duo lasted just long enough at Quintanos to hatch the idea of starting up in the rag trade, and set about making groovy sweaters under the banner of Truth & Soul. Syl provided part of the funding by working at hip men's boutique The Different Drummer on Lexington Avenue and 63rd Street – which also provided him with a practical grounding in the sales end of the fashion business.

'It was like a hippie kind of clothing store,' remembers Syl. 'For Billy and me, coming from Queens, Manhattan was like years and years away . . . There were all the cool places and the shops as well as the age that was happening right there in front of us.

'Right across the street from that shop where I used to work was this toy repair shop upstairs. It was called the New York Dolls' Hospital. That's when I first thought of the name "the New York Dolls". I told everybody . . . "I'm gonna start a band called the New York Dolls." I thought it was a fucking great name!'

Syl and Bill had narrowly missed re-encountering Johnny, who'd enrolled in the school in the autumn of 1968 but didn't stick around. Instead of honing his performing style in the formal manner, Johnny opted to further his rock'n'roll studies. He quickly became a regular at live venues such as the Fillmore East, the Scene and Nobody's, a bar described by Patti Smith's guitarist Lenny Kaye as 'the first legitimate rock'n'roll theatre in New York'.

Writing in his 1981 *New York Dolls* biography, future Smiths mainman Steven Morrissey asserted that the Dolls 'were the first real sign that the sixties were over'. As that decade drew to a close, Johnny, Syl, Billy and Arthur were crossing paths on a regular basis. Their shared interests and outlooks, along with the insular nature of New York's non-hippie rock scene, meant that it was only a matter of time before they came together.

Teenage News

'Rock'n'roll is about attitude. I couldn't care less about technique.' – *Johnny Thunders*

By 1969, Johnny's focus on the Rolling Stones had narrowed into a full-blown obsession with Keith Richards. For many young rock rebels, the guitarist represented the epitome of elegantly wasted cool. On encountering the Stones, once you'd got past Jagger's leering pout, your eye would be inexorably drawn to the man on his right, holding the music together with incongruously sloppy precision.

Richards in action presented a classic rock tableau – cigarette in mouth, death-grey complexion, rooster-thatched hair and a Tibetan prayer scarf hanging around his neck. He appeared to move in slow motion, reaching into his soul's malefic inner depths to retrieve the primal spirit of the blues and infuse it with rock'n'roll. To the teenager getting into music and its recreational offshoots, Keef ruled. The look, the outlaw attitude, the genre-defining use of rhythm guitar.

Although Johnny had yet to fully cultivate an outrageous cartoon version of his hero's coiffure, he'd already managed to develop his own decadently glamorous image. He also had the attitude. The don't-give-a-shit finger at authority, the tireless devotion to honing his guitar style, and that indefinable swashbuckling swagger that comes from the soul, rather than second-hand from the pages of *Creem* magazine.

Keen to get to the heart of the action, Johnny, Janis and Gail acquired an apartment in the East Village on First Avenue between Ninth and Tenth Streets. In those days, venturing east past First Avenue could mean taking your life in your hands. 'You just didn't go there, it was like no man's land.' Gail recalled in Stephen Colgrave and Chris Sullivan's *Punk*. 'When we moved in, we found someone had left a load of furniture in the place, including an old piano that we didn't have room for. As we tried to move the piano, the front came off and we saw all these big bits of pot inside . . . So Johnny called up a friend of his from Queens and sold it. As far as I know that was his first involvement with drugs. When he got into something, he went the whole way.'

Johnny's fascination with the Stones extended into a general admiration for the British take on the blues and rock'n'roll. Such anglophile predilections, and the availability of a friend's press card that would gain him free entry to gigs, persuaded Johnny and Janis to scrape together the airfare and head to London.

At that time, London was home to a healthy underground scene, with clubs like Middle Earth at the Roundhouse and small venues playing host to names like the emerging Led Zeppelin, Free and Tyrannosaurus Rex. 'I went to see what was happening, check out the scene,' explained Johnny. 'I saw about sixty bands and was there for about three months; Tyrannosaurus Rex at the Roundhouse, Steamhammer, all these incredible bands.'

Years later he would record a version of Marc Bolan's early single, 'The Wizard'. This lightning immersion into London's musical subculture had made Johnny even more determined to form a band.

Despite George and Arthur's enthusiasm for the Fogg, the band drifted apart when Stu Wylder and Kenneth Finger left for out of town colleges. George and Stu remained friends and spent their summer break working in a sign-making plant in order to raise some cash – a stint that provided George with a new identity. 'We were working in a factory that made those giant signs for gas stations – the ones that were 30 feet tall,' he explained. 'Stu was working the ovens, putting in these giant moulds and filling them with whatever they use to make the signs with and I was doing the assembly of the signs when they cooled down. My last name ends with "cik", but every time it was written they would write, "rick". So I got tired of always correcting these idiots, so I just gave in and when they would ask for the spelling I would just say "R-I-C-K". That's how the Rick came about.

'The Rivets part came about because of my job. After all, I was riveting these signs and they would call out, "More rivets needed here," "You missed a rivet," or, "Move it Rivets, you're falling behind." So combine the two and you have Rick Rivets. Besides, it's got two R's like rock'n'roll, or Rolls Royce – so I could use my initials and they could mean many things – I mean, it's better then Sirhan Sirhan or whatever.'

While Rick was forging a name for himself, Arthur – who had dropped out of a short-lived course studying hotel management at Pratts University – was growing tired of New York's gaudy delights. Inspired by Sparky Donovan's tales of an eventful trip to England, where he'd got to hang out at Abbey Road Studios and chat with Paul McCartney, he was keen to check out the outside world.

'Arthur was on a quest to find a place where we could start over,' recalls Rick. 'One of the places picked was Durban, South Africa, as we had read about the diamond mines and gold pouring from the mountains just as our grandparents thought that the streets in America were paved in gold – until they got here and found out they were paved in horse shit.'

Durban was ultimately ruled out on the grounds of being too remote and decidedly un-rock'n'roll. Later, Arthur was leafing through a copy of *National Geographic*, when an article about Amsterdam grabbed his attention. 'We read that this was a freethinking country that had liberal drug laws and legal prostitution, so what better place to go?' enthuses Rick. 'Arthur went first while I stayed back to sell my car and get money for this trip. When I started getting all these letters from Artie about how great it was, my car was sold and I was on the plane heading for the land of drugs and women. Besides, Shocking Blue had just had a hit with "Venus" and Artie just had to meet the singer – so what better reason to go someplace?'

While he awaited Rick's arrival in Amsterdam, Arthur made ends meet by selling snacks in the Vondelpark. 'He had a little sign that said, "Arthur's Cream Cheese Sandwiches", and he sold them for three guilders, or something like that,' reveals Syl.

'Once we were settled in and had our fill of hash and ladies we set out to find members for our new group – which was to be called "The New Amsterdam Dolls",' recounts Rick. 'All we needed was a singer and a drummer, as me and Arthur had played together. The first person we tried was a singer, but the only problem was he didn't speak much English and trying to find a drummer with a full kit was near next to impossible. So, after many attempts to find the people we needed to start this band, things started falling apart and the only thing to do was head back to New York.

'Before we headed home there were several run-ins with the law over a stolen motorbike and possession of hash – me and Arthur had gone to the flea market to buy some transportation and for about $40 each we purchased two motorbikes. As we were leaving to go home we got separated, and Arthur was stopped by the police who charged him with possession of a stolen motorbike. Now I was with him, and saw him buy it – so as far as being stolen, it wasn't Arthur who stole it but the geezer who had sold it to him. After being taken to jail, a small amount of hash was found on him and then they checked his papers and saw that they were expired.'

With the Fogg dissipated and Arthur and George back in New York, the two pals set about finding somewhere to live and a means of raising some cash. Arthur scored an apartment on Tenth Avenue, near Avenue A, while George found a place at the Broadway end of Tenth. 'I had taken a job with the United States Post Office and Arthur had taken a job with the telephone company, repairing the phones in and around Central Park,' Rick explains. For Arthur this was a good deal, as he got his own truck and could have his lunch breaks in the park during the summer. 'On the other hand,' adds Rick, 'I was indoors working on the parcel post line, throwing boxes to the containers they would be shipped in.' Outside of working hours, Arthur and Rick remained determined to get a new band together.

Meanwhile, Syl and Billy were making a moderate success of Truth & Soul. They continued to make the psychedelic sweaters inspired by ethnic Colombian designs. Billy's sister, Mercedes, even brought over a masterloomer from Colombia for extra authenticity. Their designs got a good review in *Women's Wear Daily*, and the duo struck a deal for mass production with the Nausbaum knitting mills in Brooklyn.

'We were doing Truth & Soul because we weren't doing too good at school,' Syl explains. 'Back then it was just a *schmertzer* business, as the Yiddishers would call it. We were making really good money. I was making $5000 a time and that was four times a year.' Having accrued a pile of cash, Syl, Billy and his brother, Alphonso, decided that a European vacation was in order.

Billy and Alphonso headed for Amsterdam, where they stayed for a year, having a good time and getting stoned. The more aesthetically orientated Sylvain accompanied them for a time, before heading west to immerse himself in London's musical and fashion scenes. He had clothes, cars and Marshall amps shipped back to the Murcias' home in Queens and observed the nuances of British fashion with great interest. Syl was particularly fascinated by the scenes around Kensington Market and the Kings Road, which was at its peak of hipness. 'We liked to go and see bands like the Pink Fairies,' recounts Syl. 'We'd buy cars and drive them with English plates in New York. We came back with a Jaguar which only cost $300 . . . For taxes to bring a car over it was only about $30.' Sylvain often shopped at hip boutiques like Granny Takes A Trip and Paradise Garage, where he met the latter's owner, Trevor Miles – who would soon hand his shop over to two designers named Malcolm McLaren and Vivienne Westwood.

Once back in Queens, Syl and Billy decided to make profitable use of the Marshalls by holding regular sessions in the Murcias' basement. One of their first recruits was Johnny, who the duo had pegged as a likely candidate on account of his striking rock'n'roll looks. Syl can even recall seeing him in the audience in the Stones movie *Gimme Shelter*. After years of eyeing one another across streets, schoolyards and dancehalls, Syl and Billy took the plunge and asked Johnny if he'd be interested in hooking up with them. 'He had really nice girlfriends and stuff,' explains Syl, 'so I said to Billy, "We better get him in our band so we can grab up some girlfriends."'

Initially Johnny played bass, with Syl showing him chords and passing on some of the chops he'd picked up from Mike Turby while in the Pox. 'We had our rehearsal place in Billy's mom's basement,' recalls Syl. 'That's where we first learned how to play and jammed – mainly blues instrumentals. At first Johnny didn't want to play, then he said, "I'll play the bass," because the bass has only got four strings and he figured that would be a lot easier.'

Even if Johnny wasn't particularly at home on the instrument, the trio had a whale of a time playing rock and blues instrumentals and some T. Rex songs. Syl suggested 'the Dolls' as a possible name for the nascent outfit.

By 1971, Marc Bolan had moved his band on from bongo-pattering odes to field mice to become the UK's first exponent of glam rock. While David Bowie was still wearing his frumpy 'man's dresses' and performing heavy metal songs about mental patients, Bolan had the little girls screaming and pissing on their seats. Johnny was already a fan, and could really relate to the way in which the spangled icon adapted Eddie Cochran licks into instantly catchy top ten material. Bolan's *Electric Warrior* album paved the way for the UK's glam rock explosion where acts like Slade, the Sweet and Gary Glitter would shortly take up residence at the top of the British chart.

Glam rock represented a reaction against the bourgeois intellectualisation of rock by lumbering progressive behemoths such as Yes and Emerson, Lake and Palmer. As Sylvain observes today, the extended virtuosity of stadium bands held little relevance to a bunch of kids from Queens. 'It was such a big thing that we were totally turned off of it – the big stadium rock, the Led Zeppelins, and all this stuff that was like 30,000 people in the house. It was like, "Who the fuck cares?" There'd be a 25-minute solo on this and a 25-minute gargling solo on that. It was fucking boring as hell. Rock became establishment. It became business. It became no fun. It wasn't sexy. It was all packaged and repackaged and shoved down your fucking throat. The way MTV has been for the last 25 years.'

Whereas the lyrical content of Yes's impenetrable flights of whimsy were pored over by the band's nerdy fans, glam wasn't supposed to be taken seriously. It put the bubblegum element back into music, and had its roots in the primal rock'n'roll of the 1950s. In the States it would emerge as 'glitter rock' with the New York Dolls as its flamboyant heralds.

Proceedings in the Murcias' basement abruptly halted when Sylvain was required in London, where Mercedes and Heidi Murcia were making sweaters for Kensington Market. Johnny had started falling out with Janis, and began the chaotically nomadic lifestyle he would pursue for the rest of his life. Gail asked him to leave the East Village apartment and he started crashing at the Chelsea Hotel – which, thanks to Warhol's *cine-verite* sex and drugs movie *Chelsea Girls*, was already shrouded in artistic legend, way before Sid and Nancy took up residence.

One night, Johnny was standing outside a pizza parlour and noticed two familiar-looking dudes attempting to steal a motorbike. It was Arthur and Rick, who recognised him from the Fillmore, Central Park and Nobody's. 'It was one of those hot New York City summer nights where you just went out and tried to stay as cool as possible,' remembers Rick. 'Me and Arthur were quite drunk and had seen this really nice Harley that I decided to steal. We had a van at the time and were riding around the West village when I saw this bike parked. So I stop the van and try to start it up but couldn't figure out how to start it. I said to Arthur, "Let's put it in the back of the van and bring it over to Tenth Street and we can re-paint it and get some plates and we'll have a bike to ride around instead of this van."

'So, me and Art are trying to lift this bike into the van but it was just too heavy. After about a half-hour we were starting to look suspicious and decided to take off with the bike hanging out of the door of the van. We'd made it as far as Bleecker Street, when Arthur says, "Hey, there's that guy from the Fillmore." So, I said to Art, "Why don't you see if he plays anything and maybe we can get him for the band?" I pulled over and all these people are looking at us – because we are obviously drunk and had the bike hanging out of the van. Arthur goes running over to Johnny – I think Johnny thought that we were gonna rob him because of the way Art approached him – but after Arthur introduced himself a conversation began.

'It turned out that Johnny had a bass and lived around the corner from Arthur. We told him we were trying to get a band started and asked if he would be interested. He said, "Yes," and we made arrangements for him to come over the next day and jam with us.

'We had seen Johnny for years at different shows and at the Fountain at Central Park, and he stood out because of the way he dressed and his hair. He seemed to be into the same groups we were into, so we just figured he would be great for a band. Johnny just stood out in any crowd because of the way he looked – so you couldn't help but notice him if you were into that style of dress. We would always nod hello when we would run into him but we never spoke to him until that night on Bleecker Street. That night was the beginning of the Dolls.'

'He was so good looking and beautiful,' confessed Arthur, 'I said, "I don't care if he knows how to play an instrument or anything – I'll teach him if necessary."'

The trio were augmented by Ozzie, a friend of Johnny's, who played drums. 'I think it was Johnny and Janis and Ozzie and his girlfriend who shared the apartment on First Avenue between Ninth and Tenth Street,' Rick recalls. 'Johnny kind of said that he had a drummer – so we went with Ozzie because he had that Billy Murcia look with the Marc Bolan curls and the platform shoes and I think he was Colombian also, so we decided to give him a try.'

The group had just begun building up a repertoire of Rolling Stones and Chuck Berry numbers, but it became evident that Johnny was struggling to get to grips with his bass. 'So he asked Arthur if he wouldn't mind changing from guitar to bass,' explains Rick. In typically accommodating fashion, Arthur relinquished his rhythm guitar duties and Johnny was reunited with the instrument he'd fallen in love with as a kid.

Ozzie's tenure at the drum stool was cut short on account of his limited skills. 'We rented a studio and went in and did a bunch of covers and he just wasn't very good,' observes Rick. Johnny remembered that, with Syl still in London, Billy Murcia was at a loose end. Although Sparky Donovan would have been Arthur and Rick's first choice, the duo agreed to take Billy in order to placate Johnny. 'When the subject of Sparky came up, Johnny had mentioned Billy and we didn't want to lose Johnny, so we really didn't push the issue,' reveals Rick. Sparky also lived on Long Island and was often reluctant to make the trek into town.

'When Sparky found out that me and Arthur had put a band together I think he was hurt that we didn't ask him, but we were desperate and kinda out for ourselves,' Rick explains. 'It could also have been the fact that Johnny didn't want to play with three blond guys that were all a head taller than him – with Billy he had someone that was his size.'

Billy readily agreed to hook up with Johnny, Arthur and Rick, and the quartet started practising in earnest. 'The first time we ever played together was in Artie's basement on Tenth Street,' recalls Rick. 'Johnny lived on First Avenue, between Ninth and Tenth, so he was just around the corner. This was around July of 1971. We did "Carol", "Route 66", "Pipeline", "Interstellar Overdrive", "Little Queenie", "Jack Flash" and maybe a few others.' It was during this period that Johnny settled on a new *nom du guerre* of Johnny Thunder (which he swiftly pluralized), after the DC comic book hero who starred in *All Star Western* comics.

'Now that it was in stone that Billy would be the drummer, the band got on with the task of coming up with some material,' explained Rick. 'All of the past bands that me and Arthur had been in together were cover bands that played clubs, bars, dances and anyplace that would have us. With this new band we had decided that we were going to do originals only. It turned out that me and Arthur had a few songs and Johnny had even more songs.

'By this time Johnny had moved into a different apartment, so Ozzie was never to be seen again and I don't know what ever happened to him. Billy lived near me in Queens in the rooming house his family owned. Arthur had taken up residence there as well, so it was up to me, the only one with a car, to drive them back and forth to practice.'

'The Murcia family had this big house and they would rent rooms to the Colombians, who – I would guess – had just came to the country and didn't know how to get around,' explains Rick. 'There were some amps there as well as drums. I think we actually did practice there a few times. The only thing was that Johnny didn't want to take a subway to Billy's. It was easier for him to have the three of us come into the city than for him to take the subway to Billy's house.

'Also, the basement was the home of Truth & Soul. They had their knitting machine down there and Billy would make these cool sweaters in an hour or two. He was a man of many talents, and if he'd stuck with it [he] could have made more money then the Dolls ever did.'

Johnny's reluctance to take the subway out to Queens, and the unsuit-ability of a domestic boarding house for the savage noise the nascent Dolls would soon be kicking up, meant that alternative premises were required. With a rehearsal facility on 31st Street proving a financial drain, cheap was good. 'I don't know how we found the place – either Arthur or Johnny – but we soon had a place on 81st Street and Columbus Avenue that was a bike rental place in the day and a studio at night.'

The eponymous owner of Rusty's Cycle Shop was immediately re-chris-tened 'Beanie' by his new nocturnal tenants, on account of his ubiquitous woolly hat. 'That was a strange guy,' David Johansen later declared in an interview with *Rock Family Trees* creator and *Zigzag* founder Pete Frame. 'Very eccentric guy. A real round guy shaped like a ferryboat. He used to sleep with his mother, as far as we could decipher.'

Rusty had a pair of big Fender Bassman amps and a drum kit – very use-ful, as the group only boasted three guitars between them. They paid their five bucks and every night Beanie locked them in at midnight , 'so we would-n't steal anything.' This detainment served as an aid to creative focus, as any band members who fancied slipping away were stuck inside the small space until Rusty liberated them in time for the following day's business.

Ensconced in the damp shop, Johnny, Arthur, Rick and Billy set about lay-ing the foundations for the New York Dolls, slugging vodka to ward off the cold 'This was like the black hole,' declares Rick. 'We would arrive and he would lock us in this small bike shop that had a room in the back with two amps and a drum kit. Johnny would play and sing through one amp and me and Artie would play out of the other. This was around September 1971.

'We would usually go to Johnny's place and he would show us any new songs he had on acoustic guitar and we would learn like that and then bring them to the "studio" to work on with amps and drums. In the beginning it was cool, as we used to get a bottle of vodka and Johnny would bring some downs and we had a good time.'

In addition to their assortment of cover versions, the band had started working on some original songs written by Johnny. This new material had been developed at his apartment on acoustic guitars and included 'It's Too Late' (which would later pop up on *Too Much Too Soon*), 'Oh Dot', 'I'm A Boy, I'm A Girl', 'Take Me To The Party' and 'Why Am I Alone'. Arthur and Rick contributed 'Coconut Grove'.

Despite this progress, the band was still without a name. Although Actress may have been suggested by Janis, it didn't stick. 'There was never any band that I was in called "Actress",' asserts Rick. 'This whole thing is a misnomer that keeps perpetuating itself through the years; Johnny's girlfriend Janis might – and I say *might* – have said at one time or another, "How about calling the band Actress?" Upon which someone said, "No, that sounds stupid." End of story. The band was never called Actress at any time and all I ever remember was the name Dolls – The Dolls.'

However, Rick's habit of taping rehearsals served to perpetuate this myth when his tape of the group's 10 October 1971 session was eventually released as *Actress: Birth of the New York Dolls*.

Two of the nine songs to feature on the disc would later emerge with different names and arrangements – 'That's Poison', which became 'Subway Train', and 'I Am Confronted', which Johnny rewrote as 'So Alone'. These songs are notable for how Johnny's controlled-explosion guitar style and gutter-whine vocal drawl appear almost fully developed.

The Murcia/Kane rhythm section is competently functional, with Billy displaying cliffhanger Keith Moon tendencies in his scattershot beat keeping. Rick Rivets is confined to a rhythm role while Johnny steals the show, singing and playing lead. 'That's Poison' roars out as an anthem of bleak urban desperation and angst. Johnny's familiar banana-skin guitar licks and fills spill out in all their ragged glory, louder than everyone else and spitting pure street venom.

'I am Confronted' showcases the flip side of Johnny's songwriting – the wounded angel ballad. Six years later, he'd confess, 'I prefer the slow songs.'

'Maybe good times will come for me', he wails, before bemoaning, 'Don't know what to do.' The song is infused with all the vulnerable messiness that would characterise his best slow numbers, his style already blooming into one of the seventies' most distinctive sounds. 'I Am Confronted' would never make the Dolls' repertoire, but Johnny wouldn't forget it. After rewriting it as 'So Alone' for the first Heartbreakers line-up in '75, he transferred the title to his debut solo album – which, curiously, the song didn't actually appear on, until it was reissued as a CD a decade after its original release.

Despite handling his vocal duties with consummate wasted charm, Johnny wanted to concentrate on honing his devastating new guitar style. Rick Rivets was less than delighted with the idea of seeking out a new frontman, as Johnny was one of the few vocalists that he'd encountered who wasn't suffering from acute ego overload. As he declares, 'Where could you find someone who even came close to looking as good as Johnny did?' However, Rick was outvoted and arrangements for auditions were duly made.

Enter David Roger Johansen from Staten Island.

David had been working on sound and lighting for writer, director and performer Charles Ludlam's ultra-bohemian Ridiculous Theatre Company. An introduction to his future bandmates came through a neighbour, Rodrigo Soloman, who'd previously rented one of the Murcias' rooms. 'He played congas and I played harmonica and guitar, so we used to get together at night, smoke reefer, drink beer and jam,' recalled David. 'We were into a lot of things – cutting ham, making clothes, playing congas, making shoes – into all kinds of hustles. I was doing this theatre bit, stuff like that. He knew I was into singing in a bluesy kind of way. He knew Billy Murcia because they'd both come to the States from Bogota, Colombia, around the same time . . . and when Billy and Arthur were looking for a singer he told them about me.'

On Rodrigo's recommendation, Billy and Arthur turned up at David's Sixth Street apartment in the platform boots which Billy's mother had brought back from London. 'I'll never forget that day,' Johansen told Pete Frame. 'I opened the door and I saw these guys. They had two bottles of this Olde English 800, which was like a raunchy Colt .45 type drink. I thought they were crazy. I was quite taken by them immediately.' Arthur and Syl – who was back in New York at the time – were immediately struck by Johansen's uncanny, big-lipped likeness to Mick Jagger and his 'kooky' personality.

Born on 9 January 1950, David Johansen grew up in a lower middle-class family and attended a strict Catholic school. His father was an insurance salesman, while his mother had Irish roots. Johansen senior was musically inclined and introduced his son to a wide variety of musical styles by playing the *Anthology of American Folk Music* compilation on a regular basis.

This anthology collected together obscure pre-war 78s and consisted of everything from traditional country, blues and Cajun music to Appalachian murder ballads. The quirky selection was assembled in 1952 by filmmaker and musicologist Harry Smith – after whom David would name his own band, a half-century later. In a 2001 interview with UK music critic Barney Hoskyns, David recalled listening to the *Anthology*, 'My father, who was into light opera, had this very perverse side to him about music – which is one of the things I share with him – he had an ear for an odd song that had some kind of existential angst to it. And he would delight in playing it for children.'

Like Johnny, David had little interest in the strictures of formal education. 'I got thrown out of high school,' he told *Punk*'s John Holmstrom. 'I had a male teacher who was real hung up on me, and he used to beat the shit out of me every day . . . Then when it came down to the end of the term when we took the test and everything, I really, really busted my balls to get it together and everything. He failed me anyway with a 69 . . . which is just passing. So I kept on questioning that and he just kept on beating me and one day I just kicked him in the balls.'

After his expulsion from high school, Johansen drifted into studying art through the Art Students League, where he concentrated in portrait painting and graphics. ('I used to draw a lot.')

David was also good with words, and spent much of his bedroom adolescence writing lyrics, including one called 'Lonely Planet Boy' that would wind up on the Dolls' eponymous debut album. In addition to his enthusiasm for the girl groups, David's musical tastes leant towards Motown and the blues. 'The first record I ever bought was 'Tail Dragger' by Howlin' Wolf,' he recalled, 'a ten cent single at the Do-Del record shop in Staten Island. I put that on, and it was like, what world is this from?'

Although David shared Johnny's blues leanings, unlike his future *compadre* he was not a devout anglophile. 'When I was young I used to get the fresh thing off of English bands, but nothing musically,' Johansen told *Punk*'s Ken Draznik in 1979. 'I know a lot of kids who dig on it. Like Freddie and the Dreamers. It never turned me on though. When I was young I liked a lotta stuff. It's hard for me to say. The first thing I probably really liked was Gary US Bonds. I liked all the girl groups. I liked the old Motown sound.' Later, Johnny would declare, 'David was a real mod, I used to see him in blue jeans and moccasins.'

The young David Johansen also listened to a lot of blues. He was particularly taken by the sound of the Paul Butterfield Blues Band around the age of twelve. Butterfield was white and regarded as the foremost mid-sixties interpreter of the blues, with his raging harmonica and a stellar band that included future Dylan sideman Mike Bloomfield. David was also a fan of soul singer Howard Tate – a Philadelphia-based vocalist who made some sublime records in the latter half of the sixties, including 'Ain't Nobody Home' and 'Look At Granny Run Run'.

At the age of fifteen, David put together his first group, the Vagabond Missionaries – named after the evangelists who abandoned all possessions for their faith. 'At one point the Vagabond Missionaries were like the biggest band on Staten Island,' he crowed. 'We were just kids but we used to make 50, sometimes a hundred, bucks a week off it, working three nights a week. We used to do a lot of our own material, also we'd do hits of the day, like "Boogaloo Down Broadway", "Midnight Hour", things like that.'

Johansen says the Missionaries were more influenced by soul music than the UK bands often cited as Dolls influences. 'This band was at the same time the English bands were coming out so we hadn't had a chance to be influenced by them.'

The Vagabond Missionaries dissolved when the other group members 'all got married or went to work for the phone company, stuff like that.' Bent on pursuing his musical career, the now sixteen-year-old David formed Fast Eddie and the Electric Japs, whose gimmick was that they had all Japanese equipment. 'Sometimes I was Fast Eddie, sometimes I was a Jap,' he later revealed.

The band played standards in the colleges and the local Catholic girls school, and got as far as playing New York's West Village clubs like Cafe Wha' and Café Au Go Go. The ensemble escaped the city to tour the Northeast with better-known groups like psychedelic outfit the Group Image (whose singer Barbara would later marry Arthur Kane).

Apart from a few originals, the set was mainly Motown covers like Stevie Wonder's 'Uptight'. This went against the contemporary grain, as 'every other rock band was doing psychedelic stuff,' explained David, 'I guess that made us a novelty act.' With appropriate literalism, the Electric Japs performed in front of a Japanese flag which one of the band's father's had brought back from World War II. (The band's drummer was a Puerto Rican junkie called

Joey Carillo, who went on to a fairly successful career in jazz fusion.)

Johansen recalls, 'It was very R.D. Laing in that band, because we had all grown up together, and we knew each other very well – like it was an insanity-in-the-family kind of thing. We knew each other's idiosyncrasies to the T – it was fun, but how long can you take it? You want a little adventure in your life. I wanted to play rock'n'roll music in high school . . . I had it in the back of my mind as a kind of fantasy.

'It kind of petered out. At the time everybody was going through their own various getting-ready-for-life experiences. That can tend to be time consuming. The school of hard knocks, whatever you want to call it.'

From his early teens, David had 'terrorised Greenwich Village' and hung out in Manhattan. He was particularly drawn to the action around MacDougal Street in Greenwich Village. 'Takes about 45 minutes from Staten Island,' explained David. 'Hop on the ferry, twenty minute ride, then ten minutes on the subway to the Village . . . . We'd go to the Café Au Go-Go, Muddy Waters would play there.'

Johansen was also a massive fan of Janis Joplin – 'I loved Janis Joplin like a queer loves Judy Garland' – and followed her everywhere including to San Francisco in 1969, when he stayed in nearby Berkeley. In New York, he was a regular at the Fillmore East from the late sixties through to the early seventies. In a 1995 *Q* interview with Mat Snow, David painted an amusing picture of his youth: 'We thought our gang, The Up Against The Wall Motherfuckers, were political at the time – it gave us *carte blanche* to be assholes. I had this gift to be able to jump up on a stoup and incite a riot. My mother used to say I was a Commie dupe. You had the war then. Times were different.'

In addition to being the local radical hothead, Johansen unsurprisingly – given his inherent theatricality and big-lipped Lauren Bacall looks – 'got into a theatrical trip for a while,' landing a small part in a Theatre of the Ridiculous production. His girlfriend of the time, Diane Poluski, was a former model who hung out in the court of Andy Warhol. She'd played Holly Woodlawn's pregnant sister in *Trash* and introduced David to many of Warhol's entourage.

While the rest of the future Dolls boys cruised Nobody's – described by transgender rocker Jayne County as a hangout for 'young guys from Queens who wanted to be Rod Stewart' – David hung with the art and drag crowd at Max's Kansas City, although he wasn't averse to slumming it with the lowlifes found in less rarefied establishments – especially if they were female.

Situated on Union Square, at the south end of Park Avenue South, Max's had become established as a pivotal New York watering hole, attracting luminaries from art, music and literature including Truman Capote, the Stones and William Burroughs. Between 1968-69, future Blondie siren Deborah Harry worked there as a waitress, by which time the bar was approaching the vertex of its popularity with the hip elite.

Max's was also a regular haunt for the inmates of Andy Warhol's Factory, whose bill was rumoured to be in excess of $3000 a month. Exotic pseudo-superstars such as Viva, Ultra Violet, Brigid Polk, Candy Darling and Eric Emerson took up residence with their mentor in the bar's backroom. The clique quickly developed a reputation among Max's staff for being the rudest customers in the place and for never leaving tips. Eight-hour Warhol movies were shown and the Lou Reed incarnation of the Velvet Underground – who had opened the venue in December 1965 – played their final shows there in 1970. Johansen was introduced to the Warhol set via his girlfriend and managed to fit in.

When Arthur and Billy came knocking at David's door he recognised them as somebodies from Nobody's, but overcame any innate Max's snobbery as they wore 'the same kind of drags' as him. 'We knew each other because we wore these thrift store clothes and nun's shoes – like men's shoes with a stack heel,' explained David. Intrigued, he agreed to hook up with the rest of the group at Rusty's, where they blasted through a couple of covers.

As well as his scandalised vocalisations, David demonstrated his Sonny Boy Williamson/Paul Butterfield-style harmonica chops. Visually and stylistically, Johansen gave the group a theatrically charismatic focal point. It was love at first sight. 'Johnny was just sitting there, going like this on his guitar, Arthur plugged in, Billy banged on some drums, I started screaming and that was it,' he explained.

'I was originally the lead singer, but then we got David in,' recalled Johnny. 'We sort of liked the way he looked . . . and he could play harmonica pretty good.'

'When we met we were all very similar. In dress, in attitudes, we knew what we thought about things and how we had to do it,' Johansen told *Disc*'s Lisa Robinson in 1973. 'None of us really ever went to school . . . The Dolls for me is a vehicle for getting my thoughts across.'

'We met each other because we were street people,' he told *Circus* in 1974. 'We were after the easiest way to get high with the least amount of money. When you leave the house for an evening's entertainment with only two bucks in your pocket, you know you're gonna wind up in the same place. We wanted to do something artistic. This was the best thing we could do. We were just hanging around. We weren't anybody – just the darlings of beer society. One day we decided we should do something, so we did.'

Like 'Actress', 'the Dolls' was one of a number of potential names that had been suggested, then forgotten about, as the developing band concentrated on learning songs and achieving some rudimentary mastery of their instruments. Now that they had a line-up that made playing gigs a genuine possibility, the question of what to call the quintet of Thunders, Johansen, Kane, Rivets and Murcia resurfaced.

Syl's original suggestion of 'The New York Dolls' was resurrected, although, in what was to become his trademark style, David couldn't resist subsequently embroidering the tale for public consumption. 'Sylvain came up with this name the Dolls and I tagged on the New York,' he told Pete Frame. On another occasion he said it was the name of a gang he was in on Staten Island. In 1973 he told *Record Mirror*, 'I met Arthur at a screening of *Beyond the Valley of the Dolls* – we were both into dolls, I suppose.' Arthur himself reckoned it sounded like something from a 1930s Broadway musical. Talking to *Punk* in 1976, David declared, 'We took our name from Barbie and Ken dolls. It was something you could mould into whatever you wanted it to be. That was the idea – Dolls was supposed to be a name that you couldn't define because it was whatever you wanted it to be.'

Speaking in 2005, Rick Rivets asserted that it was Arthur who added the

'New York' element to Syl's 'Dolls', as a means of acquiring an instant local following. 'I think it was most likely Arthur who put the New York in – like the New York Yankees,' recalled Rick. 'There is the New York Dolls Hospital that Syl said he worked near, but we used to pass that place all the time years before the band was ever together. We used to see that place in the 1960s, when we would cut school and Arthur would take the car and we would ride around with our girlfriends checking out New York City and all the different parts. And I remember passing the New York Dolls Hospital and saying that we should go up there and take some pictures of ourselves around the pieces of broken dolls – like the Beatles did with the 'butcher cover' – but it never panned out 'cos we were probably too stoned to leave the car.'

David's penchant for mythologizing the band's formation has also been evident in various subsequent interviews. Even though the original members had been rehearsing for some months at Rusty Beanie's when he turned up, Johansen sometimes tried to portray the group's origins as a complete happenstance – a group of guys hanging out at Nobody's, eyeing up girls. People asked what they did. 'We're in a rock'n'roll band,' they'd reply. When they asked David what they were called, he would reply, 'The Dolls.'

'One day we just decided to go jam at a place, and I said, "I'll sing," so we just did, and we started doing it every day,' he insisted.

David recalled that the newborn Dolls 'bust it out up there' at Rusty's for 'about three months' after he joined. As the quintet set about assimilating their frontman, a steady stream of friends dropped in to party and check out the group.

Among these visitors was a drummer named Jerry Nolan. 'Jerry never needed an invitation to Rusty's,' observes Rick. 'He was a very down to earth guy who never came down looking to take Billy's job, so he was always welcome. He was in another band at the time, and I think he would often come down with the bass player or by himself.

'It was always great when Jerry came down, because when Billy would take a break Jerry would always ask if he could jam, and him and his bassist would often jam with me and Johnny and we would do that song "You Don't Love Me No More" – which Johnny would later feature in his live shows. It was always a pleasure to see Jerry, the consummate professional.'

Shortly before Christmas, the band made their live debut – entirely by accident. Over the road from the cycle shop was a rundown welfare hotel called the Endicott. Welfare hotels are city-run hostelries, sump pits of abject poverty and crime. They house the homeless but are considered far down the ladder of importance by the city bosses.

The welfare workers had organised a Christmas party for the residents, but the group they'd booked pulled out at the last minute. A couple of guys had heard the Dolls' rehearsals booming out from across the road and asked the band if they'd fill in. 'It was a party for the welfare people that lived at the hotel and we were given free food for playing some music for them,' confirms Rick. 'The folks that were there were really grateful to have us give them a little joy at such a lonely time of the year.'

Faced with a mainly black and Puerto Rican audience, The Dolls launched into a set consisting of covers such as Otis Redding's 'Don't Mess With

Cupid', 'Showdown' by Archie Drell and other R&B covers. 'They got a real hoot out of it,' recalled Johansen. 'We were terrible, but we felt real proud.'

In addition to hosting the New York Dolls' inaugural outing, the Endicott Hotel marked Rick Rivets' first and last gig with the band he'd helped form. 'That was probably the best time I ever had with those guys,' observes Rick, 'because they actually seemed to be sincere about having the Christmas spirit and really caring about someone else besides themselves.'

Having returned from London, Syl was less than delighted to discover that the group had appropriated the band name which he viewed as his, 'When I came back George, David, Johnny, Billy and Arthur were the New York Dolls – with my fucking name,' he asserts. 'I was so fucking pissed off, I said, "If you've got my name then I'm in the fucking band."' After overcoming his initial vexation, he became something of a fixture at the cycle shop. 'Sylvain showed up one night after he got deported from Amsterdam for not paying his hotel bill,' remembered David. 'He was a natural for us and he knew the other guys.'

This had the effect of marginalising Rick. 'It was starting to become uncomfortable, going to practice and having someone hanging around that, you just know, wanted your gig,' he recalls. Additionally, David's brash, diva-like nature rubbed the guitarist up the wrong way. 'David Johansen comes in and right off starts going, "Well you play here, and you stop here, and we're gonna do this song, and blah, blah, blah." Bad first impression. He had a bad habit of holding on to the bottle or joint whenever it was passed his way. It was always, "Well are you gonna pass it or drink the whole thing?"' Deciding that 'it wasn't fun anymore', Rick began planning to decamp and form a new band.

The final straw came on New Year's Eve 1971, as Rick recalls. 'We were supposed to play this New Year's Eve party, and the guy who was throwing it changed his mind at the last minute, and there were about a hundred people outside of his loft during a snowstorm begging him to open the doors so we could get warm. He let us in just as we were about to break every window in the place and beat the crap out of him if he didn't open the door. It was probably one of the worst New Years ever – and I've had some bad ones.

'So that night was the last time I saw the band, as we all went our own way after the ball dropped, and Arthur stopped by the next week to tell me that I was replaced by Syl. And really I couldn't have given a flying fuck, as it felt like a giant weight was lifted off of me.'

'Originally, Rick Rivets was the other guitar player, but he started fucking around, coming to practice late and stuff like that, and so we canned him, and got Sylvain in,' asserted Johnny. 'He'd been in a band with me before the Dolls, and it was him, in fact, who named the New York Dolls, even though he wasn't in the group at the time.'

'What I think happened was that George was not having a good time,' Syl observed in 2005. 'Something had happened and he was getting too drunk. Then he just didn't want to do it anymore. Then they asked me to be in it – I said, "It's about time, thank you very much."'

With their line-up settled, and a debut performance under their belts, the New York Dolls were ready to show their finery to the world. Now the shocking seventies could really begin.

The
Darlings of
Beer Society

'We like to look bored to the bottom of
our bowels.' – *David Johansen*

In the grand manner of all cool groups, the New York Dolls had their look
down from the very outset. While long nights were spent in Rusty's cycle
shop working on their sound, the band's image coalesced naturally.

Syl and Billy's involvement in the fashion industry meant that they had well
developed ideas about style and design, as well as access to the latest trends
from both sides of the Atlantic. Individually, the Dolls were already out-glam-
ming the rest of New York – in part, thanks to Truth & Soul's London connections; they were able to snarf up the cream of Kensington Market's platform shoes, loon pants and satin jackets before anyone else in the city.

The primary element of the early Dolls' collective image was cheap glamour. Aside from the prized items passed on to them by Syl and Billy, the impoverished trio of Johnny, Arthur and David were generally dependent on their
imaginations and ready access to a number of thrift shops, which were common on the Lower East Side. Anything gaudy, camp or kitsch was fine. Frocks
were even better. The dolls were *A Rock Band*, and aimed for a cartoon-like
distillation of their chosen medium's primal essence. They wanted to thrill the
kids, shock the squares and, above all, to look totally unlike the hippies. 'The
musicians in New York were into fashion,' explained Dee Dee Ramone in an
interview with filmmaker Lech Kowalski. 'It was a competitive thing and the
Dolls had the look down the best – they'd wear their girlfriends' clothes.'

David Johansen approached his duties as frontman as if it were a scripted
role, and made sure his wardrobe fitted the part. His resemblance to Mick
Jagger gave him a head start. Those lips, combined with his penchant for

evoking classic feminine Hollywood imagery, resulted in his striking mix of androgynous street urchin and pouting, rubber-lipped starlet.

Johnny Thunders had exaggerated his Keith Richards look to incorporate a striking leather jacket and platform boots mutation. The boots were huge, white objects which he would sport, scuffed and worn, for over a year. Like Keith, if Johnny liked an item, he would wear it into the ground. By early 1972, his hair had become an erupting Ronnie Spector bearskin and his clothes were street glam and black. Though not averse to some sparkle or feathers, Johnny generally undercut anything too feminine with more butch items. A garter would be set off by a swastika armband, or a flowing silk scarf matched with a cowboy shirt.

From any distance greater than about ten feet, Johnny's initial impact was mainly down to that hair – the biggest in the Dolls and, indeed, all of rock-'n'roll at that time. 'When they came on stage, it was outrageous to see these boys,' recalled Mariann Bracken. 'To see Johnny with the tight pants and the platform shoes, and the eyeliner, and the hair teased out. It was very shocking – I was beginning to wonder whether my brother was gay or not.'

At the start of the Dolls, Sylvain swathed his small frame in the spoils of his Kensington Market trolley dashes – platforms, flared jeans, and long-sleeved Mickey Mouse t-shirts. Then he started introducing a variety of second-hand exotica ranging from Boy Scout shirts to cowboy tops, sometimes boosted by kiddie accessories like a toy holster, before introducing chiffon and frills. Syl was the first to sport garish makeup, although his *amigo* Billy wasn't far behind. Both had curly black hair, which lent itself to ready teasing into a mass of Bolan-esque corkscrews.

As to how man mountain Arthur Kane arrived at his unique combinations of ballet tutus, nurses' uniforms, sparkly pantyhose, outsize babies' pacifiers and hot pants is not known. As ever, Arthur marched to the beat of his own very singular drummer. Roy Hollingworth's landmark *Melody Maker* feature, a few months later, described him as 'strange, supine bassist Arthur Kane, blonde, and with white makeup, tights, high-heeled shoes and a mouth full of surly posing.'

Historically, New York City has often looked to the UK and Europe for its fashion tips. The glam movement, as kick-started by Bolan, would have far-reaching repercussions, persuading everyone from the Stones to Elton John to daub themselves in sparkle. In 1971 even Bowie had yet to cut his hair and ditch his floppy hats and Oxford bags.

Stateside, the Dolls took cues from Detroit's White Panthers, the MC5 – who'd sported rock'n'roll spangles in 1968 – and Alice Cooper, who paved the way for the band in a number of respects. Also from Detroit, Cooper and his band were essentially a bunch of tarted-up hoodlums hell-bent on putting on the most outrageous show in town. In addition to their stage gear of dresses and fetish wear, the rude and raucous Cooper boys confronted the audiences with increasingly lavish stage sets which included an execution *tableau* complete with electric chair.

On a nightly basis, Alice ended up in a straitjacket and dismembered dolls bit the dust. Hammering, high-energy guitar thrash performed in drag to confused crowds broadcast a profoundly mixed message, combining aggression with ersatz glamour. During the late sixties, when denim-worship was at its peak, only the Doors, the MC5 and the Stooges – themselves inspired by the auto-destructive brilliance of Hendrix and The Who – had transformed the live setting into such visceral theatre.

'The only other group I can think of who attack the audience and get the beast enraged and moving is the Stooges,' asserted Alice Cooper in *International Times*. 'Iggy just destroys the audience. He spits on 'em, picks a fight, once he got knocked out and the band just kept on playing until he came round and got into singing again. I like doing things like grabbing girls' feet and spitting on them real slow so it dribbles down them and they freak out and faint.'

In early 1972, Johnny became a proper Bowery boy when he and Janis moved into a loft above a Chinese noodle shop at 119 Chrystie Street, at the edge of the Lower East Side. The space was convenient for Rusty's, and Billy and Sylvain also moved into the small loft as rehearsals intensified.

Chrystie Street begins at Houston Street where Second Avenue ends. One block west, the Bowery runs parallel, carrying on from Third Avenue. A few blocks east is Ludlow Street, where Lou Reed and John Cale had started the Velvet Underground in the mid-sixties. Even now, the general layout of the neighbourhood remains largely unchanged, tenements forming concrete valleys that once ran with hustlers. By the new millennium, the area had been stripped of both danger and colour as a result of Mayor Rudy Giuliani's 'zero tolerance' campaign – an initiative designed to milk the cash cow of tourism without addressing the reasons why the area became so dangerous in the first place.

Johnny and pals had scored themselves a pad in the heart of one of these dangerous areas. This was no bohemian utopia – it was shunned by the artistic community who preferred to shelter more safely, north of Houston in the East Village.

The Bowery had begun in the nineteenth century as the chic centre of New York theatre life. However, by 1850 the social elite had upped sticks to Broadway, as immigrants from Europe poured in and tenements went up to accommodate them. The dandified stage-door revellers were supplanted by a less effete form of 'Bowery boy'. The diverse ethnicity of the area's underclass led, naturally enough, to a desire to band together for protection and comfort. Amongst the young, this meant gangs. In addition to such exotically named crews as the True Blue Americans and the O'Connell Guards, the Bowery was home to New York's most notorious gang – the Bowery Bhoys, an Irish Catholic outfit notorious for gouging out their enemies' eyes.

Just as the street gangs of Johnny's youth and the Shangri-Las' lyrics were dangerous and stylish in equal measure, the Bowery Bhoys dressed sharp and hung tough. The gang went in for extended sideburns, slickly oiled hair, stovepipe hats, durable boots and scarves. They chewed tobacco like James Dean chewed gum, and usually carried knives strapped to their legs. The look caught on across the city and the concept of the gangsta wannabe was born.

By the end of the 1900s, the Bowery was a major centre for night-time action, crammed with saloons and low-rent music halls. The district's hookers acted independently from the city's whorearchy, and were still going strong in the early twentieth century. By then, the Lower East Side was a crammed mass of rat-infested tenements.

As the subway enabled greater mobility during the twentieth century, the population of the Lower East Side started spreading out, leaving the poorest sections of the local population behind. The Bowery boy gave way to the Bowery bum, as flophouses proliferated, violent crime flourished and hard drugs became prevalent.

By the time the Dolls hit town, one of the principle reasons for walking downtown past Houston was the acquisition of heroin, whether it be from corner dealers or in shooting galleries, some of which started as opium dens in the previous century. For those of that disposition, copping 'Chinese rocks' was like a trip to the corner store. Later in the decade, the Heartbreakers would dedicate their first album to 'the boys on Norfolk Street', a dope-addled location a few blocks east which Johnny described as 'like another world.' It's not like that now, but right through to the 1990s, Norfolk Street was on a par with Alphabet City for dangerous drug-related activity.

In the 1970s, musicians gravitated to the Lower East Side because it was cheap compared with most of Manhattan south of Harlem. But some artists grew up there, such as Willy DeVille, who later bunched together a bunch of soul-leaning hoodlums to form Mink DeVille. They were one of the CBGBs bands that sprang up in the wake of the Dolls, but Willy actually grew up around the Dolls' adopted stamping ground.

In the seventies, Willy emanated street suss and sartorial cool with his razor-sharp suits and pompadour hairstyle. His music, when not prowling the back alleys and gutters already traversed by Lou Reed, echoed the urban romance of Leiber and Stoller and the girl groups. DeVille described the Ronettes as 'a backdrop you took for granted' as he grew up. His tough upbringing defined his take on rock'n'roll: 'My theory on music, just as music, is that if you can't fuck to it, it's no good. I like music you can do it to. It's gotta pump,' adding, 'Our music is street music. It's American street music.'

DeVille was in one of the Lower East Side gangs – and lived to tell the tale. 'Most of those are all dead though, you know, you don't live too long . . . dead, in jail . . . we didn't assemble ourselves in a conscious thing to have a gang. We all kinda hung out on the corner together, y'know, like most of the kids.'

In 1972 the New York Dolls would be strolling through the crowded streets of that neighbourhood sporting ladies' shoes, feather boas and make-up. But they had the style to get away with it. 'See it all depends on the way you walk in what neighbourhood,' explained DeVille. 'If you walk like you're uptight, everybody'll know you're uptight. You can pretty much survive anywhere if you're loose and you can hang out. If you're cool, no matter where you are, people *know*, y'know?'

Johnny, Janis, Syl and Billy's loft in Chrystie Street was basically one large room with a bathroom. The inhabitants partitioned off their respective living areas with ex-army tents. They were invariably broke and survived on hand-outs from friends and relatives, and by shoplifting. 'We took over this loft and we could look out of our back window at the backs of the flophouses on the Bowery,' recounts Syl. 'Those lofts go for a million dollars now.'

'This place was horrible,' recalled David to Pete Frame. 'There were all these prostitutes down there. There'd be whores giving blowjobs when you came in the door. They wouldn't even move. They wouldn't even bat an eyelash. You'd go in the door and you'd have to climb over them to go up the stairs.

'It was a horrible place, but it was very cheap though. It only cost about 200 a month . . . Sometimes when we didn't have the money we'd get other roommates in who had jobs to stay with us and pitch in. We used to play there once a month – we'd have a party. Two bucks to get in.'

These rent parties provided the Dolls with an opportunity to hone their act before a small and enthusiastic gathering. The group would set up in the kitchen area and play the songs they'd been working up, such as 'Frankenstein' and 'Jet Boy'. Festivities would rage into the early hours, as the parties became havens for the local dealers, hookers and assorted nocturnal exotics. From the very start, the Dolls were cutting their musical teeth amidst chaos and debauchery.

The group survived with the aid of their families, particularly Johnny's mom and sister. 'We made many trips, sent a lot of food parcels and Western Unioned a lot of money,' recounts Mariann. 'He'd call up and say, "We've got no food," so I'd cook stuff and bring it over. Johnny didn't have to starve.'

'Personality Crisis' is the first song that Syl remembers David and Johnny writing together. David's inspiration for the complex lyrics came from a camp character he encountered in the Theatre of the Ridiculous who would regularly wail, 'Oh no, I'm having a personality crisis.'

By May 1972, the quartet had gathered sufficient confidence to make their live debut at a proper venue. This took place at the Palm Room, a basement club housed beneath the Hotel Diplomat on West 43rd Street. At the time, the room showcased rock groups, but it would later become a popular gay disco hangout where Gloria Gaynor was inaugurated as the Queen of Disco in 1975. 'We found out about this benefit for this anarchist that was coming up, a "free-somebody" programme at the Hotel Diplomat,' David told *Melody Maker* in 1978. 'Some kid who had another band told us about it, and we said, "Get us in on it!" We didn't play the benefit for political reasons – we played it because it was a gig.'

'That was the first time we ever got dressed to play,' recalled Johansen. 'Just a nice pair of pants and a nice shirt. We got a great response. There were a couple of people from the music business there – Danny Fields for one told me he thought the band were great, and all this heavy stuff, so I figured we would stick to it.'

'I think we all felt something was lacking in music,' Johansen told Roy Hollingworth in 1972. 'It wasn't exciting any more to us. Everyone was hanging about on stage, being morose . . . We didn't dig that. We reckoned what bands were lacking was pizzazz. We knew we had pizzazz, we knew what we wanted to do. We wanted to play rock . . . The time is right for some good rock again.' And loud, too – Johnny was already developing a costly knack for blowing amplifiers.

On 29 May, the Dolls made a return to the Palm Room, under the banner 'An Invitation Beyond The Valley'. The event was partly organised by Warhol's organisation and featured Jackie Curtis as support. Jackie was a speed-freak junkie transvestite who'd gained notoriety for performances in several Theatre of the Ridiculous productions. The line in Lou Reed's 'Walk On The Wild Side' – 'Jackie is just speeding away/Thought she was James Dean for a day' – is about him/her.

Although they had dominated the New York underground and art scenes for much of the 1960s, by 1972 Warhol and his Factory studio acolytes had crossed the cusp of their arch-trendiness. Much of Warhol's musical history revolved around his part in establishing the Velvet Underground as the epitome of New York cool during the 1960s. The band – originally comprised of twin creative powerhouses Reed and Cale, backed by Sterling Morrison and Maureen Tucker, and with Aryan chanteuse Nico providing icily atonal vocal embellishments – established a form of musical primitivism that would inspire subsequent generations of untutored musicians.

Warhol's patronage of the Velvets caused the worlds of art and rock to collide in an entirely new way, and set New York's hip agenda for the next half-decade. By the time the Dolls appeared as small blips on the Factory style radar, the Velvet Underground was shorn of its biggest talents and on the verge of collapse.

Although it was by no means immediately apparent, the Diplomat gig would mark the beginning of the Dolls' ascent towards occupation of the niche vacated by the Velvets at the nexus of the Big Apple art/rock confluence. 'The Velvet Underground were the older generation,' observes Syl, 'and we were the younger – sort of club kids – and we were taking over their turf.'

Support at the Palm Room came courtesy of Shaker, who featured Jerry Nolan on drums. When the Dolls took their turn, their raw energy and sheer volume was enough to leave an impression on the hundred or so friends and thrill-seekers that made up the audience.

The Warhol Factory/Jackie Curtis tie-up provided the Dolls with their next two outings. Supported by Jackie, they landed a two-night booking at one of Brooklyn's many gay bathhouses. The proliferation of these hangouts – which had existed covertly since the end of the nineteenth century – was indicative of growing confidence among the gay community, which became evident in the aftermath of 1969's Stonewall Riots – a landmark event, as it was the first time that a large group of homosexuals resisted arrest under the subjective and arcane 'indecency' laws.

In 1971, the Continental Baths – situated below the Ansonia Hotel on 73rd Street and Broadway – was the most opulent and well-known bathhouse in the city. The Bacchanalian 'Tubs', as they were known, were a focal point for the early disco scene, along with the Hotel Diplomat. There were steam rooms, discos and scenes of the wildest, drug-fuelled abandon. Tubs owner Steve Ostrow was instrumental in liberalising the city's laws on sex clubs, fighting a constant battle with the authorities and the police to establish a legitimate gay scene there.

In Brooklyn, the Dolls found themselves providing musical accompaniment to the action that was going down in the cubicles. On the first night the band dragged up for the occasion, but most of their potential audience opted to carry on fucking. The next night they wore leather, which intrigued the revellers sufficiently for them to emerge from their booths.

Arthur had been supplementing his income by selling MDA – the early form of ecstasy – which first found favour in gay establishments. His lack of pushy sales patter ensured that there was always plenty left over for personal consumption, and the band got through the gigs in a euphorically altered state.

Now that they were a proper gigging band, the Dolls abandoned the chilly charms of Rusty's cycle store and relocated their practices to a proper rehearsal complex called Talent-Recon. The studios were managed by a local performance artist and all-purpose character by the name of Satan the Fire Eater, who appropriately donned horns and a forked tail for his act.

Here, they continued to work up the new songs. 'Black Girl' was updated to the less specific 'Bad Girl' and would subsequently become a first album standout. These sessions also produced the epic 'Frankenstein', a bombastic, complex melodrama in which Johansen unleashes a stream of confused outrage around the transgressive theme of falling in love with a monster. The song was laden with creaking doom chords, dramatic drum rolls and an increasingly urgent delivery, which evoked a sense of Dr. Frankenstein's lab being turned over to some manner of orgy.

To keep rehearsals fresh and pad out their set list, the Dolls also refined cover versions of Sonny Boy Williamson's 'Don't Start Me Talking' – prodded by the blues-wailing Johansen – and 'Showdown'. The latter was first recorded by Archie Bell and the Drells and tells the story of a gang fight at a local dance hall, possibly the most New York sounding song the New York Dolls ever did. Around this time, they also tackled versions of the Kinks' 'All Day And All Of The Night', Chuck Berry's 'Back in The USA' and 'Seven Day Weekend' by Gary U.S. Bonds. They also started perfecting a salacious crawl through Muddy Waters' '54 sex-sleaze classic 'Hoochie Coochie Man'. It had been his first hit and oozed peacock-strutting voodoo sex-magick.

Shaker rehearsed in the same complex, and Jerry Nolan sometimes leant Billy his drums. Also around was Jerry's teenage pal, Peter Criss – who was in the early stages of putting together the band that would soon emerge as Kiss. 'Jerry was really good friends with Peter Criss and I think they grew up together learning how to play and liking the same famous jazz drummers like Gene Krupa,' explains Rick Rivets. 'There was a famous picture of Peter, Jerry and Gene Krupa. Peter and Jerry were about twelve or thirteen, dressed in suits with ties and there they were with their idol. They both looked real sharp and were very cool for a couple of kids.'

Criss and his three denim-clad buddies watched the burgeoning Dolls with considerable interest and took notes for a complete makeover. They painted their faces to look like grotesque clowns, aliens or animals and decked themselves out in leather and studs. They played up the sleaze in the most obvious ways – such as bassist Gene Simmons' predilection for poking out his almost prehensile tongue – and churned out the most basic, lowest-common-denominator rock'n'roll anthems.

Initially, Kiss rode the wave of interest generated by the rise of the Dolls, but quickly attained stadium status with their popularist approach. By 1975's

Alive album, the band were established as champions of the kind of pop-metal that was so basic it bordered on parody. They appealed primarily to children, who snapped up their simplistic, expertly marketed fare with enthusiasm.

There was little of the wit or sexual ambivalence that characterised the Dolls. Essentially conservative, Kiss represented a sanitised form of rebellion that could be readily marketed to middle America without anyone – aside from the inevitable religious zealots, who were prone to taking things over-literally – feeling threatened. This made the band an utterly safe product, packaged in a veneer of pantomime rebellion.

Most importantly, songs like 'Ladies In Waiting' told the world that these guys were definitely not homosexual. 'When Kiss put on makeup, it was like a truck driver putting on makeup,' observes Syl. 'If I was a truck driver and I thought I want to put on makeup and play around and I want to be a super-hero like Batman. Kiss was like Batman.' Likewise, Syl rejects any comparison between Kiss and the Dolls – 'they had nothing to do with the Revolution. Just because they wore make up – which was basically inspired by us – and they got their name from our song "Looking For A Kiss".'

The Dolls also encountered Eric Emerson and the Magic Tramps at Talent-Recon. Emerson was a bona fide New York maniac who'd danced in Warhol's Exploding Plastic Inevitable. As a result, he hung out with the Factory set and became involved with actress Elda Gentile, with whom he had children. Eric and Elda had just split up when she checked out the Dolls in rehearsal. She was particularly smitten by Sylvain's ebony curls and Pierrot looks and made a b-line for the guitarist, who ended up moving into Elda's First Avenue apartment.

Elda had a vocal group with Holly Woodlawn – also of 'Walk On The Wild Side' fame – and Diane Pulaski, David Johansen's live-in girlfriend. They were called Pure Garbage but quickly split up. Deborah Harry subsequently encountered Elda at Max's and suggested they start a new group with her friend Rosie Ross, which became the Stillettoes. Deborah's partner Chris Stein later became their roadie and played for the Magic Tramps, before Elda got the idea to ask him to join on guitar. Eventually, Debbie and Chris formed Blondie, while Eric got run over by a truck on 28 May 1975. 'They found Eric Emerson one early morning in the middle of Hudson Street,' recalled Warhol. 'Officially, he was labelled a hit-and-run victim, but we heard rumours that he'd overdosed and just been dumped there – in any case, the bicycle he'd been riding was intact.'

In 1972, there was a shortage of rock venues in New York. Playing gay bathhouses strung out on MDA might have been a blast, but the Dolls were starting to develop bigger ideas. In the absence of a manager, Janis scouted about in search of a decent venue, and came up with the Mercer Arts Center on Broadway. The Center was attached to what had been the Grand Central Hotel, which – during its 1870s heyday – had been one of the city's largest and most exclusive hotels. By the turn of the century it had become run-down and sold to the city for use as another welfare hotel.

The Mercer Arts Center was the dream of air-conditioning millionaire Seymour Kaback, who loved the theatre and wanted to build the perfect complex to realise his lofty cultural aspirations. He acquired the old building and divided it up into smaller performance areas, named after famous figures such as George Bernard Shaw and Oscar Wilde. There was a jazz lounge, a cinema for art-house movies, a room for Theatre of Cruelty presentations like Arrabel's *They Even Put Handcuffs On The Flowers*, and a bar in the foyer. He hadn't allowed space for a rock'n'roll Mecca.

'It was a renovated place,' recalled Jerry Nolan in 1977. 'It was a cross between Victorian-looking design like chandeliers and a really spacey modern *Clockwork Orange* type of place, yet it had still had some of the old things still left, like chandeliers in certain parts of the walls. It was a great combination of old Victorian and modern.'

Business hadn't been good – on many nights the place was near empty and bar takings were often negligible. In early June – with a degree of desperation – in-house booking agent Mark Lewis hired the Dolls for a test show in the Mercer's Kitchen – a small fifteen-by-60-foot space at the back of the building, more often used as an experimental video theatre. Headlining the bill were the Magic Tramps and their studio landlord, Satan. Billed as 'The Dolls of New York', the band made sure that many of those who'd attended the Chrystie Street rent gigs were aware of the show, and around 30 of the band's coterie of low-rent revellers made the small room seem packed.

Phonograph Record's Alan Betrock caught the show and described the Dolls set as 'Straight out teenage rock'n'roll', adding, 'by the finale, the small room was packed full, and the sweaty bodies danced, shook and cheered for this unknown group.' The Dolls were immediately re-booked for a second show on 13 June. 'We were getting so many kids in there that they gave us one of the back rooms, which was called the Oscar Wilde Room,' recalls Sylvain. 'We commanded a pretty interesting crowd that were mainly artists and writers – all kinds of outcasts all put together . . . We were young and screaming our generation's next move.'

With the Dolls' instant impact persuading the Mercer's management to give them a seventeen-week residency in the 200 capacity Oscar Wilde Room, the night stalking characters that had started following the band began to use the venue as a regular hangout. A small scene was born and the Center's finances took an upturn, with the Dolls being paid a paltry five dollars a gig. 'They didn't even want us at the Mercer Arts Center until they counted the bar receipts,' Johnny later told *Rolling Stone*, who described him as, 'a ferret-like kid who calls himself Johnny Thunder and looks like a hybrid Keith Richard-Rod Stewart.'

'We were the only thing that was happening in that entire place,' David told Lisa Robinson in *Disc & Music Echo*. 'One time they decided that they didn't want rock there, and they just had their plays, and their *avant-garde* happenings, and they lost a *fortune* at the bar that week! So they had to ask us back.'

Populated with exotic females of both sexes, the crowds got larger and more outrageous with each Dolls show. 'We had quite a hot scene going in those days, them halcyon days,' reminisced David. 'The Mercer was a great showcase for us, because people could go and drink, and dance, and see us,' added Arthur. 'The Mercer was great,' enthuses *Pork* stage manager and scene mainstay Leee Black Childers. 'They would have Wayne County playing in one room, Ruby and the Rednecks in another, and the Dolls in another . . . you could just run from place to place and see them all. There was always so much happening in that place.'

'Everyone dressed up and came to the gigs and danced down in front of the stage,' recounts Jayne County. 'It was the perfect excuse for every freak in New York to come down and play house – dress up in Mum's clothes, hear raw music and take every drug known to man. I remember [noted rock critic] Danny Goldberg saying in a sort of shell-shocked way, "They are the most significant band to come out of NY since the Velvet Underground." And they were.'

Another of those struck by the Dolls' energy was photographer Bob Gruen, 'There was bleacher seating that was so steep it looked like a wall of people, and a stage with the New York Dolls playing in the middle – the loudest, fastest, most exciting music I'd ever heard,' he told the *New York Trash* website's Carlo McCormick. 'Everyone seemed to know each other. It was a big crowd and in the middle, a band that was just so wild. The way they dressed! They were wearing some things that girls might wear, but they weren't dressed like women. No woman dressed like that!'

When legendary gonzo rock critic Lester Bangs picked up the buzz developing around the Dolls, he headed down to the Mercer and was immediately impressed by the outrageous look of the group's following: 'I thought I was a reasonably cool looking guy for the time but was I wrong! My friend and I walked in the auditorium and were blown away by the crowd. We said, "If the crowd looks like this, what does the band look like?"'

One of the elements common to many of the Dolls' musical and stylistic influences was the desire – or at least the tendency – to shock mainstream audiences. Whether it was the leather menace of Gene Vincent, the chemical-driven anarchy of Iggy and the Stooges, or the baby doll dismembering antics of Alice Cooper, the Dolls had – collectively and individually – homed in on artists that went against the grain. For any healthy young buck looking to spice things up with some transgressive behaviour, in 1972 there was no surer way of doing so than camping it up in a frock.

Drag queens and all manner of androgynous pick 'n' mixery turned the Oscar Wilde Room into a surreal melting pot, while David Johansen's thespian inclinations already predisposed him toward a high camp, 'Faggeresque' persona. As *Phonograph Record*'s Ron Ross would subsequently observe; David was already 'a trend unto himself in New York'.

At first, Johnny never looked anything less than a rocker from the more glamorous side of the gutter, but gradually began to soften his looks as his bandmates piled on the makeup in increasingly liberal quantities. Arthur continued his own strange couturial odyssey. 'I went the furthest with it in the first place,' he gently declared, 'we played a Yippie benefit show when I decided I wasn't going to wear any pants, and we had to figure out what to do with no pants on. All I had on was a leotard dance top and a pair of opaque stockings and boots.'

It was at the Mercer that the Dolls, feeding off the antics and appearance of their crowd, blossomed into the New York Dolls of larger-than-life legend. They emphasised different aspects of their image with every show, trying out new looks and also honing the stage set which would make up the bulk of their first album.

Interview magazine's Ed McCormack reached into the Rolling Stones book of metaphors to describe David Jo – as he had coquettishly taken to calling himself – as 'Mick Jagger's skinny kid sister'. David had little time for the Stones comparisons. 'We're a lot faster than the Stones', he observed – before another Doll added, 'and younger.'

Lester Bangs noted that Johansen 'dressed like Greta Garbo'. Although he liked to portray his sexuality as being ambivalent and experimental – 'I'm tri-sexual, I'll try anything' – Johansen was rarely without a girlfriend. The gender-blurring 'David Jo' was simply another type of performance. And he played the part perfectly.

The rest of the band was staunchly heterosexual, but the way in which the dangerous, taboo-smashing glamour they were projecting magnetised their biologically female following encouraged them to keep frocking up.

From the very start, the Dolls were their very own five-man multi-media event. Their intensely visual stage show and Warhol connections combined down and dirty rock'n'roll with a kind of high-concept art-camp. Although the band had developed a shocking, era-defining look that would turn on the art set as much as it did the rock cognoscenti, it had happened organically, without any collective contrivance. 'We were so far ahead of our time that we didn't even realise it,' observes Syl. 'We never sat down around a big table and worked out a master plan to dress up as girls and shit – I mean, Johnny was homophobic!'

There was nothing else like the New York Dolls. Their sound and their look, as well as the sheer 'otherness' of the audience that they were bringing into the Mercer, marked them out as blisteringly different. Never slow to catch the unique scent of a *zeitgeist*, Andy Warhol's celebrity-obsessive *Interview* magazine wasted little time in covering them. Usually the magazine was pre-occupied with gossip and the latest doings of Bianca Jagger or Jackie Onassis. For the publication to home in on a relatively unknown band that had no manager, let alone a record deal, was both highly unusual and indicative of the seismic waves the Dolls were creating among New York's style elite.

Interview contributor Ed McCormack went on to provide the Dolls with their first major slice of national exposure, when he submitted a piece to *Rolling Stone* detailing Bowie's two consecutive visits to the Mercer in September 1972. Under the headline 'New York City's Ultra-living Dolls', McCormack goes on to describe the Dolls' 'punky Stones-influenced rock-'n'roll and their funky transsexual style', before coining the immortal line, 'before going onstage the Dolls pass around Max Factor lipstick the way other bands pass around a joint.

'Not since the original Velvet Underground has any local band cultivated such a loyal cult following among neo-decadents in New York, and – more surprising – managed to do so without benefit of a recording contract.' The interview took place at the Fourteenth Street apartment shared by Sylvain and Billy – who McCormack describes as being passed out on the sofa while the others drink and get stoned. 'We like to look sixteen and bored shitless,' declared Johansen – an uncanny foreshadowing of the whole punk scene that would ignite four years hence.

As the weeks of their Mercer residency rolled by, the Dolls were becoming the hip band to see. Former Velvets Lou Reed and John Cale came by to check out the scene, as did Alice Cooper and Bette Midler. On the night he first caught the Dolls, Lester Bangs found himself sat next to the prog-rock Harry Potter, Todd Rundgren, 'dressed all in pink. I mean, complete with pink hair, pink make-up and pink gloves.'

At the same time the Dolls were making their presence felt in New York, David Bowie was beginning to take off in the UK with the July release of his *Ziggy Stardust* album. Ever the cultural sponge, Bowie had partially based his Ziggy alter-ego on characters from around the Mercer scene – in particular, Wayne County, Cherry Vanilla and Leee Black Childers. The previous August, Bowie had checked out their outrageous production of Warhol's play *Pork* at London's Roundhouse.

When Bowie visited New York the following month he hitched up with the Warhol crowd again, as well as Lou Reed. In her book, *Man Enough To Be A Woman*, Wayne – now Jayne – County remembers Bowie coming to see *Pork* every night then popping backstage to chat. 'But all the while he was studying our makeup for his own future use . . . David Bowie just stole everything. His whole look came from us and the cast of *Pork*.'

When *Pork* began its yearlong run at the Roundhouse on 5 May 1971, it was by far the most outrageous thing yet seen on a London stage. The dialogue was based on conversations Warhol had taped over the years with one theme in common. 'It was conversations that took place about different kinds of shit,' Wayne told *Zigzag* in 1977. 'Pigeon shit, cat shit . . . comparing them with each other, everything. One sick thing after another. We used nothing but a bunch of nymphos, queens and prostitutes running around the stage naked. A girl member popped her tits out in front of the Queen Mother's house and got arrested.'

One of the loudest and proudest transvestites in New York, Wayne County – who took his name from the location of the notorious women's prison in Michigan – was born in the small Georgia town of Dallas in 1952 and, as a child, liked to take part in neighbourhood plays. He escaped the draft by turning up in semi-drag and announcing that 'her' husband wouldn't let 'her' go to Vietnam. In 1970, he hopped a Greyhound bus to New York City and hustled his way into a couple of plays. In *Femme Fatale* Wayne played a psychotic lesbian prison inmate alongside Jackie Curtis and a young Patti Smith, who played 'a dyke gangster'. Patti also appeared in another play with Wayne, *Islands*, which saw her cast in the role of a speed freak.

Wayne then wrote, directed and starred in *World, Birth of a Nation*, which he described as 'a rock musical with no music. The words were all from songs by Dylan, the Velvets, the Stones.' The play featured John Wayne giving birth to a baby and the author playing Florence Nightingale. 'This was before the Dolls. The boys in my play wore women's shoes, make-up ribbons in their hair . . . and that's all! Oh . . . their pubic hair was coloured. Warhol was there and he was jumping up and down in his seat! Every second there was something going on,' recalls Jayne. 'People dying, fucking, killing, police raiding, people cutting each other's cocks off and eating them! In the dressing room everybody was fucking each other while they were putting on their make-up.'

Having made inroads into theatre, Wayne decided to venture out with a rock band at around the same time as the Dolls first started rehearsing. He called his group Queen Elizabeth and utilised the rock-solid foundation of Jerry Nolan, who'd joined from Shaker. 'I was in rehearsals with my band Queen Elizabeth and the Dolls beat me debuting by two weeks,' Jayne County recounted in 2005. 'I was really shocked when I heard about them. I was getting all my material together, and the props and the music and all. Singing songs like "It Takes A Man Like Me To Find A Woman Like Me", "Queenage Baby", "Max's Kansas City" and [wearing] black women's underwear, fishnet stockings, garish make up, the whole bit.

'I was walking down Christopher Street when a friend of mine stopped me, and we started chatting. I was telling him all about my band and how excited I was, and that we had our first gig at New York University, when he suddenly stopped me and said, "You know there is a band playing at the Mercer Arts Center, called the New York Dolls. They are men in make up and they wear women's shoes and articles of women's clothing, but they're not drag queens."

'I couldn't believe it. I questioned my friend all about the Dolls – I just could not believe that someone else had the same idea as me! I was dumbfounded actually. They were playing every Tuesday, so I went to see them and took my band who got very upset that they had beat us to the punch. But I assured them that what I was doing was much more extreme and theatrical.'

Queen Elizabeth's live debut ended in abrupt but triumphant chaos. 'The dean of the college pulled the plug out because we were so disgusting!' boasts Jayne. 'He said we were turning lunchtime into a 42nd Street smut shop. It was true . . . and the people were liking it!'

Wayne County took the transsexual outrage element to its furthest limits as he honed his act around New York's less salubrious niteries. His routine often saw him wobble onto the stage sporting a baby doll nightie, pull out a rubber dildo and squirt the crowd with milk. Another party piece was perching on a toilet bowl and realistically appearing to take a dump using dog food – 'It would've been disgusting otherwise' – which he'd then lob at the audience. Wayne was especially proud of his custom-made shoes where 'the bottoms were balls and the front a cock'.

Like the Dolls, Wayne understood that shock tactics could provide a ready shortcut to getting yourself noticed. He later explained that he did it 'to get attention, to shock. I liked to upset people. I thought it was funny because it was done in a comedy manner.' Little wonder that Queen Elizabeth would quickly become established as the ideal band to support the Dolls.

Wayne shared a flat with Leee Black Childers, who'd stage-managed *Pork*. Leee, who hailed from Louisville, Kentucky, was the personification of Southern charm, which further riled his hometown rednecks as he was also gently camp. However, he always carried an air of quiet authority under the preening queenery. Leee was also good at spotting potential talent – in both senses.

'I met Leee on Christopher Street in West Greenwich Village,' recalls Jayne. 'There was a real street scene in NY at the time . . . People would sit on stoops on the street and watch the freak show go by. Take all sorts of drugs, LSD, pot, peyote, hash, TCB, THC, and angel dust. People were really stoned out of their fucking minds! Some on acid appeared to be reciting Shakespeare to the sky. Others were nodding out on downs or throwing up, and others were munching away on pizza and bags of junk food while discussing the future of man and planet earth and his relationship with the universe. And others were strung out on speed – rapping a mile a minute about everything that came to mind. Or just talking very quickly to themselves.'

World, Birth of a Nation also starred Cherry Vanilla, a young New York DJ, as 'a nymphomaniac necrophiliac nurse'. Having befriended Wayne and Leee, Cherry also featured in the London production of *Pork* – playing the part of Warhol associate Brigid Polk – and also claims to have helped shape Bowie's Ziggy Stardust image. 'He was just walking round without a gimmick . . . By the time I finished with him he was hot. Real hot.'

In *Punk*, Leee asserts that Bowie 'mainly hoisted the look and the clothes individually', citing a complete replication of Warhol superstar Cyrinda Foxe's outfit on his American tour as an example. 'He then signed me to MainMan and kept me under wraps,' insists Jayne, 'of course, it would not have looked good at all if people could see where he got his ideas from.'

By the time Ziggy hit Carnegie Hall in September 1972, Leee, Cherry and Wayne were all on the payroll of Bowie and his manager Tony DeFries' operation, MainMan. Wayne was under the impression he'd be making an album, Leee was a suitably decadent part of the Bowie publicity machine, and Cherry was charged with finding ways of persuading DJs to play his records. 'Then David Bowie started turning up at Dolls shows, like you know, with a notebook!' exclaims Jayne. Certainly Bowie was impressed by the Dolls, reportedly telling them that they had 'the energy of six English bands'.

In a 1977 *Zigzag* interview, Cherry outlined her philosophy for masterminding much of Bowie's 1972 promotional campaign with the maxim, 'Never do with your hands what you can do with your mouth.' From her customary fellatic kneeling position she became the inaccessible star's intimate point of contact with the music business. 'I screwed disc jockeys across America to get David Bowie's records played on the radio.' Cherry also asserted that, like the Dolls, Bowie's homosexual allusions were 'all hype. He never sleeps with guys. I've slept with him and believe me he knows how to turn people on. But he never sleeps with guys. We just let people think that.'

The Dolls' newfound favour with New York's hip elite meant they could now commandeer the good tables in the back room at Max's Kansas City. In this dimly lit, 20-by-30 space, the group quickly found that their influences were fast becoming their contemporaries, as they hobnobbed with the likes of Iggy Pop, Alice Cooper and Lou Reed. The Dolls were invited to swanky parties at Warhol's invitation, Johnny started going out with Alice's ex-girlfriend,

Cindy Lang, and David extended his personal sphere to embrace Cyrinda Foxe – much to the dismay of Warhol, who had envisioned her marrying a nice rich man. The ever-cheery Reed thought the Dolls were 'cute', adding, 'Something might happen with them – I seem to inspire transvestite bands.'

The Dolls now had some status within the scene's pecking order. Iggy and Lou, who only a couple of years before had been considered upstart punks too weird for the mainstream, now found themselves in the position of elder statesmen, emperors of sleaze and excess. Wayne was the DJ, spinning a party-humping selection of sixties garage rock and James Brown, while Cherry was the club's queen, dishing out intimate oral handshakes in the back room.

The Dolls' growing reputation merited a spot on New York's *Channel Two News*, where they were described as 'a cross between the Rolling Stones and Alice Cooper'. Reporter Joel Siegel focused on the outrage, deeming them 'illiterate, hostile and deafeningly loud' against a feedback-drenched performance of 'Frankenstein'.

Although the Dolls were thoroughly enjoying the fruits of being a local phenomenon in this most high-octane of cities, if the group were going to bring their dragged-up sonic assault to audiences outside of New York, they were going to have to bring in the straights.

Faces/Rod Stewart manager Billy Gaff had been among the steady flow of industry bigwigs who caught the band at the Mercer. 'He had us open for Long John [Baldry] in Long Island,' remembers Syl. 'So they sent a limousine for us, but we were so smashed and we were carrying on with mad women, of course, for who knows how many nights prior. I remember Billy being so sick that he had to barf out of the window of the limo on the Long Island Expressway. The poor thing was not feeling good already. Now I realise how sick Billy really was. I didn't realise it then.

'So we went out to open up for Long John and got there so fucking late that we had to close for him. He had already finished his show, but he got us out there playing to whoever stuck around. We were probably awful because we were out of our faces and probably sloppy as hell. And we were probably sloppy on a good day anyway!'

Alice Cooper's manager, Shep Gordon, was also interested in taking on the Dolls, but David and Johnny believed he was just employing the sort of collect-and-confine tactics that Bowie had allegedly used on Wayne County. Or maybe he ultimately backed off, on account of the possibility of complications arising from Johnny's fling with Cindy Lang.

Faced with the burlesque of the Dolls' live performances, their ear-splitting volume and heroic booze and pill consumption, the industry suits had understandably opted for a cautious approach. The Dolls were new, but the A&R men were – by and large – old, and would take some persuading. Having caught the band at the Mercer entirely by accident, Marty Thau decided that he was just the *hombre* to do the persuading.

Thau had worked at *Billboard* magazine as an executive advertising trainee during the mid-sixties, before starting to manage local groups in 1966. This brought him to the attention of Neal Bogart, boss of Cameo-Parkway Records, who appointed Marty as National Promotions Manager. He was a roaring success, scoring 28 hits in his first year on the job. Among these was such studio-conceived bubblegum fare as 'Yummy Yummy Yummy' by the Ohio Express and the 1910 Fruitgum Company's huge hit, 'Simon Says'.

By the early seventies, Thau had tired of the incessant hyping of manufactured acts and tedious singer-songwriters. 'So I resigned and went towards the area of the industry that had always intrigued me the most, which was the music.' He became partners in a company which sold Warner Brothers the rights to Van Morrison's *Astral Weeks* and *Moondance*, plus John Cale's *Vintage Violence* and his collaboration with experimental musician Terry Riley, *Church Of Anthrax*. Marty also had a brief spell at Paramount as head of A&R, but still found that sitting behind a desk wasn't to his liking.

'At a celebration one night with my wife – dinner somewhere, walking around on a nice, warm spring night – we passed by the Mercer Arts Center. There was this little sign advertising the New York Dolls, two bucks in the Oscar Wilde Room. I said, "Sounds interesting, let's go."'

'At first I couldn't get past the sight of them,' recalled Marty on his *Tres Producers* website. 'While everybody in America was wearing army coats and earth shoes, here were these guys decked out in leather and leopard skin, with bouffant hair-dos, black nail polish, lipstick, six-inch platform boots, chopped jeans, feather boas, armbands and pantyhose. It was a style beyond femininity.'

Speaking to *Zigzag* in 1980, Marty remembered, 'I thought, "These guys are either the worst group I've ever seen or the greatest group I've ever seen." I concluded they were the greatest, but very young, very inexperienced and primitive. These were the qualities I liked . . . they were pretty outrageous. I watched and listened to the Dolls and I heard these arrangements. I didn't hear wasted lines or excesses. I just thought it was great and to the point and somewhere in that group one or all of them have a very fine understanding of pop-rock music.'

Thau's initial attempts to secure the band a contract were rebuffed, Buddah told him that they liked the band but not David, while MCA thought that Johansen was a star, but the rest of the Dolls sucked. However, Marty had an ace up his sleeve – Maurice Levy, boss of Roulette Records, had offered to finance a singles-only label if Marty was in charge. 'My intention was to first record some singles with them. I was going to form a label and I spoke with someone who was going to put up the money. In the course of the weeks that followed, when I made contact with the Dolls and started to get a feeling about them, I was very impressed with the mentality, sophistication, view of people and what it takes. I just shelved the record company idea and decided to take them on as manager and director of their affairs.

'I flashed back on Steve Leber and David Krebs, who I knew over the years, and were trying to sell me things when I was at Paramount. They had this new company, Leber-Krebs. I felt their forte was they would bring a talent in management to this, because of their talent in promotions. So I figured we had it all covered – management and promotion, tremendous enthusiasm. We were getting spectacular press as well.'

Krebs, who had booked the Stones' US tours, also handled Aerosmith –

another wild bunch who were just getting started. Band and future management met over the red tablecloths of Max's backroom and the Dolls managed to behave themselves long enough for a mutual agreement to be made.

While contracts were being drawn up, Marty put the Dolls into Blue Rock studios in Mercer Street, Soho, on the Lower West Side. Here they recorded demo versions of the songs they'd been playing live, including 'Human Being', 'Frankenstein', 'Bad Girl', 'Jet Boy', 'Personality Crisis', 'Looking For A Kiss', Sonny Boy Williamson's 'Don't Start Me Talking', Bo Diddley's 'Pills' and Otis Redding's 'Don't Mess With Cupid' – all three covers having been in their set from the start.

The recordings were never intended for release, being simply a representation of their live set of the time. Compared to the versions of the same songs that would emerge on the band's two subsequent studio albums, the tracks were raw, with plenty of the stripped-down muscle and untutored charm that would come to epitomise the Dolls. The tracks are unmistakably slower than later live or vinyl versions, but show each member's capabilities stripped of mixing desk gloss.

David caterwauls through 'Looking For A Kiss' and a deadly 'Human Being' with arch deliberation, while Johnny and Sylvain demonstrate a similar form of twin guitar tag work to that which Keith Richards would later achieve with Ronnie Wood. Their growing understanding is evident from the way Johnny churns and blasts sledgehammer chords while Sylvain adds counter-riffs, melodies and engine room backup.

The covers are dynamite, with 'Cupid' marrying the spirit of Stax Records with a sixties New York sock-hop. Many bands see covers as a means of either padding out their set or providing an easy reference point to stoke the crowd. The Dolls were already turning it into an art form by virtue of their astute choices from the dustier corners of their influences' back catalogues – you won't find 'Cupid' on an Otis Redding's greatest hits collection, and even Bo Diddley had forgotten how to play 'Pills' when the Dolls called out for it at one of his New York gigs.

At the end of June 1972, the New York Dolls gathered at the Leber-Krebs office on 65th Street to endorse their management contracts. They had no legal advice or lawyer present, just signed on the dotted line – both individually and as a band. They even signed away their publishing and songwriting royalties. On the plus side, everyone got new amps, $100 for clothes and a $75-per-week retainer.

As the Mercer residency rolled on, the media attention continued with features appearing in both *Rolling Stone* and the UK's *Melody Maker*. Most significantly, Roy Hollingworth – *Melody Maker*'s Englishman in New York – turned in a page feature under the headline, 'You Wanna Play House With The Dolls?' The article was published on 22 July and announced the Dolls with an inky fanfare: 'They might just be the best rock and roll band in the world. And whether you believe that or not, you're going to have to take notice of them . . . The New York Dolls.'

Hollingworth was so taken with the band that he attempted to add an interview to his piece and visited Chrystie Street, where he encountered Bo Diddley on the record player, people pissing in the sink, some girls and five Dolls.

The ever-loquacious Johansen did most of the talking, setting out the Dolls manifesto. 'I think we all felt something was lacking in music. It wasn't exciting any more to us. Everyone was hanging about on stage, being morose . . . We didn't dig that . . . The time is right for some good rock again.' Roy concluded by saying the Dolls were 'just the best, new, young band I've ever seen. Yes, young.'

Also present at the historic interview was Leee Childers, who came to take photos on the recommendation of leading rock writer Lillian Roxon. Leee snapped the first definitive Dolls shot – in Johnny's closet at Chrystie Street. He must have shouted, 'Everybody pout now!', but the charisma is all there.

Caught with his hand sassily on his hip, Johnny steals the shot in his swirly black crushed velvet number. Johansen is a mass of hair and polka dots, while Syl is resplendent in big shades and a girls' Lurex cardigan. At the top is Billy Murcia, sporting the most conventional early seventies rock'n'roll image with his curly mop, tight jeans and necklace. While his bandmates are frozen in the moment, Arthur appears simply frozen – an anaesthetised glam Golem, preserved in the aspic of booze and pills. Even though Ziggy Stardust had already landed, the photo still stood out as heralding something new, alien and exciting.

In 1972, a good splash in one of the music weeklies could create the kind of fever both with the general public and within the music industry that could make or break careers. Bowie's January '72 turbo-thrust into public awareness came via a *Melody Maker* interview with Michael Watts, where he announced, 'I'm gay.' In the Dolls' case, Roy Hollingworth's piece made some UK punters salivate to hear about this new rock'n'roll phenomenon gestating in the Bowery. Subsequently, the likes of Mick Jones, Morrissey and Bob Geldof would recall their initial exposure to the Dolls as being immediately essential to their palette of influences.

Encouraged by the press attention, Marty decided to promote the Mercer shows as weekly happenings. 'They'd done a few before I came along but I wanted to make it a regular weekly event, build it up. We threw a spectacular so that in every theatre three or four bands played non-stop. We drew 1200.'

With their potential audience expanded to include those who'd come to check out the Dolls alongside the Modern Lovers' cool nerdism, Wayne County's latest outrage, or Suicide's wall of electro-noise, the Dolls ceased to be the exclusive property of the hip elite. The band gained a roadie-cum-sound man in Peter Jordan – introduced to the band by seamstress Barbara Troiani, who had the thankless job of maintaining the Dolls' delicate but much-abused wardrobe.

With their stock rising, Marty dispatched the Dolls to play some gigs outside of their safe-as-houses home ground. They played Kenny's Castaways on the Upper East Side – described in a *Melody Maker* of the time as 'a rather tacky singles bar' – and the Coventry, across the 59th Street Bridge in Queens. The Dolls would spawn a scene at this club dominated by its large dancefloor, seeing the regular appearances by mediocre Queens rock bands interspersed with bigger Manhattan names such as Rick Rivets' new outfit, the Brats, Kiss and Teenage Lust – who Johnny described as 'the worst band in the world.'

A booking at a Mafia-run jock joint in Long Island called Mr D's ended in a barroom brawl amongst the regular guys in the crowd – maybe because their girlfriends were glued to the beautiful degenerates staggering around the stage. The band ended up running for their lives, then fighting among themselves.

By autumn, there was still no sign of a record deal. Despite the recent publicity and the growing crowds at the Mercer, it seemed as if the band were just too outrageous for the major labels. On several nights the Arts Center had been picketed by anti-gay protesters – which would have discouraged label execs who wouldn't wake up to the idea of the pink dollar for another decade. Marty figured that the industry 'thought they were literally transvestites, drug addicts, perverts'.

A few months later David admitted to Lisa Robinson that the band were facing an uphill struggle to make orbiting A&R types realise the Dolls' worth. 'When these record company people come and see us I think we turn them on. Their wives get drunk and start dancing, and they go crazy. But then they think about their kids . . . and that's what stops them. They start thinking about their kids.'

'The record company people who have come to see us have been freaked out, and we're not really doing anything except standing there playing,' added Johnny. Speaking to *Rolling Stone,* David at least picked some crumbs of comfort from the publicity. 'My father thinks I'm a mutant. But now that I seem to be amounting to something, getting my name in the papers and stuff, he's beginning to dig it.'

Fortunately, the Dolls had rock journalist and A&R man Paul Nelson on their side. Nelson's day job was at Mercury Records and he loved the Dolls. He thought they might be the new Stones. He stuck his neck out on a number of occasions, convincing sceptical superiors such as label vice-president Charles Fach to check out the group. However, on these occasions the only reliable quality demonstrated by the Dolls was their propensity for coming on late, in various states of sloppiness.

As a means of breaking out of this unproductive spiral, a change of strategy was decided upon – take the New York Dolls to the UK to try to get a record deal. The combination of good press and a more open-minded climate generated by the rise of Ziggy Stardust and glam rock made it a more likely prospect than the staid US. Leber contacted London promoter Roy Fischer, who'd handled Alice Cooper, to see if he would promote the Dolls in the UK. He agreed, if they would record a couple of songs for him that he could release as a single.

At Leber's expense, the New York Dolls set off for the UK. 'We got a pretty good write-up in *Melody Maker,*' explained Johnny, 'and our reputation spread pretty fast, especially in England, it seems, because the promoters of a Rod Stewart and the Faces concert called me up and brought us over to England to be the support group.'

Less than a year after lurching out of Rusty's cycle shop to play a show for a group of Bowery down-and-outs, the Dolls were heading to Wembley's Empire Pool to play the biggest gig of their lives.

We Should Be On By Now

'The Dolls were like a gang . . .' – *Jerry Nolan*

The opportunity to capitalise on the buzz created by Roy Hollingworth's *Melody Maker* article ensured that the Dolls and their management approached the band's forthcoming UK dates with considerable optimism. However, a gig at Wembley supporting rhythm 'n' booze rockers the Faces represented a quantum leap for a group that had 'never played in front of more than 300 people'.

The rapid growth of glam rock in the UK meant the Dolls would stand a better chance of reaching audiences already receptive to raucous rock'n'roll played by burly men in makeup and spangles. When the band landed at Heathrow to be met by Roy Fischer's promotional horse and cart in mid-October, a peek at the British top 40 would have enhanced their sense of having arrived in a land of opportunity.

Recession-hit Britain was looking to escape the drab realities of power-cuts, wage freezes, three-day weeks and miserable weather by buying into the flash and sparkle of glam. Alice Cooper's 'Elected' and The Sweet's 'Wig Wam Bam' sat comfortably in the Top Ten, while T Rex's 'Children Of The Revolution' and Slade's 'Mama Weer All Crazee Now' remained in the charts, having been in the top three a few weeks earlier.

Never slow to pick up on a gimmick, the UK labels had wasted little time in cashing in on the glam craze. Future sex-crime wave Gary Glitter was a re-upholstered sixties crooner who'd been given a Bacofoil makeover and was enjoying his second straight hit with 'I Didn't Know I Loved You ('Til I Saw You Rock'n'Roll)'. Within weeks the chart would be awash with further glam opportunists like Chicory Tip and Wizzard.

Further evidence that the British climate would be right for the Dolls was evident from the way in which some of the group's earliest influences were enjoying a revival. The Shangri-Las' 'Leader of the Pack' had been re-released and hit the chart in the same week that the Dolls arrived, as had Archie Bell and the Drells' 'Here I Go Again'.

The age demographic for British glam fans was decidedly young, with kids as young as six dragging parents into Woolworth's to buy them the latest offerings by The Sweet or Slade. Their older brothers and sisters would home in the more sophisticated glam served up by Roxy Music – who'd recently had a huge hit with 'Virginia Plain' – or Bowie, who was still taking *Ziggy* around the States when the New York Dolls made the opposite trip.

The natural vigour of these youthful audiences ensured that those old enough to get into gigs created a live environment where screaming, leaping around and generally having a good time was far more important than admiring clever guitar chops. Such enthusiasm inevitably led to the odd row of trashed seats, or an ageing doorman being trampled underfoot by hyped-up kids. Always willing to fill space with a moral outrage, the British press ran stories attempting to stir up the usual tiresome indignation at the behaviour of these 'yobs'.

Of the British glam bands, Slade and Mott the Hoople led the way in terms of rabble rousing. Visually, Slade (like The Sweet) took the boundaries of glam couture to a new shinier plateau, establishing a precedent for 'bricklayers in drag'. Mott's crowd was older, better dressed, and committed to their heroes in the way that future followers of populist bands like The Clash and the Libertines would be. Like the Dolls, Mott the Hoople – who had recently hit the jackpot with Bowie's 'All The Young Dudes' – had spent their early existence toiling against the grain by sticking steadfastly to simple, wild rock'n'roll. Both groups were fiercely proud of their roots and wore their influences with pride. If the Dolls were to have any hope of finding favour in the UK, it would most likely be among the sort of unpretentious working-class kids that followed Mott.

A brief press call provided David with the opportunity to show the UK his tonsils. He began by laying out the band's manifesto: 'We are the most professional unprofessional band there ever was. We want to form our own society, a society where everyone is on common ground,' before clarifying the band's sexuality. 'Just let anyone punch us on the nose and they'll know what we are. But we're not butch.'

The shots of the Dolls' horse-drawn departure from Heathrow were hardly a stylistic triumph. The band looked thoroughly incongruous in the back of Fischer's old haywain, and the resultant shots conjured up a glam-meets-Constable *tableau vivant*. Once the group were out of the press's sight, they transferred to more modern transport, which whisked them directly to Escape Studios in Kent.

Over the course of 15-16 October, the Dolls fulfilled their part of the Roy Fischer bargain by recording 'Looking For A Kiss', 'Personality Crisis', 'Bad Girl' and 'Subway Train' (formerly known as 'That's Poison'), for their British patron. The group were housed in a converted oast house that formed part of Escape's secluded rural complex.

Having discharged their recording commitments, Marty and the Dolls repaired to the Whitehouse Hotel in South Kensington, while Steve Leber favoured the decidedly more upmarket Dorchester.

The Dolls' first UK engagement was a low-key warm-up show in London at the Speakeasy, the trendy basement club near Oxford Circus. The Speakeasy was nothing to write home about. There was a bar when you walked in, which was where most of the general hanging out took place. To the rear of the bar was a restaurant, which was usually overflowing. Finally, the band room, which could hold about a hundred, was visually limited and often suffered from poor sound because of the low ceiling. On certain nights a good band and a hot crowd could conjure up the right atmosphere.

'The Speak' was principally ultra-hip because of its clientele – London's rock elite. Its late hours made it a favourite for post-gig carousing and cavorting. The place was always crawling with groupies and there are many tales of drunken rock stars running amok. But its reputation and 'impress me' ethic also meant that groups invariably got a cool reaction. The Dolls sound wasn't brilliant, and they duly received a rather lukewarm response. On the whole, not a great start to the tour.

As Roy Fischer also handled bookings for the Groundhogs, it made sense for the Dolls to support the band – as they did on 26 October at the Alhambra in Birmingham. The Groundhogs were a blues power trio led by veteran guitar virtuoso Tony 'T.S.' McPhee, who was prone to taking off on twenty-minute demonstrations of his latest effects pedal. Their audiences were usually straggly, dowdy and encased in greatcoats, which came in handy when they sat on the floor. The Dolls must have come as a shock.

The next gig was to be the big one: Sunday 29 October at the Empire Pool, Wembley. The arena was an 8,000-seat hall located next door to Wembley Stadium. The gig was part of the Wembley Festival of Music, organised by the Stars Organisation for Spastics. The Dolls were appearing between the raucously unhinged Pink Fairies – who were already a favourite with some of the group – and the Faces, who were now in the major league, largely thanks to the huge success of Rod Stewart as a solo artist. Their crowd had always been laddish, football-loving and drunk, although a fair spattering of teenyboppers now came to scream at their tartan-clad frontman.

Before the gig, the Society's patron, the Duchess of Kent, met all the participants and presented them with a bottle of champagne. The mind boggles at the thought of the Duchess greeting first the drug-crazed Fairies, the perma-pissed Faces, then the downers-and-booze-sodden Dolls.

Introduced by motormouth DJ Emperor Rosko – who modelled his shtick on US character jocks like Wolfman Jack – the Dolls found themselves standing on a stage in front of a crowd that was about 40 times larger than any they'd ever faced. Unfortunately, many followed the Faces with the staunch partisanship of football fans, and duly viewed the New York Dolls as an away team, rife for abuse. Worse still, the Dolls were an away team in ladies' shoes.

The Dolls were greeted by catcalls and constant vilification from the Faces crowd, who started throwing things as the sound went downhill and the group stood isolated and alone in the huge space. *Melody Maker*'s Mark Plummer wrote, 'The New York Dolls played what was possibly one of the worst sets I've seen . . . Musically their set was dire and failed to gel, their two guitarists played all the old tired licks.'

At the time, the UK music press were largely preoccupied with the Osmonds' recent arrival, and the blanket coverage accorded the boy-band's invasion shunted any mention of the Dolls to the sidelines. However, white comic-reggae butterball Judge Dread – who was enjoying a period of chart success with his saucy postcard brand of novelty skank – offered up a reactionary and unintentionally funny soundbite: 'Them horrible New York Dolls,' he bellowed, 'them glorified transvestites make me proper ill. A few years ago people like that would've been stoned to death for looking like they do.'

The more technically minded Mark Plummer homed in on Johnny breaking a string on the Plexiglass guitar he'd acquired because it was the same model Keith Richard employed on the Stones' 1969 US tour. Few other guitarists attempted to play this model, which was taken off the market in 1971. They weighed a ton and were difficult to keep in tune. But they could sound amazing with a single pickup that could be switched from treble to bass.

The gig wasn't all bad news. The Dolls amused themselves by throwing toilet rolls into the crowd, and Elton John – who had recently glammed up his act on the way to superstar status – was impressed: 'I thought they were brilliant. It was exciting, it was fun. I just wish I could have been born five years later and struggled into some of those costumes.'

After the gig, Kit Lambert, boss of Track Records and manager of The Who, took the Dolls and their small entourage out to dinner. Lambert and partner Chris Stamp had started Track in late 1966, with a roster featuring The Who and Jimi Hendrix. Lambert had heard Jimi in a London club and vaulted several tables to work out a deal on a beer mat. Track had acquired a reputation for being aggressively independent, and by the early seventies had become established as a respected label. Lambert was flamboyant but astute, and was keen to sign the Dolls. He showed the visitors a high time, taking them to exclusive parties and introducing them to The Who. But even though Thau and Leber were fairly certain that Track would be their new home, they still played the field in case there was a bigger offer to be had.

Another label keen on signing the Dolls was Rolling Stones Records, which the band had launched in 1971 with their *Sticky Fingers* album and was looking to expand its roster.

A few nights after the Wembley show, the Dolls had a gig at London's Imperial College alongside Status Quo and arty rockers Capability Brown. Mick Jagger flew in from his Irish base to see the Dolls for himself. Perhaps his vanity was extending to signing a band that featured a cartoon dead ringer for himself as a frontman. He wasn't overly impressed, being quoted in *Melody Maker* as saying, 'Yeah, I've seen the New York Dolls. We were almost going to sign them up at one point. I went down to the Imperial College gig and – uh, their lead singer – I saw 'er and I just didn't think much of it at all.' Shanne Bradley, who'd go on to play bass with Shane McGowan's punk outfit the Nipple Erectors, found the Dolls far more exciting than the jaded Jagger: 'so Noo York flashy, loud 'n' trashy – in three minutes they'd emptied the hall of long haired science students.'

Thau and Leber deflected overtures from Charisma, EMI and Virgin – especially Richard Branson's paltry offer of a $5,000 advance to make the

Dolls one of the earliest acts to sign to his newly-established label. They knew all along that Track were ready and waiting. 'It was pretty much there for us to decide,' recalls Thau. 'We were talking. The idea was to make a European deal and maybe a world-wide deal.'

As their management held out for the best possible contract, the Dolls continued to enjoy the attention that comes with being the latest hot property to hit town. Fully aware of their duties as representatives of America in a foreign land, the quintet was far too polite to refuse any of the booze and pills that were offered by the quaint natives.

Billy extended the theme of transcontinental détente by hitching up with a girl called Marilyn Woolhead who he'd met at the Speakeasy. Marilyn had a never-ending supply of Mandrax – a powerful sedative that proved to be highly addictive and was eventually banned in 1977, similar to the American Quaalude. Like most good downers, mix with booze and you'll stagger about incoherently and pass out on the spot. Ten hours can be lost with no memory afterwards of what happened, or how you got into that hedge 50 miles from home. Consequently, Billy – who, along with Arthur, had the biggest appetite for booze and downers – spent much of his time in England mandied out.

On 4 November, the Dolls left London to support Lou Reed for a show that was to showcase the best of New York transplanted to Liverpool Stadium. Reed was in the UK promoting his freshly minted *Transformer* album, and was dulling the grind of touring with copious amounts of speed and booze. He was also prone to spells of erratic behaviour – as the Dolls discovered ten minutes before they were due to go on stage. Reed had decided that he didn't want the Dolls to perform and that, if they played, he would refuse to do the gig. He offered no explanation for this sudden proclamation, prompting speculation that he feared being upstaged by his former associates from Max's backroom.

Recalling Reed's hissy fit, Syl observes, 'We had plenty of time to go on. We were there for soundcheck. I think what happened there, my own feeling is, he was the generation before and we were the brand new kids on the block. Red hot, happening and everybody wanted to be like us and everybody wanted to be with us. It wasn't quite open arms to us because we were the new kids, especially back in the Max's Kansas City days. Mickey Ruskin, who owned it from the late sixties into the early seventies, needed our success to run his business. It was good when we sold out the upstairs five nights in a row. It was fantastic for them. But then we were basically 86'ed from the downstairs though, for all kinds of reasons. Stupid things, like we were busted for snorting cocaine. But they were snorting cocaine and having sex in the booth and they weren't busted for that!'

Left with little option but to pull the gig, the dejected Dolls returned to their Kensington base to revitalise their trampled morale ahead of a high-profile support slot with Roxy Music in Manchester on 9 November.

Despite the conviviality of the London scene, Reed's incomprehensible pettiness had left a sour taste that was evident when the band hooked up for dinner at their hotel, the following day. David was pissed off. The Liverpool trip had been frustrating and humiliating, the hotel was less than five-star (even by British standards) and he was missing Cyrinda, who was in Los

Angeles shooting a promo for 'The Jean Genie' with David Bowie.

On the other hand, Billy – who had been hugely excited about the prospect of touring England – was making the best of things courtesy of Marilyn and her mandies. 'I bumped into Billy in the hotel lobby,' recalled Syl in a 2004 *Uncut* interview. 'He goes into his shirt pocket and pulls out all these halves of mandies. He says, "I was offered so much, I took all the other halves, but I didn't take these."' Unsurprisingly, Billy was a bit groggy and sat at the table beside Marilyn and another female companion, provided David with a ready target at which to vent his frustrations. As Syl explained to Nina Antonia, 'Johansen was sitting there and he started in on Billy . . . "Listen you fuck up one more time and you're out. I don't give a shit who the fuck you are, what the hell are you doing, this is my band, I'm the singer, this is my career, dahdahdahdah." He bawled Billy out so bad.'

Too upset and bleary to defend himself from David's verbal lashing, Billy left the table in tears. When he stopped by Marty Thau's room to borrow £5 shortly after, it would be the last time that anyone connected with the New York Dolls would see him alive.

After Marty had given him some cash, and headed off with Steve Leber to a business meeting with former Move and T. Rex manager Tony Secunda, Billy returned to his room. There, by a macabre combination of bad luck and coincidence, he accepted an invitation to a nearby party, from a complete stranger who'd rung the hotel looking for somebody else. This maybe isn't as odd as it might seem – Billy loved nothing more than to party, and was happy to do so with whoever was available. He headed off with Marilyn in tow.

Once Billy had made the short journey to the nearby party, he attempted to dull the memory of the cancelled gig and David's tirade with a combination of Mandrax and champagne. Before long he was out cold. When it became apparent that Billy wasn't responding to any attempts to rouse him, what can best be described as a half-assed effort at resuscitation was made. The stricken drummer was stripped and wrestled into a bathtub filled with cold water, and attempts were made to pour black coffee into him. During this chaotic process Billy suffocated.

Round at Tony Secunda's, Marty was thrashing out the finer points of a $100,000 deal with Track, when a phone call made his and Steve Leber's manoeuvrings irrelevant. 'It was pretty much there for us to decide,' recalled Marty. 'We were talking. Then I got this phone call. "Marty come quickly to such-and-such address, Billy Murcia just died." Billy had gone to a party and died. We concluded after that, had he been with people who were a bit more concerned about what was happening to his person instead of worrying about their own skins, the police and the scandal, and running out and leaving him, it might have turned out different. It was really a sad, tragic waste of life.'

Rick Rivets echoes Thau's sentiments, observing that the people who were around Billy when he overdosed, 'totally fucked up, and Billy would have been alive had they been responsible enough to call the proper authorities right away. That is something that they will have to live with, but I think

'Everybody pout…', the Dolls at Chrystie Street, 1972 – Left to right: David Johansen, Sylvain Sylvain, Billy Murcia, Johnny Thunders (at rear), Arthur 'Killer' Kane.

When we were five – Billy Murcia (far left) backstage with the Dolls, left to right: Johnny Thunders, Arthur Kane, Sylvain Sylvain with David Johansen in the fore-ground, in October 1972.

'The Dolls had the look down the best' – Dee Dee Ramone. Stack heels on the Mercer's staircase, Mercer Arts Center, New York, 1973. Left to right: (At rear) Johnny Thunders, David Johansen, Jerry Nolan, (foreground) Sylvain Sylvain and Arthur Kane.

David cuts a dash in his best drags, 1973.   *Knitwear guru Syl at the Mercer in 1973.*

'Arthur was one in a million. The only one.' – David Johansen.

'I went furthest with it …' – Arthur Kane at the edge of style, 1973.

Johnny models his thrift-store football t-shirt and plastic bangles, 1973.

Johnny and Syl at the Mercer, 1973.

Dolls on white satin – the Mercury album sleeve shoot 1973, and below right: the debut album.

Above: David Johansen in incendiary live action at Gerties night club, Dallas, Texas, 1974. Opposite page: The Dolls (plus diminutive cowboy) in front of Gem Spa Candy Store, NYC, in 1973. Four years later they'd be back to pose for Punk *magazine in a short-lived reunion.*

David Johansen with his girlfriend at Gerties night club, Dallas, Texas, 1974.

they were more concerned with saving their own asses then trying to save Billy's life. What could have happened to them anyway if they called the police right away? Nothing. Even if they had some drugs in their apartment. A life would have been saved and they might have gotten a fine that I'm sure the Dolls management would have paid. Big deal. It's not like they would have been thrown in jail for ten years. That's the consequences of getting high with people you don't know.'

Reflecting on his friend's death in 2005, Syl identifies the tragedy as 'An awful accident,' adding, 'he was at the wrong place and he was probably with no one that could really help him. Time is too short, especially when you're in trouble. You don't have much time at all. Billy wasn't doing too good physically anyway – I remember we were opening up for Kevin Ayers in some place and Billy was getting sick. Violently throwing up right there as he's playing, right on the drums. Then he was having to play on top of that, which was really horrible. He actually had a bad stomach. I don't think he knew about it and he just kept carrying on like crazy. It just got the better of him. I really think that's all it was. I don't think anyone ever tried to hurt him.'

'Billy's mum always thought it was some kind of murder or something,' recalled Sylvain in *Uncut*. 'I had to ring up his sister, Heidi, and tell her from London. I just heard this scream and, God, it was the loudest scream. It crossed the whole ocean. It crossed the whole ocean.'

'We didn't even think about the band,' explained David. 'We had to get Billy home. We had to bury him. We had to take care of his mother. She was such a beautiful woman. It was overwhelmingly sad. We were young, and to feel intense grief like that was something we weren't accustomed to yet.'

Marty Thau realised that this tragic mystery death was the sort of thing that the media would seize upon with gusto. He created a barrier between the band and the press while the Dolls escaped back to New York on a 7am flight. Obviously, with the attention they'd already had and the extreme 'elegantly wasted' aura, everyone assumed that Billy had died of a drug overdose. But it wasn't as simple as that, and, as both Thau and Rivets have observed, it could have been avoided. The band was devastated because they'd lost a brother.

Syl relates a touching story how the Dolls were huddled together on the plane, sobbing their hearts out. When the stewardess asked them why they were crying, Sylvain replied, 'Well, yesterday we were five and today we're four.'

Oddly, the inquest into Billy's death revealed that no drug traces were found during the post-mortem and the official verdict was given as 'death by drowning'. It seems that the authorities were, like the media, happier to write Billy off as a drug casualty who'd died entirely through his own recklessness, rather than recognising the role played by neglect and panic on the part of those who were on the scene at the time.

Back in New York City, the shattered Dolls had to come to terms with Billy's death. Sylvain moved from Elda's apartment into Billy's old room at

Fourteenth Street. He never seemed to get over the death of his friend and always spoke of him with evident sadness. For his flatmate Johnny, solace was found in chasing the dragon, which marked the start of his serious heroin use.

Arthur's unexpected early return home came as something of a surprise to Rick Rivets, who had been looking after the bassist's Third Street flat while he was on tour. 'He was gone about a week when I hear a knock at the door and it's Artie. The first words out of his mouth were "Billy died." This was the tour that was supposed to make them into stars, as record companies were interested and they did some major shows, and all was looking good until the night that Billy went out by himself. If one other member of the band were with him he would be alive today but those people freaked and Billy is gone.'

The Dolls were already starting to look like rock'n'roll casualties, and their career was only getting off the starting blocks.

Billy's body was flown back to his family in a metal casket, and the funeral took place in early December at a cemetery in Westchester, upstate New York. The ceremony gave some sense of closure to the band's nightmare trip to Britain. Having had a month to come to terms with what had happened, the remaining quartet began looking to the future. Syl told *The Village Voice*, 'Of course we're still going to carry on as a group. We're looking for another drummer and we hope to come out strong in the New Year.'

Shortly after Billy's funeral, the surviving quartet met with Marty and decided to continue, 'We cast around for drummers and decided on Jerry Nolan.'

So far as rock'n'roll and street credentials went, Jerry Nolan was eminently qualified to become a Doll. He exuded a unique charisma halfway between seasoned tour pro and street gang warlord. He talked fast, was streetwise, and passionate about music. By late 1972, Jerry was regarded as possibly the best drummer on the scene. He was the obvious man for the job as he'd sat in with the Dolls during their rehearsals at Rusty's and Talent-Recon and the band all knew and liked him. 'Jerry was such a professional,' asserted Sylvain, 'he was already playing the Catskill Mountains with this and that band . . . He was playing with rock bands that were playing places like the Metropole. It was all a different ball game from us really.'

The only other genuine contenders to replace Billy were Marc Bell, who would later appear in Richard Hell's Voidoids and finally show up in the Ramones, and Sparky Donovan – who tried out, but lived too far out of town to be a viable option, and returned to the Brats. Crucially, Jerry had always wanted to be in the Dolls. 'When the Dolls started they were great . . . very raw. A real rock'n'roll band. Nobody could top them.'

Before he lifted a stick, Jerry knew he'd pass the audition held at Charles Lane studio. 'There's only one guy who can fill that job and do it well,' he told David. 'I'm the guy.' After the formality of the audition, the band headed to Max's to celebrate.

From the very start, Jerry's streetwise nature and assured manner meant that there was little question of him being the uncomfortable 'new boy' in an already established group. He became the band's oldest member, having been born in Williamsburg, Brooklyn on 7 May 1946.

Williamsburg is connected to the East Village and Lower East Side by its eponymous bridge. Traditionally, the area provided homes for many of New

York's Hassidic Jews, whose number was vastly expanded during the 1940s by immigrants fleeing the Nazi holocaust in Europe.

These refugees settled amongst their own people, alongside neighbouring Polish, Irish, Italian and Afro-American communities. As the post-war economy wound down, many local industries relocated as the local population mushroomed, jobs became scarce, and poverty and crime became prevalent. Successive waves of immigrants from Puerto Rico and the Dominican Republic only served to exacerbate social problems that were turning the area into a cauldron of pent up frustrations.

During Jerry's youth, this situation was yet to reach the crisis points that manifested during the 1970s and 80s, but the area's diversity and material poverty provided him with grounding in the facts of street life and its tinny transistorised soundtracks, which emanated from a thousand tenement windows.

Like Johnny, Jerry got his initial musical jolt from his older sister. 'When I was six or seven years old I went to my first concert. My older sister took me to see Frankie Lymon and the Teenagers in the Alan Freed Show. He was the first rock'n'roll disc jockey. He gave rock'n'roll its name. He founded rock-'n'roll, in a sense. He brought black and white kids together in the same dancehalls. He brought black and white kids playing on the same stage and he introduced R&B, he introduced rockabilly and made it come together. When it clashed it became rock'n'roll.'

That first concert left an indelible impression on Jerry, and he always cited Frankie Lymon and the Teenagers as a major influence. The fresh-faced veneer of Lymon's ultimate teen party anthems like 'Why Do Fools Fall In Love?' and 'I'm Not A Juvenile Delinquent' masked a turbulent private life and a chequered past. At the age of ten, Frankie was pimping around Harlem, fixing up black hookers for white guys. He was a star by the time he was twelve, being pictured with Marilyn Monroe and Jane Russell, but also became a heroin addict when the hits stopped coming. Frankie was arrested for stealing drums to finance his habit, got married three times, and finally, in 1968 – the day before he was due to go back in the studio to attempt a comeback – overdosed at his grandmother's apartment. He's now buried in the Bronx in an unmarked grave.

Shortly after this rock'n'roll awakening, Jerry's mother remarried to a soldier who was stationed in Hawaii. The family moved to the paradise island for three years. Here, a young black GI gave Jerry his first drumming lesson. In addition to equipping him with the rudiments of his future trade, these lessons provided Jerry with some much-needed self-esteem. The constant relocations that are the lot of an army brat made it difficult for Jerry to concentrate on his studies. He didn't enjoy school and had started to blame himself for his academic shortcomings. 'The first thing that I ever did that was good, that got respect from other people, was playing drums,' he explained in a 1973 interview with *Phonograph Record*'s Ron Ross. 'I wasn't noted for being Jerry the failure in school, I was noted for being Jerry the drummer.'

Then his stepfather was posted to Lawton, Oklahoma, where they stayed for another two years. During this period, Jerry joined his first band at high school and made a lifelong friend in saxophonist Buddy Bowser, who would go on to play on the first Dolls album. At the age of fourteen, Jerry was getting occasional gigs playing drums in local strip joints. He was in his midteens when the family returned to Williamsburg in the early 1960s.

In June 1977 Pete Frame conducted a lengthy, largely unpublished interview for *Zigzag* with Jerry and Johnny Thunders. Here Jerry related his sometimes shocking early life story. He would never speak so candidly and honestly – not to mention graphically – again. All Pete Frame was after was some information to add to one of his magnificent *Rock Family Trees*, but he got far more than he bargained for:

'When I moved into Williamsburg, Brooklyn, I had to definitely prove myself. Not once, many, many times. That feeling of proving yourself never leaves. You always have to prove yourself . . . As long as you fought in front of everybody. Whether you won or lost wasn't important at all. The fact that you fought was important. That was gaining respect and acceptance. Now to win, you're just maybe a better fighter and you can be in a higher level of a gang. You can be president or vice-president. Gangs have a lot of organisation . . . they tended to be run on almost military lines. A lot of gangs were more powerful because they had better strategy.

'I'll tell you, when I'd see gang fights it was very heavy. There was a lot of killings, a lot of people hurt bad. There was a lot of gunfire, a lot of stabbings. It was really heavy and very, very frightening. It's more frightening to think about it now than it was then, because when you're in it you're there all the time. You learn to act your role and play your part. You learn how to move and how to be in with the in crowd. And you accept it. It's almost fun.

'The first time I ever seen anyone killed and seen a lot of blood I was quite young . . . There was a dozen or so kids just raided our neighbourhood. Last minute type of shit, y'know? Unexpected type shit. I don't know the reason. Someone beat up on a girl, a cousin of this guy Robert, one of the older members of the gang. This guy ran out and got a hold of these guys and they were fighting and they both had knives. One guy had a gun and was firing at a girl and missed, so this guy went up to this kid that had the gun. He fired at him and missed too.

'Somehow this other kid got a hold of him and stabbed him directly in the heart with a knife. That was the first time I ever seen someone get killed and a lot of blood. When he pulled the knife out it was the first time I'd seen a really grotesque looking stab wound – like the meat and the veins just came right out. It was just dangling from the knife. Pieces were hanging from the knife. That blood really came out. It was so red and so thick and so quick the way it happened . . . the expression on the kid's face and the scream and falling down in the black gutter and this red, thick blood making the gutter look white. Because the blood was so different – even though the gutter was black, the blood stood out quite bright.

'There was nothing I could do because by that time you could hear the sirens and everything. I looked similar to this guy that stabbed him anyway. A lot of people used to mistake us. I've actually had my life threatened and gotten into some fights because I looked like this guy. Everybody split, and everybody was screaming. The kid hit the floor. There was a big puddle of blood and Robert was still in the same area, kicking him and shit. He didn't think twice about stabbing him. Didn't seem pissed off. He still kept on kicking him in the head, still holding the knife. You could see the cops coming in the distance and I just split. I was walking up the block and I started to feel really dizzy. It was really hitting me – all that blood. I lost my head. I had to actually sit down and get myself together. It had a big impression on me.

'The guy got caught and sent up. He was away for three years, but it was self-defence, to a degree. The guy shot at a girl. There were plenty of witnesses and the guy shot at him anyway. So he definitely got away with it. But I understood. That was the neighbourhood I grew up in. That was the type of thing that happened a lot.

'Where I came from in the age I came from it was not racial as much as it was over territory. Just territory. Y'know – "I come from a cooler, better neighbourhood than you do and I'm gonna show you." A lot of it had to do with people talking. If one gang were hanging out at their club and stuff like that and they heard another gang was badmouthing us – that was enough to start a fight. Or if some member of another gang was in your neighbourhood badmouthing or just doing something fucked up or acting too bad, that was enough to start something. It could be over chicks. It could be over racial things, which wasn't that much. Most of the time it was just an excuse. It was pretty much territory. If someone from another gang came into your territory, then the shit could hit the fan. Then you were looking for trouble.'

In addition to providing Jerry with the sense of volatile fraternity he would later find among the Dolls and the Heartbreakers, life as a member of the Phantom Lords gang provided him with an outlet for his practical nous. 'I could make some pretty good zip guns. I'm very good at making guns. I could go out now and make a gun just off the street. There's a few ways of making a zip gun. It's made out of tape, wood and car aerials. For your quick, cheap, fast zip gun you get a car aerial and a .22 shell will fit right in the fatter part. There's your barrel. You can only get a couple of shots out but that's all you need. You need plenty of tape. You need a certain amount of carpentry work on the handle and you have to know how to make a trigger. You have to get hold of some .22 shells. Bullets. One shot at a time – you have to reload it. It might blow up in your face – it's not worth it if you don't make it right. Some of them used to backfire and blow up right in your face but that all depends how much time you put into making 'em. Nowadays they don't make 'em so much because it's easier to buy a gun.

'What the kids used to do in them days was take store fronts that were empty and pay the landlord some dough and rent it out over a month. They'd hire jukeboxes, repaint the place, build a bar, paint the windows black with just a little peephole in the door. Boom! We'd go up the police station and buy a Police Athletic League sticker for ten bucks. We'd contribute to the Police Athletic League, and because you had a P.A.L. sticker in the window a cop would walk past and go, "Oh these boys are nice, they're trying to stay off the streets." That was fine to a degree because we could sniff glue, smoke pot and fuck bitches in the cellar of the club.

'The clubs were really stylish. One of the clubs I was in was called the Bamboo Lounge. We were one of the first gangs to give clubs real conservative names for a front. Meanwhile, we were really the Young Lords, which was a younger part of the Phantom Lords. The Phantom Lords were the older teenagers and the Young Lords were fifteen or sixteen, like me and some friends of mine.'

'The Young Lords survived by ripping off rival clubs, girlfriends, everyone. The president of our gang's mother owned a candy store. We used to steal money from her store every day to paint the place. We used to make money from the phones – have the phone company bring in a phone and we'd get a percentage of the phone and we'd get a percentage out of the money in the jukebox, which was a lot of dough.

In addition to being a cash cow, The Phantom Lords jukebox provided Jerry with more direct musical influences: '"Rockin' Robin" by Bobby Day, all Dion and the Belmonts, Frankie Lymon and the Teenagers, some rock'n'roll things like Chuck Berry – they just had to be really popular. Elvis Presley, Gene Vincent, Eddie Cochran were definitely popular. The Shirelles, things like that.'

During the early 1960s, Jerry 'joined a whole bunch of bands and joined in with the instrumental boom. Everyone was playing instrumentals, doing Stickshift and Bill Black's Combo and all that shit. I did that for a laugh. The first group in high school was the Strangers. The next group was the Naturals. In 1961 and 62 I was in really hardcore instrumental groups – the Vibetones. I never did surf music. I hated surf music. The Vibetones were my first complete band. They had keyboards, a bass player, two guitars, then finally we got in the vocals as well.'

Jerry wasn't too impressed by the British invasion that came after the Beatles and Rolling Stones in 1964. 'I dug the British invasion to a degree because they just did what I was doing and was doing for so long with a different approach. They did a good job of reviving. It was a revival to me but to a lot of kids younger than me it was sort of brand new. They thought the Beatles wrote all those Chuck Berry tunes. I was affected to a degree by it but it wasn't nothing new at all to me. I was almost pissed off that it'd take something like that and everyone thought it was brand new. I was trying to do this for years with Buddy, this black kid I'd been friends with for years.

'I got into rhythm and blues and soul, all that "gotta gotta", all that shit. I was just trying to find what I liked the best. I did all kinds of music, even Latin-type shit, jazz, but I hated that. Then I just got back into rock'n'roll. It was sort of a feeling inside. I knew what I liked the best. After trying all types of music I came back to the original form, more with vocals.

'Living in the Midwest you had very hardcore instrumentation. Everyone was a guitarist. Everyone was really into their instruments. On the East Coast, everything was vocals. All the kids sitting on the street corners, all these jitterbugs, singing vocal groups with no music. Acapella. I got into groups that were combining the vocal form of music and the instrumental form from the Midwest. So I was lucky to get into the R&B aspect of it . . . rock'n'roll, lot of vocals and shit.'

Ultimately, Jerry had to choose between a career in the Lords that would most likely have soon seen him dead or in prison, or – hopefully – a longer one in rock'n'roll. 'Once I started getting into music I realised how it was better to release my frustrations and exaggerate myself through music than it was killing someone, pulling a knife or shooting someone. I got away from it . . . from aiming a gun and being the one who pulls out a gun or being shot at or doing the shooting. I've gotten away from that, but now I'm the one who's doing the ducking in the midst of it. I'm not sure I go for that either. I enjoy music more. There's a lot of violence in this business, but it's better to get it out dancing or wrecking your equipment playing on stage. It's better to do it that way than hurting someone, that's for sure. I don't like to see bodies thrown in front of me all the time. Lifeless bodies and people losing their lives every day. I really don't enjoy seeing that at all. I don't think that's fun in any way. I think rock'n'roll and music can be fun because, even when I was growing up in this neighbourhood, rock'n'roll was new then.'

He played everywhere. At times, his existence equalled being a gang member for violence and danger. 'I seen somebody get shot and killed by a shotgun one when I was doing a gig at this club. When I first started getting into music I brought my band down to a club where we used to have a social club. We'd done the gig and I was putting my drums in a cab. I was on my own, just going home. Then this fight broke out between the Hellburners and the Phantom Lords. There was this friend of mine who I used to look up to as an older brother. I thought he was something I wanted to be when I grew up because he was really cool – long, slim and well-dressed. He had this outrageous scar. He was very handsome but he had a scar that went from one end to another which came from being slapped in the face with a razor. He pulled a sawn-off shotgun out of his trench-coat and blew this guy away. One shot – right when my cab was parked because of a red light. It happened so fast. Gang fight. It only took a minute or two. The cab just took right off. I told the cab driver that I thought I chose the right business.'

By mid-1971, Jerry had successfully auditioned for Motor City glam goddess Suzi Quatro, who had been making a name for herself in the all-girl quintet Cradle. 'Suzi Quatro was doing a gig with all her sisters in the city and the drummer had quit. They found out about me through some people, so I auditioned and joined the band that night. We went back to Detroit and I stayed there for four or five months, the whole summer. I was in the band with her and her sisters. We couldn't get a record deal. I thought they were good actually. A little bit too good. They were pretty advanced for a female band.'

Recalling Jerry's tenure with Cradle, Suzi explains, 'My younger sister Nancy and I took the band van to New York in search of a drummer – we found Jerry. He was actually the only male drummer who played in our all girl band. I thought he looked interesting . . . we drove back to the family home in Detroit and started rehearsing. Trouble was, he fell in love with Nancy – which would eventually cause problems and we had to let him go.'

The band split when Suzi got a phone call from the UK, went to London and hitched up with sixties-producer-turned-glam-rock-impresario Mickie Most's RAK Records. Aided by the Nicky Chinn/Mike Chapman songwriting hit machine, Suzi was poured into a leather catsuit and hit pay-dirt with earthy stompers like 'Can The Can', '48 Crash', 'Daytona Demon' and 'Devil Gate Drive'.

Jerry returned to New York in late 1971 and lost no time in occupying any free drum stool that caught his eye. Among these were Kicks – a band featuring future hair-metal axe strangler Billy Squier – and Wayne County's Queen Elizabeth, whom he joined as a permanent member. By then, Jerry had developed a style that managed to weld the metronomic feeling of Charlie Watts with the energised sledgehammer force of Ginger Baker.

At the same time as drumming for Queen Elizabeth, Jerry continued to gig with both Shaker and Kicks. This kept him out of trouble and he soon earned a reputation for having the kind of constitution that could play hard all night and soak up copious amounts of booze and pills – as well as for taking naps on bar tops. 'I'd do a gig with one band at one end of the Mercer Arts Centre, then I'd run over to the other end and do a gig with Wayne County. One time we opened for the Dolls – just me and some guitar player. That's what I was into then, just trying to find a band. Then the Dolls went to London and Billy died. They came back to New York and I joined the Dolls.' Jerry's replacement in Queen Elizabeth was Tommy Erdelyi, who would later inspire the 1976 punk explosion as one of the Ramones.

Now that he was a New York Doll, Jerry needed to look the part. Johnny – who was delighted to discover that the drummer shared his newfound passion for heroin – took Jerry up to the Fourteenth Street apartment he shared with Syl, and set about turning the streetwise mook into a creature of feminine allure and charm. Which didn't really pan out. As most photos of the band would attest, Jerry generally seemed ill at ease in his knotted chiffon blouses and liberal panstick. 'It was still taboo and it wasn't really where he was at,' recalls Syl, 'I think he felt a little bit uncomfortable.'

However, Jerry realised what was required of him to be a fully-fledged Doll, and approached the dressing up as if it was in aid of a costume party. To sweeten the equation, he demanded a new pink Ludwig drum kit and two spares from Marty. He was more than capable of knocking seven shades of shit out of any of the three kits, and woe betide anyone who wanted to take issue with his girly makeover.

The new Dolls line-up played their first gig at the Mercer Arts Centre on 19 December 1972 – barely six weeks after Billy's death. This was a big one. After Billy's passing the popular perception of Dolls had altered from the band being touted as brash new underground to the band being viewed as a glamorous sideshow of sex, rock and death. 'The whole thing was fucked up, and of course it made us ten times bigger,' Sylvain recalled. 'How awful is that? We came back to New York and we were superstars.'

This time the Dolls were booked into the 450-capacity Sean O'Casey Theatre, one of the largest rooms in the Mercer. The joint was rammed, while Steve Leber had also invited a sizeable slice of the Manhattan music industry. 'Out of an audience of 500, there were maybe twenty real kids who were there to rock. The rest of 'em were record company people,' recalled David in an interview with Ben Edmonds of *Creem*. 'So we came on stage, and all we could see were these balding old relics with their polished heads, snorting coke and thinking that they're so outasite . . . [Atlantic Records head] Ahmet Ertregun and [Rolling Stones guitarist] Mick Taylor decided that we were the worst high school band they'd ever heard. Mick Taylor told us, "You guys got six months to polish it up." I told him to go screw.'

The hit-and-miss Dolls turned in one of their sloppy howlers, failing to catch fire until the second set – by which time the execs had left. 'I guess, all of a sudden there was a drug-related death and the group were five times hotter than they ever were,' observed Marty Thau. 'Hundreds were turned away and it was like a record industry convention that night. It was great for the fans who knew what a Dolls show was about but the presidents laughed up their sleeves. They should've stayed for the second show – they would've seen something spectacular.'

'We sucked and they didn't get it,' explains Sylvain. 'They never got it. They're probably still wondering, "What the hell was that?"'

Although his upbeat personality and sense of fun was dearly missed, as a drummer Billy wasn't in Jerry's league. Nolan's presence made the band a far more cohesive unit. Instead of maintaining the kind of steady rhythm that can be heard on the Actress demo, Jerry embellished the Dolls' sound – adding new fills and packing a far greater punch. The robust manner in which the Dolls had managed to regroup after their London debacle and the vastly expanded interest shown in their comeback, made this latest rejection all the more galling.

Marty realised that the Dolls' image was so diametrically opposite to the established All-American credentials required by the industry that the band would always be likely to scare record companies away. Indeed, they were described by *Creem* as 'the most walked-out-on band in the history of show business.'

A description of the band in the *New York Daily News* the following year succinctly nailed the characteristics that would attract the kids, and repel the suits, in equal measure: 'Sneering, sporting women's clothes, shoes, make-up and hairdos, contending they add pizazz to their music, the recently emergent New York Dolls are classically offensive. Their raw, screaming music supports the obvious hostility of their stage image.' 'People have the wrong idea about us,' protested Arthur. 'They think we're a bunch of trans-sexual junkies or something.'

In the US, Bowie got away with much of his androgynous experimentation simply because he was so alien, and the idea that the British were all fag-gots anyway helped to explain away his queer image. The Dolls, on the other hand, were good American boys, and good American boys simply did not go on stage in pantyhose and hot pants. Even the wilder indigenous rockers like Black Oak Arkansas could have walked into a redneck bar without too much trouble. 'The Dolls were just too much against the grain, too real,' asserted Marty. 'That, coupled with all the confusion about their sexuality, which was really weird. There were people who literally thought the Dolls were trans-vestites. I said, "Go out on the road and see the beautiful young girls they attract – maybe you'll have a bit more understanding of what they're about!"' Jerry Nolan was once attacked by a gang of black kids who thought he was a faggot,' explains Jayne County. 'Straight boys would learn first hand what it was like to be a queen on the street, even when they weren't gay. It was an education! I got attacked by a bunch of white kids. Black, white, Puerto Rican, Italian – it did not matter. If they thought you were a fag and you were walking through their neighbourhoods, you were in trouble. If you hung out mostly in the 'gay' area you were usually safe. And there was a gay bar on every corner in the West Village at that time. You could go from bar to bar and never get bothered. But when the glam kids started invading the straight rock clubs and bars, there was usually a lot of confusion because people had a hard time with the look. The 'gay' look, or glam look, or androgynous look. It would freak out people 'cause people weren't familiar with the scene yet. They thought it was some sort of new faggot movement.'

'Once, even in Max's, Billy Doll got called a faggot by this table of tourists, and he went over and grabbed their table and flipped it over on top of them . . . It was an era in New York that compares easily with Paris in the 1920s, Berlin in the thirties and England in the sixties. It was all very Weimar Republic. At some of the Dolls shows it became hip to wear swastika armbands. Not because they were anti-Semitic – they didn't even know what that was – but because it was decadent and fashionable.'

Then there was the music – which was far too fast, loud and raw for the fondue-set execs that filed in (and often straight out again) to check out the Dolls. 'They say that we're very crude and don't use our guitars in the traditional sense of the instrument. But we use those guitars to make sounds that mean something to us,' countered David. 'We don't make sounds that would mean anything to a bunch of hillbillies.' Marty's asking price of $250,000 wasn't helping, either.

There was still one hope. Paul Nelson continued his tireless efforts to get Mercury Records to sign the band. However, he found himself flying in the face of some heavyweight opposition – the label's president, Irwin Steinberg, had been at the Wembley gig to check on Rod Stewart, who was probably Mercury's foremost act. He'd also caught the Dolls and told Nelson, in no uncertain terms, never to mention their name again.

Forced to take a roundabout route to getting the band signed, Nelson managed to persuade the company's head of publicity, Mike Gormley, to fly in from Chicago to catch the Dolls at Kenny's Castaways. Gormley was impressed and agreed that Mercury should sign the band. Encouraged by this, Nelson decided to try one last stab at collaring Steinberg.

On discovering that his boss was in New York, Nelson stayed up all night in the restaurant of his hotel and ambushed him at breakfast. If he was going to be fired he didn't want it to be in the office. With Gormley's support and a growing array of press clippings, he finally got his way. As Ben Edmonds observed, Mercury 'made an investment in their own future that they probably don't understand.'

Marty Thau got word that the label were about to offer a deal and gave the band the go-ahead to expand their road crew, in anticipation of subsidised touring. Keeth Paul came in as soundman, while Desmond Sullivan and Max Blatt joined Peter Jordan as roadies. They even acquired a personal valet to take on the major task of looking after the Dolls' wardrobe – Vietnam veteran Christian Rodriguez, who had worked as a colour co-ordinator at Truth &

Soul and was nicknamed 'Frenchy', because he pretended he was French to impress the ladies. Frenchy also filled other necessary functions with the Dolls, like looking after the increasingly stoned Johnny and acting as an all-purpose minder.

On 11 February 1973, the Dolls returned to the Mercer to headline 'An Endless Valentine's Day All-Night Party', which also featured Wayne County, electro proto-punks Suicide and Eric Emerson and the Magic Tramps. Costing $5 to get in and running from 10pm until dawn, the show attracted the cream of New York's beautiful people, who'd gone to town in terms of drag and pushing out the glitter boat.

In his *NME* review, underground press veteran Barry Miles focused on the Dolls' louche, ambisexual following. 'The total effect was quite sinister after London which still tends more towards the warmth and friendliness of lace and velvet, whereas NY is cold and distant in silk and satin, the faces remote in dead white make-up like wandering ghosts of a lost humanity.'

The Dolls' New York gigs drew an exotic herd of punters, who not only tried to look like their heroes but take their androgynous glitter flash in different directions. This inevitably inspired waves of copyists, who adapted elements of the Dolls' bold style to suit their own ideas. As some of these fashionistas and imitators formed bands, a burgeoning scene developed in the group's wake.

Bands such as Kiss – of whom Jerry observed, 'I don't think they're any good at all' – and Aerosmith were also on the rise with their basic forms of tarted up rock, while other bands included the Stillettoes, the Brats, the Harlots of 42nd Street, Twisted Sister, Luger, Ruby and the Rednecks, Teenage Lust and Another Pretty Face.

'Everybody else took notes and took it to the bank,' explains Syl. 'But we fell and broke our legs because we were running so damn fast. We were actually inventing it all, not even knowing what the hell we were doing.' As Blondie guitarist/songwriter Chris Stein later asserted, 'The New York scene dates back to the Dolls.'

'At the time the only band I thought had any potential were the Miamis,' recalled Jerry. 'At that time I thought they were better than the average band. They used to be Queen Elizabeth, then Wayne split and got a new band and Queen Elizabeth became the Miamis.'

Rick Rivets had wasted little time in putting together his Brats. Initially he teamed up with former Fogg drummer Sparky Donovan and drafted in neighbourhood pal Bill Spence on bass, with a hippie vocalist and a second guitarist known only as Cat rounding out the ensemble. The unnamed quartet had played a couple of local gigs when Rick got talking to guitarist and record store owner Keith Ambrose at his Queens shop, the Music Box. Impressed by Ambrose's Rod Stewart-style feather-cut and anglophile musical influences (the Kinks, the Yardbirds, The Who), Rick invited him along to a rehearsal. Before long Ambrose had joined, and the band swung their direction away from Allman Brothers covers and towards the gutsier, garage influenced rock that was far more in keeping with Rick's tastes.

However, this new direction was not to everyone's liking, and both Bill Spence and Cat made their excuses. The line-up was bolstered by the addition of David Leeds, who Rick met at Max's Kansas City, and they set about rehearsing at David's loft on Bleecker, putting together a set containing a smattering of Sparky Donovan originals as well as the usual Stones and Chuck Berry standards.

Finally, the band selected their name from a shortlist suggested by Alice Cooper, who had recently started hanging out with the group: discarding names like Husky Babies and Jelly Filled Liver Donut, the group settled on the Brats, adopting a glam image significantly more butch than that of the Dolls – who they supported at the Diplomat Hotel's Crystal Room on 16 March. 'It wasn't a bit strange playing on the same bill as the Dolls, because we shared the bill quite a few times,' recalls Rick. 'Anytime the Dolls played anyplace in New York I would go, because Arthur was still my friend and nothing like a band would change that. And we were pushing for them to make it so that maybe the scene would open up and all the bands would get their shot.'

Lou Reed, who hopped aboard the glitter bandwagon with *Transformer* the previous year, was growing disdainful of the growing glam fixation he saw becoming prevalent in New York's nightclubs, 'I just think that everyone's into this scene because supposedly it's the thing to do right now,' he scowled. 'The makeup thing is just a style now, like platform shoes. If people have homosexuality in them it won't necessarily involve make-up in the first place. You can't fake being gay, because being gay means you're going to have to suck cock, or get fucked.'

Unlike Reed, David Bowie retained his enthusiasm for both the Dolls and glam in general. As he continued his alien invasion of America in his Ziggy persona, he passed long hours on the road writing his follow-up album. Consequently, the resulting *Aladdin Sane* is suffused with Americana and Stateside influences that the magpie-ish Bowie had picked up along the way. Poignantly, he refers to Billy Murcia's death on 'Time' – one of the album's standout tracks – where he sings of 'Time – in Quaaludes and red wine / demanding Billy Dolls.'

The glam/glitter rock groundswell, Marty's willingness to drop his asking price considerably, and Paul Nelson's tireless lobbying finally proved sufficient to break down Mercury's resistance. On 20 March 1973, the New York Dolls signed a two-album deal with a $25,000 advance plus an allowance for new equipment. The band's weekly retainer was upped to $200 for each group member.

While Syl celebrated by scoring a new Les Paul, Marty and Paul Nelson took David to the label's Chicago HQ to meet the suits. He was still wasted from a drinking session the previous night, and dozed off during the very meeting that had been called to work out how he could take on the role of the Dolls' media mouthpiece. Marty's next idea was to get Bob Gruen to film a message from the band to their backers from the dressing room at Max's. This backfired too, as his subjects were post-show drunk and couldn't manage anything approaching coherence. Many of Irving Steinberg's worst fears were already being realised.

Still, the group was there to make hit records, not to showboat for the board of directors. At last the New York Dolls were going to record their first album.

You Can Take The Dolls Out Of New York . . .

'The New York Dolls came along and they were
like everything. They were incredible and blew my mind.
The way that they looked, their whole kind of attitude.
They didn't care about anything. They were a group that
were all about style.' – *Mick Jones, The Clash*

The New York Dolls had packed a lot of action into the first year of their existence. Although the band had barely played 50 gigs since their formation, they had built up a set that contained more than enough good material for an album. *NME*'s Michael Gross reported that the Dolls had been poring over their live tapes, 'to see where the sound should be changed and where it should be left well enough alone. One day those may appear as a hell of a bootleg.'

By the end of March 1973, the search was on to find a suitable producer to put the gloss on their debut. Surely any producer professing to be in love with the rock'n'roll world would see the Dolls as an exciting challenge. They had their own wish list, with gun-toting Wall-of-Sound wacko Phil Spector at the top. That idea was an instant non-starter, as Spector was in the midst of one of his frequent spells of hermitude. Marty Thau was keen on securing the services of Brill Building behemoths Jerry Leiber and Mike Stoller – who'd recently had a huge hit producing the Dylanesque bubblegum favourite 'Stuck In The Middle With You' for Stealers Wheel. However, the duo were almost certainly out of the Dolls' minimal price range and were scaling down their activities. Instead, Marty looked up former Shangri-La's producer Shadow Morton, but he was recovering from a recent car accident and was unfit to produce.

Roy Wood – who'd gone from the psychedelic pop of the Move to the orchestral prog-pop of the Electric Light Orchestra to glam opportunists

Wizzard – was considered, but he'd recently suffered a nervous breakdown and had consequently turned down a production offer from Mott the Hoople. Bowie would have been an obvious choice, but he was too busy making *Aladdin Sane*. 'We went to twenty producers – none of whom would have anything to do with us,' recalled David. 'Time was running out because the studio was block-booked and the record company were pressuring us. We had to get a producer fast, and Todd Rundgren said he'd do it . . . he was the best available.'

Rundgren had caught the band at the Mercer and had been an occasional drinking buddy at Max's. Stylistically, he was an odd choice – a self-taught multi-instrumentalist singer-songwriter, whose output leaned toward the kind of close-harmony jangle pop associated with the Byrds and mid-period Beatles. He also dipped his toe in progressive waters, experimenting with a wide range of influences that included Motown soul, Latin American jazz and watered down Zappa-esque stylings.

In 1973 Rundgren was hot, having impressed the previous year with his *Something Anything* double album that had spawned a top ten hit in 'I Saw The Light'. This glammed-up one Renaissance-man band – described by *Rolling Stone*'s Jon Landau as the 'Mozart of his generation' – would knock out three albums during 1973: *A Wizard/A True Star*, *Runt* and *Todd*. The eponymous title of the third album, and its self-indulgent content, provided some indication of how the press plaudits were beginning to go to his head.

As much as securing Rundgren's services solved one headache, it instantly created another, as the producer was in demand and was compelled to fit the Dolls into an already hectic schedule. His other outside production that year was Grand Funk Railroad's huge *We're An American Band* album. This, in addition to the pressure for product from Mercury – who, having been sceptical about signing the band, wanted a near instant return on their investment – made conditions less than ideal.

'The Dolls were something of a local phenomenon, rising above the rest of the bands in that particular scene,' Rundgren later told *Q* journalist Mat Snow. 'I was amused by them. At the time it seemed a little bit silly, these guys walking around in hot pants, wearing girls' clothes all the time, and the fact that they imitated the Stones but were so half-assed about it.'

Rundgren's success as a recording artist meant that he didn't need to produce the Dolls album, especially as his credentials as an all-round whiz kid were firmly established. 'The main reason that I did the Dolls album was because it was a New York City Record. There was no reason to get David Bowie or some other weirdo to produce it; the only person who can logically produce a New York City record is someone who lives in New York. I live here, and I recognise all the things about New York that the Dolls recognise in their music,' he explained.

Having experienced a measure of success with his precise, technically orientated production methods, Rundgren attempted to apply this approach to the Dolls. This type of ascetically studious process was okay for a lone boffin like Rundgren, but was scarcely suitable to the raw attack of Johnny Thunders turned up past the scale of ten, New York's hardest-hitting human drum machine, and the queen/king of the scandalised camp vocal.

True to form, when the Dolls arrived to begin recording in mid-April, they were still immersed in their endless party. Keen to keep the good times rolling, the band simply moved the revelry from Max's into Studio B of the Record Plant on 44th Street. The quintet had no experience of heads-down studio reality and its laborious creative process, and turned up with a complete entourage of crew, girlfriends, journalists and hangers-on. 'The atmosphere in the studio was carnival-like, I guess, because they did have such a large entourage,' recalled Rundgren. 'I found it sort of annoying, but the band were only loosely held together anyway.'

Creem journalist Ben Edmonds visited the sessions and described the chaotic kinesis he found. 'Singer David Johansen strolls over to the plate glass partition which separates the studio from the control room, and scotch-tapes an advertising flier he's just found to the window so that it faces the booth. "Too fast to live, too young to die," it reads, "LET IT ROCK!" He spins around the band launches full-throttle into "Trash", an electric explosion that seconds his gesture with a vengeance, and without which his action would've been empty and melodramatic. In that moment it becomes perfectly apparent that the New York Dolls – far from being an easy target for anybody's labels – are in the midst of creating a category that doesn't even have a name yet.'

'I still see the engineer, Jack Douglas, from time to time and he fills me in what really went down,' Johansen said later. 'Apparently, Todd would tell him, "I gotta go home and make some phone calls. If they get any ideas call me." I think Todd needed a bullwhip and a chair. He wasn't intimidated by us; just exasperated. We had about twenty people in with us; everybody was drinking and smoking pot. We didn't know that you were supposed to go to a studio and knuckle down. For us it was just another part of this non-stop party we were living.'

When it came to recording, Johnny acted like he was on stage and went for maximum volume, while Sylvain tried to temper the sonic carnage with some subtler musical compliments and toppings. Meanwhile, a permanently drunk David had all the little lyrical vignettes he'd been honing at the live gigs in his head, ready to be spilled out. Arthur just lurked around vacantly, providing a steady bass rumble, whereas Jerry took instant umbrage to the way that Rundgren attempted to graft the kind of restrained drum sound he'd used on his solo albums to Nolan's primal beat-blitz. 'A lot of people thought Todd Rundgren was great,' he would complain, 'but he sucked with us. He really fucked us up.' When Marty Thau suggested that Rundgren place Jerry's drums higher in the mix, the producer simply snorted his contempt. Johnny agreed with the criticisms of their ex-drinking pal, insisting that 'he fucked up the mix really bad'.

Subsequently, whenever he was called upon to make a radio appearance, Johnny always tried to make a point of dedicating 'Your Mama Don't Dance And Your Daddy Don't Rock'n'Roll' to Todd.

After all the criticisms directed at Rundgren by Johnny and Jerry, it came as some surprise to hear Sylvain sing his praises in 2005. 'Getting Rundgren was the icing on the cake. The most perfect cat that we could ever figure out. He really made us work. He really saw the little nooks and crannies to really bring out. He took that art project and made it into an incredible piece of music that will live forever.'

For his part, Rundgren blamed the Dolls for the muddy mix. 'The record would have been a lot better had they not got in such a hurry to finish it. They insisted it was mixed in the same studio we were working in, the Record Plant, where the only room available to mix in was at the top of the building and I always thought the sound was dodgy. Then they insisted on being there when it was mixed, which was the worst mistake.'

However, the broad consensus of opinion regarding Rundgren's production is exemplified by Jayne County. 'Todd ruined the Dolls first album. They sounded nothing like that. He thought by watering them down and taking away a lot of their raw trashiness, he could make them commercial. What a mistake!'

With their album in the can, the Dolls continued to play regularly to rabid crowds at Max's. *NME* made up for being scooped by *Melody Maker* the previous year by sending Nick Kent to tell the world about the Dolls again, in a 'This Is America' special. He hadn't heard the album yet, but his experience of seeing the band on their home turf prompted some choice observations: 'It's almost as if Donny Osmond ditched his brothers, started taking downers and grew fangs, picked up with a bunch of heavy-duty characters down off 42nd Street, and started writing songs on topics like premature ejaculation.' More pertinent was his point that 'their image could be so terribly pretentious, but it all seems so perfectly natural.'

Kent was impressed by the cover versions littering the set, mentioning Willie Dixon's 'Hoochie Coochie Man', the Coasters' 'Bad Detective' and the Cadets' 1956 hit 'Stranded In The Jungle' – 'the absolute all-time greatest novelty rock song ever'. It recounts the travails of a guy whose plane has come down in the jungle and can't get home to the States. The song also provided David with another opportunity to affect a new role on stage, his voice becoming a Tarzan-esque howl while the others made ape noises and Jerry weighed in with appropriate jungle drums.

In July, *NME* carried another New York scene report, this time by Michael Gross. Dominated by a large photo of David, erroneously identified as 'the mysterious Sylvain Sylvain', it provided another account of the group's fervent New York following and über-hip status, plus a potted history and favourable gig review. The piece contained observations about Johansen's 'incredible resemblance' to Jagger, identified a similarity between Arthur and Who bass titan John Entwistle, and noted that Johnny combined 'the power of Keith Richard with the terse economy of [The Band's] Robbie Robertson'. Gross went for the geographical metaphor by comparing the Dolls' sound to 'spending a night on the Times Square subway platform with a warm loving body'.

Although Johnny wanted to call the album *The New York Dolls' Greatest Hits*, it was released as *The New York Dolls* on 27 July 1973. In many ways it represented a significant triumph over adversity and hostility – Mercury had little understanding of what the band were all about, and thus no idea how to handle or market them. Rundgren essentially thought that his charges were a bunch of Stones-copying party troglodytes, and time constraints meant there had been only a week to capture the live set that had been slaughtering New York for the past year. And yet despite all this, the Dolls pulled it off. The sheer strength of the songs, and the force and *élan* of the Dolls' playing, elevated the album into the realms of rock's greatest all-time debuts.

Once Rundgren had departed to concentrate on his latest slab of creative onanism, the Dolls were left to vent their frustrations at one another. Jerry identified David's ego as a source of their producerial problems, 'David had a bad habit of calling the shots about things he knew nothing about. He wanted to pick the producer and settle for this mix, that tone . . . he had everything to do with making the wrong moves and fucked up everything.'

Publicly, at least, David was having none of it. He was loudly proud of the album and gushed incontinently to the press about what he obviously considered to be his baby. 'I mean, I wrote those songs, and my unbiased opinion is that they're great,' he boasted at *Record Mirror*'s Martin Kirkup. 'That album is gonna be a classic in five years. I know it! Nobody's even really listened to the words yet . . . We've got pop prowess, I think. I don't think we're like anything else. People always have to make analogies, of course, but we are something new.' Privately, David chose to hide any reservations beneath his confidence in the Dolls appeal – 'don't worry, they'll take anything we put out.'

The New York Dolls roars off the starting blocks with 'Personality Crisis'. A cornerstone of the Dolls' live set, the song was a solid choice to announce the band to the great record-buying unwashed.

Johnny's Chuck Berry licks and Rundgren's good-time ivories crash in, as David's lycanthropic wail heralds an escape-velocity descent into New York City. *'Yeah, yeah, yeah / No, no, no, no, no, no, no'* – already there's a scandal on the sidewalk. His lyrics bundle us directly into the heart of the Dolls' private universe – a scene populated by hustlers, wannabes and the terminally self-obsessed: 'We can't take her this week / And her friends don't want another speech.' Everything is frantic; a blurred snapshot of bitching, social climbing and nuked aspirations is laid out over Johnny, Syl, Arthur and Jerry's dirty rock'n'roll. 'Personality Crisis' tells the world who the Dolls are and, specifically, where they're comin' from, honey.

Opening with David's sleazed-up appropriation of the Shangri-Las' 'When ah say ahm in love, you best believe ahm in love, L-U-V' from 'Give Him A Great Big Kiss', 'Looking For A Kiss' puts the Dolls' influences proudly on display. This is Arthur's 'teenage hard-on music'. Johnny's riff is the fundamental guitar sound of rock'n'roll – an Ur-lick with an extended lineage that could be traced backward through T Rex's 'Get It On', via innumerable suburban sixties garages and the righteous groove of Diddley and Berry, to the primordial birthing pools of blues-influenced rock, deep in the Mississippi Delta. Instrumentally, the Dolls hotwired their influences into the present by mainlining adrenaline into the mix. Johansen's lyrics take the Shangri-La's doomed love theme a stage further by comparing the merits of the search for l-u-v against those of narcotic abandon. His verdict: 'I need a fix and a kiss.' This is romance, Lower East Side style. Introducing the song at Max's, David deadpanned, 'This is a song about the days when love was free, before all the boys burnt out their energy fibres and their girlfriends went to work in massage parlours.'

With songs such as 'I'm Waiting For The Man' and 'Heroin', Lou Reed had been the first to represent New York street life with such graphic *verité*. The

Dolls trod the same streets wearing a different kind of drag – where Reed had no other focus than to revel in the expectant misery of seeking out his man on the corner of Lexington and 125th Street, Johansen is beset by hedonists looking to shoot up in his room. On the whole, the Dolls seemed to be having more fun with their drugs than the melancholy Lou.

David's 'Vietnamese Baby' transplants the doomed romance theme to Saigon. Although the track isn't overtly political, its topical title and examination of the helplessness of lovers amidst the backdrop of war marks one of the few occasions that the Dolls' lyrics ventured away from the dramas of their home turf. Despite this broader scope, they are still delivered by Johansen in the context of dialogue. The track also features several sonic metaphors such as the opening gong, Johnny's machine-gun effects and Jerry's militaristic drum coda.

Another Johansen composition, 'Lonely Planet Boy' opens with a plaintive sigh and a riff that Johnny would subsequently recycle for 'You Can't Put Your Arms Around A Memory'. This lonesome ballad was written before David hooked up with the Dolls, and features some atmospheric sax noodling from Jerry's teenage pal Buddy Bowser. A pure slice of road-borne angst, the song came to be featured at gigs in a Stones-style acoustic interlude.

'Lonely Planet Boy' provides further evidence of the fundamental influence the early 1960s girl groups had on the Dolls. However, as David explained to *Sounds'* Martin Kirkup, these influences came to him distorted by the specific hyper-realism of Lou Reed. 'I first saw the Velvets when I was about thirteen actually, and I was very impressed by them. I imagine that they influenced us. Like Lou would have those girlie vocal things – "doo doo wah" – and that's from the same things that influenced me most, the chick bands. People say that "Lonely Planet Boy" on our album is influenced by the Velvets, but I know it's the Ronettes really.'

The opening four songs on *The New York Dolls* can be viewed as a form of preparation for the listener. They display the distaff poles of the band's stylistic range: from the in-your-face hectoring of 'Personality Crisis' to the whispered entreaties of 'Lonely Planet Boy'. They also introduce the doomed romance theme and re-present it in diverse settings: the New York scene ('Personality Crisis', 'Looking For A Kiss'), the endless American roadscape ('Lonely Planet Boy'), and Vietnam ('Vietnamese Baby'). Next, rather than shifting geographical emphasis, Johansen's lyrics supplant one doomed lover with a monster.

Almost operatic in scope, 'Frankenstein' is the longest song on the album, taking almost six minutes to build successive layers of growing angst and hysteria as David rails against those who would limit the scope of his desires, before the song reaches a desperate climax with the question, 'Do you think that you could make it . . . with Frankenstein?'

Frankenstein here is an obvious metaphor for a lover becoming a monster. 'Frankenstein' is the Shangri-Las *in extremis*; zapped by electricity from unspeakable devices and surrounded by spare parts taken from the dead. Johansen's bravura vocal delivery more than matches Syl's music. This is David Jo at his scandalised, bullying best – as *Trouser Press*'s Ira Robbins subsequently observed, 'Only the criminally self-conscious could find this performance unstimulating.'

'The song is about how kids come to Manhattan from all over,' explained David. 'They're kind of like whipped dogs. They're repressed. Their bodies and brains are disorientated from each other – it's a love song.'

It's hardly surprising that 'Trash' – another Sylvain and Johansen composition – would be selected to pave the way for *The New York Dolls* as the band's debut US single. Although the album contains several tracks that epitomise the Dolls – 'Personality Crisis', 'Looking For A Kiss', 'Frankenstein', 'Subway Train' and 'Jet Boy', in particular, none does it as absolutely as 'Trash'. Led in by Jerry's toms, which rise above Rundgren's muted production, David's vocal is rich with coquettish sloppiness, defining his indomitable cheap-but-proud sluttiness. His drawled pronunciation of the title, 'Tray-ash', preserves his sassy on-stage persona in everlasting plastic. Somewhere between his vocal and Sylvain and Johnny's twin guitar assault, the two axemen create an intricate web of backing harmony that counterpoints between Syl's sumptuous, otherworldly sweetness and John's rhythmic interjections. 'I stole those chords from Eddie Cochran,' says Syl. Like 'Personality Crisis', the song is a declaration of identity and intent – This is who we are and if you don't like it you can go fuck yourself – 'Please don'tcha ask me if I love you / If you don't know what I'm doin'.' This is the same attitude that would typify much of the punk canon that the Dolls inspired. The break, 'How d'ya call yoah luvvah boy', is pure girl-group tittle-tattlery.

'Bad Girl' dates back to Mercer Street, with Johansen's words having started life as 'Black Girl', a biographical account of his infatuation with a sexy neighbour. His lyrics are very much in the tradition of lascivious blues, as practised by the likes of Andre Williams: 'A new bad girl moved in on my block/I gave her my key, said you don't have to knock.' Sadly, the amorous David's pleading is in vain and the theme of hopeless desire is maintained.

Like 'Bad Girl', 'Subway Train' is another updated version of one of the Dolls' early originals, 'That's Poison'. For the young Dolls, becalmed in the outer boroughs, the subway provided an umbilical link to the city, where all the action was at. These journeys became almost a rite of passage, a progression toward new experiences, represented here by Johansen's transplantation of relationship hassles onto the subway. In addition to being set there, 'Subway Train' extends the motif by building up to full pace in the style of an accelerating train, while Johnny and Syl's guitars *sound* like the subway. If Kraftwerk had grown up in New York rather than Düsseldorf, they'd have written this instead of 'Trans Europe Express'.

In view of the Dolls' predilection for cover versions, it's surprising that the only non-original number on their debut is an energetic reworking of Bo Diddley's 'Pills'. Another direct indication of the primal rock'n'roll side of the band's influences, the song was both stylistically and literally appropriate. Syl tells the story of the Dolls meeting Diddley at one of his gigs and telling him they did 'Pills'. 'You do pills? That's good, 'cos I don't,' replied the Gunslinger, before having the Dolls ejected when they started calling out for the song during his set. 'He thought we were trying to sell drugs!' laughs Syl.

Although credited to Thunders/Johansen, 'Private World' was co-written by Arthur – a fact that David pointed out at most Dolls gigs. Kicking in with a bass line that sounds like Arthur was attempting 'Louie Louie' on Quaaludes, David's cry of 'breakdown!' sends the track careering into spirals of chugging instrumentation. Lyrically, the song explores the idea of being in your own space while everything around you is chaotic and distracting. This aptly described the situation that the individual Dolls – particularly Arthur – found themselves pitched into. 'Private World' represents the first example of the quintet joining a long tradition of bands writing about their tribulations as a working group – a lineage that would be extended by generations of Dolls-influenced bands, notably The Clash and the Libertines. 'We were no longer teenagers out having fun. We were in the business now. I started getting this railroaded feeling even before the album came out,' explained Arthur, who had recently been described by David as 'the only living statue in rock'n'roll'.

The album closes with 'Jet Boy', which dated back to the band's early sessions at Chrystie Street. Taking its cues from the Stones, Stooges and MC5, the track takes the theme of lost love to Manhattan's skies. Accompanied by stomps, handclaps, wailing guitars and an afterburner rhythm section, 'Jet Boy' strikes a fistful of valedictory chords. The middle-eight resembles the train sequence in the Stones' episodic serial killer epic 'Midnight Rambler', a frenzied onslaught of suddenly erupting energy, which stokes the track to further heights of snarling defiance. Arthur had also been influenced by the bass run in the home stretch of the Stones' 'Nineteenth Nervous Breakdown'. As if to confirm the hand-me-down nature of rock'n'roll, three years later The Damned joyfully appropriated the piledriving opening riff for their first single, 'New Rose'.

For the album cover, Mercury set up an afternoon photo shoot at a Third Avenue antique shop. The session placed the bemused Dolls amidst a sea of moose heads. It was all very last minute and the band hated it. Mercury said it was too late to do anything else but the Dolls managed to negotiate a two-day reprieve. 'We were supposed to [pose] without our makeup, like we were dolls among the antiques,' Syl told *Toronto Sun* reporter Kieran Grant. 'We looked like we do on the back of the cover. It was okay, but it had nothing compared to what the Dolls really were. I called up all my friends in the rag business and said, "Hey, I got $900 and I need a dynamite shot." These friends suggested [photographer] Toshi, who was doing *Vogue* covers. He got the crew and this guy named Shin for the hair and another guy for the makeup. That couch we were sitting on, we found that on the street and brought it up. We put the white fabric on it – I remember tacking it on. It was really a trashed couch, with a white satin cover.'

Assisted by make-up artist Dave O'Grady, the Dolls applied their thickest coating of industrial-strength cosmetics and teased their hair in to a unique assortment of out-there bouffants. Arthur looks trashed and slutty, cradling a martini with a cigarette in his mouth in his fetching off-the-shoulder halter top and gobstopper beads. Syl resembles a disco Pierrot, complete with rosy doll cheeks, roller skates (which he donned purely for effect) and a kids'

cowboy shirt. Johansen preens into a compact mirror, his hairy legs pushed into a spectacularly *outré* pair of platform mules. Johnny just looks mean as the band's man in black, even if he is wearing a kids' cowboy shirt. Finally, Jerry took another uncomfortable stab at displaying his feminine side, striking a pose that suggests he could well have been busting for a piss.

'I look like Simone Signoret, Johnny looks like Anna Magnani, Jerry looks like Lee Remick, Syl looks like Polly Bergen and Arthur's got a Dietrich thing going on,' David later told Nina Antonia.

For sheer shock value, the image could only have been topped if they'd have worn false breasts. In 1973 it was still possible to send the average redneck into apoplexy if your shirt was just too damn fancy. Reflecting on the sexual climate of the day, Bob Gruen recalled, 'It wasn't just a matter of being homophobic. It was illegal to be homosexual. People don't remember this, it wasn't hatred or fear – it was the law. To say that the Dolls, guys who wore makeup, were your friends was like saying you knew a criminal.'

DJs wouldn't play the album because they couldn't get past the cover, which amazed David – 'When a kid comes in and sees that picture he's gonna forget about the Allman Brothers and he's gonna have to buy it.' However, this wasn't the Stones' dragged-up like dowagers for the cover of 'Have You Seen Your Mother, Baby', or even the Mothers of Invention donning frocks for far-out yoks. To most red-blooded, all-American, God-fearing heterosexualists, the Dolls looked downright deviant. Even if they weren't gonna listen to the album, nobody was likely to forget an image like that.

The back cover shows the group loitering with intent in front of Gem Spa, a tobacconists and newsagents situated on the corner of St Mark's Place and Third Avenue. St Mark's was the epicentre of New York's art-rock community. The Dom, where the Velvets used to play and Warhol had his factory, is still there, as is the clothes store Trash & Vaudeville, which is run by ex-Stillettoes Tish and Snookie.

Despite Mercury springing for a few press ads plugging the album, the label was far more interested in promoting Canadian soft-rockers Bachman Turner Overdrive, who'd they'd just signed. BTO were good clean boys, who kept away from their girlfriends clothing and could be counted on to behave responsibly. Randy Bachman was a member of the Mormon Church, so wild sex and strange drugs were never likely to be an issue. Mercury understood BTO and found them far easier to get behind than the difficult Dolls.

The fact that the Dolls were almost completely unheard of outside of New York and London meant that only a select group of hipsters were likely to be motivated to rush out and buy the record. Instead of touring the States for six months, then releasing a single, followed by more dates, and *then* an album, the Dolls hit the road to promote the disc on the day after its release.

The Dolls wanted a string of hit singles and believed that the album was packed with suitable candidates. Their material was simple, had plenty of hooks and was, to an extent, based upon the chart-topping template that had served the Shangri-Las, Ronettes and Crystals well. However, when 'Trash' and 'Personality Crisis' was released as a seven-inch in July, it made little impact. According to Marty Thau, Mercury 'expected to sell 500,000 or more' copies of the album, but were uncertain as to how to market their unique investment and thus did little to push the preceding single.

Once *The New York Dolls* hit the stores this pattern was repeated. Given the torpid nature of the US mainstream music scene, it was hardly shocking that such a raw sounding group failed to find a niche amongst the mellow soft rock on FM radio. It seemed – as the Ramones were to discover three years later – that the American public wasn't ready for an amped up progression on the girl-group sound. In many respects, when one considers the lack of promotion, airplay and the Dolls' non-existent profile outside of New York and London, it was remarkable that the album managed to climb even as high as 116 on the *Billboard* chart.

Although *The New York Dolls* would subsequently be reviewed or featured in scores of 'Best Of…' articles (in 2003 *Rolling Stone* nominated it as the 213th Greatest Album of All Time), in 1973 there was little interest in writing up the album, let alone showering it with praise. Although Bud Scoppa offered some genuine enthusiasm in soft porn mag *Penthouse*, it was hardly likely to give the album much of a push. An unaccredited *Billboard* scribe provided more mainstream support, noting, 'The Dolls obviously have a gimmick (their appearance, of course), but more important they have the resources to back up the gimmicks. The material is original and is the kind of wall-shattering sound that so few bands can achieve successfully.' Oddly, the reviewer took the opportunity to fling some compliments in Todd Rundgren's direction, which leaves one wondering just how impressed he or she would have been if they heard the band in their full un-muddied glory.

In New York City, the album was bigger news and added encouragement to the decadent lower Manhattan beat boom forming in the wake of the Dolls. Highly influential rock critic Lillian Roxon popped up in the *Sunday News* with a feature headlined 'The "Fun City Sound" Is What's Happening In Rock'. She cited the Dolls as 'the best of the New York glitter explosion', while describing the album as 'the definitive New York sound album. It gets you up and dancing and feeling fourteen again. It's what being young and in New York is all about.' Roxon compared New York to Liverpool before the Beatles broke out.

In *Disc & Music Echo*, Lisa Robinson also compared the NY scene to Liverpool in the early sixties, along with San Francisco in 1967 or 'Rome before the fall'. Johansen was on form for the interview, dashing out arch one-liners like, 'I never wore glitter in my life. I mean, it probably gives you cancer.' He dismissed any attempts to lump the Dolls in with a New York glam rock scene. 'I never related to that scene at all. We've been called glitter kids, street punks, a fag band, and well publicity is publicity but . . . Sure we dress differently every day, and maybe we do things differently, but I really believe our music is fantastic, and that's all that really counts, right?'

In 2005, Sylvain revealed that he was most impressed by the album being favourably reviewed in staunch jazz publication *Downbeat*. 'We were the first band to be featured in *Downbeat* magazine, the *Billboard* of the jazz world,' he laughs. 'You can't be more down than *Downbeat*! We were the first rock'n'roll musicians to ever be reviewed.'

Just as the UK press would subsequently rope in bands like Eddie and the Hot Rods and The Jam to pad out articles proclaiming the 1977 punk explosion, their American forerunners identified any band possessing the merest hint of sparkle as indicative of New York's developing glitter scene. These included Wayne County and Queen Elizabeth, Suicide, Kiss, Luger (who featured a keyboard player called Ivan Kral, who'd go on to the Patti Smith Group), Teenage Lust, Ruby and the Rednecks, and Rick Rivets' post-Dolls outfit, the Brats.

By mid-1973, the number of bands orbiting New York's newly identified scene had swollen to encompass a host of colourfully named, vaguely glamorous outfits such as, the Harlots of 42nd Street – who were a bunch of acid rockers until they caught wind of the Dolls and glammed up – Fast, the Marbles, the Planets, the Miamis, Another Pretty Face and Day Old Bread. Even John Lennon hopped aboard the glam wagon, producing a demo for a band called New York Central, which enabled them to secure a record deal with RCA. Subsequently they changed their name to Elephant's Memory, and their drummer Tony Machine would later resurface in the post-Jerry Nolan incarnation of the Dolls.

Starting on 28 July at the Tiger Stadium in Masillon Ohio, the Dolls set out on their longest string of gigs to date, an intermittent three-month sojourn that included a trio of shows supporting Mott the Hoople during August. In his *Phonograph Record* review of the gig, Lester Bangs described the impact of the Dolls on unprepared provincial audiences: 'Here's this shreddy football field covered with farmer kids and fatboy yokels in sweatshirts with the sleeves torn out and those goofy Hillbilly Bear hats guaranteed to make you look like a moron . . . and all the yummy little greenbanks chicks, and filtering thru the crowd is these whizzy weirdos in like purple leotards and platforms even tho' they're six feet tall already, and all the lokel yokels are honking, "Ooogh! Faaaggits!" Imagine the surprise of these haysox, then, when the Dolls hit the stage and it's the selfsame faggots they was just about to beat up!'

While the band was contemplating conquering new frontiers, their old home venue at the Mercer Arts Center suddenly collapsed. The MAC was run by Sy and Cindy Kaback, who were in the building when the entire structure suddenly began to buckle, 'We had been hearing weird noises all day. We called the 24 hour Building Department hotline to try to get an inspector to come out and tell us if it was safe to open all the shows that night and were told to call back Monday,' recalled Cindy. 'I was on the phone to the fire department when the building went down. I kept asking them to come and they kept asking me what was wrong. I kept saying, "The walls are making very strange noises." And they kept saying, "Have you been drinking?" Then bam! We were disconnected and I flew up in the air from the impact. Everyone in the office went out the fire escape in the dark holding hands. When we reached the street the fire department were there and they said, "Don't go back into that building!" We said, "Yeah, no kidding." No one from the Mercer Arts Center was hurt, but four people in the welfare hotel above it were killed.'

Deborah Harry blamed the collapse on its long history as a welfare hotel full of incontinent bums: 'It was so old and decrepit from years of people pissing on the floor and throwing up in the corner that it just caved in.' It's been said that, when the building collapsed, the Magic Tramps were rehearsing inside and narrowly escaped with their lives.

After squeezing on between Mott and soft-boiled subversive country rockers Dr Hook (who opened by declaring, 'Hi, we're bigger faggots than the make-up faggots') in Ohio, the Dolls hooked up with Ian Hunter and company for a second support slot on 3 August at the Felt Forum – a five thousand-seater within Madison Square Garden. Todd Rundgren was introduced by legendary DJ Murray the K who led on the Dolls. They opened with their rendition of the theme from the *Courageous Cat* cartoon, which was a band favourite. The show – which was created by Batman originator Bob Kane – was a parody of the Dark Knight and ran for 130 episodes from 1960. (A version of the Dolls' take on the theme, which was created especially for the show by Transartists Productions, can be found on the 1996 Mercury compilation, *Rock'n'Roll*.)

Having established their upbeat sense of abandon, the Dolls then careered through the set they'd be playing in Europe a few months later, starting with 'Personality Crisis', followed by most of the album, plus a few covers like their killer version of the Shangri-Las' 'Give Her A Great Big Kiss' and 'Stranded In The Jungle'. These shows also featured a couple of songs that would pop up on the second album – 'It's Too Late' and 'Human Being', which dated from the Chrystie Street sessions.

During the show, Johansen went for a theatrical effect by sporting a black top hat and white dress shirt front that he would also favour for some of the later UK gigs and offered the audience peculiar advice such as, 'If you're a garbage pail in the house, stick out your pail.'

Their set garnered a panning from *NME*'s Linda Solomon, who started by admitting she was not a fan. 'Out pranced the Dolls like a plague of locusts, punching in with "Personality Crisis" from their new album . . . The band blew themselves out in their first five minutes.'

Sounds' Chuck Pulin was kinder: 'The Dolls are a famed New York band with a tough punk rock following, they play good, no nonsense rock and play it hard.' Pulin's use of 'punk' identifies the Dolls as part of a lineage that stretches back to garage bands such as the Seeds and the Count Five and was also applied to the Stooges and the MC5. He also alluded to the fact that the Dolls' pre-gig partying wasn't slowing down any, 'Their whole number was going down heavily but backstage was even more crazed than out front.' This continued afterward, as the Dolls partied at the Plaza Hotel with a MainMan contingent headed by a swaying Iggy Pop and Wayne County, as well as funk superstar Sly Stone: 'Boys kissed boys, girls kissed girls and the CBS folks went crazy as more and more people pressed uninvited through the door,' observed Pulin. The following October, *After Dark* magazine reported that Iggy – who was in town for a stint at Max's – had walked into one of the Felt Forum doors and had spent the bulk of Mott's set laid out in the emergency room.

The Dolls' final gig with Mott was on 7 August at the Alpine Arena in Pittsburgh, where they were joined on the bill by emerging rock behemoths Blue Öyster Cult. This was followed by a return to home territory with a trio of concerts at My Father's Place on 14-15 August – a former Long Island bowling alley, which had been converted into a 400-capacity bar and concert venue by promoter Michael Epstein. The venue hosted early gigs by Billy Joel and Bruce Springsteen, as well as some of Bob Marley's first US dates. The Dolls shows were advertised on local radio and they comfortably filled the Bryant Avenue venue for all three mid-week shows. The band returned to the venue in April 1974, and their performance forms the basis of the *Pink Pedal Pushers* bootleg.

While the band were back in New York, Syl took David, Johnny and Arthur to a fashion show at the MacAlpine hotel and introduced them to Malcolm McLaren and Vivienne Westwood, who he knew from visiting the Let It Rock shop during his London jaunts. Since his initial meeting with Syl three years earlier, McLaren had embraced his role as a Kings Road retail proprietor and haberdasher with vision and enthusiasm. He had converted Trevor Miles' Paradise Garage into Let It Rock, where, surrounded by the detritus of the previous two decades of rock'n'roll, he sold reproduction clothing to the suburban teddy boys who began to patronise the store.

However, McLaren was no mere revivalist, content to market old trends to individuals who had few ideas of their own and were happy to relive the youth of their fathers as if it were some Utopian golden age. For him, the Dolls represented the great leap forward, away from the nostalgists and age-ing hippies. Having first encountered the whole band on their doomed trip to London the previous autumn, McLaren was immediately struck by this 'gang of girly-looking boys, looking like girls dressed like boys' as they piled into Let It Rock on a brief shopping spree. Inspired by the Dolls' 'tiny lurex tops, bumfreezer leggings and high heels', the future Sex Pistols Svengali began the process of remaking his stock and rebranding his small King's Road outlet that would ultimately become Sex, resulting in the birth of punk rock style in Britain.

Writing for *The Guardian* in 2004, Malcolm recounted the first time that he heard the Dolls: 'How much it hurt my ears! And then I started to laugh – laugh at how stupid I was. How bad they were. Bad enough to be good. By the fourth or fifth track, I thought they were so, so bad, they were brilliant. I was smitten – like my first real desire, first kiss, first everything. I had seen the Beatles, the Rolling Stones, the Yardbirds, the High Numbers, John Lee Hooker, Muddy Waters and Screamin' Jay Hawkins, but this was the first time I had fallen in love with a group.'

After throwing a party at the MacAlpine, which was also attended by Andy Warhol and many of his Factory set, McLaren and Vivienne Westwood returned to London full of enthusiasm for the developing scene that they had witnessed in New York. He changed the name of his shop to Too Young To Live, Too Fast To Die, and added elements of the fashions prevalent among the Dolls and their followers to his own pre-existing situationist ideas, and aspects of the biker chic exemplified by Marlon Brando in *The Wild One*.

Rather than get out on the road and promote *The New York Dolls* to audiences outside of their home turf, the Dolls' next move was to play two shows a night at Max's between 22-27 August. This was a safe option, which enabled the band to play before packed houses and rake in some easy cash. In retrospect, it could be argued that this kind of short term thinking played a significant part in the band's failure to break nationwide, but then the Dolls were hardly the most career-oriented of ensembles.

The Max's residency found the band on good form, sticking to almost the same half-hour set that they'd played while supporting Mott. David spent much of the time between songs bantering with the enthusiastic crowd, taking song requests, and in one instance introducing 'Bad Detective' as 'about a topic which is still widely discussed around here – it's about heroin smuggling in South East Asia.'

Photographer Roberta Bayley – who'd briefly worked for a few weekends at Let It Rock two years earlier – caught the band regularly during this period, and later explained that the Dolls were having too much of a good time being queens of the New York scene to worry about much else. 'They were getting more girls in Max's than the Rolling Stones could get in that one particular moment. They were bigger than anybody just within that world, which – that's the only world you're in, is the world you're in. If Max's back room is your world, and you're the biggest person there, then you're the biggest person in the world.'

Although undermined by a lack of airplay and their apparent reluctance to leave New York, the Dolls were beginning to stir up some interest in Los Angeles, largely due to the press coverage filtering through from Lisa Robinson in *Disc* and Rodney Bingenheimer's columns in *Phonograph Record* and *Go*. Marty Thau had booked the band to play four nights at the famous Whisky A Go Go on Sunset Strip, and concrete evidence of the Dolls' rising profile on the West Coast was provided when the gigs sold out in a mere four hours.

During all this activity, Johnny kept in touch with his family back in Queens. 'When he came here, he just said to me, "I just put out an album with the Dolls," and put it on the table,' recalls Mariann. 'I don't think I ever played them. I didn't like the Dolls' music at all. Johnny would just say, "We're going here, we're going there." He was never big-time about it. Johnny loved animals. He had a Labrador called Pretty Girl. Then he found a dog in an alley in the garbage – a mutt who he called Onion. The two dogs had puppies and Johnny had to get rid of them when he went on tour with the Dolls, so he dropped them off with me.' Of all the Dolls, Johnny was the only one whose family turned out to wave him off on tour.

On 27 August, two days before the Dolls were supposed to leave for LA, a drunken Arthur crashed out at the apartment on Second Street and First Avenue he shared with Connie Gripp, a notoriously volatile 'dancer' who regularly turned tricks on Times Square. For a hooker, Connie was extraordinarily possessive. Rick Rivets, who subsequently lived with Connie for about four months after she and Arthur broke up, recalls her as being 'evil, and that's with a capital E.' He adds, 'To say Connie was a handful is an understatement. She had to be one of the most screwed up people I have ever known. The two of them made quite a pair as they were both tall had the same hair and dressed alike. They were quite outstanding; it's just too bad that she didn't know how to control her substance use.'

The Dolls were attracting plenty of female interest and Connie couldn't bear the thought of Arthur being thrown into the latter-day Gomorrah of the Sunset Strip, which was renowned for the predatory nature of its ultra-young groupies. However, the Dolls could hardly be viewed as anyone's innocent prey and, with one eye on the possibility of some hot and heavy action, enforced the time-honoured 'no girlfriends on tour' rule. This was too much for Connie – while Arthur lay sleeping, she tied together his ankles. The gentle-natured bassist came round to see her standing over him with a kitchen knife in her hand. In the ensuing struggle to wrest the blade from her grasp Arthur suffered a deep and painful cut to his thumb. 'The bone was hanging out,' recalled Arthur. 'Then she, with no clothes on, went out on the front fire escape. She had an outrageous body. For kicks she would go out on the avenue with no clothes on, then watch the cars crash.' While Connie was on the fire escape, Arthur crawled into a cab and got patched up at Bellevue Hospital.

Connie had succeeded in severing a tendon in Arthur's thumb, and the extent of the injury required him to wear a cast that would prevent him from playing bass for two months. Chief roadie Peter Jordan stepped in to cover for Arthur. 'We got Peter to play because he was also a musician, who was also one of our earliest people who was quite dedicated to us. He worked for us for nothing and we're still indebted to Peter for everything. He was really good to us. So Peter took Arthur's place at that point,' explained David.

Arthur was enormously disappointed to miss out on playing Los Angeles, although he covered up for Connie by maintaining that he'd caught his thumb in a guitar case. Despite being unable to play, Arthur's presence remained pivotal to the Dolls and he went along on the trip, appearing in photo sessions and supplying occasional backing vocals. Generally, he would stand at the back of the stage swaying to the music and drinking, while Peter Jordan occupied Arthur's normal spot behind Syl on the right of the stage. With his naturally blond hair and unassuming stage presence, Peter provided a reasonable approximation of Arthur's human statue routine, although he wisely opted not to attempt any replication of Kane's unique stagewear.

Connie was right to worry about the girls. There had already been features in *Rock Scene*, *Star* and *Melody Maker*, which mentioned the groupies who hung out on Sunset Strip and frequented local scenester Rodney Bingenheimer's English Disco and the Continental Hyatt House Hotel – which was known locally as the 'Riot House', on account of the excessive hedonism that was *de rigeur* whenever a major rock band was in residence. The girls, who were all around fifteen years old, dressed to thrill, and pursued their quarry with single-minded determination. 'Hollywood in the early seventies was really crazy,' explains Syl. 'These trash Hollywood mothers in their leopard skin slips started throwing their daughters at us.'

These girls had inherited the mantle of the G.T.O.'s – Girls Together Outrageously – who'd become so notorious that they'd made an album for Frank Zappa's Straight Records in 1969. The album, *Permanent Damage*, was a collection of primitive chants, skeletal songs and sleazy conversations presenting LA groupie culture to the world. The girls billed themselves 'the only female rock'n'roll band' and set about wresting the axis of groupie/musician relations away from the guys. As Miss Cynderella told *Disc*, 'We got a bit tired of male groups having little girls chase them about. We thought it would be a good idea to have a female group being chased by little boys, like a female Rolling Stones. And it worked.'

The G.T.O.'s wore an eye-blasting mix of thrift shop rags, exotic hippie finery and lingerie. Coincidentally, the girls' backing group for a while was a group called Runt – led by a young Todd Rundgren. After dalliances with the Stones, Keith Moon, Jim Morrison and other prominent glitterati, their leader, Miss Pamela, went on to become Jimmy Page's LA squeeze in the early seventies before 'retiring' with Michael Des Barres of glam-metal band Silverhead. Coincidentally, she'd also encountered Arthur and Rick Rivets during their stay in Amsterdam, describing them as 'two Dutch hippies'.

Thanks to the G.T.O.'s, groupiedom became an alternative career option for LA's aspirant rock chicks. By 1972 there was a new bunch ruling the Strip. Fourteen-year-old Lori Maddox was pursued by Jimmy Page (as is described in Stephen Davis' *Hammer of the Gods*). She was pictured with Led Zeppelin in *Melody Maker*, along with her fourteen-year-old friend Sable Starr, who later numbered them as conquests alongside Iggy Pop and David Bowie. Davis describes Sable in Plant's suite, hurling champagne bottles at the billboards below.

Pamela Des Barres was disparaging about the new girls in her 1992 book, *Take Another Little Piece of My Heart*, describing it as 'a fading scene'. 'You couldn't trust the new LA groupies, who were desperate, discouraged, grovelling ego seekers. The love of music had become secondary to preening in *Star* magazine, standing next to Anybody In A Band. It was scary out there.' In her previous book, *I'm with the Band*, she described Sable as 'the most hideous of these tartlets'.

In 1973, no visiting rock band was safe from the attentions of such rabid groupies. The Dolls duly booked themselves into the Hyatt and as the hottest, prettiest rock band around placed themselves directly in the crosshairs of the libidinous Sunset Strip sirens. With his more traditional rock'n'roll looks, innate sense of style and natural cool, Johnny represented the prime groupie target and was duly sought out by Sable Starr, in her capacity of number one groupie. According to Syl, Johnny and Sable's liaison was inevitable from the moment the Dolls arrived in LA. 'Over here we had Lisa and Richard Robinson putting us in *Rock Scene*. The girls in California were reading it, and Sable said, "Man, when that Johnny comes out here he's gonna be my boyfriend!" and stuff like that. They were doing that with us and we were doing that with them because they had the *Star* magazine which was all the California groupies.'

There was little in the way of a cat-and-mouse dating game once Sable arrived at the Hyatt and presented Johnny with a natty pair of Frederick's of Hollywood briefs. 'She gave him a blow-job and that was it,' revealed Syl. 'Oh, I loved Johnny so much,' recalled Sable when she accompanied the Flamin' Groovies on their 1976 UK gigs with the Ramones. 'It was instant head over heels in love, the whole thing.' 'I met Sable when she was fifteen and I was eighteen,' insisted Johnny. 'When I first met her . . . she was a weird chick but kinda nice.'

David was less keen on the groupie action, he shared a room with Marty and preferred to spend his downtime lounging by the pool, 'I ain't lettin' those bitches near me,' he told Lisa Robinson. 'I don't mind them hanging around as long as they don't want anything and as long as they don't get *traumatic*.'

The moment Johnny met Sable is captured on Bob Gruen's *All Dolled Up* DVD, as she adoringly hands him the box of undies. From that moment on, 'they were joined at the hip,' says Gruen. His DVD shows young love blossoming at Rodney's English Disco, where Sable announces her abdication as Queen of the Groupies to marry Johnny. Syl wasn't so lucky, confessing to a dose of 'Hong Kong clap'. It required a hefty penicillin shot from the young Michael Jackson's doctor, who helpfully asked, 'Why couldn't you have just gotten a blowjob?'

In addition to facilitating the start of Johnny's liaison with Sable, the LA trip also marked the point at which he consummated his relationship with the needle. Although Johnny had indulged in smoking heroin with Jerry, he'd largely been an uppers man, and still was at this point. The arrival of Iggy Pop at the Hyatt gave Johnny a cohort with whom he could explore the twilight world of intravenous heroin use.

At this time, Iggy was still managed by MainMan. Acknowledged as the living embodiment of rock'n'roll outrage, he was locked into a downward spiral of drug-fuelled auto-destruction that would lead to the final implosion of the Stooges the following year. Despite being well on the way to becoming a fully fledged member of the chemical trashcan set, Iggy remained beautiful, engaging and charismatic, and exuded enough wasted cool to ensure that he ranked high as any groupie's catch. He had already been with Sable, but was now getting serious with her sister Corey.

Iggy had been into heroin since finishing 1970's *Fun House* in LA. Smoking or snorting smack has its buzz, but necessitates greater consumption of the drug. Many junkies see the needle as an instrument of love, administering instant gratification. If they're with someone, they like to turn them on too – even if it means banging the neophyte up with a slice of their own valuable stash – thus establishing an instant rapport where the outside world needn't exist. More practically, if an individual user builds up a network of junkie pals, it becomes easier to cop a hit when cash is short or there's a supply drought.

This is what happened to Johnny in Los Angeles. 'That was the start of Johnny's heroin addiction,' asserts Syl. 'All I can really say about that is I didn't see the needle going in. I didn't see the penetration. It all starts, of course, with the girlfriends. Johnny's girlfriend was Sable Starr. Sable's sister Coral was going out with Iggy. Iggy wasn't doing too good. He was kind of like living off other stars and he was bouncing from one girlfriend to another in Malibu or wherever he was in Hollywood. Then, when we came in – of course, we were like the darlings and we had everything.

'So Iggy and Johnny became brothers in law. They were always in Johnny's room whatever hotel we were at – the Hyatt House or the Ramada Inn, whatever one we got thrown in or out of. That's when I saw Johnny finally high on smack. They were all doing it. I used to back away because me and Billy had got in with that in Holland and shit. I knew about that in New York too, because during the Vietnam war it was like three dollars a bag here . . . You'd get a nickel bag for marijuana but you could get a three dollar bag for smack. They called it a *tres* bag of heroin. Whenever there's some kind of war on, with Afghanistan or whatever, there's tons of fucking heroin comes in here. So it was always around, but it was in LA that I saw him change and he was never the same again.'

Sylvain identifies heroin as the main reason why Johnny's latent homophobia became evident – initially through his reluctance to drag up for gigs. 'Johnny was definitely very uncomfortable with that. At first he was totally in tune. Something happened as soon as he hit that needle. I think that's when it really changed. He started to, like, feel weird with what we would wear and it made him feel uncomfortable. You could tell the guy had a problem with it . . . It was weird because he was always much nicer to his male friends than he was to his girlfriends. He hurt all his girls – heroin is the drug for that.'

Speaking to *Mojo* in April 1996, Iggy would site this particular period of excess as the point at which he decided to make a break from the Stooges, in an attempt to clean up his lifestyle. '. . . A lot of the people involved with me then were unsound . . . Johnny Thunders was one of them.'

Within days of that introductory blow-job, publications such as *Star* and *Rock News* presented Johnny and Sable as the Burton and Taylor of glam rock. The couple talked about going to the chapel and getting married. The rock gossip pages developed an instant fascination with the relationship between rock's latest wild man and the teen-queen of Sunset sleaze.

But the Lolitas of the Sunset Strip were only part of the cavalcade of lunacy that greeted the Dolls' first Californian visit. The Whisky shows were chaos, crammed with beautiful young things going ape. 'I loved it,' crowed Johansen in *Circus*. 'Those kids just wanted to be part of the pandemonium.' The group even managed the distinction of actually being thrown out of the Riot House, after a naked groupie covered in baloney appeared in the lobby via the elevator. Apparently, the groupie was both tenacious and whiny, so the band had tied her to a chair, garnished her naked body with fine mortadella and loaded the whole ensemble into the elevator, which they sent down to the lobby. From here they went to the Ramada, where Iggy and the Stooges also happened to be staying. Once there, an entire box of washing powder found its way into the hotel swimming pool, and the Dolls were again looking for a new place to crash.

While in town, the Dolls filmed two TV appearances – *The Real Don Steele Show* surrounded by the girls from Rodney's, and the influential *Midnight Special*, where they shared the bill with Mott the Hoople. Peter Jordan stood discreetly behind the amps as Arthur mimed his bass parts for 'Personality Crisis' and 'Trash'.

Between the shows at the Whisky and the filming of their *Midnight Special* appearance, the Dolls journeyed up to San Francisco to play the Matrix club on 5-6 September, where they were supported by pantomime rockers the Tubes – who would later score a transatlantic hit with 'White Punks On Dope'. Despite Arthur's continued incapacitation, the Dolls were functioning with uncustomary precision during these shows – testament to the fact that playing a regular stream of dates was turning them into a tight touring unit. The exception to this was a cover of Herman's Hermits' 'Something Good', which rattled along in a shambolic manner, while Johnny opted out, preferring to stand on the side of the stage and sink a brew. David continued to polish his banter, introducing 'Private World' with 'the music was written by Arthur who's disabled this week due to an unfortunate culinary accident,' and using the break during 'Trash' to deliver an extended monologue on the theme of doomed romance.

Following the success of the Los Angeles gigs, further shows had been arranged which would see the Dolls exploring (what were for them) the uncharted regions of America's South. For Johnny and Sable, it was time for the new lovers to temporarily separate. 'I sent her home to New York while we carried on the tour,' explained Johnny. 'When we got back the police were looking for her at the airport and everywhere!'

This wasn't so funny at the time. Sable was only fifteen, and her wealthy parents from the exclusive Californian enclave of Palos Verdes had become worried, as she hadn't been heard from for days. They knew she was with someone from a notorious bunch of New York ne'er-do-wells and consequently called the police. The fuzz ascertained that the Dolls were bound for Houston, Texas, and that they were looking for a young blonde female. Consequently, when Cyrinda Foxe turned up to meet David at the airport, she got hauled in by the Texas Rangers. Subsequently, Sable made contact with her mother and asked her to ease off with the cops.

Unsurprisingly, the combination of the Dolls and the god-fearing Deep South was inherently volatile. In mid-September, they played Houston's Liberty Hall and a short run of shows at Gertie's in Dallas, which prompted some local press reaction concerning the bunch of drug-crazed faggots who were coming to town. Most vociferous were the Mothers Of Memphis, whose publicity had ensured a sell-out but also an oppressive police presence. The cops didn't bat a mirror-shaded eyelid as co-headliner Iggy went through his raging paces, but the moment a fan leapt onstage to kiss David, they started wading into the kids, nightsticks flailing. David was then accused of starting a riot and hauled off to the cells, charged with female impersonation for wearing his women's shoes. 'But I'm not impersonating anybody,' protested the aggrieved frontman, 'I'm perfectly satisfied with what I am.'

After David was bailed out, the relieved touring party got out of the unenlightened South and hit Detroit for a show on 22 September, where they stormed the Michigan Palace. The Motor City has always loved high-energy rock guitars, and provided the Dolls with their most receptive audience outside of their New York stronghold.

The Dolls continued touring through the following month, including several shows with Mott the Hoople and management stablemates Aerosmith. On 4 October, they played Atlanta's Municipal Auditorium, followed by another gig the next day at Florida's West Palm Beach Auditorium. On 11 October, they visited the Auditorium Theatre, Chicago. Mott and the Dolls went upstate New York on 16 October to Rochester's Auditorium Theatre, followed by a gig at Kleinham's Music Hall, Buffalo. On the 26th the Dolls supported Mott for their major New York City showcase at the spectacular Radio City Music Hall. In between Mott dates, the Dolls also managed gigs in Milwaukee and Missouri, where they supported redneck rockers Lynyrd Skynyrd ('They came up to us afterwards and said, "Y'all boogie like hell,"' recalls Syl), Boston, Philadelphia, St Louis, Minneapolis, Pittsburgh, Toronto and Connecticut.

Johansen would be disparaging about Mott when talking to *NME*'s Nick Kent later in the year. 'They *used* us on that tour. I mean, the times when we were getting booed onstage, I'd say, "Listen if you think we're bad just wait until you see Ian Hunter!" It was hysterical . . . all the time, after gigs we'd go up to their room, steal their drink, fuck their groupies and leave 'em wondering what happened.' He also alleged that Hunter told his guitarist Ariel Bender to check out Johnny's moves.

Sour grapes? Talking to Mott fan club president Keith Smith, former Mott keyboard player Morgan Fisher said, 'According to the books there wasn't much friendliness between Mott and the Dolls because they were really out to do their thing and blow us off the stage. But I watched them nearly every night because I was totally fascinated by them. It was the first punk band I'd ever seen in my life. All their clothes and their transvestite dressing up. It was amazing. I think we got on all right. I didn't think there was any rivalry backstage.

'There were a few things said in the press but then there's always things said in the press by support acts. It sells tickets. David Johansen, the singer, was a bit of a Mick Jagger. He had a big mouth and liked to say controversial things . . . I thought they were a dynamite band and in the end it was a good combination.'

On 30 October, the Dolls hosted a triumphant homecoming Halloween party at the Waldorf-Astoria Hotel Grand Ballroom, the future location for the annual Rock 'N' Roll Hall Of Fame bean-feast. *NBC News* reported that a thousand or so punters, some ticketless, smashed the glass doors to pour into the venue. The masquerade ball got underway with the best costume competition, which was judged by actor/singer/dancer/choreographer Tommy Tune, *Interview* editor Rosemary Kent and designer Chester Weinberg. They chose a Mae West look-alike and a fan who'd dressed as an exotic alien to win the prize of a night on the town with the Dolls. (The runner-up got a night for three in a Newark motel.) The Dolls, who featured their usual set with the addition of a bluesy new group composition called 'Lone Star Queen', dressed up too. David favoured white evening dress plus feather boa and black top hat, Johnny was dressed in a black satin tuxedo and, for the first time, his controversial swastika armband, while Sable also trashed taboos by strutting around in black face and suit. Syl dressed as Charlie Chaplin, man-mountain Arthur donned football uniform and Jerry came as his old girlfriend, Bette Midler.

The New York Dolls was finally released in the UK on 19 October – an example of the way in which US record companies often released albums on home soil long in advance of their European release dates, thus creating a healthy market for imports. Obviously, those who couldn't wait out the weeks for the UK release were forced to fork out the extra pound or two. Nick Kent had secured himself an import copy and waxed lyrical in the *NME*. Under the headline, 'Welcome To The Fabulous Seventies', Kent raved and

You think you can handle a piece a' me? – David flips the bird, while the other Dolls look on, 1973.

(Post) Teenage Fan Club – Syl amuses some admirers at the Mercer Arts Center, 1973.

Horny devils, David and Jerry get to grips with their demon, 1973.

'Don't Bogart that whole thing.' Johnny and Arthur partake of some recreational substances, 1973.

'Straight boys would learn first hand what it was like to be a queen on the street.'
Wayne County [right] snuggles up to Jerry, 1973.

'I had this gift to be able to jump up on a stoup and incite a riot.' David lets rip,
while Arthur lurks in the shadows.

Leopardskin Syl and David play Gerties night club, Dallas, Texas, 1974.

Arthur (left) providing eye candy and backing vocals with Syl at Gerties night club, 1974.

Achtüng! Syl camps it up on tour, 1973.

New York's finest present arms, 1973.

The strange and terrible beauty of Arthur 'Killer' Kane, 1973.

Trash! The Dolls hang out in the Mercer's basement, 1973.

'Straight out teenage rock'n'roll' – Syl and Johnny get in tune, 1973.

'Uh, how do you call your lover boy?' – David addresses his public, 1973.

Glam guitar gods Arthur, Johnny and Syl in full flow, 1973.

salivated, 'The New York Dolls are trash, they play rock'n'roll like sluts and they've just released a record that can proudly stand beside Iggy and the Stooges' stupendous *Raw Power* as the only album so far to fully define exactly where 1970's rock should be coming from.'

Kent appreciated that many people would hate the album, and that the Dolls were 'defiantly unprofessional and tasteless', 'barely competent', and that the disc lacked the dynamics of the MC5's *Back In The USA*, although they possessed 'that pure teen consciousness that the latter so painfully lacked . . . you're hearing musical street fights, a bastardised brand of hell-cat cacophony teetering on pure anarchy but held together by the kind of attitude that has always stood as the quintessential factor of the rock and roll statement . . . [a] total lack of self-consciousness and a commitment to full-tilt energy workouts no matter what level of proficiency you're working at.'

Over at *Melody Maker*, Shangri-Las fan Richard Williams observed, 'While the Stones are funkier and more assured, what the Dolls have is all in terms of sass, vulgarity, energy and fun. They make the Stones just a little tired.' Unlike Nick Kent, he criticised the thin production: 'Rundgren's innate sophistication goes too far towards losing the cheap 'n' nastiness which is so priceless, and on a rubbishy monoaural gramophone the album simply does-n't work.' Williams also mentioned that when Tony Stratton-Smith was think-ing of signing the Dolls he considered hiring Shel Talmy, who produced the early Who and Kinks singles. He concluded by declaring that the Dolls' debut was 'easily good enough to join that select pantheon of true seventies rock records – "Cold Turkey", *Raw Power* and the MC5's *Back In The USA*.'

Despite this release-lag, Mercury were already making noises about a sec-ond album, but any opportunity to write new material was pushed onto the back burner in favour of promoting the album in Europe. This would be an emotional visit. It was less than a year since Billy died. The Dolls were return-ing on a wave of press and public expectations, as well as the morbid curios-ity that any rock'n'roll fatality brings.

In preparation for their British gigs, the Dolls spent the next two weeks honing their set at Baggy's – a Manhattan rehearsal facility set up in a ware-house space by former Soft Machine road manager Tom Edmondston. Through the studio they met and befriended former MC5 and Stooges soundman Bob 'Nitebob' Czaykowski, who joined the Dolls' road crew.

David kept the publicity steam hissing ahead of the UK tour by dropping a series of choice soundbites. 'Look, we're saying something that Teen Earth is interested in,' he announced to Lisa Robinson for *Disc*. David admitted to being tired from touring ('I'm a mere photostat of what I once was'), but seemed genuinely excited about coming to the UK, wondering if the Dolls would get the same response as the Osmonds – who were creating bub-blegum shockwaves throughout the British music press. 'We've got new drags for this European tour that would blow the mind of the Queen her-self,' he parped.

In an attempt to play down his crossdressing, David said he didn't usual-ly wear makeup except if he looked 'really bad'. Bearing in mind that he was currently favouring a white evening tuxedo on stage, he almost seemed to be swinging from controversial transsexual (as exemplified by the fetching black crop top he wore at the Whisky) to good old-fashioned Hollywood-style glamour. 'Drag just means my clothes,' he explained. 'We're not a band of five hillbillies on stage scratching their fleas away. It's more intense drama. It's more a reflection of what's happening right in front of us, a reflection of our audience . . . When I'm on stage, I'm in ecstasy. One of my happiest times is when I'm onstage. In a sense I'm an actor, and the band is an act.'

Roy Hollingworth stoked up the sense of anticipation with a review of a gig in Atlanta which appeared in *Melody Maker* during the week that the quintet were due to arrive in the UK. His introduction heralded the arrival of the Dolls in suitably overstated style, 'This is the story of the last rock and roll band. The New York Dolls. There won't be another . . . What follows will mean nowt.'

Johnny was described coming offstage in Chicago and vomiting copiously into a vase of flowers in the dressing room. He also sparked a wave of outrage by sporting a swastika armband on his black leather jacket, in the photograph that appeared on *Melody Maker*'s cover. The likes of Keith Moon and Stooges guitarist Ron Asheton had been appropriating items of Nazi regalia for shock value for several years, as had many bikers. The usage had little to do with an endorsement of fascist values, but was rather a naïve attempt to create a stir by using taboo imagery. Such symbolism didn't go unnoticed by Malcolm McLaren, who would use the device in a more sophisticated manner, resonant of anthropologist Claude Levi-Strauss' ideas about symbols and signifiers.

There were hate letters in the music papers of the 'It was with a mixture of scorn and disgust that I noticed the Gestapo-type swastika armband worn by Mr. Thunders' nature. One letter even blasted the paper for featuring 'Pouff Rock' and the Dolls, who were apparently only famous for their 'drag appearance'.

The image of Johnny Thunders skulking in the cover shot was one of the most dramatic and compelling images yet seen in rock'n'roll. His explosion of hair obscured most of his scowling face, while his body was encased in black leather, complete with studded leather gloves. The swastika was just a detail. Next to this Alice Cooper looked like a pantomime dame.

Johnny's surly menace was heightened by the juxtaposed figure of Johansen cavorting next to him in white tuxedo, bow-tie and top hat, clutching a bottle of Pernod. His made-up grin made him look like a cross between Jagger and Batman's Joker. A cigar-chomping Sylvain appeared as a malevolent fairground barker in bowler hat and lashings of face paint. Oddly, Jerry and Arthur were both pretty much devoid of slap, dressed fairly conservatively while facing the camera with wasted half-grins. This was the magic of the New York Dolls, distilled into one image that was preserved in the amber of *Melody Maker*'s front page.

On 20 November the Dolls arrived to start their European tour, which would kick off with five gigs in the UK before going on to France, Germany and Holland, taking in several TV appearances along the way. The group were based at the plushly intimate Blake's Hotel in South Kensington, which had been opened by actress Anouska Hempel and was favoured by the likes of Keith Richards for its discreet charm.

The Dolls entertained a string of visitors and supplicants, including Malcolm McLaren and Vivienne Westwood, plus *NME* young guns Nick Kent and his then-girlfriend, Chrissie Hynde. At the time, Kent occupied a unique position in the music press, flying the flag for Keef, Iggy, and now the Dolls. His writing transcended the usual music paper fare – breaking out of traditional journalistic reportage, he looked, acted like and hung with the groups that he wrote about. His features around this time, which were heavily influenced by *Creem*'s Lester Bangs, helped change the face of rock writing. The street-sharp Chrissie came from Akron, Ohio, wrote for *NME* and, after a stint working in Sex, went on to global fame with the Pretenders. She was rumoured to have been Arthur's main squeeze on the UK visit.

The tour started on 22 November with university gigs in Warwick, York and Leeds, where, in an interview with *Melody Maker*'s Steve Lake, David dismissed any suggestion of the band being mere Rolling Stones copyists, 'We're a bit bored with hearing about the Stones. I personally don't care, it doesn't bother me. A lot of times we tend to parody things that happened in the mid-sixties – and not only the Stones, but a whole bunch of other people.'

Audience reaction varied from the euphoric enthusiasm of Dolls devotees, to morbid curiosity or apathy from old rock'n'rollers and blind hatred from 'proper' music fans and the closed-minded. This latter reaction applied to 'Whispering' Bob Harris, the mumbling, sanctimonious host of BBC2's music show *The Old Grey Whistle Test*, for which the Dolls recorded one of the TV appearances of the decade. The group careered recklessly through 'Jet Boy' and 'Looking For A Kiss'. Johansen, sporting a polka-dot chemise, did his rubber-lipped cutie pout four-square into the camera, while Johnny, decked out in skull-emblazoned old leathers (*sans* swastika), lurched all over the place and thrashed the Vox Teardrop guitar Arthur had bought him in Leeds.

Harris, who was generally predisposed toward bland singer-songwriters and progressive rock dullards, could barely contain his disgust. Looking directly into the camera as the last strains of 'Looking For A Kiss' reverberated around the studio, he whispered, 'Mock rock,' with all the venom and passion usually associated with a three-toed sloth. But that very comment, from this bearded exponent of musical Mogadon, was a defining spark for the bored hordes who'd been waiting for something like this to come along. In some ways, it was as significant as the Sex Pistols-Bill Grundy interview would be, three years hence. The only son of a chief inspector in the Northampton CID, who had once arrested trouser-splitting sixties legend P. J. Proby, Harris was an early embodiment of the dreary old guard, and would later be involved in a fracas with Sid Vicious at the Speakeasy club. He nearly experienced an earlier pasting that night in the studio. 'I shoulda walked over there and then and hit him over the head with my fuckin' bass,' laughed Arthur in 2004. 'He was like Aleister Crowley,' smiled David, 'sitting in his chair with his arms folded making pronouncements.'

Irrespective of Harris' usual disdain for anything with a discernable pulse, there were many among the *Whistle Test*'s audience who grasped the significance of the Dolls' performance. In his Clash biography, *Passion Is A Fashion*, Pat Gilbert describes the young future Joe Strummer and his mates being 'gobsmacked' at catching the programme in the student union bar of

Newport Art College. 'They thought the Dolls were magnificent. It filled them with hope that something so conspicuously trashy could get on the TV. They sought out a copy of the group's self-titled debut album.'

Elsewhere, young Steven Patrick Morrissey from Stretford, Manchester was also having his life changed. The man who would become an indie icon the following decade was then a schoolboy rock fan, and Number 87 in the Mott the Hoople fan club. He published a fanzine-style book on the Dolls in 1981. 'They were as important to me as Elvis was important to the entire language of rock'n'roll,' he said in *Uncut*'s 2004 Dolls special. 'They were the best group ever to come out of America.' In the press ads for his 2005 live album, Morrissey is clutching the white Vox Teardrop guitar – signed by Sylvain with the inscription, 'Trash 1973'.

The Dolls also made a big impression on thirteen-year-old Nina Antonia from Liverpool. 'I saw a picture of them in *16* magazine and fell in love with Johnny Thunders,' recalls the woman who'd go on to write the first biography of the group, and almost single-handedly continue to fly their flag long after the band had dissolved. 'At the time, the Stones seemed old to me then, even more so than Bowie and Roxy, but the Dolls really were a young band, doing like bubblegum blues. That's what I loved about the Dolls.' Called upon to cover Johnny Thunders and the Dolls for *Mojo*'s 2005 Punk Special, Nina cited their *Whistle Test* appearance as a defining moment for the whole punk movement. 'That night in 1973, the New York Dolls fired the starting pistol.'

A pair of gigs at Biba's newly-opened Rainbow Room on 26-27 November provided the Dolls with a trendy, high-profile re-introduction to UK audiences. Biba's started life as an ultra-hip boutique, synonymous with glamour and high fashion, with its own brands of clothes and makeup, and accessories. It defined early seventies glamour. Biba's had ambitiously taken over the old six-storey Derry & Toms department store on Kensington High Street. The striking gold and black, deco-influenced building came on like a hip Harrods, glamorous and pricey, but well-timed to strike a chord with a new, post-hippie generation who'd appreciated Bowie and Roxy Music.

The refurbished store's crowning glory was the Rainbow Room on the top floor, which opened as a restaurant and coffee bar in the day and now planned to put on groups in the evenings. It was a lovely looking space. Sympathetic lighting gave it a muted, multicolour luminosity, and scatter cushions topped off the cool, swish ambience, unusual in the drab, grey London of 1973.

Biba's had booked the Dolls for the Rainbow Room's gala opening night. This was something of a coup – New York's flashiest youngbloods set to storm the capital in its hippest new venue.

After the soundcheck, Arthur and Sylvain cruised the store's lower floors, where they acquired the wide rubber belts they often sported in subsequent photos. Arthur got caught swapping the price tag on a black jacket with leopard skin lapels from £40 to £12. Store security pounced and wanted to have Arthur arrested but, as the Dolls were playing that night, Biba's management begrudgingly let him off. Johansen would later dramatise the incident when talking to *NME*'s Nick Kent. 'Y'know, we were caught changing price-tags on the clothes at Biba's. They were gonna get heavy, so Marty just came along and said, "I don't wanna hear any more about this incident." They dropped it.'

When the band returned to the hotel after the soundcheck to give a press conference, they found that a tap had been left on in Arthur's bathroom, causing significant flood damage. After a delay, the Dolls emerged to face such probing enquiries as, 'How much hosepipe do you push down your trousers?' (Johansen's answer: 'None, it's all me.') The hotel's downstairs bar was heaving with press, Johansen holding court, complaining that he'd been awake for three days, while guzzling champagne from the bottle. Surrounded by the other Dolls, he did most of the talking. *Disc*'s Peter Harvey described Jerry and Arthur 'quietly kissing' on his left, while Sylvain looked 'almost straight' and Johnny resembled 'a bedraggled peacock'. Later Arthur showed him his scarred thumb. 'That's where a chick tried to cut off my hand. It's always those wild scenes, y'see.'

The on-form Johansen was on sound-bite overdrive, describing the Dolls audience as 'decadents of all ages', while adding, 'We attract only degenerates to our concerts.'

'We have come to Britain to redeem the social outcasts,' he crowed. 'We have just conquered the USA. The Press find us prolific . . . I've been compared to Linda Lovelace. She's a symbol of the youth of America.'

Amidst the verbal sparring, David managed to lay out the Dolls musical manifesto, 'We just want to rock out. We play short and sweet songs. We don't want to play boring music, it's inconsiderate. We just bash it out however it comes out. The kids don't have to think about us, they can just dance. We sing about what is going on.'

The quaint phrase 'poovery' was invoked by the nationals, but it didn't derail David's flow – 'we like all those queens and we're the tackiest boys from New York City.' This prodded one reporter to ask what 'tack' means. 'I think it's an arch-attitude towards a particular thing. It's just like that terrible jacket you're wearing. That's tack, if I ever saw it.'

Warming to his theme, Johansen took the press conference up to his room, where he offered such insights as, 'I'm the most prolific singer of the twentieth century,' and 'I am nineteen, I have been for years.'

That night's gig was a bit of history, the Dolls' one proper London showcase. As it happened, it would be the last time they would play the capital for more than 30 years.

Kris Needs: *For a nineteen-year-old raised on the Stones and currently running the Mott the Hoople fan club, the New York Dolls were heaven-sent. I had been blown away by their album and fired up by the press reports to the point of near-obsession. When it was announced that the Dolls would be playing two London shows, I sprang into action and managed to secure two tickets for the first night, which was prematurely titled The New York Dolls Christmas Ball. £2.50 was quite a lot for a gig in those days, but it also included a meal in the plush decor of the Rainbow Room. The food predated* haute cuisine – *you didn't get much. But I wasn't here to play gourmand.*

Sitting at our table about halfway back, I soon realised that we were seated behind the NME table. Here I saw up close for the first time the people I'd read avidly, week after week. Nick Kent, sashaying and swaying in a pink satin shirt like a glammed-up stick insect, looked elegantly wasted. 'So journalists can look cool too,' I thought. There was a sassy-looking girl with Keef hair who I later realised was Chrissie Hynde. Another guy looked like he'd stepped out of the MC5, in shades, Afro and denim. That was premier Bowie-Mott correspondent Charles Shaar Murray. There were other courtiers on the rock-lit high table, which probably included Roy Hollingworth. That whole gathering radiated knowing cool – possibly because some of them had already seen the Dolls and maybe met them. They were all on expenses and obviously didn't pay to get in. It was then that I realised that I wanted to be like these guys one day.

The undistinguished meal was followed by an even less memorable support band. Beggars Opera could not have been less suitable for this gig, having risen out of the UK progressive rock trough. The band had a kind of gothic element to their endless keyboard noodlings. I sat there, stomach in knots, waiting for the Dolls.

Suddenly up flared the lights, and on tottered the Dolls in an amazing array of feathers, rubber, leather, high heels and rooster coiffures. Even after seeing the Stones, Bowie and Mott several times that year, nothing could have prepared me for that first shot of the Dolls. It remains the most heart-thudding entrance I've ever encountered. Left to right, there was Arthur – statue-still, sleepy-eyed and clad from head-to-toe in tight yellow Lurex. Next to him Sylvain hopped about in white satin blouse, big white guitar and his cowboy holster. Centre-stage was Johansen – all in white with long turquoise scarf and wide red rubber belt, which looked uncannily, like those on sale downstairs. The finishing touch was his black patent leather women's shoes and a white fur ankle bracelet. Behind him was Jerry's gorgeous pink drumkit. Behind that, Jerry in a smart shiny jacket and a more toned-down street look than the garish bouffant inflicted on him for the album cover. Stage right was dominated by the human tornado that was Johnny Thunders. If Keef had always been my favourite Stone, Johnny would be my main man in the Dolls. He skidded, slashed and circled, pausing only to rip out those stun-burst solos from the yellow guitar that would accompany him for years. With all that garish colour dazzling off his band-mates, Johnny was again the man in black, except for his faithful white knee-length platforms. Halfway through the set he peeled off his tail-coat to reveal a curious one-armed black-leather-and-studs bikini top and a blue version of the big rubber belt. He also wore a garter belt around his thigh in the fashion that Sid Vicious would adopt a few years later.

Seconds later, they dove straight into the opening chords of 'Personality Crisis'. I thought I'd died and gone to heaven. God, it was loud – someone said they were using the Stones PA system thanks to a favour from a mutual friend of their road manager Ian Stewart. It sure sounded like it. I was amazed that many of the dinner table audience remained seated as the Dolls proceeded to blaze through 'Looking For A Kiss', 'Bad Girl' and most of the first album. There were a couple of songs I didn't know, which must've been 'Babylon' and 'Mystery Girls', plus the expected barrage of covers. I was looking forward to them and wasn't disappointed as they stampeded through 'Stranded In The Jungle', 'Pills' and a killer version of the Shangri-Las' 'Give Her A Great Big Kiss'. At the time, I'd been a massive Shangri-Las fan for nearly ten years and didn't know they'd worked this one into the set. I literally fell off the chair I was standing on with whooping delight. I'll never forget the thrashing hurricane of Thunders skidding up to Johansen's mike for the 'What colour are her eyes?' conversation bit and then careering off again, splattering discordant riffs all over the place.

As the set steamed on, the Dolls reached their climax around 'Jet Boy' and were soon gone. The crowd hadn't gone apeshit, being more of an 'impress me' nature and probably with free tickets. But it's safe to say that the gig radically altered my perception of what a rock'n'roll band should do. With the Dolls, I managed to get up front and witness at close quarters the greatest display of riotous and unfettered rock'n'roll I'd ever encountered, apart from Mott the Hoople in their early days. The Dolls were everything you hoped they'd be and more – brash, street-cool and outrageously flamboyant. Forget the crap about not being able to play – the Nolan-Kane rhythm section was a powerhouse bedrock on which the twin guitar onslaught of Thunders and Sylvain could duel, intertwine and spark. And Johansen was a great front man in his camp, pouting fashion. There was something magical here. A spontaneous combustion and attitude, which could've taken on the world, especially a few years later. Having been to hundreds of gigs since, I realise how great the New York Dolls were.

Michael Watts reviewed the gig for *Melody Maker* – the sixth time he'd seen the Dolls – and was finally convinced 'that they're a great kick in the ass to the corpus of rock and roll.' Watts was the journalist who catapulted Bowie to national prominence with his famous 'I'm gay!' interview in January 1972 – so he was no stranger to outrage.

He likened the Dolls to the primitive outfits of ten years before, 'when everybody sounded amateurish and was trying to master their chops'. He asked if it was 'a heresy' that the Dolls were taking rock music, which had progressed into something of an ascetic art form, back to its roots. 'It probably is, but rock and roll needs its anarchists and heretics, and the New York Dolls lob Molotov cocktails into the opera houses that some wish to build . . . the Dolls, with their crude musicality and exaggerated posturings, are the new children of pop mimicking their elders and blowing rude noises; just generally letting out the stuffiness. They make you feel sixteen again . . . if you hate them you can't forget them.' He concluded, 'what counts is that they're speaking for now.'

On 28 November, the Dolls flew to France to continue their European promotion with two weeks of gigs and TV shows which would also take in Germany, Holland and Belgium. The group landed in more controversy as Johnny projectile-vomited all over the press corps anticipating the Dolls' arrival at Orly airport.

Nick Kent was again along for the ride, and later turned in one of his personalised accounts for *NME* which further cemented the Dolls' image as rock'n'roll bad boys. After leading off with a tale about how John Lennon saw a video of the Dolls and called them 'faggots', Nick went into an eye-witness account of Johnny's myth-stoking regurgitation. He was five minutes off the plane and staggering towards the airport entrance where the record company had prepared a reception for the cream of the European media. After Johnny erupted, Kent observed, 'the members of the band look stone-faced and wasted, wondering if maybe he's going to fall into his own vomit.' David continued to revel in the role of the man with no shame by launching into a typically inappropriate Nazi collaborator impersonation: 'Vee did not co-operate with ze Naz-ees.' He found this so funny he would do it again at the German press conference. 'It was all over the press,' Syl enthused, 'the Dolls arrive in France and they are degenerate, drug-addicted faggots.'

Later that day, the Dolls performed their first French gig in Lyons, followed by a show in the fading industrial city of Lille the following night. They then journeyed to Paris, checking into the Ambassador Hotel before enjoying a night off, during which time Malcolm McLaren added his presence to the ranks of the band's European campaign entourage.

At mid-day on 1 December, there was supposed to be a press conference at the Ambassador Hotel for media from all over Europe. The hung-over quintet failed to surface, so Marty declared a free bar – at Mercury's expense. The Dolls finally materialised late afternoon, by which point the tab had exceeded $8,000. As in London, a well-lubricated David did most of the talking.

The Dolls had a live concert for Radio Luxembourg scheduled for after the press conference. Their late appearance and the free bar meant they rolled up late for the gig in a thoroughly smashed state. They then staggered sloppily through the show, which later surfaced as a great band-in-disrepair bootleg called *Paris Burning*.

'All I know is that I had fun at those shows,' David told *Melody Maker* in 1978. 'I was usually drunk. A lot of people thought we took fun a little too far . . . some of the conservative elements of the recording industry . . . I don't know how you can take fun too far.'

The Dolls' Paris showcase was booked into the Olympia on 2 December. Viewed from the outside, the Olympia looked like a small town cinema, but the 3,000-seat venue was a well-established cornerstone of the city's music scene. The stage door had seen a procession of big names that included everyone from Edith Piaf to an unknown Jimi Hendrix, who appeared there supporting the French national monument Johnny Halliday. Billed as *Les Poupees de New York,* the Dolls were set to appear for both a matinee and an evening show. Nick Kent described the band, who had gathered in the hotel bar in readiness for the matinee as 'behaving in their usually invigorating boisterous manner' – Syl shooting off a cap-gun and Arthur sporting a ballerina outfit, 'looking to all intents and purposes like he'd just been run over by a truck-load of Valium'. The Killer – in a 'quite amazing monotone' – asked Kent if he knew Stacia, Hawkwind's pneumatically-endowed nude dancer. After again showing off his scarred thumb, he spoke about his relationship with Connie Gripp – 'I'm worried that she might come back and try to kill me.'

The Dolls were genuinely excited about playing the Olympia, which explained their uncommon punctuality. The matinee show was dogged by sound problems, with the PA blowing out for five minutes, taking the electricity with it. Kent uses words like 'cacophonous', 'distorted' and 'grotesque' to describe the sound. He also recounts Johnny staggering around the stage 'in obvious pain, attempting to motivate himself and the band simultaneously and succeeding only in beating his instrument into an ever-more horrendous state of tunelessness.' According to Kent, halfway through one song Johnny paused for five minutes to throw up behind an amp, although Sylvain would later explain to Nina Antonia that he was taking a much-needed leak.

On 3 December, needing to attend to commitments elsewhere, Thau and Leber abandoned the Dolls in Paris, leaving Frenchy in charge of the tour from this point. His fast task was to secure a cash injection from Mercury to keep the band on the road. They were late for a TV appearance, and then a crowd riot erupted around the stage at the city's Bataclan, as riot police armed with clubs dispersed 4,500 locked-out fans. Once the show got underway, Johnny found himself subject to considerable provocation from a section of the crowd. In retaliation for the tirade of abuse, one individual who'd been grabbing and spitting at him was whacked over the head with a mike stand. The gig had to be abandoned as the band beat a retreat from the howling mob and brutal, vengeance seeking police. 'It was bad,' reflected Sylvain. 'Somebody could have got killed.'

The following day the Dolls headed east to Germany for more press and TV, where they played 'Looking For A Kiss' on the *Musikladen* show in Bremen. The press conference was held at Salambo's Boudoir in Hamburg – a historic location, formerly known as the Star Club, where the Beatles cut their musical teeth fuelled by a diet of amphetamines and hookers. Now the place hosted live sex shows. You can see the Dolls slouched in the doorway on the back cover of *Too Much Too Soon*. At the conference, Johnny – who'd already done little to win over the press by turning up in a swastika armband – further diminished his stock by observing that German beer tasted 'like junkie's piss'. Syl upped the ante by asking, 'Why are all krauts so fucking fat?' 'It's all them Jew-meat sausages', offered Johnny.

'We were all over Europe and every country was a different experience,' Johansen told *Circus* the following year. 'In Germany we had it out with the press. The Germans asked us the dumbest questions in the world and we lost our patience with them. We started making jokes about the Nazi party.'

After their whistle-stop visit to Germany, the Dolls travelled to Amsterdam to film a performance for Avro's *Top Pop* programme, which also featured Roxy Music. The band also played a gig at a local university which was intermittently disrupted by homophobic protestors.

On 10 December the Dolls travelled to Brussels for another television appearance before returning to New York where Johnny took another stab at achieving something resembling domesticity, by moving into a new apartment on 24th Street with the waiting Sable. He was also becoming increasingly close to Jerry who, being older and more worldly, he saw as a kind of father figure.

The Dolls finished up the year with a pair of domestic shows, one at Cleveland, Ohio, on 30 December, before seeing in 1974 with a return to the Michigan Palace.

By now, the first album was nudging 110,000 in sales and had spent three months on the lower reaches of the *Billboard* chart. The Dolls had been almost constantly on the road since it was recorded and now faced the formidable task of lashing together a follow-up.

Hustler's Convention

'I think the New York Dolls are very, very relevant.
I see rock'n'roll as like a changing of the guard and
this time around, we're it.' – *David Johansen*

The Dolls entered 1974 knowing that they would shortly be required to create a follow-up to *The New York Dolls*. With sales on their debut falling some way below Mercury's till-rattling expectations, the label felt that a quick second album would be the best way to recoup some of their outlay. This was likely to be a tall order, as the band's opportunities to write new material had been severely restricted by the dual demands of touring and partying. Aside from outtakes from the first album and the Dolls' assortment of cover versions, the only new songs in the repertoire were the catchy 'Who Are The Mystery Girls' and 'Puss 'n' Boots', as well as Johnny's heavier 'Chatterbox' – all of which the band had been playing live and in rehearsals for some months. They would either have to get busy writing songs in the studio, or fall back on the covers.

Once again, the selection of a producer became a key issue. The band needed to build upon the moderate success of their debut and were looking for a producer who would guarantee a disc packed with potential hit singles. However, it quickly became clear that the process of finding a willing pair of magic hands to work the desk was following a familiar pattern. Leiber and Stoller were again top of the list, but were unavailable for the period during which the Dolls were scheduled to be in the studio. To Jerry and Johnny's horror, Todd Rundgren was briefly considered, as was Bob Ezrin, who'd bombastically reupholstered Alice Cooper and Lou Reed.

Realistically, neither of these were viable options, as Rundgren was in no hurry to repeat the task of trying to control the Dolls' less than scientific approach, and Ezrin was in great demand, ensuring – like Leiber and Stoller

– that his fee was likely to be in excess of the funds Mercury would be prepared to cough up.

Disappointed with their failure to secure Leiber and Stoller, Marty and David hit upon the idea of seeking out Shadow Morton – whom they both admired on account of his groundbreaking work with the Shangri-Las. 'We all loved the Shangri-Las,' David told Pete Frame. 'That was maybe the one out of three or four groups that the whole band had loved. Everybody has their own hero. That was one. That was a common. It was pretty unanimous to get Shadow.'

Despite Johansen's assertion that the whole group wanted Morton to produce, Jerry and Johnny subsequently admitted that they had misgivings. 'He was just wrong,' insisted Johnny, who felt that the producer's drinking was a problem. Jerry felt that the appointment was just David 'calling the shots'. Today, Sylvain says Morton was 'never my pick'. Arthur, in customarily easygoing style, went where he was poured.

'Basically Shadow was like old school,' says Sylvain. 'To me he was a bad choice. He was really friends with Marty Thau and David. We all loved the Shangri-Las but David really . . . I mean, to him, anybody that worked with the Shangri-La's [was special]. He was just about to do anything to get this guy to work with us.'

Given the Dolls' enduring admiration for his past work, the selection of George 'Shadow' Morton should have been a dream ticket. However, since his mid-sixties heyday Morton's stock had declined steadily. After working with such diverse acts as Janis Ian, Vanilla Fudge and the Blues Project, he had drifted away from producing to pursue an alternative career as a racing car driver, which ended in disaster when a serious crash left him with several broken bones and temporary paralysis. In 1971 he'd been hired by Mott The Hoople to produce a single, 'Midnight Lady', which failed to chart. More recently, he'd concentrated on combating his alcoholism through an interest in Tibetan religion. By the time David and Marty tracked him down, Shadow was drifting from the primrose path and spent much of his time as a Long Island barfly.

At first, Morton thought that the New York Dolls were a girl group, 'He hadn't a fucking clue who we were,' recalls Syl. However, the producer's surprise at being confronted by the band in all their thrift-shop finery was assuaged by the $10,000 fee he was promised. 'He was shocked that we were dragging him out of the woodwork,' Arthur later told *Q*'s Mat Snow, 'just because we were Shangri-Las fans.' Marty was delighted, 'We're very pleased,' he explained to Lenny Kaye for his *Melody Maker* studio report, 'we think it's a perfect case of mix and match.'

Despite this initial optimism, Shadow's drinking, Johnny and Jerry's growing junk habits, and the intensifying pressure from Mercury to deliver a hit record undermined any possibility of a smooth creative process. Once all parties settled down to work at New York's A&R Studios, on 28 January 1974, the combustible nature of these underlying issues became evident. There was escalating tension between David and Johnny. Johansen had now firmly established himself as the Dolls' frontman, singer, principal songwriter and media mouthpiece. Of all the Dolls, he was obviously the most eloquent and, confident in his own abilities, saw taking control in the studio as a sure-fire means of ensuring the album would be a commercial success. Johnny was a more sensitive, complex character. Beneath the hair and street-tough image, there was a vulnerable person who could turn wildly unpredictable when intoxicated or marginalised.

David had a closer relationship with Morton than his bandmates, and this ensured far more of his compositions were recorded than those of the Dolls' other two main songwriters, Johnny and Syl. 'On that album I felt like I was a second class citizen,' observes Syl. 'Shadow Morton actually told me that the management had told him to push David and Johnny's songs. I had written "Too Much Too Soon" for the album but it never came out. It was part of it when we were trying our demos and throwing around songs, ideas and all that. We had done it but Shadow told me it wasn't being used. Johnny later did it on one of his acoustic albums. Johnny loved that song. *He loved that song.* There's a little piece of magic in it.'

Johnny's attempts to get some of his songs on the album were only marginally more successful, as the guitarist was forced to fight his corner to ensure 'Chatterbox' made it to the final cut.

In addition to the resentment caused by the competition for songwriting credits, a further layer of hassle was created by Morton. The producer wanted to earn his money and leave his trademark stamp on the record by employing female backing singers and dubbing on unusual sound effects. This again served to divide the band; David was enthusiastic about such embellishments, as they referenced his influences, while Syl, Johnny and Jerry would have preferred that the band stick close to their no-nonsense rock'n'roll roots. Speaking in 2005, Sylvain sees the vaudevillian aesthetic of cover versions such as 'Bad Detective' and 'Showdown' as indicative of David's future direction (fully realised when he adopted his louche Buster Poindexter persona during the 1980s). 'David was what people would consider to be reinventing himself, before reinventing himself as Buster and all that. *Too Much Too Soon*, I say today quite jokingly, was the first Buster Poindexter record. The black backing singers, it was fucked. I'm not saying that you should always stay the same but it *was* too much too soon. That was perfect. You couldn't title it better.'

Lenny Kaye visited the studio for *Melody Maker* and provided the only eyewitness press account of the sessions. The journalist – who would subsequently go on to become Patti Smith's guitarist – arrived on the scene as Johnny was putting down a guide vocal on 'Chatterbox' while Syl, Arthur and Jerry played live. The plan was that the vocals would be redone later, along with overdubs. Kaye's report conjured an odd picture of disparate elements within the band attempting to pull together, while the serenely disconnected Morton sat with his cowboy hat pulled down, reading a book on Tibetan mythology while the Dolls' sonic chaos coruscated around him.

Irrespective of his reduced status, Shadow wasn't averse to blowing his own trumpet when Kaye asked him what made a good producer. 'Me,' he replied. 'That's all. Energy level, belief, instinct . . . it's what happens after the board gives all it's got to give. A producer makes a hit because he deals with a quality of the people that sit in the studio that are capable of making hits, and then he counts on a lot of things. He counts on the situation, he counts on energy, he counts on a little bit of God, he counts on a little bit of luck, a little bit of music . . . I don't consider myself a good producer. I consider myself one of the best producers.'

David agreed with Morton's inflated self-assessment, but backed up Johnny's subsequent assertion that the producer was 'a drunk', observing, 'it was great working with him – he was funny, but you had to keep the booze away from him.' Marty had no such reservations and felt that the big time was just around the corner, gleefully declaring, 'I took the best of that [Mercer] scene and now it's time to collect.'

Or maybe it wasn't. Even to the ears of a fervent Dolls fan, *Too Much Too Soon* projected the sound of on-the-road strain and self-inflicted abuse, a toxic bull-charge through the band's influences and signature chops, sliding all over the place, sometimes keeping going through sheer energy – artificial or otherwise. Kaye's report led Dolls devotees to expect the new disc to be everything that the first album should have been. He described what he heard that day as 'a testament to how far the group has come since the days they took as much time tuning as actually playing'.

However, once again the finished mix fell short of the sounds that were dancing in Dolls fans' expectant imaginations. The final production is unsteady, muddy and over-separated, while the performances are a weird collision between amphetamined energy and downered-out somnambulism. After so long in the creative wilderness, Morton probably couldn't believe his luck and obviously believed that a few quirky sound effects and Shangri-Las lifts would merit his ten grand fee. Unfortunately, rather than surpassing expectations, it seems the former maestro had exceeded his sell-by date.

The combination of Morton's drunken sloppiness and the Dolls' customarily haphazard approach served up an album that was riddled with flaws. Despite this, *Too Much Too Soon* was still infinitely preferable to most other aural confections available that year. The disc is suffused with an essential pissy attitude in every curled guitar shard, wrecked surf chorus or pouting aside. This peculiar energy drives most of the songs forward, accelerating just ahead of entropic collapse, as Johnny's scattershot riffing aquaplanes above Jerry's manic drum salvos. Syl and Arthur are never less than perfectly sympathetic, while David's repertoire of vocal characters is wider though his spat-out delivery is no less petulant.

Johansen could still evoke the street punk but the quartet of cover versions enabled him to extend his range of roles – from jungle survivor to Chinese detective or venerable blues man. And, when necessary, the depths of his soul could be mined to gripping effect on tracks like 'Human Being'. In this respect, David's adoption of specific personas for each song was redolent of Mick Jagger who, by the early seventies, had already established a grab-bag of personalities depending on what kind of character he was trying to project. As David told Lisa Robinson, 'In a sense I'm an actor and the band is an act.'

Too Much Too Soon kicks off with 'Babylon', one of the songs that didn't make it onto the first album. David explained that, in this instance, Babylon is actually a stop on the Long Island Expressway, just past Amityville. He told the press that this could be taken to represent any suburban small-town where the girls get on the train and go into the city. Always keen to add some more texture to the mythos, he told others that it was an ode to a suburban drag queen.

'"Babylon" is about people who live in Babylon, Long Island, who go into the city every night dressed to kill,' Johansen told *Circus*. 'These people have to get home before sun up. You know, like vampires they can't get caught by the sun. This girl finally splits Manhattan where she gets a job in a massage parlour.' Hence the line, 'She's been massaging all day, but she's thinking about you daddy.'

From the moment David summons his gang with a rooftop wolf-whistle, there's no time to waste. 'C'mon Boys' – the Dolls gotta run, drive, get away to where it's at. Syl and Johnny's guitars chug and wail in urgent counterpoint, while Jerry Nolan drives the song toward those Babylon girls and the endless party. The track immediately re-establishes the Dolls' low-rent hedonism. As with 'Frankenstein', as the number gathers velocity his entreaties become increasingly urgent. But unlike the unreal sexual dilemma broached in 'Frankenstein', this time David's in a rush to get his boys to where the action's at. Morton's production style is immediately obvious, with each sonic component emerging with singularity from the vacuum-packed mix.

'Stranded In The Jungle' is the first of the four cover versions that lay out a bunch of the Dolls' prime influences for all to see. Although these covers were a means of padding out the group's thin corpus of unrecorded fare, they also indicate the breadth of their musical backgrounds. Once again, the Dolls showed that they were an offshoot from a lineage that grew out of a genre-defying melting pot.

As Screamin' Jay Hawkins, the mighty ghoul-blasting blues shouter who gave throat to 'I Put A Spell On You', told Gerri Hershey in her seminal eighties book *Nowhere To Run*: 'Can't get to soul without R&B. And gospel. And what they call rock'n'roll, which ain't nothin' but R&B. Labels are bullshit. You wanna get to the sixties, you gotta start with the forties and the beginning of rhythm and blues, late forties, early fifties. Somewhere along the mid-fifties, people started doing gospel and blues too. You can't make a clean separation anywhere.'

The Dolls didn't try. To them, the Shangri-Las, Coasters, Eddie Cochran, Frankie Lymon, MC5, Rolling Stones and Howlin' Wolf could all ride on the same inspirational boxcar. Ultimately, the band cared little about where a song came from, so long as it made people dance. 'Rather than have them sitting there listening, we want them dancing on the floor,' insisted Johnny. 'We want them getting off to us. We're rock'n'roll. Sure we have few technicalities about our music, but my God we have feel . . . when we play everyone casts their shackles aside, and dances.'

Originally recorded by the Jayhawks, 'Stranded In The Jungle' had been a novelty hit for the Cadets in 1955, 'I've always loved the song', declared David. The Dolls turned it into a screaming doo-wop pantomime, smartly switching from ape-call narrative to big city tear-up and back again. Jungle drums, chattering chimps and clicking cicadas cue in David's report from beyond the reaches of civilisation. The combination of Morton's use of sound effects and the Dolls' vaudevillian performance is straight out of *The Muppet Show*. In many respects, the track bears similarities to some of Frank Zappa's doo-wop pastiches, with no cliché left unreferenced – from the shrill 'yeah, yeah, yeahs' of the backing chicks to David's use of multiple characterisations to give voice to the loin-cloth panic of the lyrics. Viewed in the context of the album, 'Stranded In The Jungle' has the effect of de-railing the urban momentum generated by 'Babylon'.

Normal service is resumed with 'Who Are The Mystery Girls?', which emerges through a miasma of wailing guitars to establish itself as one of *Too Much Too Soon*'s standout tracks. While David screams cynical street wisdom from the powder room, the rest of the band back him up by utilising all the classic elements of the Dolls unique sound in perfect synthesis: Johnny's sarcastic lead, Syl's cohesive knack of filling the gaps left by Thunders, the priapic Kane/Nolan beat, hand-claps and girl group flourishes.

Again, Morton's production efficiently files down the sharpest edges of the Dolls' nails; the bass and drums are reduced to a throb, Syl's guitar is similarly muted, relegating him to Johnny's backing man (rather than essential six-string twin), and the sheer Joan Crawford venom of David's vocal is stripped of its haggard hoarseness. Despite this, his get-her delivery of 'What do you know about love?' is unmatched in terms of making it abundantly clear that you *so* don't know shit . . .

'(There's Gonna Be A) Showdown' concerns a rumble in the dancehall. Written by Kenneth Gamble and Leon Huff, it was originally a top 30 hit in 1968 for Archie Bell and the Drells. Gamble and Huff had started building Philadelphia's reputation for quality soul music in the mid-sixties, after enjoying their first hit with the Soul Survivors' 'Expressway To Your Heart'. They subsequently became involved with Philadelphia International Records and quickly established a mighty stable of black artists, including groups like the Three Degrees, Delfonics and Stylistics.

'Showdown' suffers from Morton's stodgy production, which conveys an impression of the song being recorded in a wind tunnel. When the Dolls played the song live, its glorious chorus could get a whole crowd singing along – a rude, raucous declaration of pugilistic intent. Nick Kent observed that the production sounded like it was put down on horse tranquiliser. Despite this, the sheer energy of the Dolls carries the song home. It was an inspired choice of cover. 'They did songs they could actually act out – that's what's really funny about it,' explained Nina Antonia in 2005. 'Looking back at the songs they did, I think someone should do an album of songs that the Dolls covered. For example, on *Manhattan Mayhem* there's a storming "Give Him A Great Big Kiss", recorded in the studio in 1973, and the meanest rendition of Muddy Waters' "Hoochie Coochie Man".'

One of *Too Much Too Soon*'s best tracks, 'It's Too Late' dated from the Chrystie Street sessions of eighteen months earlier. The first 30 seconds feature a Dolls roll call: drums, harp, lead, bass, rhythm, before settling down into a decent slab of Stones-influenced garage. Johansen subsequently explained that the song was dedicated to downmarket British glamour-puss Diana Dors, who receives a name check in the second verse. 'She was the inspiration of that song, but to know you'll just have to listen to it.'

Unfortunately, the song's uninspired backing scarcely lives up to Johansen's lyrics – despite the vocalist's lung busting efforts to fill the myriad gaps with harmonica blasts. 'It's Too Late' is further evidence of how the shortage of new material undermined *Too Much Too Soon*. This was a track which had been passed over for the debut album, and was included here simply because the Dolls hadn't accrued anything else on a par with 'Mystery Girls'. Too much too soon, indeed. David is once again laying down the lyrical law. A poor little rich 'baby' is admonished at length, 'But how's she ever gonna love you when she can't *parlez-vous* your *Francais?*'

'Puss 'N' Boots' marks the only Sylvain songwriting credit on the album. Co-written with Johansen, it's a succinct example of the Dolls at their most gutter-crawlingly in-your-face, yet pop-sensitive and economic. Shadow unwittingly pre-dated the sampling frenzy of the next decade with his lifting of sound effects, the abrupt ricochet gunshot at the end of the song hoisted from the Olympics' 1958 novelty classic 'Western Movies'. (This West Coast trio were up there with Dolls favourites the Coasters when it came to fun-packed R&B soap operas.)

David got the title for 'Puss 'N' Boots' from a journal aimed at foot fetishists. 'It's about a person who gets into a lib movement and goes crazy,' Johansen told *Circus* scribe OB Lewis. 'The puss in boots movement. The movement to liberate pusses that weren't in boots.' Helpfully, the magazine added, 'It's the perfect song to bang your head against the wall to.'

Johnny had stuck to his guns and succeeded in getting one of his compositions onto *Too Much Too Soon*. Like 'It's Too Late', 'Chatterbox' had been knocking around the fringes of the band's repertoire for some time. It had been known as 'Milk Me', and earlier in the year he'd been calling the song 'Jailbreak Opera'. On vinyl, the song is 2.25 of snarling vitriol, delivered by Johnny in a thin but attitude-riddled whine.

The rawest track on *Too Much Too Soon*, 'Chatterbox' is pure Thunders, containing all the lyrical themes and hooks that would epitomise his Heartbreakers material, two years hence. Broadly similar to the Stooges' 'Real Cool Time', the lyrics recount the vocalist's attempts to convince the object of his affections to have him over for some hot 'n' heavy action. Except, unlike Iggy, Johnny's chick is giving him some lip; 'I said ya squawk a lot.' Musically, it sounds like Thunders won a battle of wills with Morton, and the song emerges with its buzzsaw venom largely intact.

'Bad Detective' was another cover version. Originally recorded by vocal harmonists the Coasters in May 1964, the song was one of a whole clutch of hits that had been written for the quartet by Jerry Leiber and Mike Stoller. These included cuts such as 'Yakety Yak' (1958) and 'Poison Ivy' (1959), as well as episodic mid-fifties mini-movies like 'Shoppin' For Clothes' and 'Riot In Cell Block Number Nine'. In *Nowhere To Run: The Story of Soul Music*, Gerri Hirshey observed, 'Leiber and Stoller worked well with the individual singers' voices, letting them speak or sing in musical playlets that often had hilarious pantomime routines for those all important stage shows.' 'Bad Detective' exemplified this, a supercharged cartoon romp through Chinatown, with chopsticks guitar motifs and nonsensical vocals that became camper by the minute. It's fifties B-movie tack, but belted out like the MC5 meets Abbott and Costello. Arthur spent three hours creating the surreal vocals.

The album's final cover is a storming rendition of Sonny Boy Williamson's 'Don't Start Me Talkin'', which abandons the episodic humour of 'Bad Detective' and 'Stranded In The Jungle', pitching the Dolls feet-first into a blazing slab of prime blues power. The Kane/Nolan rhythm section chugs along powerfully, while David's harmonica rips jaggedly across Johnny and Syl's twin assault. The song arrives as consecutive bursts of action, which match the energy levels of the band live. This time around, David adopts the vocal persona of a raging bluesman, albeit one who is 'goin' down the beauty shop to get my hair styled'.

Too Much Too Soon concludes (too soon) with a pell-mell guitar descent into 'Human Being', which reintroduces the Dolls' doomed-love motif. Benefiting from a lack of Morton's embellishments, David lectures the bar room on human nature; 'And if I want too many things/Don't you know that I'm a human being?' As with 'Frankenstein' he utilises a lengthy song sheet to build desperation and drama. The track accelerates toward a thundering climax before Buddy Bowser's post-coital sax exhales some blues and the Dolls turn out the light.

As with *The New York Dolls*, the main bone of contention with *Too Much Too Soon* was the production. Talking to *Zigzag* in 1977, Johnny made his dislike of both Morton and Rundgren's methods clearer than crystal meth. 'Listen to the albums, man. Sounds real musical but there's no drums. We never had no drums on any of the albums.' He also singled out David as a cause of some of the perceived faults. 'The first two albums were butchered. They were great songs and we could have done great performances, but David was the type of guy who didn't want to do a song twice in the studio. But sometimes you have to! He didn't give a shit about anybody in the band giving a good performance, as long as he sounded okay.'

'Important parts of the songs were never brought out. Nobody spent enough time getting our sound, especially Johnny's guitar sound,' explained Jerry. 'Nobody pays enough attention or spends enough time capturing it. They're more worried about telling Johnny that they can get it over in the studio, but you got to really go out of your way to get the sound. You gotta study and have the time. But when you get it, it's well worth it. If you really listen close you can almost hear some of Johnny's sound and style. You can listen close and hear a lot of things but why should you *have* to really study. You should feel it instead of listening for it. It should hit you really quick. You shouldn't have to look for something or listen to something. It should all be there all ready for you, so you feel it. You're not supposed to think about how deep or how intellectual the group is. It's just the feel. It's supposed to feel [snaps fingers] right on and together.'

'I don't care if people say the second album isn't any good,' David told *Circus*. 'I think we're really good. I don't think anybody can offer as much as we can, as far as rock and roll is concerned right now . . . I'm into believing that we're really doing something out of sight. If [the critics] like the albums, then they're the persons we made the albums for. If someone doesn't like the album, then we didn't make it for him.'

Johansen reiterated his position in conversation with Pete Frame in 1978. 'It's easy to say it didn't work out the way we wanted it to – that was a common one – when we never wanted it in the first place. But I'm quite satisfied with both those albums. If you listen to them today they hold up quite well. They sound real mainstream today. When you're establishing precedents and recording techniques you might get slagged off at first but, eventually, if you're right it will be seen. They set a precedent as far as recording techniques are concerned.'

Contrasting Morton with Rundgren, David observed, 'Shadow was the more creative of the two.' Morton's next project was a nine-piece girl band called Isis.

Cinematically billed as *The New York Dolls In Too Much Too Soon*, the album is dedicated to Diana Barrymore, whose biographical account of her tragic family life, (which was made into a 1958 film starring Dorothy Malone and Errol Flynn) provided the LP with its title. Related to actors John and Drew Barrymore, she died of a tragic drugs and booze-related death, although David, who described the disc as 'a eulogy' to Barrymore, liked to say that she was killed when somebody rammed a tennis ball down her throat. 'She had a foul life anyway,' he pragmatically asserted.

The album cover is a performance shot taken from the band's *Don Steele* appearance. This is a curious choice, especially given the inherently visual nature of the quintet. Although Syl and Johnny show up well, David's face is partially obscured and Arthur and Jerry are lost among the bright lights toward the back of the frame. Considering the negative reaction from DJs that greeted *The New York Dolls'* sleeve, it seems likely that Mercury opted for an uncontroversial image in order to maximise potential exposure.

A far more engaging image of the Dolls can be seen on the back cover, which was taken during their recent visit to the Star Club in Hamburg. The band look like they've been partying since the photo session for the first album – apart from a content-looking Johansen, whose purple latex strides are the brightest colour in the shot. Black-clad Johnny's face is the colour of chalk, while Syl appears in a satin catsuit. Jerry's tough stance cuts a meaner figure than his uncomfortable-looking simper on the first album. Arthur clings to the cavorting Syl as if the guitarist was the only thing anchoring him to the planet.

This time around, the Dolls took the more conventional step of playing some dates in advance of the new album's release, to build up a groundswell of excitement outside of their hardcore following. The biggest of these shows took place on 15 February 1974 at New York's 4,000-capacity Academy of Music on Fourteenth Street, near Union Square, which later became the Palladium. Mercury stumped up for some promotion and David recorded a radio advertisement that featured him declaring, 'Man, I'm getting tired of this seeing your face every night through the winter. There's one thing about this winter. We've got the New York Dolls coming to the Academy Of Music on Friday night, February 15. We got our own St Valentine's Day Massacre, honey, since all the deco got stacked up. That's this Friday, honey. You better be there.'

The gig was a near sell-out, with Elliott Murphy opening up. At the time, Murphy was being touted as a new Dylan – largely on account of his 1973 *Blonde On Blonde* soundalike album *Aquashow*. He had all the requisite impedimenta: the harmonica holder, shades and acoustic guitar. However, this tended to be undermined by equal measures of insincerity, pretentious lyrics and his annoyingly-thin voice, not to mention a peculiar fixation with *The Great Gatsby*.

To herald the Dolls' set, Bob Gruen had filmed them in a short black-and-white gangster-spoof called *The Lipstick Killers*. After emerging from behind a newspaper proclaiming, 'LIPSTICK KILLERS ELUDE FEDS IN METRO MAN-HUNT', the Dolls, sporting pinstripes and hats, line up mugshot-style as 'Rocky' Johansen, 'Pretty Boy' Nolan aka 'Scarface', Giovanni Genzale, 'Killer' Kane and 'Legs', alias 'The Dancer' (Syl). The gun-toting Lipstick Killers are then shown straddling Bob Gruen's Volkswagen as it careers, Mack Sennett-style, up Fourteenth Street to the Academy. After the Dolls were shown charging through the foyer, the film finished with a voice boom-ing, 'There's no telling where the Killers will strike again, it could be in your neighbourhood,' at which point the Dolls appeared in the auditorium, firing replica machine guns and two hours late.

Almost as soon as the Dolls launched into their customary opener, 'Personality Crisis', the sound system cut out. After a short delay they stormed through a triumphant homecoming, with the crowd throwing Chocolate Kisses onstage during 'Looking For A Kiss' and bringing them back for three encores, which included a heaving rendition of Muddy Waters 'Hoochie Coochie Man' and a full-tilt thrash through Chuck Berry's 'Back In The USA'.

Nick Kent was there to cover the Dolls homecoming on behalf of *NME*, observing, 'Their popularity has reached such proportions in their home town that the only way it appears one can get laid in New York these days is to be part of their entourage. Their concert at the Academy Of Music was easily the best I attended throughout my thoroughly depressing stay in the city.' Kent also remarked on how the number of Dolls look-alikes in the crowd was 'proof that there is some kind of life-blood pumping away in New York rock,' before concluding, 'The Dolls are the best and the last of their breed, jack-knifing their way with style, across the . . . infinity of parodies that currently makes up the true substance of rock'n'roll right now.'

The day after the Valentine's show, the Dolls took their *Too Much Too Soon* roadshow out of New York. Although Mercury were keen that the band tour behind the album to a greater extent than with their debut, their itinerary was left to the band's management and tended to follow no logical geo-graphical progression. Additionally, these shows were often in small venues and organised at short notice, which was partly on account of the band's substance-stoked unreliability, but also indicative of Leber and Krebs' grow-ing preoccupation with Aerosmith.

On 16 February, the Dolls played Bloomington, Indiana with Southern boogie dullards Lynyrd Skynyrd, before travelling to Cambridge, Massachusetts for a gig on the following day. The Dolls' next booking was an eventful show at the Capitol Theatre in Passaic, New Jersey. The gig was only a third full as it had only been announced a week before, but managed to make the pages of *Circus* after the ushers and bouncers started streaking down the aisles. The report says that the Dolls were 'momentarily stunned, but then cheered on the nude dudes, declaring the concert a "streaker's festival".'

In early March, the Dolls headed north to play Vancouver and Seattle, before returning to LA to play Santa Monica Civic Auditorium on the 16th, with a further gig taking place the next day at the 1,000-capacity JJ's club in San Diego. The LA gig had been fitted around an invitation for the band to take part in animator Ralph Bakshi's latest venture, *Hey Good Looking*. Bakshi had made his name with his groundbreaking animation of underground comic strip *Fritz the Cat*, and this new venture was set in the fifties with the Dolls playing a rock group. Unfortunately the project ran into financial problems and the Dolls, who were caught thieving from the props department, ended up on the cutting room floor when the film eventually came out as a fully animated feature in 1982.

The Santa Monica gig, which saw *The Lipstick Killers'* West Coast premiere, consolidated the Dolls' position in LA. However, less welcome was Johnny's increasing unpredictability – at a party the next day, he accused Sable of getting too frisky with Arthur and laid into her in the bathroom, banging her head into the wall. This marked the start of a continuing cycle of violent abuse that would ultimately precipitate the end of their relationship.

In addition to his growing infatuation with smack, Johnny had recently been cultivating a deadly affection for methedrine – one of the strongest forms of amphetamine. In addition to the effects common to most types of speed, methedrine also produces euphoric sensations similar to those associated with MDMA. However, crystal meth can keep the user awake for days on end and causes acute hallucinations, paranoia, heightened aggression and a reduced resistance to illnesses. Once Johnny started alternating between meth and heroin, he suffered these effects in full, which served to make him unstable and argumentative.

An example of this unpredictability occurred during the brief trip to Canada. While the rest of the Dolls were waiting outside their hotel for Johnny to come down from his room and join them in the van, someone said he was on the phone and would be down in a minute. After an hour, there was still no sign of Johnny, so David went up to his room to see what was going on. Here he found the guitarist still on the phone – blankly listening to the dialling tone.

'Look, I don't want to denigrate anybody, but when Johnny and Jerry started rooming together, deciding that heroin was God, then it was tolerable for a while but we'd go places and they couldn't get it and it would cause problems,' explained David. As a fellow devotee of the bottle, David could handle Arthur's boozy excesses, but Johnny and Jerry's smack consumption got his goat. 'It just became untenable, and I'm not a co-dependent person. I got to a point when I thought: we're not going to do this.'

'First Johnny, then Jerry started shooting heroin. I noticed changes in their appearance and behaviour, plus Arthur's alcohol intake escalated and he had to be constantly watched,' recalled Marty Thau. 'David and Syl were obviously aware of what was going on and became increasingly unhappy over this turn of events.'

After a show on 6 April at Providence, Rhode Island, the Dolls embarked on another exercise in preaching to the converted. Billed as the Manhattan World Tour, the band took in reliable venues like My Father's Place, Kenny's Castaways, the Coventry and Max's. This run of shows could be viewed as indicative of how the Dolls' management were resigned to the fact that the band were never going to crack the big time, and were content to consign them to an eternity of small club concerts. However, viewing the policy with hindsight, Syl contends that it had its own kind of logic. 'Marty and Dave came up with that. Since we'd been all around the world and everything, now we'd do another sort of world tour. So we did a show in Manhattan, Queens, Brooklyn, Staten Island and The Bronx. New York basically. The five boroughs, which was the whole world.

'This was 1974. Every night we introduced somebody new. We introduced Kiss, the Ramones had just come out. They had just played their first shows. I think this might have been their first show.'

The tour started at My Father's Place, Long Island, on 14 April, which was broadcast live on WBAB radio. The next two dates were at Max's, which were followed by a landmark gig at Club 82 on Fourth Street and Second Avenue on 17 April. This had been one of Manhattan's most glamorous drag venues between the 1940s and late sixties, playing host to a bevy of transvestites and female impersonators. Latterly, 82 had lost some of its sparkle once such establishments could operate openly, but still employed a team of lesbians to man the door and bar.

In keeping with the spirit of their surroundings, the Dolls dragged up more thoroughly than usual. Johansen sported a black wig and Cyrinda's striped dress while a shorter-haired Jerry looked typically ill at ease in his polka dot dress. Syl donned a cheekily revealing pair of chaps and Arthur stuck with his hot pants, pantyhose and turquoise boots. However, Johnny steadfastly refused to drag up preferring to go topless. The Miamis supported and acted as the Dolls' 'gentlemen dates'.

'That was the only club that we ever did anything like that, really devised shit,' recalls Sylvain. 'It was run by this lesbian woman who was gorgeous, called Tommy, and ran it like a brick shithouse. It looked all tropical. The Copacabana goes gay, if you will. The centre of it was the actual stage, like a square. Completely around the stage was the bar. We would hang down there. The prostitutes were on Tenth Street and after their work hours they would go down to Club 82 and drink down there. They would have like drag shows and do performances. We were the first rock'n'roll band to play there. Tommy never used to want that. Just like Micky Ruskin at Max's Kansas City. But business was bad for them. They needed new fun and excitement again.

That's where the New York Dolls came in. They still talk about what we did at Club 82 because it was the most exciting thing. It came at a time when the Dolls had been on their way up and then on their way down and this was like the sort of the valley of their career.'

On 19 and 20 April, the Dolls played the Coventry before a show at the respected Bottom Line the following night. This intimate, cabaret-style venue was more used to coma-inducing singer-songwriters such as Jackson Browne and Tom Paxton, and was probably the most establishment-orientated music venue the Dolls ever played in New York. The Bottom Line seemed to like the Dolls and they went over well – although afterwards, a drunken Arthur smashed the dressing room mirror with a bottle. 24 hours later, at Kenny's Castaways, they blew up the sound system.

In May, the Dolls achieved the remarkable distinction of being voted both best *and* worst group in *Creem*'s readers' poll. At least they beat Queen and Aerosmith in the first category, but were nonplussed to have surpassed the Osmonds in the latter. In addition to highlighting the polarising affect that the Dolls had on audiences, this paradox of popularity and notoriety provided the record company with good advertising copy for *Too Much Too Soon* when it was released in July. The full-page advertisements displayed two identical pictures of the group under the headings – 'The band voted the best new group of 1973' and 'The band voted the worst new group of 1973.'

The music press opted to vote the Dolls into the 'worst' category, and roundly panned *Too Much Too Soon*. 'The new album is another wall of noise; cut after cut of annoying screeching, with David's feeble voice drowned out of each cut,' wailed *Circus*. *Melody Maker*'s Michael Watts admitted to enjoying the Dolls in his Biba's review but wasn't impressed here. A big fan of the most conservative progressive rock, he described the band's instrumental skills as 'possibly the worst on record', their songs 'scant on melody' and bemoaned 'the lack of progression' on the previous album. There was some consolation as he admitted that, 'None of this, though, is to the point. A sense of humour, enthusiasm and sheer rock'n'roll *joie de vivre* surges out of the speakers; now and then, indeed, individual songs even manage to stand out . . . But the Dolls are best just making a good, loud noise.' Three years later, the same journalist would do a hatchet job on the first Clash album.

One might imagine that there were few more Dolls-friendly reviewers than *NME*'s Nick Kent. But he wasn't impressed either, going as far as to assert that the Dolls were close to 'blowing it completely'. Kent observed that he had expected the second album to smooth out the production problems of the first and deliver the necessary killer punch but felt, 'The second album pinpoints a considerable deterioration on the powerhouse potential of its predecessor.' He criticised Morton's production and described the sound as 'often fairly appalling, the instrumental work is at times incredibly sloppy and the mix throughout is just plain bad.' He even described Johnny's 'Chatterbox' – the song that he'd described as a 'gem' in his Academy of Music gig review – as 'a complete waste of time and vinyl'. Kent was a little more positive about 'Puss 'n' Boots' and 'Babylon', which he compared to the MC5. In conclusion though, he observed that, 'the overall impression . . . is that this album is messy and shot through with unfulfilled potential.'

Despite the sniffy reception accorded *Too Much Too Soon*, the Dolls took to the skies in search of new audiences. Accompanied by saxophonist Buddy Bowser and taking their guitars as hand luggage, they racked up frequent flyer credits with concerts in Ohio, Michigan, Florida, the Carolinas and Connecticut. There didn't seem to be any regard for logistics, strategy or human endurance. The result of all this zigzag wandering was terminal on-the-road psychosis and excess. Inevitably, the band became increasingly reliant on the numbing effects of booze and drugs to block out the drudgery. It was hardly surprising that Arthur demolished his hotel room in Cleveland.

Johnny found some non-pharmaceutical solace when the Dolls hit New Orleans on 17 July, despite the fact that band and crew arrived to find that night's venue – the Warehouse – inexplicably burned to the ground. The two days that Johnny spent in the city saw the guitarist immersing himself in the jazz sound of New Orleans. From that point he would always say that his life's ambition was to go to New Orleans and play with the jazzmen. He even acquired a trumpet and stand-up bass. The music of New Orleans is evocative, beautiful and timeless. In Gerri Hershey's *Nowhere To Run,* the city is described as the place where 'more kinds of black music . . . survive, intact and undisturbed by the vagaries of marketing and record charts'. New Orleans' inherent musicality originated from the African Slaves during the eighteenth century. Forcibly removed from their homelands, the slaves embellished and adapted traditional rhythms and vocalisations, ultimately paving the way for the development of jazz and blues during the first half of the twentieth century. During this period, New Orleans became home to a proliferation of marching bands while rootsy 'tribes' like the Wild Magnolias created scorching soundtracks to the massive Mardi Gras festival.

The city also became famous for its piano men, like Huey 'Piano' Smith, Fats Domino, and Professor Longhair, the patron saint of New Orleans R&B. Others followed, including the Neville Brothers, Allen Toussaint, Dr John, Lee Dorsey, Bertty Harris, Clarence 'Frogman' Henry, Irma Thomas, the Meters and those Dixie Cups. Johnny would have known some of these names, but had to go to the Crescent City to experience the full impact of its uniquely hedonistic musical heritage.

Having soaked up some culture, the Dolls then moved on to Los Angeles for four nights at the Roxy between 23-26 July. Unfortunately, tiresome goth-panto the *Rocky Horror Show* – a musical for Meatloaf fans looking for safe danger – was running there at the time. The theatre obviously thought the Dolls would lend their simpering production some credibility, but the street reality of the band and its crew rubbed the cast the wrong way as they barged their equipment all over the stage and dented some precious props. Harsh words were exchanged and the theatre cancelled the Dolls' remaining three shows. This resulted in accusations of tardiness by the local press, not to mention disappointed fans who'd snaffled up every ticket in advance. The group were also drastically late for a record company dinner, which hardly served to improve their relations with Mercury.

There was some consolation when the Dolls managed to pull off a live triumph on the nationally-syndicated and highly-regarded *Don Kirshner Rock*

Show. The show was filmed before an audience in Long Beach Auditorium to go out at prime time on a Friday evening, the band's half-hour set showcasing highlights from both albums, including 'Showdown', 'Stranded in The Jungle', 'Trash', 'Chatterbox', 'Don't Start Me Talkin'', and 'Personality Crisis'.

'You'd never know it, but that wasn't really our audience they showed. We were there with bands like Rufus, or something else,' revealed Syl in an interview with the *Toronto Sun*'s Kieran Grant. 'We were having a hard time up there. The audience wasn't going for it, and Johansen had been boozing it up a little too early that day . . . When I see it now, we look pretty damn good, but fuck, it wasn't as easy as it looked. The audience was starting to boo us. You took away our girls and our groovy scene, we didn't know what to do.'

The cancellation of the LA gigs served to sour relations between Marty Thau and Steve Leber. Marty still believed that the Dolls had the potential to become a massive attraction, churning out killer singles, while Leber was an old school booking agent who found the band's excessive behaviour and lack of concrete success difficult to stomach. Leber decided to continue putting the Dolls into the small clubs – in junkie terms, to maintain rather than get high.

Perhaps surprisingly, Syl now thinks that this was a sensible move. 'I think the smartest thing a band can do is to be exactly where the kids want them the most. If it's a stinking little club you've got to fill it to the rafters so you can't fit another finger in the joint. And outside it looks like the fucking Beatles are playing downstairs again. It got a little tougher when they put us in the little clubs in Detroit and further out places.'

It's worth noting that, as the Dolls declined, the third party in the Thau-Leber-Krebs management consortium was seeing his own charges' star rising swiftly and effectively. Aerosmith were basically a sanitised, more radio friendly take on the Dolls' shtick – which meant they could appeal to the average denim-clad, Budweiser-swilling rocker without him having to wade into the scary waters of sexual ambiguity. Aerosmith towed the line and their record company, CBS, stood squarely behind them as a result. The Dolls, on the other hand, felt that they were being suppressed by their record company, and ignored by the Leber-Krebs management axis.

Further evidence of the way in which the Dolls' organisation was unravelling came when a July British tour was summarily cancelled due to alleged 'visa problems'. The gigs, which had been advertised in the UK music press, had been set to include a headlining spot at Olympia, in London's Earl's Court, and an appearance at the Buxton Festival.

The cancellation of what would have been the Dolls' third visit to the UK demonstrated that the band were a long way down the list of Mercury's priorities, and disappointed their British fanbase. Marco Pirroni – original Siouxsie and the Banshees guitarist and tubby driving force behind Adam and the Ants' early 1980s chart domination – gave his own take on why the Dolls failed to ignite the UK: 'In early 1974 the New York Dolls were also interesting because of their trashiness. Their sound was an influence, but they made the unforgivable mistake of having long hair and wearing platforms. So people in Britain wrote them off a little bit.'

One person who could forgive the hair and boots was a young Mott the

Hoople fan called Mick Jones, who would later go on to form The Clash. He first talked about being blown away by the Dolls in letters he wrote to his school friend Robin Crocker – then in Wormwood Scrubs, serving two years for armed robbery. In 1974, Mick had a group called the Delinquents. He wrote, 'As for our band, we're really good/bad/mediocre. I've been trying to get an image like the New York Dolls. Me and Paul are gonna get our hair curled and John "Hermit" Brown is going to get his hair straightened.' Stuck in prison, Robin had no idea who Mick was going on about. 'That was the first I'd heard of them;' he recalls. "Mick gave me a crash course when I came out. Straight away I just loved it.'

A year later, when Mick was trying to put together a group with Tony James (who would later form Generation X and work with Johnny Thunders) they advertised in *Melody Maker* for musicians. Any hopeful applicants had to be into the Dolls, along with the Stones, Mott and the Stooges: 'Decadent third generation rock and roll image essential. New Dolls-style.' The pair assembled what became known as the London SS, a legendary ensemble who never played a gig but would contain many of the main movers from the subsequent punk movement. Morrissey applied, but wasn't considered because he came from the North. At rehearsals they'd run through 'Personality Crisis'. 'The New York Dolls were an invisible skein linking Joe [Strummer], Mick and many of the other key players in punk,' observed Pat Gilbert in his Clash biography *Passion Is A Fashion*.

By August 1974, Johnny's behaviour was becoming increasingly problematic. On one occasion, Sylvain was sitting in his Greenwich Village basement with girlfriend Janet Planet, when Johnny's sister Mariann phoned in tears, asking what was the matter with her brother. She said he'd locked a maintenance man in her cellar, then ran off. A little while later, Johnny turned up at the front door, wired to the gills, having just done a whole ounce of methedrine. Unsurprisingly, given the brain-frying amount of crank he'd imbibed, Johnny was rambling and seeing things. 'He was never the same after that,' says Syl.

Equally predictably, Sable found the beatings and Johnny's drug-fuelled, sleep-deprived craziness too much to bear, and attempted to commit suicide by slashing her wrists. Syl discovered her just in time and took her to Bellevue Hospital. Faced with the choice between an extended stay in the hospital's psychiatric wing or returning to her parents, she opted for the latter, leaving Johnny to raise hell on his own. 'Johnny was crazy,' declared Sable. 'Crazy and vicious. Sick, disturbed. So after he tried to kill me four or five times, I thought I'd take a trip back home.' It was at this point that Johnny quit using meth, opting to stick to smack, which at least had the advantage of making him less aggressive.

In the US, scoring smack is an often grim ritual of getting to know the relevant vendors or spots where it's possible to cop. Look for the man on the corner, mumbling the name of the brand he's selling for a few dollars per glacine bag – 'Red Devil' or 'Public Enemy'. It can be a risky business, with a good chance of getting ripped off. If you've just arrived in a city it's very difficult to score without knowing the local connections. On tour, this inevitably led to problems among the Dolls' junkie faction. No dope simply meant no gig, as the process of withdrawal – which includes gushing bodily fluids from every available orifice – would simply not allow it. Johnny and Jerry's problems were solved when Steve Leber unwittingly engaged a new tour manager who also happened to be a drugs dealer. 'The guy used to knock on our door and sell us heroin,' says Sylvain. While this cosy arrangement solved the short-term problem of scoring, the long-term effect of regular heroin use was unsurprisingly amplified. Eventually, even Sylvain and David were tempted to dabble – but fortunately had the good sense not to land themselves with an addiction.

On Mondays 12 and 19 August, the Dolls returned to Club 82. No matter how much fun they had at the venue, it was still another small club gig. Arthur sang Ricky Nelson's 'Poor Little Fool' and, for a change, the band veered away from pushing the album in favour of a mess of covers, which included an indulgent fifteen-minute jam on Junior Walker's 'Shotgun'.

Melody Maker's Chris Charlesworth was there and noticed the Dolls' lack of progress venue-wise. He wrote that Club 82 was, 'hardly the kind of venue for a band with two British tours and two albums under their belt. An obvious step down, in fact, and a sure fire pointer that all is not well in the Dolls camp . . . In a club, a small, sweaty, noisy, crowded basement like the 82, the Dolls are perfect. On a concert stage, exposed before the eyes of a few thousand, their imperfections stand out like sore thumbs. Perhaps that's why I finally understood the Dolls on Monday.'

Charlesworth – accurately, in retrospect – compared the deflating of the Dolls to that of another band later honoured for pivoting a generation – the Velvet Underground, whose final gigs in New York were on the same level. In two years, the Dolls had gone from being red hot, with the world at their feet, to a glorified bar band playing toilet gigs in order to keep afloat. There was internal conflict and constant drug hassles, which stifled their creativity and ensured that little new material was ever attempted. Some waggish cynics even suggested that their pharmaceutical facilitator-road manager was brought in by Leber and Krebs to keep the Dolls sedated.

A gig at the Joint in the Woods in the wilds of Parsippany, New Jersey, that August, summed up the dire situation. The Dolls showed up two hours late, dead drunk. Johnny dropped his guitar while Johansen forgot his words, and an amp blew. While the Dolls might not have been completely falling apart, they were obviously in trouble, and this was exacerbated by the manner in which the group had begun dividing into factions. On the one hand, Johnny and Jerry were united by their smack habits, while David and Syl had managed to keep their shit together to the extent that they both entertained notions of progressing the band creatively. Arthur, who was drinking far more than Sylvain and Johansen, was left to his own devices, which usually involved a doomed cycle of repeatedly clambering aboard then falling off the wagon.

'Arthur had a drinking problem,' David would later acknowledge, with understatement. 'At that time and at certain other times he would be too incapacitated to play. Arthur came back at various times. He went through a period when he lost a lot of his self-confidence and things. But he was always on the road with us.' As David later explained to *Q*'s Mat Snow, Arthur's innocent, open nature generally compensated for his drunkenness, and kept him in the band, 'What could you do with him?' smiled David. 'He was like a big doll. He was so sweet, and such a drunk. We used to put him in rehab, and he'd come out and you'd find he had bottles hidden all over the place. When you're that age, what the hell can you do? You're having enough trouble keeping your own pants on. We tried.'

This view of the amiable bass Yeti is reiterated by Rick Rivets. 'Arthur was a very gentle person and he was not the kind of person who if he drank would get loud – quite the opposite. He would get very quiet and would talk in a soft manner and never would get obnoxious or bother anyone. He kept to himself and would watch sci-fi movies on TV or listen to records. Of all the times we went drinking together I can't remember him ever getting loud or unruly. He was always a pleasure to be around and would come up with some very witty comments that would have us laughing for hours as he had a very good sense of humour.'

But when asked in 2005 if Arthur was a happy drunk or a miserable alcoholic, Sylvain replied, 'No, no, he was a sad case. The poor guy.' The 'romance' of heroin addiction and its attendant withdrawals isn't far removed from the reality of needing a drink in the morning, so that you can actually pick up a glass to do so. Arthur was in the hopeless trap where it's still possible to kid yourself that one glass of booze is just a kick-start for the day. In reality, he would've been thinking about nothing else but the next drink, rather than trying to come up with a new 'Private World'. So Arthur, now plastered in the alcoholic sense, remained in New York, attempting to dry out while the band went off on their next set of dates. He was an integral part of the Dolls and could never be fired. Peter Jordan simply resumed his stand-in role as the Dolls kicked off a further round of gigs at the Minneapolis State Fair on 1 September.

Too Much Too Soon sold 100,000 copies and made 167 on the *Billboard* album chart. Mercury gave the green light for a third album, but, given the parlous state of the band, getting them into the studio was always likely to be a tricky proposition. David and Johnny were at loggerheads and their working relationship had broken down. Their personalities and aspirations were totally opposite – David was flash, loud and was upfront about the fact that he wanted to be a mega-star. To Johansen, Johnny's insistence upon remaining 'true' to his rock'n'roll roots appeared shortsighted and old-fashioned. When drunk, David could be boorish and hectoring, whereas Johnny's smack habit made him withdrawn and furtive – thus establishing a chalk and cheese dynamic. He preferred to let his guitar do the talking. Johnny's band ally, Jerry Nolan, was a more forceful character. Apart from providing Johnny with a surrogate father figure, he was his drug buddy. Jerry turned against David over what he saw as the vocalist's role in the mis-production of the two albums and Johnny followed suit. This led to an inevitable climate of mutual antagonism which, while the band could still play gigs and rehearse together, ensured that writing any more teenage anthems was next to impossible.

Leber and Thau were also at odds. Marty still wanted to get Mercury behind the Dolls, while Leber was content to keep sticking them in little clubs. He promised them a trip to Japan if they cleaned up and got rid of Thau. Johnny and Jerry liked the idea of going to Japan and recording a third album, but there was little hope of a unanimous band vote. Mercury, losing both faith and patience at the lack of return on their investment, began suggesting session men as a reliable means of getting a third Dolls album in the can. They mooted bubblegum kings Kasenetz-Katz – who Marty would have known from his Buddah days – as possible producers. Given the duo's methods, this would almost certainly have meant David planting his vocal over a pre-recorded backing track, and found little favour with Marty or the band.

The Dolls started September in Vancouver, Canada, before returning to home territory for a gig at Jimmy's on 52nd Street on the 13th. These dates were followed by a gig in Denver, Colorado, before the band headed South to Florida for a four-day stint at Dallas' 16 Club between the 16th and 19th. They then headed back up to Canada for a gig in Toronto on 21 September and Montreal on the 27th. The recording of this gig shows the Dolls gouging even deeper into a repetitive furrow. They were still playing much the same set as they did six months earlier, aside from the addition of a rump-shaking version of Eddie Cochran's 'Something Else'. Maybe as a kind of resignation to their eternal bar band status, the Dolls also started featuring a cover of 50s R 'n' B rocker Larry Williams' 'Dizzy Miss Lizzy' around this time.

Marty Thau decided to bow out at the end of the month. Two years before, he had thought he was taking on the best rock'n'roll band in the world and that he would clean up. Although he still had faith in the Dolls, the lack of support from Leber, Krebs and Mercury and the creative stasis caused by internal divisions had created a situation whereby the band were moving in ever decreasing circles.

'[Leber and Krebs] were too strait-laced in their views,' said Marty. 'It got to such a point where I was so frustrated with my partners and the confusion amongst the Dolls, who were being torn at by every force around them, that I just said, "I'll step back for six months, for the purposes of not sinking the ship. You're not gonna phase me out 'cos I have my contracts as well. Let me see if you can deliver," and they proceeded to drive the Dolls down to the clubs in New Jersey.

'At that point I approached the Dolls and said, "Look, we're either gonna get it straight with Leber and Krebs and go back to our earlier working relationship and close our eyes to all the forces and opinions about us from everywhere, and do a third album," which Mercury was gonna finance, "and it'll come."'

Of course, getting straight was easier said than done. 'I tried to tell the Dolls to show them they could work and make a record, instead of just partying,' recalled Marty. 'Ultimately, all they had to do was write some new songs.'

Recording engineer Jack Douglas, who David kept in touch with, had agreed to produce a demo of Syl's 'Teenage News' at the Record Plant. It was a disaster. Johnny, who had a new song called 'Pirate Love', didn't turn up. Jonesing Jerry went off to cop and Arthur had a bad case of the shakes. Nothing got done. Throughout all this, it seemed like only Sylvain was keeping his shit together, but this letdown – for once they were doing one of his songs – was his own signal that the Dolls were collapsing. Syl desperately wanted the band to carry on and fulfil its obvious potential. He tried to maintain morale and acted as an intermediary between the warring camps. 'The song that was supposed to save the New York Dolls but we never got to use it,' mourns Syl of 'Teenage News'. 'It was not only our comeback but our final demise.'

There were still gigs to do, but the Hollywood Street Revival And Dance – which took place at the Hollywood Palladium on 11 October – had the air of a golden oldies review as it roped together a grab-bag of names who were celebrating trash rock'n'roll.

Los Angeles had enjoyed parallel scenes to New York during the sixties. In the first half of the seventies, after the Velvets had countered the sunshine love sound, its whole plastic starlet flutter was ruled by Rodney Bingenheimer and veteran reprobate Kim Fowley. The duo headed this LA glitterati-farty trash celebration, which even saw the former GTOs showing up. Iggy Pop also put in an appearance, along with former Turtles and Zappa backing singers Flo & Eddie. The show was a celebration of a scene based on celebrity, glamour and excess, but in many ways was similar to one of those sixties tribute packages with the Searchers and sub-Beatles beat boom bands.

NME's Richard Cromelin described the event as 'a wake' for a scene whose sell-by date had already flashed past in less than fifteen minutes. He laid into the Dolls – 'It's really a trash band, with a bad, mushy sound, and now a definitely tiresome image that can't hold them up much longer . . . the Dolls are hooked to a time that's inexorably rolling away, and their only redeeming feature is the perversely fascinating way they cling suicidally to their path to oblivion.'

The LA show saw a brief rekindling of the ongoing Starr-Thunders romance, to the extent that Sable accompanied her wayward guitarist back home. The reunion didn't last, as Johnny remained prone to bouts of drug-induced violence. Sable opted to stay in New York where she ended up sharing a flat with Nancy Spungen.

These were not the good times. Staunch Dolls supporter Paul Nelson quit his desk at Mercury to take up a job on *The Village Voice*, New York's weekly lifeline, where he would join the new strain of cult rock journalists such as Robert Christgau, Jon Landau, Lester Bangs and Dave Marsh. The hammer really fell when Mercury's big cheese Irwin Steinberg, having not received any new demos, pulled the plug on any further Dolls-related expenditure. He demanded that the group pay back all loans and expenses, including hotel damages.

On 7 October 1975 Mercury officially washed its hands of the New York Dolls. Phonogram's East Coast A&R Director Donna Halper explained, 'The New York Dolls contract expired on 8 August 1975. We had a two LP deal with them and it was decided at that time not to renew their contract. The reality is that neither of their LP's sold very well. Not only that, but they were costing us huge amounts of money because of their tendency to destroy hotel property. I truly believe that the company tried to be fair and patient with the Dolls, but as talented as they were, they were a continued source of aggravation for us.'

Marty Thau still held strong views about the ill-fated relationship between the Dolls and their record company. 'From the beginning when I found them to 1975, Mercury Records didn't think they were selling as well as they should have sold. The facts were: the first album sold 110,000 copies, the second sold maybe 100,000 copies, but because of all this interest and excitement in them they thought they'd go gold. I'd say, "Hey, I think this is pretty impressive what they've done. With all that's going against them, all they symbolise to a whole set which won't budge an extra inch, this is only a matter of time. It's pretty early. When the Dolls are gone, final sales of that album will be gold, platinum, whatever. They'll all catch up." But to the record company it was just too confusing and bitter a pill to swallow. They really didn't know . . . it's hard to sell something if they don't understand it, but I accepted that.'

As businessmen, it would be naïve to assume that Leber and Krebs had become involved in the Dolls for any other motive than to make a profit. When the band didn't turn into an instant money-spinner, they were happy to consign their charges to the bar-band treadmill.

Florida fanzine *New Order* carried an 'I Remember the New York Dolls' feature in its inaugural 1977 issue. Here Tony Porsche recalled a December 1974 Dolls gig at a Fort Lauderdale dive called the Flying Machine. The picture Tony paints is not a happy one: 'by this time the Dolls weren't the self-assured punks they once were. Johnny and Jerry were fed up and junked up. Arthur was too wasted to care. David and Syl made a vain attempt to look professional.' After mentioning that many kids couldn't get in because security was checking IDs at the door, Porsche remarks, 'Half the audience just wanted to see some genuine Nu Yawk weirdos and the other half had nuthin' to do. The Dolls knew this.' It was apparent that the endless party was finally over – both band and audience seemed to be going through the motions. 'Nobody clapped, nobody moved, nobody even booed, they just stared.'

Better Red Than Dead?

'The "no future" concept that spawned punk started with the Dolls. They paved the way and, in the process, made all the mistakes.' – *Marty Thau*

The Dolls' descent to bar band status coincided with a new musical revolution stirring in the New York underground. Just as the scene that had surrounded the Dolls revolved around an assortment of bands that regularly played the Mercer Arts Center, this new uprising was likewise centred on a specific location – a former biker bar at 315 Bowery, opposite the dead end of Bleecker Street, called CBGB & OMFUG.

In December 1973 the rundown bar had been taken over by Hilly Kristal, who had previously managed the Village Vanguard Jazz Club on Seventh Avenue, before opening a country music bar on Thirteenth Street. The initials stood for Country Blue Grass and Blues, with the OMFUG representing Other Music For Uplifting Gormandizers. It was originally going to be another steel guitar and checked shirt establishment, but there wasn't enough country in town and Kristal would quickly discover that finding gormandizers to uplift was equally difficult.

The first artist from the New York underground scene to play CBGB's was Wayne County, who debuted at the club early in 1974. The transgender queen of punk outrage (now known as Jayne County) recalls, 'I played CBGB's four whole months before Television with my band Queen Elizabeth. It was for a crowd of Hells Angels. They used to hang out there a lot before it became "cool" and the Ramones and Patti Smith started playing there. In fact, I'm the one who told Dee Dee Ramone about CBGB's. He was complaining about there being so few places to play in New York City, so I told him about it.'

'Looking fine on television' – *the Dolls mime for the cameras, 1973.*

The glammest gang in town – Johnny, Jerry, David, Arthur and Syl, 1973.

Little ole wine drinker Johnny takes a break, 1973.

Putting glam fashion on a pedestal – Arthur pushes the sartorial envelope on The Don Steele Show, *1973.*

Top left: Dinner and dancing – a ticket for the Dolls' Biba concert, 26 November 1973. Top right: Disc *magazine announces the Dolls' 1973 UK invasion. Above: Everything you'd hoped they'd be and more. Kris Needs attended the Dolls' 1973 Biba gig, where he took this rare live shot.*

David and Johnny get close at Biba's, 1973.

'Like a prima ballerina ...' David performs his 'Personality Crisis' routine, 1973.

The Dolls camp it up in Gay Paree, 1973.

The New York
Dolls in Too Much
Too Soon, *their
second album,
1974.*

Syl, David and Johnny harmonise, 1974.

Syl puts his best stack-heeled foot forward, 1973.

In Pete Frame's 'Dolls Family Tree', Television guitarist Richard Lloyd explained how the band blagged their way to a booking. 'In April [1974], Tom [Verlaine] and I were walking down from his house to the loft in Chinatown, and we passed this place, which the owner, Hilly Kristal, was outside fixing up. We asked if maybe we could play there and he told us he was going to call the place Country Blue Grass and Blues. So we said, "Yes, we play stuff like that" . . . He gave us a gig, so we got a whole bunch of friends down and convinced him to give us every Sunday for a month.'

The bar's tawdry location added to its excitement. In 1974, the Bowery-Lower East Side was still considered dangerous, even to the point of being a no-go area for more timid revellers. The club was dark, narrow and illuminated inside by neon beer signs. Next door was the Palace Hotel, another of the city's flophouses and a major haven for the ubiquitous Bowery bums. The doorway of the club reeked of hobo piss, a fragrance that tended to follow you inside.

Although Wayne County was the first notable act to play at CBGB's, it was Television's residency that really established the venue as the place to hear cutting edge rock'n'roll. Their bass player, Richard Hell, was well connected with the earlier scene and was going out with Sylvain's old girlfriend Elda Gentile. Both Elda and Debbie Harry had left their intermittent girl group, the Stillettoes, and had taken much of their old band along with them. Reforming as Angel and the Snakes, the frontwomen were joined by Amanda Jones, plus Chris Stein on guitar, Fred Smith on bass, and Billy O'Connor on drums. 'Chris calls it the last of the glitter groups,' recalled Debbie. 'It was a sort of campy Shangri-Las-Supremes type of girl trio. We had a lot of fun but we weren't too musical, you know. The record companies at that time were not interested.' Angel and the Snakes managed a mere two gigs at CBGB's, before splitting to begin a process that would result in the formation of Blondie.

Debbie and Chris were invited to rehearse at Performance Studios, around the corner from Max's, by Tommy Erdelyi – who they knew from the Mercer as 'Scotty', the guitarist in a neighbourhood glam band called Butch. Debbie and Chris had recently caught Tommy's debut as a drummer with the newly formed Ramones and had invited the band to play at CBGB's.

Just as the legacy of the Velvet Underground had influenced the early 1970s milieu that the Dolls had dominated, the Dolls' energetic approach to rock'n'roll provided the fertile loam in which bands such as the Ramones and Blondie took root. 'The Dolls demonstrated that if you possessed the essence of rock'n'roll, it didn't really matter how good you could or couldn't play,' Tommy Erdelyi told *Mojo* in 2005. 'It wasn't like I didn't already know this, but the recognition hit me like a thunderbolt.'

Aside from Television, who took their cues from the Velvet Underground and the symbolist poetry of Arthur Rimbaud, the Dolls' kinetic reworking of the girl-group pop aesthetic was an evident influence on several of the bands that would come to typify the scene. In particular, the Ramones and Blondie quickly developed their own unique interpretations of the Shangri-Las' bubblegum sensibility. Johnny Thunders was the first of the Dolls to catch on to the CBGBs vibe, and it wasn't unusual to see him get up to jam at Blondie's early gigs.

Guided by Bob Gruen, *Melody Maker*'s Chris Charlesworth covered the activity around CBGB's for a major feature which appeared under the headline of 'Tacky!' The article was topped with a photo of the inappropriately named Another Pretty Face, whose makeup and pouts were an obvious attempt at evoking a slab of pure Dolls style – although the result was more akin to British sub-glam gurners Chicory Tip. Charlesworth observed, 'Excitement, sweat, crude and simple music and a "take-it-or-leave-it" attitude mingle together in this new generation of bands.'

He went on to compare what he witnessed at CBGB's and the more established Club 82 with the pub rock scene that was becoming prevalent in the UK, while describing the music as 'pretty duff', and 'shameless punk rock'.

The Dolls' influence on what was to become globally recognised as punk rock was chiefly derived from their willingness to get up and play, regardless of any technical shortcomings. However, in 1974, Charlesworth noted that it was the band's *outré* imagery that appeared to be providing many of these new bands with significant inspiration. 'Shock and outrage is the name of the game: the more freakish, the more outlandish the fetishes of the personnel and the more bizarre their clothes the better. It's not much more than grabbing a guitar, learning a few chords, applying lipstick and bingo!' He concluded by identifying the Dolls' influence. 'Regardless of musical merit they cannot be accused of jumping on the bandwagon as they started it rolling in the first place. The Dolls are really outside the confines of underground New York by now: they've released a couple of albums and toured on a countrywide basis.'

Within months it would be evident that something exciting was happening at CBGB's, and it wouldn't end there. As the new subgenre coalesced, it quickly became apparent that many of the CBGB's groups would take the Dolls' musical reductivism to new minimalist levels. These bands would also carry this innate simplicity over into the way they looked – dressing down rather than glamming up.

Rather than establishing the New York Dolls as venerable forefathers, this had the effect of making the band seem like old hat. Additionally, the sense of glamour that suffused the Dolls' sound and image was abandoned in favour of the grittier fashions of the street. This time around, those who were in the gutter had little interest in looking at the stars.

'See, what the CBGB's thing was all about in the beginning was to be able to play our own music, what we wanted to play, instead of fucking hits,' reminisced Willy DeVille. 'Hilly Kristal was the first to say, "Play what you want." So that's how that started. Then somebody came up with the name "Punk" . . . this is the new bunch of bands. All the bands that have been playing together for the last fifteen years, they're older guys, they're out of ideas. . . The music is coming from the street.'

These new bands regularly credited the Dolls with paving the way for their subsequent success. But even if the Dolls were looked upon as punk progenitors, their current state of disarray and reputation for unreliability and misbehaviour ensured they found it difficult to get gigs. Whereas the debut albums from Blondie, the Ramones, Television and art rockers Talking

Heads would receive global acclaim, the Dolls became increasingly marginalised. The lineage had moved on and the Dolls found themselves drifting behind the surge of the incoming cultural tide. 'The music at CBGB's was so different from anything we were hearing elsewhere, and it was even different to the Dolls,' as Leee Black Childers would explain.

In London, Malcolm McLaren was horrified to learn of the decline of the Dolls, but recognised the band's need for a makeover. He'd continued to run his boutique, but had also set the wheels in motion to start a band drawn from some of the young ne'er-do-wells hanging around in his shop. McLaren remained enraptured by the Dolls and had already begun assimilating elements of their style into his fashion designs. Viewing the Dolls as the perfect template for the group that he was assembling, he instructed guitarist Steve Jones to learn how to play to their first album. 'Malcolm had this big thing about the New York Dolls,' said Pistols drummer Paul Cook. 'He was fascinated with them. He loved New York and thought it was all so great.'

Malcolm felt strongly that the Dolls shouldn't go under. In January 1975, he hooked up with the band and offered to provide some organisational assistance – much to the surprise of Marty Thau. 'I used to see Malcolm McLaren, who loved the Dolls, at their shows,' he said. 'Suddenly he was in New York and trying to resurrect them.'

'Malcolm was kind of sick of London for a while,' David told Pete Frame. 'He wanted a change and wanted to broaden his horizons, so to speak. He was a pal of ours and helped us a lot. He helped us arrange some shows and things like that. He was good to us. He didn't ask for any particular monetary compensation and he was learning from us as well. There was no pretence about it. It was all pretty up front.

'We had written a song called "Red Patent Leather", which was a red concept song. It was all about red, everything that was red – Indians, the communists, red patent leather – all kinds of overtones. So we decided we wanted red patent leather pants, shirts and everything. So we got Malcolm to make them for us. I figured the natural backdrop for that would be a red drape, so we might as well make it a communist flag, because that's really red. So then we came out and said, "This is a communist party!" when we did our shows.'

'Vivienne got us outfitted,' recalls Syl. 'Malcolm McLaren and Johansen never had much to say to each other, but they locked eyes and said, "Well, now that everything is red, what about the red flag?!" Malcolm, of course, always has a political agenda to everything he does.'

Each outfit was created out of leather, rubber and vinyl, personalised with zippers, pockets and chains which pre-dated later Sex/Seditionaries creations. Johnny's boasted a skull-adorned bum-bag. 'The outfits were like rubberised and so tight and hard to get into you needed talcum powder!' laughs Syl. McLaren, who saw the Dolls' makeover as a chance to promote his clothes, also provided a waistcoat and shirt ensemble for Jerry, plus a baggy red gabardine suit for David.

Malcolm also acquired a new loft rehearsal space on 23rd Street, which gave the band somewhere to practice. However, by this stage, rehearsal was low on the list of priorities for most of the band. Johnny and Jerry were full-blown junkies while Arthur's long-term booze problem continued to affect his increasingly distant performances. McLaren arranged for Arthur to receive medical insurance and put him into a New York clinic to dry out. 'It was a well known place, where a lot of famous people go because of the privacy and the area where it is located,' explains Rick Rivets. 'I don't know how long he was in, but he did complete the stay and I guess he might have relapsed some time after.' Malcolm also tried to get Johnny and Jerry into a drug rehabilitation programme, but they stubbornly refused to go.

Irrespective of his enthusiasm, and determination to rescue the Dolls from their largely self-inflicted decline, McLaren's arrival did nothing to address the factional conflicts within the band. Jerry, in particular, saw him as being in league with David, and readily identified Malcolm as not to be trusted, subsequently describing him as 'a parasite'. Johnny followed suit, and expanded his resentment from David toward this weird looking English guy who was trying to dress them up in communist fetish gear. When interviewed for *Please Kill Me*, Legs McNeil and Gillian McCain's groundbreaking oral history of the New York punk scene, Syl revealed that Jerry would say, 'Johnny, look at this guy . . . how we gonna become like the Beatles with this schmuck?' 'And Johnny would think, "He's right. This guy's an idiot." They didn't take Malcolm seriously, which was a mistake.'

If McLaren was trying to get the Dolls up and running, he was also using the experience to test the water for what could be possible back in London. By putting the Dolls under a communist flag, he realised he could potentially create a moral panic. In another move reminiscent of those adopted by John Sinclair and the MC5 half a decade earlier, he told journalists that the Dolls were now a 'people's communication centre'.

In keeping with this spirit of year zero reconstruction, the group wrote and rehearsed a new set, which all but supplanted its timeworn predecessor. New songs appeared, such as David and Syl's cod-funk 'Funky But Chic', 'Girls' and 'It's On Fire', along with the aforementioned 'Red Patent Leather'. David and Johnny managed to cooperate for long enough to pen a sleazy blues called 'Downtown', while previous third album candidates like Johnny's 'Pirate Love' and Sylvain's 'Teenage News' finally got an airing. They also added some new cover versions, which included Jimmy Ricks and the Raves' 'Daddy Rollin' Stone' and Clarence 'Frogman' Henry's 'Ain't Got No Home'.

So far as Jerry was concerned, the formulation of a new set provided the only crumb of consolation to be drawn from the new regime. 'Our spirits were pretty high when it came to having a new repertoire and all that. It was great.'

After a couple of low-key warm-up shows at the Coventry in Queens and My Father's Place on Long Island, McLaren managed to fix up the new-look Dolls with four gigs between 28 February and 2 March at New York's 2,000-capacity Little Hippodrome on 56th Street.

In a move that foreshadowed some of his Pistols-era proclamations, McLaren issued a press release headlined, 'What Are The Politics Of Boredom? Better Red Than Dead. Contrary to the vicious lies from the offices of Leber, Krebs and Thau, our former "paper tiger" management, the New York Dolls have not disbanded, and after having completed the first Red 3-D Rock'n'Roll movie entitled *Trash* have, in fact, assumed the role of the "People's Information Collective" in direct association with the Red Guard. This incarnation entitled "Red Patent Leather" will commence on Friday, February 28 at 10pm continuing on Saturday at 9 and 11pm followed by a Sunday matinee at 5pm for our high school friends at the Little Hippodrome. This show is in co-ordination with the Dolls' very special "entente cordiale" with the People's Republic of China. New York Dolls, produced by Sex originals of London c/o Malcolm McLaren.'

The 'Red 3-D Rock'n'Roll movie' referred to a short film that the band had recently made for a Canadian TV station, that consisted of little more than the Dolls performing 'Trash' in an alley, resplendent in their new red garb. Although the footage has long been presumed lost, Bob Gruen took stills that day at the decrepit old movie studio in the Bronx. One would later provide the cover for the *Red Patent Leather Live* album.

Like Club 82, the Hippodrome was another venue more used to hosting drag shows than rock concerts, but the Dolls sold it out with reassuring ease. Support was provided by Television and Pure Hell, a black punk band led by a flamboyant character called Neon Leon, who would later gain notoriety by being in Sid Vicious' hotel room on the night that Nancy Spungen was killed.

In between bands, Wayne County had been hired to DJ. While this practice quickly became commonplace, in 1975 it was practically unheard of for a group to have a DJ playing records to establish an appropriate mood. Wayne was called in to replicate the ambience he'd been cooking up at Max's for a few years now, and duly served up a selection of glam and garage by the likes of Paul Revere and the Raiders, the Castaways, the Seeds, the Velvets, the Sonics, the Stones, the Pretty Things and Iron Butterfly, plus more current glitter rock by Slade, Bowie, Suzi Quatro, the Sweet and Mott. During his set, Wayne was bemused when Johansen handed him an album of Communist Workers Party songs and asked him to play it before the group came on. 'I was so embarrassed that I put the LP on and hid behind a curtain,' he recalls. Insult was added to injury when McLaren tried to stiff Wayne on his fee and ended up handing over 'a measly $50!'

To add to the chaos, Arthur had started drinking again, which meant, for the first three gigs, Peter Jordan had to stand in again. Arthur made a welcome return for the final show, but, as Wayne recalled, he 'was so drunk he couldn't play and they had to get Peter Jordan to hide behind the bass amp and play while Arthur's guitar was turned off. It was a scream.' After the second show, Jerry's habit again got the better of him, so Spider from Pure Hell stood in.

However, despite the ill-judged communist motifs, the unfamiliar set and general drug and booze-induced chaos within the band, the shows went over astonishingly well. Debbie Harry remembers the Hippodrome run as 'some of the best shows they ever did', with *New Order* fanzine's Tony Brack later concurring that one of the shows was 'agreed to be the best gig they've ever done'. Yet Bob Gruen claims 'No one ever took 'em seriously at all.'

Having reintroduced the Dolls to New York, McLaren wanted to take the band to the provinces. With the assistance of Syl's cousin Roger Mansour –

who had been the drummer with 1960s soul-influenced garage band the Vagrants – a string of shows around Florida was arranged, where support would be provided by ex-Fogg drummer Stu Feinholtz-Wylder's latest group, Age. Although this tour can be viewed as a dry run for the disastrous string of dates that McLaren organised for the Sex Pistols at the start of 1978, at the time the plan was to gig the band relentlessly in the sticks in order that they could return to New York, road-tested and ready, to reclaim their place at the heart of the Big Apple's rock scene.

With hindsight, the Dolls' flirtation with communist chic was always liable to derail this gameplan. If sporting high heels and lipstick didn't go down very well with the rednecks, the new look was likely to guarantee murderous hostility from these owlhoot audiences. This didn't just apply to the good ol' boys – many American rock fans at that time were staunchly conservative under their long hair and sloganed t-shirts. This particular move was literally a red rag. Aside from the fact that thousands of young Americans had died fighting the communist NVA in Vietnam, the Cold War ensured that much of the US equated communism with evil. Additionally, Florida was not that far away from America's Deep South, where racism and bigotry were deeply ingrained. The Dolls' music, lifestyle and image had never been widely embraced – 'So we were supposed to come out of that?' reflects Syl 30 years on. 'We're all trying to make the fucking world a better place because it fucking sucks, but this is 1975 and the Vietnam War was still going on. In other words, America is still fighting the communists, in blood. In the USA too. It wasn't the best move. Hanging up that fucking flag was the death of the Dolls.' Johnny couldn't have cared less. When asked if he was a communist he replied, 'Yeah, what of it?'

On top of the hostile receptions, the Dolls were hardly firing on all cylinders. After the first gig of their Florida jaunt, Arthur again fell off the wagon, which necessitated Peter Jordan's return. Furthermore, the *froideur* between David and Johnny increased when the guitarist began moving in on David's main squeeze Cyrinda Foxe. 'I don't think it was a very smart idea sleeping with each other's girlfriends and things like that, to put it mildly,' observes Syl. 'I don't really wanna get into the details, but with all due respect though, combine that with the ups and downs of the music business. When the band starts screwing each other's wives, then complicate that with addictions and money problems. You know you're this big thing and then you don't have anything the next day. It's not an easy thing. Hey, it can break your heart.'

The band was holed up at a trailer park in Crystal Springs, outside Tampa, which was owned by Jerry's mother's new husband. Johnny and Jerry's smack supply dried up when their local dealer was busted. The duo became increasingly hostile to David, Malcolm, the red outfits and the whole tour with each passing minute

Being housed in a trailer in 100-degree heat, with half the band going cold turkey, created just the sort of pressure-cooker environment that the Dolls could have lived without. Demonstrating an unhappy knack of making a bad situation intolerable, David provided the final straw. 'Johansen was getting lushy drunk,' recalls Syl. 'He was sort of an abusive drunk. He would tell you that you didn't matter, and he was the singer, and he could go on his own, and he didn't need your hang-ups and your bullshit. Basically, he said that to us one day after dinner, and Johnny and Jerry, after they heard they could be replaced again and again, just walked out. And I drove them to the airport.'

'Me and Jerry left because we felt we weren't getting anywhere playing our old songs in tiny clubs,' said Johnny. 'The group was getting stale and staying behind the times, not advancing in any way,' added Jerry. There was obviously a major rift between the Thunders-Nolan axis and Johansen. 'He thought anybody could be replaced, especially when Malcolm came in,' said Jerry. 'They felt they were going to take over the world, but they were doing everything but rock'n'roll music.'

'It was a drag being on the road and they couldn't cope,' rebutted David. 'As long as they had stuff, everything was OK. It wasn't as if we had a medicine crew with us to take care of that kind of stuff. It was every man for himself, so John and Jerry would have to go back to New York and score. It got kind of ridiculous.'

'We were still playing the old songs and we'd written half a new set,' Johnny recalled. 'Me and Jerry wanted to go back to New York and do some new songs and have a whole new set, instead of playing the same old stuff, and they wanted to stay in Florida and play those dates and all these hip places. We didn't think it was the right thing to do so me and Jerry split.'

Two years after the event, Jerry recognised that the very nature of the New York Dolls served to hasten their demise. 'We had a lot of people against us, but we always had a lot of people against us in the beginning, so I know that ain't the reason. I think it had a lot to do with the band and me personally. I don't like to say I blame David, but I hold David responsible for a lot of things. Important things, like the fuckup with the Dolls' sound on record that was the major downfall of the band. If you listen to our records, you don't hear or see anything about the way we really were or what we could have been. If we were recorded properly we would have had the strength of our records and we would have backed that up with our stage performances. Now if we didn't back 'em up then okay, fine, you can accept that. At least you still have that black piece of plastic. That can prove a lot. But we didn't have that, so that was our big downfall.

'Then when the group itself was having problems, no matter that they were falling apart, that was the end. I wasn't going to stand doing the same mistakes over and over again. We kept on getting in the same rut. I was fed up, I don't care what band they were. I don't care if they were the greatest band in the world, which they were at one time. Who cared if they were the New York Dolls? I was gonna leave 'em because they weren't producing what they were supposed to and they weren't giving the kids what the kids wanted, and what we promised the kids in the beginning. We made a vow amongst ourselves that we promised that we'd give those kids the right sound in what we were rebelling against and everything. We were gonna give 'em what we started the whole group for. Then we backed out in a way, especially David. He says, "They'll buy anything, I don't really care . . . ah, let it go, they'll fix it in the studio." It don't go like that, man. You gotta get that fucking right performance down, then you can work on it. I don't think I'm a perfectionist but, compared to them, I was.'

In 1978, Pete Frame asked David if there was any great unrest in the ranks before the split. 'Not particularly,' he understated. 'It just got to the point where we were getting on the verge of being repetitious as far as the Dolls image was concerned. It was getting kind of albatrosstic. People were expecting us to fulfil a certain image that certain days we weren't. It just came to a point where we said, "Fuck it, let's not do it any more."'

Johnny's explanation was typically succinct. 'It just happened. It was a personality crisis.'

Sylvain gave his take on the split to *New York Rocker*'s Ellen Callahan in 1977. 'We didn't really break up,' he insisted. 'We just never went any place because basically I wasn't in control of the situation, and obviously no one else wanted to do anything or else we would have . . . The Dolls were like five freaks, five individual leaders going off in our own directions. Even when we played we all had our own audiences.'

The smack drought had brought Johnny and Jerry's discontent to a sweating, sniffling culmination. Desperate to cop, the pair upped and flew back to New York. 'The Dolls went down to Florida with McLaren to begin a tour, and about twenty minutes later we all heard that Johnny Thunders and Jerry Nolan had left the group,' Debbie Harry recalled. 'Another twenty minutes later, we all heard about the Sex Pistols who, coincidentally, looked like a combination of Television and the Dolls. You have to hand it to Malcolm, he's got an ace sense of showbiz.'

Everyone seemed to have their own take on the sad demise of the New York Dolls. In 1977, Patti Smith – by then New York's biggest ascending star – told *New Order* fanzine that she didn't think they put enough work in. 'With the Dolls they were so much into image. It wasn't the people's fault with the Dolls. You can't just want to look like a magazine.'

When interviewer James Marshall maintained that they sounded great too, Patti replied, 'Yeah, but what I'm sayin' is they stopped working. They stopped progressing. They didn't want to tour, they didn't want to pay any dues. They went into this business thinking it's all limousines and it ain't. It's like being in the Army. It's heartbreaking stuff and it's tough work.'

'We told David we were sick of the Dolls and that we were going back to New York to start again,' insisted Johnny. 'He said, "Anyone in this band can be replaced," but when we left, that was the end of the Dolls. The *only* Dolls.'

Like Johnny, Jerry was always adamant that, after they left, 'There are no Dolls.' However, David had his own ideas. There were still some remaining bookings to fulfil, so Arthur approached local guitarist Blackie Goozeman to round out the line-up for these obligations. 'They threw Johnny out of the band,' recalled Blackie, 'and I had known the guys before that, 'cause I'd met Arthur and stuff prior to that. So, I ran into him in a bar, and he used to say, "You wanna join the band?" And I thought, "Oh, he's drunk again."' Eventually Arthur and Syl convinced Blackie that they were on the level and the nineteen-year-old formerly known as Stephen Duren agreed to make up the numbers.

Goozeman had relocated to Florida from Staten Island, after a stabbing incident prompted his father to ship him south to military school to remove him from local gang action. His tenure at the academy was short lived, as after two years he was thrown out for beating up a sergeant-major. By the time he was sixteen, Blackie – who had started by playing his brother's guitar when he was nine years old – was a regular on the local bar circuit with bands such as Black Rabbit and Orfax Rainbow. On hooking up with the Dolls, he was plunged into what he later described as a 'baptism of fire'. 'They were the only band I ever knew that sat in an airplane terminal, missing five flights in a row because one guy was getting a blowjob in the bathroom, and the other was passed out under a table, and shit like that.'

Once the Florida dates were finished at the end of April 1975, the remaining Dolls went their separate ways. Johansen returned to New York to plot his next move in the belief that, as the loquacious, charismatic frontman, he could waltz into a solo career. Sylvain and McLaren hung on to the Dolls' hired station wagon and drove to New Orleans 'to cool off and hang out,' recalls Syl. 'He was telling me all about this "next phase" he had planned, and how he was going to go back to London and start a new band.'

After catching a mild STD and befriending a Cajun midget, Malcolm decided to return to London, keen to put into practice the lessons he'd learned on the Dolls doomed road trip.

As he left, Malcolm promised Sylvain he would keep in touch with a view to bringing the guitarist over to hook up with his new group. 'The Sex Pistols was supposed to be my band,' explains Syl 'I have the seven-page letter which Malcolm wrote to me in the summer of 1975 telling me that I should be coming to England and that this is my band and forget Johansen . . . He sent me these photos taken in a photo-booth of them before they looked like the Sex Pistols. There was this guy and it said, "Yes and we're thinking of calling him Johnny Rotten." All that's now hanging in the rock'n'roll Hall of Fame in Cleveland, with Johnny's guitar, David's jacket, pictures and shit. It's in the section where they start dealing with punk rock or new wave or whatever.' Consequently, Syl agreed to part with his Les Paul guitar and electric piano to help Malcolm's latest venture get up and running. 'I'm still waiting for the plane ticket,' he deadpanned.

Arthur was left with a post-Dolls hangover he found difficult to bear. 'I didn't want to back to New York after the failure of the Dolls,' he told Nina Antonia. 'It's funny how things change, you can be on top of the world and 30 seconds later, someone else is the next big thing and you get swept under.'

Accompanied by Blackie and the remnants of the Dolls' PA, Arthur set about forming the Killer Kane Band with guitarist Andy Jay and drummer Jimi Image. 'We came to LA and we couldn't walk down the street,' recalled Blackie. 'I remember Arthur Kane making the comment one day when we were walking down Sunset Boulevard and someone was throwing something at us from a car . . . he said, "If we can make them look here then we can make them look anywhere." It was pretty rough.'

Back in New York, Johnny and Jerry were now managing to function after resuming their junk connection. Johnny temporarily moved in with his sister Mariann and her husband Rusty, who attempted to help him out by taking him on as a trainee plumber. 'That ended fast,' Rusty explained to film-maker Lech Kowalski. 'Two days of getting up at four in the morning and working for fourteen hours a day – That wasn't for Johnny. He wasn't much of a physical labour kind of guy.'

Realising that his best option was to get a new band together, Johnny briefly reunited with the now Stooge-less Iggy Pop. They talked of doing something but the pair never got past a predictably bleary loft rehearsal. This was no big disappointment to Johnny, as he had already decided he didn't want to share the stage with another frontman.

Nor did Richard Hell, who had left Television three days before Johnny and Jerry split Florida. Having been creatively marginalised by Tom Verlaine, Hell was keen to form his own group as an outlet for his songs. With his proto-punk spiked hair and safety-pinned t-shirts, Hell was in demand and had already turned down overtures from McLaren to front the London-based group which was supposed to include Syl. Johnny, who knew Richard from CBGB's and had hung out with him before the Hippodrome gigs where Television supported the Dolls, phoned the bassist and asked if he'd like to start a new band with him and Jerry.

After establishing that he and Johnny would share the vocal and song-writing limelight on an equal basis, Richard agreed to give the new group a try and the trio began rehearsing almost immediately. 'We just had to get started,' Jerry told Pete Frame. 'We didn't find the right guy but we played anyway. It wasn't too bad. We just really had to play in front of people. We had some equipment. We managed to just come up with just enough stuff. We've always had friends that help us and lend us things. One thing about people in rock'n'roll is most of 'em will help you.'

Unlike his new bandmates, Richard Hell (nee Myers) was not a native New Yorker. He'd gone to school in Wilmington, Delaware, where he'd befriended a guy called Tom Miller who played guitar. By 1968, the pair had both relocated to Manhattan, where literary activity – Hell was publishing a poetry magazine – centred on the Strand bookstore at the top of St Mark's Place, which also employed Patti Smith. By 1971, Richard and Tom had got into acid, changed their names to Hell and Verlaine (after nineteenth-century poet Paul Verlaine, sometime lover of Rimbaud) and formed a short-lived group with drummer Billy Ficca called the Neon Boys. Two years on, Verlaine tried to start a solo career with Hell acting as his manager. In November, Television came together when guitarist Richard Lloyd was introduced to Tom by scene-maker Terry Ork and they decided to start a band, bringing back Ficca and persuading Hell to move to bass. Their first gig was on 2 March 1974, at New York's Townhouse Theatre on 42nd Street. After getting some good reviews, ex-Roxy Music electronics pioneer Brian Eno was engaged to produce some demos for Island Records while Blue Öyster Cult's Allen Lanier did the same for Arista, but no deal was forthcoming.

Looking for an outlet for his own songs, Hell left Television, to be replaced by Fred Smith from Blondie. Television would go on to become one of the first groups to release a privately pressed record when they put out 'Little Johnny Jewel' on Ork in October 1975. It served to reignite major label interest and, in 1976, Television signed with Elektra. This resulted in February 1977's acclaimed *Marquee Moon* album, the perfect representation of their unique blend of opiated lyricism and biting twin-guitar interplay.

The trio of Thunders, Nolan and Hell chose to call their new group the Heartbreakers – a name first coined by Syl, which referenced the band's somewhat fatalistic attitude. 'It's like the kids that never did anything right,' explained Johnny. 'Everyone they touch goes out of their mind, like someone who comes along and burns down your house. That's breaking your heart.'

The Heartbreakers made their debut at the Coventry in Queens on 29 May 1975, which Johnny laughingly described as 'a disaster' in *Zigzag* two years later. This was followed by their first CBGB's show on 3 June. By the time they returned to the Bowery bar on 25 June, they had gained a second guitarist and singer in the shape of Walter Lure, recruited from a local band called the Demons who had rehearsed in the same 23rd Street loft that McLaren had found for the Dolls. They'd originally offered the gig to Walter's bandmate and drug buddy Elliot Kidd, who spent the rest of his life – he died in 1998 – bitterly regretting having turned down Johnny's offer.

Walter had been a regular at Dolls gigs and had captured Johnny and Jerry's attention while playing with the Demons. 'We enjoyed Walter the best out of that band,' said Jerry. 'We thought he had potential. We auditioned him three or four times before he was totally accepted in the band, but I think it was well worth it . . . At first, maybe he wasn't exactly what we were looking for but the potential was what we were looking for. We felt it could certainly grow and he could become part of it. And he liked our ideas. The music we play is more of a feel.'

Born in 1950, Lure shared many of his musical influences with the two former Dolls, having grown up on Elvis, then the Beatles and the Stones. As a teenager he'd run with a gang called the Green Dogs, but had stuck at his studies and eventually spent five years working as a qualified chemist. However, Walter's love of music was stronger than his professional interest in pharmaceuticals, and he began playing guitar in a neighbourhood group called Bloodbath, before moving on to the Demons. He was a gangling, manic presence who made the Heartbreakers' frontline into a formidable three-prong attack.

When he wasn't playing with bands, Walter could always fall back on his second career as a pharmacist. In July, an eight-ounce jar of pure Quaalude powder came into his possession – which Johnny nagged his new bandmate to hand over. Promising that he could get as much as $1500 for the stash, Johnny wrested the powder from Walter and set about dipping into the jar for his own recreational purposes. This soured his relations with brother-in-law Rusty Bracken, who became irritated by his increasingly dissolute houseguest. 'Johnny was getting fucked up. He was getting nasty,' Rusty told Lech Kowalski. 'One word led to another and I whacked the shit out of him – which made me feel pretty terrible the next day, 'cos I was about 40 pounds heavier than him.' To Johnny's horror, Rusty then flushed the powder down the toilet.

Shortly after, Johnny moved in with his latest girlfriend Julie, who was pregnant from her previous relationship. The birth of the child, who was christened Johnny Jnr., brought out Thunders' parental instincts – he assumed the role of father readily, 'Little Johnny was not Johnny's son,' confirmed Mariann. 'Julie was pregnant when he met her. He had a good heart – He took care of little Johnny as if he was his own. My mum bought stuff for him – crib, carriage – Johnny cared for him. She had two children with Johnny – Vito was born in London.'

With their line-up complete, the Heartbreakers set about making their presence felt in New York, alternating between playing Max's and CBGB's. Thanks to a combination of the Dolls' reputation and Hell's credibility with Television, the Heartbreakers were embraced by the CBGB's crowd as established elder statesmen with attitude and killer rock'n'roll chops. The band produced flyers for these shows which featured the slogan 'Catch 'Em While They're Still Alive' under a Roberta Bayley photo of the group splattered in fake blood. In an early review, *Melody Maker*'s Steve Lake dismissed the Heartbreakers as a 'hopelessly discordant joke', but future Stiff Records boss, Jake Riviera, returning from a summer US tour as Dr Feelgood's manager, described them as the best rock'n'roll band he'd ever seen.

Both Johnny and Richard had built up a substantial corpus of material, which ensured that the Heartbreakers didn't have to pad out their live set with cover versions and crowd-pleasing Dolls oldies. Live, the differences between their creative approaches were fundamentally evident. Johnny wrote as he always did – simple, timeless rock'n'roll, while Richard's literary influences led him in more esoteric directions. Musically, the sparring between Thunders and Lure's guitars resulted in moments of dynamic interplay which evoked the power of the MC5's Wayne Kramer and Fred Smith, as well as a near-telepathic understanding reminiscent of Keith Richards and Ronnie Wood's axe partnership.

Pivotal Hell songs included 'Love Comes in Spurts', which usually started Heartbreakers sets (later, once Richard had left the band, the Heartbreakers would use this track as the basis for 'One Track Mind'). 'You Gotta Lose' was Hell's most basic rock number, while 'Blank Generation' – which dated from his Television tenure – was already established as a rollicking anthem of don't-give-a-shit nihilism.

Johnny revived 'Pirate Love' from the final days of the Dolls, as well as 'Goin' Steady', an update of the fifties-sixties teenage love ditty with a killer chorus and lines like 'I'm looking for a teenage cutie.' He also re-wrote the Actress era ballad 'I Am Confronted' as the lovelorn 'So Alone'. Johnny would later complain when Jerry wouldn't do slow songs like this but, during the Heartbreakers' honeymoon period, he was allowed to stretch into areas that showcased his subtler side. Freed from the restraints of being at the base of the Dolls songwriting totem-pole, Jerry chipped in by writing most of 'Can't Keep My Eyes On You', a wired, slightly unhinged beat-vamp that featured a naggingly repetitive chorus and one of Johnny's nastiest solos. Walter contributed a melodic pop outing called 'Flight'.

By early 1976, the Heartbreakers' set also featured 'Chinese Rocks', a bouncy yet brutal representation of the junkie lifestyle originally written by Dee Dee Ramone but rejected for inclusion on da brudders' albums by Johnny Ramone, who could live with references to solvents but not opiates. 'In those days, Johnny didn't want songs about heroin,' explained Joey

Ramone. 'So Dee Dee got real frustrated and he took it over to Johnny Thunders of the Heartbreakers. That was his clique: Johnny Thunders and Richard Hell. The Heartbreakers copped the song and it became their anthem. But Dee Dee wrote the song.' Employing the same kind of logic that would later insist 50 Cent's raps represented a cautionary warning against the gangsta lifestyle, Dee Dee observed, 'I don't know if anybody's gonna listen, y'know, but it's a good idea to write an anti-drug song, to try and discourage them from using the stuff.'

Despite the strength of their set and the positive response from New York audiences, internal tensions started to mount as Johnny again saw the spotlight being directed away from him. Having left Television to perform his own material, Hell often insisted on occupying centre stage. Johnny, having had a gutful of prima donna vocalists, wasn't enjoying the sense of *déjà vu*. 'I'd already had enough of being behind a front man and just getting the one song a night,' protested the guitarist. 'That's not why we started the Heartbreakers.' Leee Black Childers recalls Thunders and Hell coming to blows on stage – 'A lot of people would go for that reason.'

Relations between the competing frontmen were hardly strengthened when Richard started getting intimate with Sable Starr. Although Sable and Johnny were no longer an item, he still carried a torch for his ex and seeing her with Hell hurt.

By June 1976, the bad vibes came to a head when Richard attempted to enlist Jerry's support in booting Johnny out of the group. Hell badly underestimated the strength of Johnny and Jerry's relationship and his plan backfired spectacularly when Johnny quit, taking both Jerry and Walter along with him. Effectively, Richard had engineered his own dismissal from the Heartbreakers. 'He wanted to sing all the songs,' Johnny told *Zigzag*. 'Conflicts of interest – so I quit the band and the band came with me and stayed with me.'

'He thought we'd listen to him and get rid of Johnny, which was a big mistake,' added Jerry. 'No way. There's a certain friendship and loyalty between me and Johnny.

'I guess Richard left because he wasn't happy playing the kind of rock-'n'roll we were into. He's into the Television-Patti Smith vein, and we had to cater to him a lot. The longer he was in the band the more he wanted. We got tired of it because it stopped us from our own creating . . . Richard's not a very good musician. He's more interested in presenting himself as a poet. A lot of poets use music to get to where they wanna go, but we're better off without people like that in our band.

'I don't think we knew it but Richard joined the band with the intentions of doing something else in time. I think he more or less joined the Heartbreakers because it was the right thing to do at the time and it was the only thing to do at the time. He had something else in mind.

'He sort of wanted to play with me and Walter and he would've played with John if John didn't do nothing or take any part in being a frontman. And we didn't dig that.'

After his departure from the Heartbreakers, Richard set about putting together the Voidoids, which enabled him to occupy the frontman spot without opposition. The group included guitarists Bob Quine and Ivan Julian, plus Marc Bell, who had auditioned to replace Billy in the Dolls. They signed to Sire for an album the following year, inherited Richard's back catalogue and released 'Blank Generation' on Jake Riviera's newly established Stiff Records in October 1976.

The Heartbreakers duly cast around for a new bassist and turned up Billy Rath, a Bostonian who'd been orbiting the fringes of the CBGB's scene and claimed to have just finished a stint working in Florida as a gigolo. Born in 1949, Billy named his biggest influences as the Zombies and the Barbarians, a sixties garage-punk group who hit big one time with 'Moulty', a song about their one-armed drummer. Although he confessed to nurturing an ambition to spend a whole weekend with a Girl Scout troop, Billy harboured no desire to be a frontman – which suited Johnny. 'He'd played with a million com- mercial-type bands,' said Jerry. 'He's a real dedicated bass player. He's not much of anything except a bass player, actually. He's just into being a bass player – and he's a damn good bass player. That's his trip. He's a loner, in a way. Quite different from the rest of the band . . . In the long run he's good for the band. I think we need a guy like that.'

After a brief period of rehearsal, The Heartbreakers returned to action with a series of gigs at Max's and CBGB's. Nancy Spungen turned in a review of the 23 July Max's show for the recently-established *New York Rocker*, which had been started by Alan Betrock of *The Rock Marketplace* as a mouthpiece for insiders on the New York punk scene. It was their first gig without Hell, but she reckoned, 'The band were amazingly tight for a first performance. Jerry's already fine drumming sounded twice as good with a great bass player. Finally, Johnny and Walter were riffing off each other; both taking leads, both providing interspersing rhythms. All four members together created a perfect chemistry, a certain magic, if you will, and the audience sure knew it. They didn't seem to mind the loss of Richard Hell at all; receiving the familiar tunes with joyful fervour.'

In addition to pushing herself forward to write Heartbreakers reviews for *New York Rocker*, Spungen set her sights on screwing her way through the band and snarfing up any spare junk in the process. In 1976, heroin was commonplace in New York and Johnny and Jerry were veteran users. CBGB's was within minutes of literally hundreds of East Village-Lower East Side copping spots. At this time, Billy and Walter were relative newcomers to the junk scene but, inevitably, would get into it too – although not to the same extent as their bandmates. Nancy looked up to Sable, another dope- vet, and set out to emulate her, even down to copying her drug habits and ringlet hairstyle. She rapidly became an addict, and copping off with drug- using rockers was a good way to keep the smack coming.

The Heartbreakers' new line up functioned explosively well, the four indi- viduals bouncing off one another to whip up urgent rock'n'roll cyclones. Freed from the limitations of having to perform Richard Hell's songs, the quartet concentrated on creating new material and began rehearsing with uncustomary dedication and enthusiasm. This period produced a slew of material that would comprise the core of the band's set for the remainder of their career. Most songs were demoed at a studio in Staten Island. 'Those were our lucid days when we could talk in a straight line,' Walter later reflected.

'Born To Lose', a defiant slab of hard rocking fatalism became the Heartbreakers' anthem. Walter had written 'Get Off The Phone' before Hell's departure and rewrote it as 'Oh What Do You Do' now reverting the song to its original form, a rousing number which spliced Bowie's 'Hang Onto Yourself' to Cochran's 'Somethin' Else'. Johnny's 'Baby Talk' hijacked an old Yardbirds riff and featured lyrics that hit a Ramonic vertex of simplicity, with the bulk of the song comprised of the title and the phrase 'I don't mind.'

Now that the band had reconstituted their set and ventured as far as Boston and Cleveland, the obvious next move was to get some of their material down on vinyl. As Nick Kent had observed earlier in the year, 'The Heartbreakers are ready to break out of their tightly bound Lower West Side pitch . . . with some decent hard-sell record company backup.' However, this was easier said than done. 'The record companies were scared of us,' said Johnny. 'We had a bit of a reputation after the Dolls and the way that went.'

'We were building up a big following, drawing a lot, always capacity,' said Walter in 1977. 'Record companies didn't want to know because of the Dolls' reputation – talk about "uncontrollability", drugs, *et cetera* – much exaggerated.'

The Heartbreakers really needed a manager, so they asked Leee Black Childers – who had by this time initiated his career as a photographer – if he'd like to have a go at cracking the barrier of label resistance. Childers' previous management experience had been with Iggy in LA during 1973, so there wasn't much in the way of bad behaviour that could faze him. In Sullivan-Colegrave's *Punk*, Leee recalls, 'I called a friend and said I'd decided to manage the Heartbreakers, and he said, "Are you crazy? They're junkies, they're nuts."'

It quickly became apparent that the legacy of the Dolls, particularly Johnny, made getting a record deal next to impossible. 'The big problem that I ran into when I talked to record companies was that they had gained a reputation of not showing up for gigs,' explained Leee in an interview with Nina Antonia. 'Or doing two songs and storming off the stage and throwing things, and of course this was pre-punk days so it was totally unheard of that anyone could act like that and expect to sell records.' He added, 'Whenever Johnny's name was mentioned record companies didn't wanna know.'

Before they'd played a note, the Heartbreakers were tagged as junkie bad boys who'd wrecked the Dolls and couldn't be relied on. Not a secure investment. In their first few months of existence, it seemed as if the Heartbreakers were picking up where the Dolls left off and were destined to be big fish in a small New York pond.

Following the Dolls' Florida debacle, David Johansen had no wish to be in any group with Johnny or Jerry – who initially believed that there might be a possibility of a reconciliation. 'I had a lot of anger deep inside when me and Johnny left,' said Nolan later. 'When finally David came to the city, I had another talk to him but it wasn't gonna happen.' Together with Sylvain – who was not optimistic about the chances of receiving any concrete offers from McLaren – he hastily put together a Dolls line-up to carry out a highly lucrative ten-date tour of Japan arranged by a Japanese DJ named Yuya, who'd been introduced to David by Bob Gruen. 'We went over to Japan in July 1975 and did a whole tour,' recalled Johansen. 'The Dolls had always been very popular in Japan and we made a lot of money. More money than I'd made in a long time. So we came back and we didn't work again until December. We had enough money to live off.' Syl and David's post-Dolls survival fund was further boosted by a lucrative sponsorship by Ibanez guitars.

Peter Jordan, who'd been looking after Wayne County's live sound and had recently recovered from injuries received trying to stop an attempt to mug his wife, was promoted to full-time bassist and joined by Tony Machine on drums – who the original Dolls had encountered when he worked as a go-for for Leber and Krebs. Rather than enlist a second guitarist, Syl moved to lead and a keyboard player – Chris Robison from Elephants Memory – was brought in. Robison was an experienced musician who'd recorded a couple of gay-centric solo albums, and was suggested by Bob Gruen's wife, Nadya. 'She thought he might be quite capable because we wanted to get a band together in two weeks and go,' explained David.

The biggest show of the ersatz Dolls' Japanese tour came on 7 August at Tokyo's massive Korakuen stadium, where the band supported Jeff Beck in front of 45,000 people. The gig was far larger than any that the old Dolls had played and took place amidst a cloudburst – 'You know how shrivelled people look when they get out of the bath?' jokes Syl. 'Well they all looked like that.' Peculiarly, Johansen claimed to have spotted three UFOs hovering over the stadium as they played. The photos that appeared in Japanese rock magazines showed that the group had adopted a new, baggy-suited, hoodlum-type look. Bob Gruen went along for the ride, capturing the gigs in Tokyo and Kyoto on videotape. Much of the band's set consisted of songs from the red leather period interspersed with old favourites such as 'Frankenstein' and 'Personality Crisis', and a recording of the Tokyo gig later surfaced as the French *Tokyo Dolls Live* album.

Although David was initially reticent about attaching the New York Dolls names to what was effectively a Johansen/Sylvain revival band, the Japanese promoter had stipulated that the group be billed under their most famous nomenclature. However, the frontman was delighted by the way in which the new line-up gelled, telling *Circus*, 'We got this dynamite band together and we couldn't believe it. We practiced for about two weeks and it was magic.'

This synergy, and the lucrative nature of the Japanese dates, made it apparent that the Dolls, even in this watered down form, could still be a going concern. When *Melody Maker* ran a report on the tour toward the end of 1976, David was delighted to hear that the unidentified interviewer thought that the new line up represented a 'great improvement' on the old Dolls. 'Wonderful, it would take an Englishman to say that. See, all these Greenwich Village idiots are riddled with sentimentality. They genuinely are nostalgic for the old band. Isn't that incredible? Can you imagine anyone getting nostalgic for the New York Dolls?'

In December 1975, the new New York Dolls made their New York debut with a midnight show at the Beacon Theatre. 'We weren't really a band then,' David told Pete Frame. 'We'd just get up for a gig every once in a while. When we needed cash we used to work almost every weekend, two or three nights a week.

'We were very tempted to go at it again full speed – but I didn't want to get involved in terminal touring again; I wanted to be home. After you tour so much you tend to come home and your friends don't want to know you. So I wanted to just slow down and dig myself for a while. I didn't want to record but I had to make a living . . . so we just did weekenders – flew out to places like Detroit, Cleveland, Toronto, all over Ohio and New York. By doing that we made enough to live, while we sorted out our plans for the future.

But, as *New Order* fanzine's Peter Brack would write about a July 1976 gig at Max's, 'The new sound is keyboard dominated early sixties British invasion rock. Something was missing.'

In fact there was quite a lot missing; the absence of Johnny, Arthur and Jerry meant that the unique dynamic that infused the Dolls with their distinctive energy and dissolute appeal was lost forever. The new material was sub-standard, and, despite Johansen's intention to sell the ghastly 'Funky But Chic' to the highest bidder, he hardly found himself inundated with offers.

As 1976 wore on and punk rock broke on both sides of the Atlantic, it became apparent that the brief success of the band which Johansen now referred to as the 'Dollettes' was more of a last gasp than a fresh start. David began switching his focus toward launching his solo career, while Syl – who had seen the Sex Pistols take shape without him – finally admitted that the Dolls were finished. 'Me, Bobby and Tony worked real hard trying to pull something together. We were always told, "Hey, we're gonna go in the studio and make an album," but it just never happened. So we decided to go our own ways.'

No
Christmas
For Junkies

'We did get a reputation for drug-taking, but then
we did do a lot of drugs.' – *Walter Lure*

By the second half of 1976, the Heartbreakers' career horizon didn't extend
much beyond alternating gigs at Max's and CBGB's. 'There was no real talk
of the future or deals,' explains Leee Black Childers. 'The band were content
to earn the quite good money they made at the two downtown clubs, which
was enough to stay high – a priority – and to live [which was] less important.'
Even Sire, who had acted as a kind of clearing house for CBGB's bands like
the Ramones, Talking Heads and Richard Hell, steered clear. 'The Dolls were
such a rebellious band,' said Johnny. 'We did what we wanted to do.'

'Nobody wanted anything to do with us in the States,' he told Pete Frame
in June 1977. 'We had bigger audiences than most other New York bands, but
the business stayed away from us . . . they were afraid to touch us. They knew
we wouldn't do what they wanted us to. They knew we wouldn't follow the
system.' The Heartbreakers consequently found themselves in a similar
predicament to the Dolls – a popular live draw unable to get a record deal. 'It
had nothing to do with the public,' stressed Jerry. 'The public loved us. We had
bigger crowds than any of the bands, man. But the business, record people,
managers and things like that, were definitely afraid to touch us. I don't think
they really thought we had something going. They follow the typical rules.'

Despite his experiences with Johnny and Jerry on the Florida tour,
Malcolm McLaren was one of a very small demographic that didn't find the
Heartbreakers – or their reputation – in any way off-putting. While the
Heartbreakers had been coalescing in New York, Malcolm had succeeded in
establishing the Sex Pistols as Britain's original punk band. Initially, this took
the form of snowballing coverage in the UK music press, alerted to the
band's existence by McLaren's tactic of making sure there were journalists at

146

most of the Pistols' early gigs and ensuring something newsworthy happened. Their shambolic appearance at the Marquee in support of Eddie and the Hot Rods in February 1976 had ended with the Rods' amps being trashed, and Steve Jones telling *NME*'s Neil Spencer, 'We're not into music, we're into chaos.'

This had been followed by a series of media-friendly events orchestrated by McLaren that included an April show at a Soho strip joint, a contrived punch-up during a Nashville gig later the same month, and a high-profile residency at the 100 Club on Oxford Street – all of which received far more coverage than any unsigned band could usually hope to receive.

The Ramones' landmark gigs at London's Roundhouse and Dingwalls in early July, and the Pistols/Clash/Buzzcocks Screen on the Green gig the following month, both served to establish the often nebulous concept of punk rock in the public consciousness. By the time the Sex Pistols headlined the 100 Club Punk Festival in late September, they had already made it onto television (with an appearance on Granada's Anthony Wilson-fronted late-night rock programme, *So It Goes*).

McLaren was courting several major labels while the mainstream media ran horrified copy decrying this dreadful punk craze. In October, the Pistols signed to EMI for a £40,000 advance (at a time when the usual figure was around £10,000), and 'Anarchy In The UK' was set to be released as their first single the following month.

To support the new single, and as a means of showcasing British punk rock, a major tour had been arranged for December. McLaren was keen to add an American band to the bill, which included The Clash and The Damned. Initially, he had hoped to persuade the Dolls to reform but had been turned down flat by David, who, along with Syl, was in the process of putting together his own backing band, the Staten Island Boys. After finding that the Ramones and Talking Heads were unavailable, Malcolm settled on the Heartbreakers as fourth choice.

'One night my phone rang. It was Sophie [Richmond], Malcolm McLaren's assistant.' recalled Leee. 'She explained that they managed the Sex Pistols . . . The band were very successful, to the point of doing a UK tour and would The Heartbreakers like to be second on the bill? I called Johnny with the offer – He laughed 'til he peed – Didn't I remember Malcolm, the guy who dressed the Dolls up all in red with some loony idea of billing them as communists? I had missed this incarnation, while on the road with the comparatively stable Iggy. Johnny thought it might be a hoot and we should do it. Jerry, of course, hated the idea. So off we went to England.'

It was hardly as if the Heartbreakers had much to lose, and they'd be arriving to join a developing scene that viewed the New York Dolls as founding fathers – ensuring them a decent reception. McLaren furnished the band with plane tickets to London, and they arrived at Heathrow on 1 December to discover that no work permits had been arranged. 'From the arrival it was clear there was no plan and no organisation,' asserts Leee. 'There were no work permits – clearly none had ever been applied for – there was no hotel, no money, only chaos. To his credit Malcolm somehow scammed us through immigration, fed us hamburgers and found us a bed and breakfast in South

Kensington.'

It was shaping up to be a busy day for McLaren – while he'd been getting the Heartbreakers through Customs, the Sex Pistols had been making a last-minute appearance on Thames Television's *Today* programme. The band had been booked as late replacements for EMI stablemates Queen, who'd pulled out on account of toothy vocalist Freddie Mercury requiring some urgent dental work. As has been extensively documented, the Pistols' drunken four-letter responses to interviewer Bill Grundy's provocative questions provoked enough complaints to jam Thames' switchboard. It guaranteed that the band were plastered all over the national newspapers, even if the early evening show had only been broadcast in the London area.

'Jerry Nolan – who never slept except when you wanted him – got up at dawn to scrounge around the streets and came upon a news stand fairly screaming the morning headlines about the Sex Pistols and the scandalous television interview they had done the day before,' recalls Leee. 'Jerry walked in and dumped the papers on my bed saying, "Now look what you've gotten us into." Shortly, Malcolm's other assistant Nils [Stevenson] came to fetch us for rehearsals. Everyone thought it was great fun, and soon so did we. Rehearsals, however, were not so fun. These bands could not play. They were awful.'

The Anarchy Tour was due to start on Friday 3 December at Norwich Polytechnic. 24 dates had been booked, finishing up at the Roxy Theatre, Harlesden, on Boxing Day. The Grundy farrago resulted in a knee-jerk reaction from many provincial councillors, and most of the gigs were cancelled within a few days of the fateful *Today* appearance.

'The tour bus left from Denmark Street and a bunch of colourful punks shivered in the cold morning to see us off,' explains Leee. 'When we reached our first destination we were greeted by mobs of photographers. Malcolm told everyone to put their coats over their heads and run for the hotel, where Nils rushed us to our rooms and locked us inside. Food was brought and the show was cancelled.'

This set the pattern for the rest of the tour. Three days after hitting the road, the peripatetic punks actually managed to perform at Leeds Polytechnic. They played the second surviving date at Manchester's Electric Circus on 9 December, before returning to London for an extended weekend, as cancellations ensured there would be no gigs for the next four nights. Whilst there, Leee bumped into The Damned's manager, Andy Czezowksi, in The Ship, a pub on Wardour Street. Czezowksi was about to open London's first punk club, The Roxy on Neal Street, off of Covent Garden. Billy Idol and Tony James' Generation X had already been booked for the new venue's first night and he was looking to recruit other bands for regular nights, in what had previously been a gay bar called Shageramans. 'Malcolm McLaren hadn't paid them [the Heartbreakers] or anything so they were literally penniless and sleeping on friends' floors,' recalled Andy. 'I offered them a gig at the Roxy, £30 – done, they said.'

After a gig at the Castle Cinema on 14 December, where the picketing Christian extremists outside outnumbered the musical extremists in the hall, the Heartbreakers kicked off an impromptu all-night jam before again heading back to London for their Roxy show, which attracted an enthusiastic crowd of around 300 and was filmed by DJ Don Letts for his *Punk Rock Movie*. Walter gleefully described the mad reactions at the Roxy as 'loony-bin scenes! We love that sort of craziness – PA columns being pulled over, people jumping up and down bouncing their heads off the ceiling, getting into fights. It's great all those people going out of their minds! We have a mutual admiration society with our audiences.'

By now, The Damned had been sacked from the tour for offering to play a gig that the Pistols had been banned from, and EMI had withdrawn tour support as a prelude to dropping the Pistols. With days in between shows spent sitting around in hotel rooms, the Heartbreakers were bemused, to say the least. 'We waited around a lot, drank a lot of beer, and ate a lot of sandwiches. But when we did play it was like whoa!' recalled Walter.

'Basically, on that Anarchy tour the Heartbreakers just blew everybody away,' adds Leee. 'They were a great rock'n'roll band . . . While the rest of the bands were still getting their act together, the Heartbreakers would just step on stage and kick ass. When you've got a great bass player, a Johnny Thunders on guitar and Jerry Nolan on drums, what you have is great rock'n'roll, and there ain't no way around that. The audiences, of course, went crazy.'

The UK music press acknowledged that the Heartbreakers were old pros, showing the young whippersnappers the proverbial thing or two. *Sounds'* Pete Silverton reckoned they had 'the best drummer' and 'craziest looking bassist', and was particularly taken by the way in which 'Get Off The Phone' ended with one of the parties in a phone conversation hanging themselves with the flex.

Almost a week later, the Pistols, Clash and Heartbreakers played the final two dates of the decimated UK tour in Plymouth. Malcolm McLaren's original plan had been to blaze a punk rock trail across the country, exposing every corner of the UK to the new movement. Instead, the bands ended up disappointed, tired and broke.

Once the tour was over, the Heartbreakers found themselves with nowhere to stay, low on funds and a long way from home. For a while, they crashed at the same Regents Park house inhabited by Habitat heir Sebastian Conran, who was then working as a roadie for The Clash and had taken pity on the American visitors. This 'white mansion' would subsequently house a homeless Joe Strummer.

Caroline Coon and John Ingham, two journalists who'd been championing punk in the weekly music press, were looking after a large house off Ladbroke Grove and invited the Anarchy Tour groups and their entourages around for a traditional Christmas dinner. 'It was perfect until the Americans arrived,' recalled Caroline in *Punk*. 'They were pigs in leather jackets and boots. They kicked their way into the house. They had no manners, no sense of respect. The family atmosphere was destroyed.' She goes on to relate how the Heartbreakers contingent ran up a huge phone bill, stole from the house and passed the smack around, making the first-timers violently ill.

'That was the minute that heroin turned up on the scene because the New York contingent brought smack with them in a big way,' added Pistols insider Steve Walsh. Leee Childers remembers being drawn to a room where he found a tearful Sid listening to Jim Reeves' Christmas album. Although Sid's mother had been an addict for a considerable time and the future Pistols bassist had been injecting speed for at least two years, this was the night that would pass into punk folklore as the point at which Sid got his first fix. Looking back on his first meeting with Vicious nearly 30 years on, Childers declares, 'I will go to my grave swearing that – weird as he was – he was not a junkie at that time. Also, I do believe Jerry Nolan's account that he introduced Sid to heroin.'

In the early weeks of 1977, the Heartbreakers attempted to underplay their pharmaceutical indulgences as Jerry told *Zigzag*, 'We've got no drug problems.' When it was pointed out to Johnny that 'Chinese Rocks' was a drug song, he sighed, 'Yeah, but that's all in the past, man.' Possibly these declarations were a tactic to ward against the band being targeted by the immigration authorities or police, but they were fooling nobody who'd actually encountered them. Leee Childers would sometimes be standing by with a bucket at the side of the stage in case junk-sick Johnny threw up.

After vacating Sebastian Conran's house, the Heartbreakers took over a flat in Pimlico. Shortly after, the whining, star-fucking Nancy Spungen washed up on their doorstep. Like all the CBGB's and Max's crowd, Nancy knew that the Heartbreakers had jetted off to try their luck with this bunch of punks in London. Before the band had left New York, she'd had flings with Johnny and, most recently, Jerry, who she misguidedly considered to be a boyfriend of sorts.

'Nancy Spungen came to England after the Anarchy Tour,' explained Jerry in *Please Kill Me*. 'I mean she followed me everywhere and told everybody stories about us that were all lies. Pertaining to sex – which we never had – trying to convince them that I was her boyfriend.' Leee Childers was keen to keep her away from Jerry. 'I couldn't imagine anything more horrible than Nancy Spungen turning up . . . So I told the band she was in town and I said, "I do not expect any of you to have anything to do with her."'

Kris Needs: *One night we were sitting about in the front bar of the Speakeasy – me, Mark Perry, Mick Jones, Topper Headon, Joe Strummer, Sid Vicious, Paul Cook; there was this girl tottering about in black leather mini-skirt, fishnets, etc, trying to bum cigarettes and talk to us. She was obviously up for anything, especially if it led to drugs. She was said to have had her sights fixed on Johnny Rotten, because the Heartbreakers had been less than overjoyed to see her. Nancy turned up at the flat that Rotten and Sid shared in St. James' Park, which belonged to an ex-prostitute. Rotten hated her so she made straight for big, gullible Sid.*

'You cannot believe how bad this woman was,' lamented Lydon in his autobiography. 'Non-stop. "Ooooh Sid," with the most annoying voice. She was so dumb, like those gangster molls you see in the movies. Where was she from? "Neeew Yooork." Why was she here? "Drruuugs."'

'The New York guys came and brought their heroin, end of story,' asserted Chrissie Hynde. 'They also brought Nancy Spungen, who turned Sid into a sex slave. It was a simple equation; everyone disliked Nancy and told Sid to dump her.'

In order to survive, the Heartbreakers needed to keep gigging. Without any record label support, PA or transport, this meant touring London in much the same way as the Dolls had orbited New York. Throughout the opening months of 1977 they played a number of London clubs, including a roof-raising rampage on 3 January at Dingwalls, the large bar in Camden Town which had been a hub of pub-rock but also played host to the Ramones the previous July.

The Heartbreakers' relationship with the Sex Pistols continued to provide the band with some much needed concert income, and a three-gig jaunt to Holland represented a welcome break for the group, who were finding life on £1 a day less than fulfilling. Leaving on 4 January, the impoverished quartet travelled to Amsterdam by road and ferry, while McLaren was at Heathrow, overseeing the Pistols' re-enactment of the Dolls' departure lounge misbehaviour of four years earlier.

The opening show took place at the Paradiso Club, where the band sampled the various types of hash and grass available as if they were compiling a Good Dope Guide. This was followed by a concert at the Rotterdam Art Centre on 6 January, where McLaren told Pistols' soundman Dave Goodman to order Steve Jones to 'stop posing like Johnny Thunders'. The band returned to the Paradiso the following night for what would turn out to be Glen Matlock's last live appearance as a Pistol, before Sid Vicious usurped his place.

Despite the fun to be had for any young rock'n'roller in Amsterdam, the Heartbreakers were becoming decidedly homesick. On the boat trip back to England, they cooked up a plan to get deported home to the US by creating a scene at Customs. The quartet, accompanied by Dave Goodman – who was under instructions from McLaren to ensure they got back to London safely – scarcely required the assistance of the rough sea crossing to make them appear gaunt and unsteady on their arrival at Dover. Once they reached the passport checkpoint Johnny fell over and dropped his dope, while Walter mischievously asked a Customs officer for a light for his spliff. Jerry looked on, swigging whiskey from the bottle as the unfortunate Goodman presented the band's passports. 'They're musicians,' he explained, gesturing vaguely in the direction of the four-man synchronised substance abuse team that were lurching around behind him. 'Oh – that's alright then,' replied the Customs officer, who waved them all through without as much as a second glance. 'I think the band felt cheated and wanted to go through Customs again, but it was too late,' smiled Goodman.

Once back in Britain, the Heartbreakers returned to the Roxy on 11 January and again on 13 February. In March they played the Speakeasy, Global Village, two nights at Dingwalls and the Marquee. They even began venturing out of town for gigs in Liverpool (Eric's) and Middlesbrough (Rock Garden).

This pragmatic approach to touring helped build a following for the band. *NME*'s Tony Parsons and Julie Burchill were quick to seize upon the Heartbreakers' unique appeal – the former describing Johnny as 'a junk sick, transvestite Eddie Cochran' and the latter hormonally opining, 'Johnny Thunders is the answer to all your teenage dreams.'

For their part, the band were simply happy to have a regular supply of gigs and income, free from all the hassles and baggage (Nancy notwithstanding) that tended to follow them around New York. 'England just has more places where we can play and continue to play,' Leee Childers told *New York Rocker*. 'Towns like Croydon and Sheffield attract totally different audiences. In New York, after you've played Max's and CBGB's, where can you go?'

'Coming to England gave us the chance to get out and about and see what was happening,' explained Walter. 'We didn't expect anything, we were just going to see how things turned out.' 'All the bands were more together,' added Johnny. 'There was competition, but not spiteful. The record company and the press were more aware.'

Although he was still homesick and missing Julie – who was pregnant again – and Johnny Jnr, Thunders had settled in to the extent that he declared, 'We're pretty much based here now. This is pretty much our home now.'

The Heartbreakers' burgeoning UK following, and a steady trickle of good live reviews, re-ignited record company interest, which in turn prompted Leee Childers to redouble his efforts to secure that elusive deal. Suddenly, the tide turned in the Heartbreakers' favour and he received offers from Arista, Polydor, France's Skydog, CBS, and even the Pistols-whipped EMI, who were playing it safe by offering a singles deal plus further options. But they settled on Track, the label that the Dolls nearly signed to in 1973.

True to Heartbreakers form, the Track deal was somewhat irregular. The band was asked to declare that they were signed to the Chris Stamp Band Ltd on relevant documents. The deal was negotiated on behalf of the band by Leee's business manager, Peter Gerber. 'It was his job to spend the endless boring afternoons with lawyers trying to come up with a workable contract between Track and the Heartbreakers,' explains Leee. 'He was that rare businessman who actually liked his clients and did the best he could for them.' There was also a stipulation that if the Chris Stamp Band Ltd went bankrupt, all the tapes would become the property of Heartbreakers Inc, a company set up by Childers and Gerber. The deal allowed Track, who were verging on bankruptcy, to avoid paying a large advance and permitted the band to retain their tapes should Track go under.

The deal, which was for an unspecified number of singles and two albums a year for three years, suited both Leee and the band. 'A company that had worked with The Who, Jimi Hendrix, Thunderclap Newman, Marc Bolan, and that guy who screamed "Fire" feared no one,' exclaimed Leee. 'It mattered not that they had no interest at all in charts, sales, profits and losses, numbers, lists, or anything that had to be looked at or examined. They were perfect.'

Between 20 and 22 February, the Heartbreakers began recording at Essex Studios, using the in-house engineer to lay down demos of three tracks: 'Chinese Rocks', 'Born To Lose' and 'Let Go'. These were later released as an EP by Jungle, and are more primitive, less energised, than subsequent versions. However, Johnny's vocals showed up well, and the tracks provided concrete evidence that the band could transfer their live kinesis to vinyl.

Kris Needs: *On 21 February 1977, I interviewed the Heartbreakers for the first time at Track's Carnaby Street offices. After nodding to Siouxsie Sioux, who was sitting on the doorstep outside, me and my mate Colin – the gui-*

tarist in our punk group the Vice Creems – met Johnny and Jerry, Walter and Leee Childers. Previously, I'd casually encountered the Heartbreakers through Leee, but this was the first time we'd met for an extended period. Both were totally friendly, instantly dispelling any trepedation which I'd built up after five years immersed in the Dolls legend.

They'd just finished recording two songs for their forthcoming single – 'Chinese Rocks' and 'Born To Lose' – and were trying to decide which one should be the A side. I was awestruck by the powerful avalanche of raunch tumbling out of the big speakers. While the tracks were playing Johnny was pacing up and down, deep in thought. The electric storm shuddered to a halt. 'Which one shall we make the A side?' asked Johnny. '"Chinese Rocks"!' bellowed Colin and Me. 'Okay then,' he shrugged.

During the ensuing interview, Johnny tended to let Jerry do most of the talking. He would just add his thoughts if he felt something needed saying. You could already tell that interviews were not his favourite pastime but, after I'd gushed like an idiot about the Dolls' Biba's gig and the Heartbreakers' new tracks, the ice was broken.

The Heartbreakers had been in town nearly three months. Punk was certainly known because of the Pistols furore, but they'd only issued one [withdrawn] single, and The Clash had yet to release their first album. Few groups would ever top the Heartbreakers' live onslaught, and right now they must've been experiencing a similar kind of buzz to that which they'd felt in New York during the Dolls' Mercer heyday. I asked if they were aware of what was happening here?

'We knew about the Pistols, but we didn't think there was such a big scene happening,' said Walter, who had just walked in, a tall, gangling figure with a loud tie outside his shirt. 'We thought it was just this one band. As for the audiences, we were expecting a lot of hippies still into Led Zeppelin and shit like that. We didn't know how we'd go over . . . but it was great once we got here.'

'The whole scene over here reminds me of New York four years ago, but they've taken it a step further,' added Jerry. 'It's the same atmosphere with a different type of music. It's very exciting for us because we're the only New York band from the same background doing the same kind of trip. It seemed like we were the only band in New York that was really rocking and trying to keep up with the times, but you soon get bored with yourselves if you don't have other bands to look at and learn from. Here we can learn a lot, and I've noticed that they've picked up a few things from us too, which is great. It's very exciting.

'I think all the English bands have a lot of potential for their age. They've got the right idea and what it takes. I love these bands . . . Some of them are going to be great in the future.'

'I've never been so happy in my life,' beamed Johnny.

'Four years ago you couldn't touch New York. They were really ahead of the times, and the bands were all learning off each other,' added Jerry. 'It was very creative and friendly but, right now, New York and the whole scene there is as fucked up as it was creative four years ago. It's gone stale. All the bands hate each other. I've never heard musicians put each other

down so much. I've been in this business nineteen years, and I've never seen such hatred and jealousy between bands. I'm glad I'm away from it all. I can't stand to be there.'

What about Television and Patti Smith?

'They're not rock'n'roll. They're light poetry stuff. What they consider punk rock over there is really folk rock. They're more into avant-garde *and arty stuff . . . late sixties bohemian-type shit. Everything's so serious, although the Ramones are different.'*

Jerry reckoned the Heartbreakers were the only true rock'n'roll band in the city. 'When we play there, we pack in the people and we don't even have a record out. For some reason we're more popular than anybody in New York. We get a younger, more energetic crowd.'

I asked if the band had a game plan.

'We'll establish ourselves here, get a reputation and then go back to the States and see if they've grown up a little,' declared Johnny.

'Now we're just going to go to the top of the world and take it for as long as they'll let us,' Walter added.

Predictably, the Heartbreakers' living arrangements continued to be problematic. Although the absence of any visas meant that their stay in the UK could be terminated at a moment's notice, Johnny was joined by Julie and Johnny Jnr. At first, they shared a flat in Chelsea with Billy and Walter, while Jerry – who didn't fancy being surrounded by screaming infants – found a place of his own in Pimlico. However, living arrangements in Chelsea quickly proved to be unworkable for all parties, and, after Julie gave birth to Vito, the Thunders clan relocated to a house in Islington with Leee and Gail Higgins Smith.

Gail had travelled to London after losing her job in a large New York department store. She'd hooked up with the Heartbreakers at their recent Dingwalls gig. Leee had asked her if she fancied being the band's road manager and she readily agreed. 'Since I knew all of them really well and had no job to go back to – and it was being paid for by Track records – I thought, "Why not?"' she recalled. 'Road managing a band can't be that different from managing salesmen – except for the drugs.'

Conditions in Islington represented only the most marginal of improvements to those in Chelsea. 'The house shared by Gail and I on Cross Street was a stopping off point for many young performers and fans,' explains Leee. 'Of these guests, I can thankfully say that none of them died at my house.' Unsurprisingly, the constant stream of visitors, combined with Johnny's need to feed his habit, hardly made for a textbook nursery environment.

Indeed, faced with the endless requirements of his charges, Leee's duties resembled those of a wet-nurse more often than a manager. Speaking in 2005, he observes, 'As for myself the credit I do take – with the aid of Gail Higgins – is keeping these boys alive and playing for the years that we were together. Believe it or not, we never missed a gig. We threw up a lot, but we were there.'

On 3 March, the Heartbreakers played the New York Weekend at the Nag's Head in High Wycombe. Promoted by Ron Watts, who'd organised the previous year's 100 Club Punk Festival, this quintessential pub backroom had played host to the Pistols, Clash, Damned, Generation X, and usually found around a hundred or so punks and local lads bent on a steaming knees-up. As the following night would feature Wayne County and the Electric Chairs and Cherry Vanilla, the Heartbreakers' gig was like the first part of a real Max's Kansas City homecoming (in Buckinghamshire) – to be repeated at the Roxy shortly after.

The gig was storming – the band rattled through most of the set that would be recorded for their debut album, plus 'Do You Love Me' as an encore. They managed to bridge the gap between classic rock'n'roll and punk – sheer musicianship suffused with don't-give-a-shit ragged glory, and infectious songs laden with addictive hooks. If punk rock was rock'n'roll speeded up, the Heartbreakers hot-wired the medium and dragged it kicking and screaming through New York's gutters, whorehouses and shooting galleries.

There was a lot of primitive fifties rockabilly swing in the Heartbreakers' engine room. Billy was adept enough to latch onto this – so whatever Walter, who usually played rhythm guitar, felt like hammering on to their bedrock could only result in a gloriously kinetic rock'n'roll energy surge. Johnny and Walter utilised call-and-response choruses to provide cohesion and stability, allowing Johnny to attack his vocal leads with reckless abandon. Sometimes, like his guitar, he was out of tune, but it was all part of the Heartbreakers' kamikaze sonic attack. Still skidding, howling and roaring, with a deft flick of the hand Johnny referenced the gracefully subtle flourishes exemplified by blues masters such as Hubert Sumlin. Classic licks were peeled off effortlessly. At this point, Thunders was close to becoming the consummate rock-'n'roller – nobody else came as close to bringing the original fifties spirit into the seventies in its pure form.

The group dressed New York street-smart. There was no makeup, glamour or contrived styling here. They looked like Jerry's Young Lords – sharkskin or leather jackets and slicked-back hair. Three years later, after their complete cultural immersion in urban America, The Clash would adopt this look. With the Heartbreakers, New York's mean streets were transplanted to English towns.

On 15 March, The Heartbreakers played two sets at the Speakeasy, which were recorded by producer John 'Speedy' Keen, and subsequently surfaced on the 1982 album, *D.T.K. Live At The Speakeasy*. Keen, who looked like a Motörhead roadie, with his leather jacket and moustache, was best known as the composer and singer of 'Something In The Air', Thunderclap Newman's enormous 1969 hit. That single – as well as the subsequent *Hollywood Dream* album – were released on Track, who supported Speedy's solo career after the band split in 1970. Although much of Keen's solo output was grandiose, introspective and melodic, he was a rocker at heart – as was evidenced by a B-side rabble-rouser called 'Fighting In The Streets'. In 1975, he told *Zigzag* that he planned to organise a gig at London's Lyceum featuring him and rock-star mates doing Eddie Cochran songs. It helped him to hit it off with the Heartbreakers. 'He just came down and dug it,' explained Johnny. This rapport, allied to the fact that he was essentially Track's in-house producer, installed him as the most obvious choice to produce the Heartbreakers' vinyl debut.

The day after the Speakeasy shows, band and producer hunkered down in London's Essex Studios and laid down five tracks: 'Get Off The Phone', 'All By Myself', 'Let Go', 'Can't Keep My Eyes On You' and 'I Wanna Be Loved'. After a couple of days, they relocated to The Who's Ramport studios in Battersea and recorded 'Goin' Steady', 'Do You Love Me?', 'Chinese Rocks', 'Born To Lose', 'Pirate Love', 'One Track Mind', 'It's Not Enough' and 'Baby Talk'.

It was a promising start – thirteen tracks were recorded in a week. However, the mixing process, which began at Ramport on 22 March, would take most of the next six months. One of the reasons behind this extended mixing period was that Keen was also working on metal behemoths Motörhead's debut. Despite this, when Jerry spoke to Pete Frame in June, he seemed convinced that the band had the right man behind the desk. 'I'm sure he'll be one producer of many. We don't have that kind of character that sticks with the same old shit. When we become that kind of band and that kind of people, that's when we become boring, staying in the same rut that we used to fight against.'

Between February and October, the Heartbreakers could be seen around London's clubs. When asked, 'When's the album coming out?', whether it was Johnny, Jerry, Walter or Billy, the reply was always, 'Pretty soon, it's being mixed.' This took place at a gamut of studios – mainly Ramport, but also Olympic, Advision and Trident.

Additionally, the band's need to keep gigging in order to put junk and food on the table ensured that studio time was regularly interrupted to travel to shows, and for the necessary recovery periods that inevitably followed hard nights on the road. Much of the end of April and beginning of May was lost in this manner, as the Heartbreakers crossed the English Channel for a short but profitable tour of Holland, Belgium and France.

By 20 May, their vinyl debut was ready to hit UK stores. 'Chinese Rocks', backed with 'Born To Lose', sold 20,000 in its first week of release and shot to number one in the independent charts. At one point it was reckoned to be outselling the Pistols' 'God Save The Queen'.

Amidst the growing tide of half-baked, tinny efforts committed to vinyl in the name of punk, 'Chinese Rocks' stood out as a dark anthem – despite the muddy sound quality. Johnny was already dismissing it, saying he preferred 'Born To Lose'. *NME*'s Charles Shaar Murray was equally dismissive, although he was more inclined to take exception to the song's overt heroin references than any musical shortcomings – 'Anyone who sings "I'm living on a Chinese Rock" deserves to be marooned on one – you cool fool!' 'We all just saw it as a hilarious statement of the ridiculous but seductive junkie lifestyle,' observed Walter.

A gritty illustration, rather than a celebration, of the hopelessness of smack addiction, 'Chinese Rocks' is hardly an advert for shooting up. Lyrics such as, 'I should have been rich / But I'm just digging a Chinese ditch,' show the desperate futility of the junkie lifestyle. This hopelessness is underpinned by Johnny and Walter's guitars, which slash and howl in a high sea of effluent, while Johnny's vocals struggle to emerge from the six-string tempest. Although the Rath/Nolan rhythm section is unsatisfactorily low in the mix, the track conveys enough of the Heartbreakers' boundless energy and street hassle experience to represent their live *sturm und drang*. Indeed, the popularity of the track was evident from a riotous crowd reaction during a gig at Camden's Music Machine the night before the single was released. Supported by Siouxsie and the Banshees, the band threw down a storming set before a packed house that hailed them as heroes.

'Born To Lose' is possibly even more of a low-life anthem. The wellworn phrase signified doomed rebellion, and as such had long been adopted by Hell's Angels throughout the US. From its first sardonic chord, the song is a masterpiece of immaculately distressed rock'n'roll. Johnny's lyrics are pure blank-generation nihilism: 'Nothing to do, I've nothing to say'.

The single was 'dedicated to the boys on Norfolk Street'. This desolate avenue is in the heart of the Lower East Side, running into Houston Street where it sits between the start of Avenues A and B on the other side of the road. 'It's like another world there,' said Jerry. 'They probably wouldn't even know what these songs are all about or what we've meant by anything we've done. We came from our world. Everybody's gone through their drug stage. At the time of that song, I guess we were going through ours. Norfolk Street used to be our sort of connection, y'know? Looking for drugs and stuff like that. That's all in the past now. It's all over.'

Given their reputation, it was no great surprise that life on the road with the Heartbreakers was anything but tranquil. There was an incident in Leeds on 3 June when the band, accompanied by Gail, were detained in their room at the Wesley Hotel by a guy claiming to be from the SAS. First he complained about the noise, then pulled out a gun and said the building was surrounded because there was a man with a shotgun on the roof. After four hours, he swore those present to secrecy and left. He was obviously bogus, so the band got the hotel reception to call the police, who fingerprinted all present and turned up at that night's gig in case he showed again. 'The Leeds Police took a lot of fingerprints to compare us with the fingerprints at the station to make sure that we weren't the people that held ourselves up,' explained Walter. Three weeks later the gunman was picked up trying to steal a car with a fake gun. Jerry would subsequently embellish the story by saying the Heartbreakers had taken the rap for a hotel pay phone robbery, and spent a day in jail.

By the summer of 1977, punk rock had swept Britain. Of the Heartbreakers' compatriots on the Anarchy tour, the Sex Pistols had hopped between record labels, toting expanding grab bags of ready cash, while 'God Save The Queen' threatened the very moral fibre of the country (according to Woolworth's and W. H. Smith, anyhow – both stores refused to sell the disc). The Clash released their landmark eponymous debut album in April, and were becoming the biggest, regularly gigging group from the initial wave of British punk. The Damned had taken on a comedic role, after beating everyone to the punch by getting 'New Rose' issued as the first UK punk single. There were a slew of bands following in their wake. Some were good – Siouxsie and the Banshees, the Buzzcocks, Alternative TV, Subway Sect. Others were simply bandwagon jumpers, like the Vibrators and the Suburban Studs.

A *Zigzag* interview with Pete Frame in early June found Johnny and – particularly – Jerry at their most candid. Pete was in the process of compiling another of his renowned Family Trees, this one chronicling the New York pre-punk bands. He had decided to curtail *Zigzag*'s coverage of hippie bands and singer-songwriters and turn over to newer music. Just to get up the hippies' noses, Pete stuck a knife-wielding Johnny on the cover, along with the headline – 'Heartbreakers – Heroin & Murder In The Bowery'.

Jerry explained that he was becoming vexed with other journalists who only wanted to talk about the Dolls. 'I don't want to live on memories. Live for now. I'm doing new things. I don't want to live in the past, or live for the past. I just remember the good times and keep on creating good things. We really create with each other. I think it's a really good team, especially me and Johnny. We might have a million and one differences, but when it comes to the music, we have a great deal in common. We like each other's ideas and respect each other's performances and things like that. That's for sure.'

Frame stated that he knew the two Heartbreakers used heroin, and wondered if Jerry would mind talking about it. 'Oh, I'll talk about it. I just don't wanna ponder on it too much because it's over. We're not into drugs any more. It was just a part of our past, like a million other things. And it was an important part of our past because it was an emotional part, y'know? It was a lot to do with ups and downs, things like that, in our life and our behaviour, and in what looked like might be our future. It got to be where it didn't look like a very good future, so we dropped out of that drug bag, y'know? It didn't mix well with the music we were playing.

'We did write about it, to a degree. I guess, you don't really wanna write about everything you see, feel and touch, but it just sort of happens anyway. You don't make it a point to do it, it just sort of comes out. Now we're singing and writing about other things. "Chinese Rocks" was written about two years ago. As far as we're concerned, anything on our upcoming album is like all over. But it'll be there for a lot of other people to enjoy and to see a bit of our history. Everything we do is gonna be old hat to us and new to the public.'

'How did you actually get on to it?'

'Ah God, it's probably the same as how a lot of people get into it,' replies Jerry, like he's talking about making a record. 'At first, it's part of the good time. It's part of the fun, due to the fact that it's always there, practically for free, most of the time. You always have this memory about being stoned and how easy it is to take, almost anything or everything, no matter whether it's good or bad. It's easy to cope. It really is. It's a too-cool-for-your-own-good drug. A little too cool.'

Johnny walked in and asked, 'What you talking about?' Jerry laughed nervously. 'He wants to talk about heroin – but I'm explaining to him that it's a thing of the past.'

'We were singing and writing about things at the time. Not on purpose, not like we wanted to. It was natural, like we couldn't help it. There were some great things about [heroin] at the time. There were some definitely good times we had doing all this, and there were also bad times. We realised that it was taking us a little too much away from what we really wanted to do. See, we don't like to get hung up on any one thing for too long anyway. And the drug scene has a bad habit of making it a habit. Understand? So it's up to us to break away from that. We may get into something else and it might be easier to break away. [Heroin] was just a little difficult to break away from. That was definitely not easy to play with. If you play with fire you're gonna get burned. But we did and we got burnt, we all got burnt real bad. But, we're not dead. We're not in bad shape at all. In fact we're quite successful to a degree and quite satisfied with what we've been through – because we are through it. We can't look back. We're evolving with other things now that we can't wait to present and get out, write and do another album, blah blah blah.'

'There's a new single called "The Medication Programme",' added Johnny with a mischievous chuckle.

'Johnny, tell him about Norfolk Street,' said Jerry, excitedly. 'He wants to know what the dedication on the [single] sleeve means.'

Johnny cranked into life. 'Norfolk Street is a street of closed up buildings, boarded up windows and nailed up doorways, some basement clubs, Puerto Ricans and black guys, very heavy junkies. Oh, they try and rip off anybody. It's not easy to walk down that street. It's a very heavy area to be in. You've got to know how to take care of yourself if you live in New York.'

'Very heavy junkies,' added Jerry. 'Very heavy heroin buying. Any white boy in the neighbourhood is definitely there for one reason. There's also black guys and Puerto Ricans who go there to cop too. They can rip off anybody. Anybody can pull out a gun and shoot or put it to your face and pull the trigger. You don't have to be any colour to do that. We've been jumped a number of times. I was stabbed . . . Anybody in our group has experienced being jumped, stabbed or mugged. It's very heavy, but that's part of the fun in copping dope. We wouldn't want it any other way. If someone came to us with the dope . . . Man, we really got off on going down to cop.'

'It was a good experience,' added Johnny.

'You learn what it's like to pack a weapon,' continued Jerry, warming to his theme. 'You learn what it's like to use it and you learn what it's like to have it held against you. Definitely marked up for experience, y'know? Survival. It's certainly nothing to brag about. It's good to be through it, but to go out of your way to be through it is not a good idea because usually the people who go out of their way to go through it are the people who don't survive. We had to go through it in order to get high. But we don't get high no more. We enjoy doing what we're doing now. This is a whole new trip.'

Unaware that both Johnny and Jerry were still addicted, and taking their declarations of being clean at face value, Pete suggested they were lucky not to have died.

'Yeah I am very lucky,' agreed Jerry. 'I could've been dead too from a fucking OD or something like that. But I'm not because I had a lot to look forward to and a lot to look back at. Because of all these people's abuse and because of a lot to look forward to. I'm not into drugs. I don't smoke pot. I don't sniff speed. I don't do anything. I don't drink. I just dig rock'n'roll and I like to come up with ideas. I dig the whole scene and the environment and the feeling. I get off on listening to records and rediscovering rock'n'roll all the time. I get off on that more than I get off on anything else.'

'Jerry used to say that a lot,' observed Alan Hauser of Jungle Records, the label which released the *Live At The Speakeasy* album in 1982, and has continued issuing Heartbreakers, Dolls and Thunders-related CDs to the present day. 'Even when he was on one, it was, "I'm not going to take drugs, that's in the past." He was still doing that in 1984! He would get very dogmatic about it. Perhaps Jerry could see where it was going in a way and telling himself. Jerry would blatantly lie about it.'

Hauser's sleeve note for the CD reissue of the Heartbreakers' debut album, *LAMF,* relates the tale of how once, during the sessions, the band sent a taxi on a round trip to Birmingham to collect drugs – on Track's account.

'I think we can afford to call ourselves the Junkies,' trumpeted Jerry in his interview with Pete Frame. 'We know more about it than anybody. We can afford to call ourselves the Junkies because we're not junkies. We're definitely anti-drugs to a degree. We don't wave flags for it or against it.'

Suppressing a chortle, Frame suggested it could be commercial suicide with the media. 'I think it's about commercial songs,' argued Johnny, citing 'God Save The Queen' and its current rise in the top ten. 'Its probably gonna be number one this week.'

'A good song is a good song no matter what,' added Jerry. 'Just like the Pistols song is such a good song. It's so good that whether they play it or not on the air, it's definitely gonna sell. I think the music is more important than anybody's name. Like I say, we're not waving any flags over drugs. In fact, we're totally against drugs to a degree. The abuse of it, y'know? The music is supposed to be a fun and up attitude and any hard drugs that we have mentioned are not fun and up if you're doing rock'n'roll. How can you wail out on an hour set of rock'n'roll fucked up on junk? How can you nod out and play rock'n'roll at the same time? Unless you're playing jazz-rock or some shit. We don't play that. Our music is real fast and up-tempo.

'Besides we're music junkies. Being into rock'n'roll made us go through everything. That made us experience what it's like to be going through a drug stage, a sexual stage, a rebellion stage. I mean, rebellion, sex and everything else we've gone through is just as important as drugs was.

'We just like the name because we're hung up on . . . nothing. We're nothing junkies! We have a habit for nothingness, not getting too hung up on anything. You read about junk food junkies, music junkies . . . It's just a great name. We don't think it's gonna pin us down. We don't think we're gonna get labelled if people know and have an open mind. The Heartbreakers was a good name but it ain't us, y'know? There's too many names like that. I think more people can relate to that name than they can the Heartbreakers. I just hope that all the people that believe in us for our talent don't back away now just because we've changed the name. There's always a business that worries about the least important things to worry about.'

Johnny and Jerry would subsequently dismiss the name-change idea as a joke but, at the time, Pete Frame maintained that they seemed deadly serious. 'That's what we want,' Jerry declared. 'It's easy to work with. They [the press] may just make something of it, I don't know. I've seen them do stupid things before. They wouldn't accept us in fucking New York because of

David finds a place to rest his hand whilst the Dolls squeeze into frame for a publicity shot, 1973.

What are the politics of boredom? The Dolls as an ersatz 'People's Information Collective' on the Red Patent Leather *sleeve.*

The way they were: The classic Dolls line-up of Kane, Sylvain, Thunders, Nolan and Johansen dissolved in the summer heat of 1975.

So alone – Johnny in a corner, 1978.

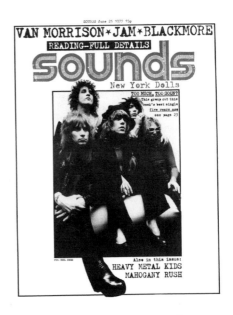

A Phonograph Record *cover feature from October 1973.*

Sounds *covers the New York Dolls, in 1977.*

Heartbreaker Johnny joins the long mac crowd, 1977.

'Don't take my knife away' – Johnny emerges from the shadows for a Zigzag cover, 1977.

Like A Mother Fucker – Johnny on the cover of Zigzag for the second time in 1978.

Johnny with Heartbreakers guitarist Walter Lure, 1977

Taking a break – Johnny in Toronto, 1989.

Poster for a Miami show featuring the short-lived Johnny Thunders Jerry Nolan Band, 1987.

Johnny accepts an offering from a Canadian fan, Toronto 1989.

Reborn Dolls – Syl and David at the WHFS Festival, Baltimore 2005.

Morrissey with David, Arthur and Syl at the Silver Clef Awards, 2004. Inset: The sleeve art from Morrissey Presents: The Return Of The New York Dolls, Live From The Royal Festival Hall, 2004.

David and Syl prepare for Kris Needs' interrogation, March 2006.

David with Kris Needs, March 2006.

a thousand other reasons. Most of 'em weren't even true anyway. But if they like us for what we are they'll accept us no matter what name we use. If they're gonna get hung up on names they're not worth getting involved in.'

'What do you think of the name?' Johnny asked Pete, who pointed out that their prospects of getting airplay would be limited, as the BBC wouldn't touch a band with that type of loaded nomenclature.

'Who needs them?' asserted Johnny.

'Isn't that what kids want?' enquired Jerry. 'If I was a thirteen-year-old girl and I was going to a concert and my mother said, "Who are you gonna see?" "I'm going to see the Junkies, Mom." I think that'd be great for the kids . . . Any big form of art, anything that's been accepted with a high rate of popularity has always been outrageous or different and so-called unacceptable. We ain't for or against anything.'

Suddenly, Johnny asked, 'You think we're a punk band?'

'I don't know what the fuck a punk band is,' Frame replied, before asking when the album is coming out.

'A month?' said Jerry, with less than convincing certainty. 'We're mixing it right now.' Jerry's unhappiness with the production of the single became evident when Frame enthused, 'you can tell it's got the power and the musicability there and it stands out from most of the other stuff around.' Responding somewhat dismissively, Jerry replied, 'We're getting close.'

Despite his disappointment with the single, the drummer remained optimistic about the forthcoming album. 'Wait until you hear the other cuts on the record! We put this single out for a lot of reasons but there's some other songs on the album that might even be more commercial than them two songs. We were even thinking of calling the album *The Heartbreakers' Greatest Hits*.'

Pete then asked the duo what they thought about some of the other New York bands, such as the Ramones. 'They all sound the same though,' answered Johnny. 'I like their slower songs. Their other songs are like one long song.'

'Yeah, but I'd rather have that than them sound different and boring with big gaps between songs,' observed Jerry. 'It was a nice, tight show. I didn't get bored once. That was important to me.'

'CBGB's, man, was cool to hang out in for about six months but now it's all kids from suburbia,' asserted Johnny. 'You'll never get any bigger if you just keep playing CBGB's.'

'I guess they feel it's an important landmark, to me it's not shit,' concluded Jerry.

The constant gigging in Europe throughout the first half of '77 turned the Heartbreakers into the ultimate rock'n'roll killing machine, but also ensured Walter and Billy spent the next few years as junkies. 'We were basically still together but there was too much idle time in London,' reflects Walter. 'The longer we lived in London, the more trouble we got into. Some of our vices were becoming more than recreational.'

Throughout their extended sojourn in the UK, the Heartbreakers had ridden their luck in terms of visas. At the start of July, the band was issued with notice to leave the country within 24 hours. This came as something of a shock, as the group had assumed their paperwork was taken care of by Track. The label was equally surprised. 'As far as we know, the band have their work permits in order and their exchange permit has been OK'd by both the English and American musicians unions,' insisted press officer Alan Edwards. Leee Black Childers lodged an appeal and was told he would get a decision by 4 July, which gave the band enough time to play the opening night of the new Vortex club in Wardour Street, Soho.

Usually a soul disco called Crackers, the Vortex ran weekly on a Monday night, then expanded into Tuesdays once the owners realised there was decent money to be made from live punk bands.

The Heartbreakers had been booked at the last minute and were supposed to play a short set after the Buzzcocks, but the 'headliners' insisted that the New Yorkers went on early. This wasn't such a wise move by the Mancunian pop-punksters, who bit off far more than they could chew by irritating the older, tougher, wiser Heartbreakers. By the time the soundcheck came around, the Buzzcocks' fey vocalist, Pete Shelley, had ensconced himself in his dressing room in the hope of avoiding direct confrontation with the Lower East Side mooks.

Most of the Vortex crowd, who included The Clash, Sid and Nancy, Generation X, Motörhead's Lemmy, the Damned and Mark Perry of Alternative TV, were there for the Heartbreakers. They didn't disappoint, delivering their set with the rampant energy of a teen world gone bad – good/bad, but not evil – and receiving a wall-climbingly euphoric response. The comedown arrived the following day, when the band were shipped back to the US.

Back in New York, Walter found himself cast in the role of social anthropologist following the broadcast of an NBC special on the UK punk scene. 'Everybody saw that and they all sorta, come up to me and stuff, and say, "Wot, is it really that heavy in England?"' he told *Sounds*' Jon Savage. '"Do people get killed at the shows and get beat up and stuff?" I said, "Yeah, Yeah, man." They loved it, thought it was great.'

Although the Heartbreakers' problematic debut album mix still hadn't been completed to everyone's satisfaction, Leee turned his attention to the packaging, calling upon Roberta Bayley to shoot some photos for the sleeve.

The group had decided that their album would be called *LAMF*, after the New York gang tradition of staking out territory with graffiti. The acronym stood for 'Like A Mother Fucker'. If visiting another gang's turf, the invaders would add the prefix 'DTK' – 'Down To Kill'.

Since the dissolution of the Dolls, Roberta had established herself as one of the foremost photographers of the scene that had developed around CBGB's and Max's. She was a regular contributor to *Punk* magazine and was responsible for the iconic image of the Ramones that graced their eponymous debut. For the *LAMF* shoot, she took the Heartbreakers to a SoHo alley at night and constructed a far more menacing gang tableau than had been the case for da bruddas' sleeve. Walter recalled the cover being shot in 'a sort of factory, sleazo area. There were so many ideas about it – everybody seemed to want to quit the band because of the cover, he didn't like it, or had different ideas. Finally, in New York, we took pictures one night, and sent it over to England: they liked this one so much, and were so tired of us fighting that they put it out.'

On 16 August Johnny married Julie in a low-key ceremony that was attended by a small group of family and close friends. Even if the impoverished couple could have afforded it, there was little time for a honeymoon as the Heartbreakers were booked to play three 'welcome home' gigs at the Village Gate, a small club in the West Village. Johnny strolled on stage and announced, 'This song was written by a bunch of ego-maniacs!' before roaring into 'Chinese Rocks'. After a few songs, some equipment problems surfaced which plagued the rest of the set.

Covering the sold out shows for *New York Rocker,* Roy Trakin celebrated Johnny's success in fronting a band where he was the main creative driving force. 'These boys don't need anyone . . . The vocals are buried beneath a glorious electrical storm. It's no secret now who was behind the wheel as far as the Dolls' music was concerned.' Trakin asked Johnny now that he was back in New York, whether he'd consider re-uniting with David Johansen. 'Yeah, sure. I'd fool around with him in the studio, but I'd never be in the same band with him again.'

The set that night opened with 'Chatterbox' – which had been reverted to its original title of 'Milk Me'. Asked if the song was a paean to the joys of hand relief, a mock-shocked Johnny told Trakin, 'I wouldn't write a song about that.' For the encore of 'Jailhouse Rock' the band were joined by ex-Tuff Darts frontman Robert Gordon – who was then fronting a band which included former Doll Peter Jordan and guitar legend Link Wray – and Syl Sylvain.

After the Dollettes had run out of steam at the back end of 1976, Syl had divided his time between helping David get his solo career out of the starting gate and putting together a band of his own. Syl retained Tony Machine and Bobby Blaine from the final incarnation of the Dolls and added bassist Mike Page to form the Criminals. However, rehearsals were derailed almost immediately when Syl was involved in a collision between a car and a van on Thirteenth Street, which left him with a badly broken leg. Although this meant that the guitarist spent the early part of 1977 in hospital, he received sufficient compensation money to finance the Criminals until they started gigging.

Sylvain unveiled his new quartet with a set that included a ten-minute version of 'Peter Gunn' – the TV detective theme by Henry Mancini, immortalised by Duane Eddy – at Max's on 23 April. According to a *New York Rocker* report, 'They did six songs and seemed a bit under-rehearsed.' However, the band must have made a reasonable impression on someone at the paper, as they were included in the *New York Rocker* Top 40 New York bands guide: 'Sylvain's post-Dolls group sports a more jazzy-rock show band sound. The band is tight and effective, the songs are varied and commercial, but there is no real solid lead singer to carry it all off.'

In the same way that the Heartbreakers bore the unmistakable imprint of Johnny's influences, The Criminals were obviously Syl's band. The guitarist's knack of grafting catchy, melodic hooks onto unsophisticated rock'n'roll ensured that the band were an accessible party package. 'The Criminals are well rehearsed, proficient and musically solid, certainly no denying that the band knows what they're doing,' wrote *New York Rocker*'s Ellen Callahan.

'They are an entertaining highly professional rock'n'roll act that will certainly add a great deal of colour and fun to the New York club scene.'

Syl was equally enthusiastic about his group. 'We wanna go all the way. We want to do Broadway shows and movie themes . . . Anything and everything . . . and a lot of hit records. This whole time has been a preparation for what's happening to me now. And what's gonna happen to us as the Criminals. We're gonna be a movement. It hasn't started yet – but it will.'

Syl's open nature and intense commitment to keeping the New York Dolls afloat had ensured that he'd maintained good relations with all four of his former bandmates. Just as Johnny was delighted to team up for an encore with his former guitar partner, David was equally happy to maintain a working relationship that now spanned five years.

The development of David's Staten Island Boys had also been interrupted by Syl's incapacitation, but by August 1977 he'd got as far as recruiting bassist Bud Verno and drummer Frankie LaRocka from Cherry Vanilla's backing band. Appropriately enough, David had first met the duo while travelling back to Manhattan on the Staten Island ferry after a visit to his parents, 'They approached me and they wanted to play with me. I didn't think that much of it at first because so many people approach you. Then finally we got together and they're quite good musicians and quite affable gents at the same time.'

Like David and Syl, Arthur also had a new band – the Corpse Grinders. 'After the Dolls broke up and I left the Brats, me and Arthur basically reformed the Fogg with Stu Wylder from our high school days,' explains Rick Rivets. 'Arthur chose the name Corpse Grinders after a 1970s B-movie.' The line-up was rounded out by drummer Jimmy Criss who joined from Teenage Lust.

Kane had broken up the Killer Kane Band and returned to New York the previous year. Killer Kane frontman Blackie Goozeman would subsequently change his surname to Lawless and become a huge success during the 1980s with hair-metal giants WASP. Although the KKB only performed sporadically, a posthumous three-track EP would be released on Rick Rivets' Whiplash Records in October 1977. The A-side is a brooding ballad, 'Mr Cool', which was backed by two livelier tracks, 'Long Haired Woman' and 'Don't Need You'.

'When Arthur came back to New York he had the demos on a cassette that was all stretched out and that is why the record sounds weird in places,' reveals Rick. 'He only had the three songs that were on the EP and he told us that he had written the songs so he was paid for the records. A few weeks later we get a letter from Blackie's lawyer saying to stop pressing the records or face a lawsuit as Blackie had written the material and not Arthur. We agreed to not press anymore and the matter was dropped. Soon after Blackie was signed to Capital with his band WASP.'

Arthur had also been working on something which he called his 'Colour Code Theory'. 'At this point in time Arthur was spacing out on either alcohol, or glue, or some kind of drug, and he had this vision that if he dyed his hair green, put silver bracelets on his arms and went to the top of the Empire State Building, that The Spaceship would come for him and take him to another world,' recounts Rick. 'So after he'd waited for about five hours and no space ship, I hook up with him and he is really pissed. So we start walking to his place to do some photos for the Killer Kane Band EP and he starts telling me about the colour code and how you have to know it if you want them to come and get you. We get back to his apartment and he has this whole map drawn on all the walls. I asked him what that was all about and he told me that this was the colour code and he couldn't understand why they hadn't come for him as he drew the map as he was told to. Basically, it was something that only Arthur could understand and he really never talked about it much after that, except every once in a while he would mention it and he would seen to get agitated.'

After a brief period in the short-lived LOK, Arthur started the Corpse Grinders with Rick – who'd recently split from the Brats on account of the increasingly theatrical direction that vocalist Keith West was imposing on the group. 'West fancied himself a Broadway singer but his only problem was he couldn't hold a tune,' asserts Rick. 'One of the main reasons I left the Brats was that I refused to play the theme song from the play *42nd Street*. This was what West saw himself as, with his top hat and cane, prancing about the stage at Max's doing show tunes with a hard rock band backing him.'

Stu Wylder was also keen to get back on the road, as he'd done little but soak up the local scene since Age had broken up following their 1975 gigs with the Dolls. 'I lived in a loft on Second Street right next to CBGB's. The Ramones lived right next door. We had a common wall and they used to rehearse there every day and I would listen to them. I got to know Dee Dee very well and his crazy girlfriend Connie who used to go out with Arthur,' recalled Stu. Debbie Harry lived right across the street on Bowery, right across from the entrance to CBGB's. What a neighbourhood! The Corpse Grinders started rehearsing in my loft so there was a lot of music being heard on the block.'

Also on the block – for one brief reunion – were the New York Dolls. Realising that the entire band was in town, Roberta Bayley gathered the quintet together for a *Punk* photo-shoot in front of the very same Gem Spa location where they'd posed with such menace for the back cover of their debut album, four years earlier.

'I knew that all of the members were in New York, and I ran the idea past David Johansen and he was okay with it,' explains Roberta. '*Punk* magazine was pretty hot right then and we were doing a Dolls retrospective feature of Bob Gruen's photos, plus we ran Johnny Thunders' lyrics to "London Boys", his response to the British punks.

'To say that it was difficult to get them all together would be an under-statement! Not that anyone was against doing it, but they all had different schedules and priorities. So I would get three "yes" answers for a particular day, and then someone would say that day didn't work for them and I would start over. This went on for weeks, until finally everyone agreed on 29 August. The shoot was scheduled for night time. Unfortunately Jerry never showed up! The guys tried to make me feel better by saying, "Jerry was never really in the band anyway"!

'Finally, on a Saturday afternoon, 9 September, a second shoot was planned. One by one, they showed up. I was really stressed because I was certain someone wouldn't show. I think David was last, arriving with Bob Gruen. We did two set ups, one in front of Gem Spa and one around the cor-ner on St. Marks Place. I shot colour and black and white, and Gruen also shot pictures of me taking photos, which is nice to have.

'One other thing I think is significant – everyone had short hair at this point except Johansen. Try to understand how important hair had been to the Dolls, especially Johnny and David – they had great hair. But with punk, hair had to go. However, not one to appear behind the times, David simply tucked his locks up into a hat.'

In many of the resultant shots, the quintet look uncomfortable and disconnected – only Syl raises a smile while David, Johnny and Jerry stare at their shoes, or off into the distance. Arthur looks directly and intensely at his estranged 'family', almost appearing to will the group to reconcile and reform.

This was never an option, although Syl may have retained enough of his seemingly inexhaustible commitment to have given the band another go. Musically, Jerry and Johnny were focused on getting back to the UK and the Heartbreakers' forthcoming album release, while David would shortly be courting label interest for his solo debut.

It was also a transitional period for Johnny, David and Arthur in a personal sense, as all three had recently married. In addition to Johnny's nuptials the previous month, David had embarked upon his short-lived marriage to Cyrinda Foxe and Arthur had tied the knot with girlfriend Babs. Roberta Bayley's shoot would be the last occasion on which the classic Dolls line-up would be pictured together.

Shortly after the Gem Spa shoot, Jerry flew back to London to add his mixes to those of Speedy Keen and Walter. It was becoming apparent that each of the Heartbreakers had their own distinct idea of how the album should sound, and consequently – regardless of whose will ultimately prevailed – were likely to be unhappy with the production. In order to preserve its live ferocity on wax, the Heartbreakers' raw sound required a light touch. Having returned to the UK with renewed work visas, the band were mixing the life from their own record. As the in-house animosity levels rose, Johnny and Jerry found that they were re-experiencing all the studio hassles that beset the Dolls.

Four months earlier, Jerry had told Pete Frame that he'd left the Dolls because of the bad production on their two albums. He all but predicted his fate with the Heartbreakers too. 'I would leave this group too if it was on an album that I don't like. If it was produced the way I don't like it I wouldn't stand for it. I wouldn't be in this group. I don't care if the next album makes them or not. I don't care how many millions of dollars they make. I'm not gonna walk around with a bad product, a bad album that I'm ashamed, not proud, of. If it ain't good it'd better be great. I'll settle for good, 'specially the first album. I'm trying to make sure it sounds great. I know we can. We already did it. It's performed right. Now I want the sound right and, if it ain't, I'll settle for good because I have to. But I'm not gonna settle for anything less than good – I'll leave or have nothing to do with anything.'

To maintain the band's UK profile while the album was still being finished, Track released an EP. The lead track was a live highlight – 'One Track Mind' – Walter and Jerry's hedonist anthem. Lyrics like, 'I got tracks on my arm and tracks on my face / There's tracks on the walls over the place,' did little to add any credence to claims that the band had cleaned up. The flip featured another couple of tracks that were going over well with UK audiences; 'Can't Keep My Eyes On You' and a cover of the Contours' 'Do You Love Me?', which was often aired as an encore. Written mainly by Jerry, 'Can't Keep My Eyes On You' dated back to the Heartbreakers' first line-up and featured some ribald lyrical adjustments courtesy of Walter. There would be further lyric changes live when the chorus was adjusted to 'Can't keep my cock in you'.

Kris Needs: LAMF *finally reached a form that Track deemed suitable and was released on 3 October 1977. I first heard it in the Track offices and had to contend with Sham 69's Jimmy Pursey leaping around the room with his trousers round his ankles, trying to spray everyone up the arse with a fire extinguisher. Initially knocked out by the album, I wrote an enthusiastic preview for Zigzag: 'I wanna play it and play it 'cos I love the Heartbreakers . . . For sheer ecstatic raunch you can't beat 'em.' Only later, hearing it on a normal sound system did it become apparent that a lot of the blazing assault, dark soul and snarling nuances which made the band so unique had been mixed down into the gutter, leaving a clogged-up wall of noise. Luckily, the songs and performances were so strong that it still beat the shit out of most of the Heartbreakers' current competition.*

LAMF kicks off with 'Born To Lose', before setting the pace for the whole album with Johnny's 'Baby Talk'. The song is basically a clever, raucous heist of the Yardbirds' 'I Ain't Done Wrong' from their *Five Live Yardbirds* album. 'I always thought we took it from "I Ain't Got You",' confessed Walter. 'I didn't know "I Ain't Done Wrong" at all. But, lo and behold, I went back to the original studio recordings and sure enough, it's right in the middle of "I Ain't Done Wrong".'

'All By Myself' was a Lure-Nolan song, which Walter sings in a Kinksy fashion. He says it was the only song he wrote with Jerry, who came up with the staccato drumbeat. The track contains the immortal line, 'I don't need society / to open up my fly for me.'

'I Wanna Be Loved' is a Johnny track that dated from the period when Richard Hell was in the band and often served as a set closer. The structure, attack and melody are classic fifties rock'n'roll in the Cochran-Vincent style – Johnny in his unabandoned element, straight and to the point.

Johnny's 'It's Not Enough' is the album's ballad, complete with chiming acoustic twelve-string. Having purged all slower material from the Heartbreakers' set after the departure of Richard Hell, he'd overruled himself in the studio to produce a plaintive song that provided gentle shade when contrasted against the coruscating energy of side one's closer, 'Chinese Rocks'.

Side two roars in with two more live favourites 'Get Off The Phone' and 'Pirate Love', both of which had been in the set from the very start. The bands' reworking of 'Love Comes In Spurts', 'One Track Mind' follows, before Johnny's 'I Love You' races by in less than two-and-a-half minutes of unrequited angst. 'Goin' Steady' chugs along engagingly, but is undermined by the mix, which reduces the bass, rhythm and drums to a distant fuzz. It's hardly surprising, as the track was subjected to five separate production marathons in four different studios.

'Let Go' is a straightforward twelve-bar rocker cooked up by Johnny and Jerry, which again left much of its live power in the studio. Although Johnny's hectoring Noo Yawk whine and Dolls-style backing vocals make welcome appearances, the muffled mix ensured that the album ended with a far smaller bang than should have been the case.

Once *LAMF* hit the stores, reviews tended to focus upon how the muddy mix emasculated the Heartbreakers' trademark sonic maelstrom. In *Sounds*, Jon Savage observed, 'The songs are [mostly] great, the playing assured, tight, adventurous . . . so what's the problem? The mixing . . . they can't seem to get it quite right.' Summing up the general consensus of pundits and fans alike, he added, 'The sound doesn't do the songs justice.'

'It was a shitty album,' Johnny bluntly confessed to *Melody Maker*'s Harry Doherty. 'That's the worst thing that happened to us. What happened was that we mixed it, right, and everybody liked the mix. Then Jerry Nolan went ahead of us while we were still in New York. We had heard a test pressing and liked it and then he started remixing the album. I was in New York at the time and I didn't even hear what went down until the album was out.' Johnny asserted that Jerry deliberately sabotaged the album because he wasn't happy with it and wanted to scupper its release. 'Y'know, he started screwing up all the mixes and so it sounded the way it did.'

'The result was a predictable disaster,' acknowledges Leee Black Childers. 'The only way to record that kind of music was to go in, do it, and get out again.'

'The recording of LAMF had gone well but we could never get the sound right on it,' said Walter. 'We were jealous of the Pistols' record 'cos it had such a great sound and we'd wanted to come up with something so vital . . . John thought it was a curse because the Dolls' albums hadn't sounded so good either . . . We were like the royalty of punk rock, so to have it fall apart because the record came out shitty was a bummer.' Jungle Records' Alan Hauser, who would later release the original mixes of LAMF, maintains that, 'Aside from all the different approaches done at different studios, the final 1977 mixes were fine. A mastering fault gave the LP the "mud".'

Unable to stomach having to tour behind another album that he was unhappy with, Jerry quit the group on the eve of the UK tour. Nerves were frayed. This group had never been commercially successful, and, when they'd had any money, they'd spent the bulk of it on drugs. Now, their biggest tour was about to start and their drummer had jumped ship. Not only that, but Johnny was without his best friend, father figure, soul mate and principal drug buddy.

Jerry attempted to clarify his decision by slinging mud at his former bandmates in an interview with *Record Mirror*'s Barry Cain. 'There's one guy in this band I don't like. I've discovered he's a coward, and I can't work with cowards. He's done things behind my back . . . he gave in to allow the album to be released. He's only interested in reading about himself in the papers . . . There's also another guy in the Heartbreakers who acts more like the middle man in a drugs deal rather than concentrating on what he should be doing. The whole thing's a joke and I want out.'

'Jerry's leaving the Heartbreakers was because of Walter,' insisted Johnny in a subsequent *Zigzag* interview. 'Everything went to Walter's head. It was all new to him to get any kind of recognition at all, and Billy was just a fucking asshole and he still is and Jerry just got fed up and buggered off. I mean, me and Jerry been playing together for seven years now and me and Jerry splitting up is worse than losing a wife or a girlfriend. We got [former Clash drummer] Terry Chimes to play drums but it was never the same without Jerry.'

'It's gonna be hard to find someone,' Walter observed, 'but for a lot of drummers on the punk scene Jerry's their idol, so we should find someone with the right style soon. It's probably better he's a great drummer and he has a lot of good ideas, but he created a lot of problems. He's the main reason we haven't rehearsed once in the last year.'

To the casual observer or acquaintance – especially interviewers – Jerry customarily projected the impression of being the consummate professional. By contrast, Johnny was as blunt as fuck. He never tried to hide the fact that he found interviews a wearisome chore but a necessary evil in the rock-'n'roll game. Jerry was always friendly and outgoing, but had an aura of danger which was more apparent if you knew he had been involved in deadly gang activity and hard drug culture. No matter how polite he was, you would never think of messing with this man. He was a cut above the normal aggressive young punk. Whereas Johnny would be seen in public nodding out or falling over on stage, Jerry rarely appeared to be out of it. He would denounce drugs at the drop of the hat, but Jerry was an addict and was responsible for encouraging and indulging Johnny's use of smack.

He also had some burning issues, which had been stoked to boiling point by the unrealised potential of the two Dolls albums. His attempts to prevent the *déjà vu* production shortcomings that undermined *LAMF* were in vain, which only served to exacerbate his frustration. Eventually, the life was mixed out of the Heartbreakers' album, and the proud Jerry felt that he had little option other than to stand down – although he would make repeated return appearances. Johnny was his blood brother, after all – even if the blood sharing came via a syringe.

As far back as the end of 1976, *New York Rocker* ran a gossip item that went, 'Drumming up trouble? Jerry Nolan may or may not be in the Heartbreakers by the time you read this, due to managerial differences within the group and certain ego problems.'

A few months earlier, Pete Frame had asked Jerry about the stability of the Heartbreakers' internal relationships. 'We're not really the type that hang out together that much. We all got different interests and different ideas about living life off stage now, more than we ever did. But that's cool. That's a part of growing up. But I'm sure musically – and lately we haven't rehearsed as much as I'm sure we'd like to . . . the more we're together as a band without anybody around the more we tend to create and come up with good ideas. Everybody slacks off at times. We have our periods where we slack off but we've come back pretty much tight and uniform. Not visually, I mean mentally.'

Regardless of where Jerry's head was at, the Heartbreakers needed to find a new drummer. Sex Pistol Paul Cook was tracked down by 'phone and played the first three gigs of the tour starting on 1 October at Bristol Polytechnic (with Cook's partner-in-crime Steve Jones getting up for the encore). The gig was beset by a number of fights during the Heartbreakers' set, which the music press blamed on 'football supporters' and 'skinheads'. Despite this, the band returned for five encores, including a version of the Monkees' 'I'm Not Your Steppin' Stone', which had been a staple of the Pistols' early sets.

Cook was only a temporary solution to the vacancy caused by Jerry's departure so the band auditioned Rat Scabies – who was temporarily without a gig after The Damned's split following the release of their second album, *Music For Pleasure* – but found his style too radical. 'Like sixties heavy metal', reckoned Johnny.

Next, a somewhat puzzling press release came from Track publicist Alan Edwards. It read, 'Jerry Nolan is no longer a member of the Heartbreakers, but a hired musician. He will be performing with the band for all the British dates through to the Croydon Greyhound on 6 November.' To those who knew that the drummer had taken a stand over the album, it appeared to be a means of rejoining his group without losing face.

Being cast in the strange position of hired hand in the group he'd formed, Jerry took the stoic route, keeping himself to himself but playing his ass off all around the country. Many put the recent schism down to the complex relationship between Johnny and Jerry. They might scream at each other and walk out into other projects, but they couldn't get properly divorced.

The group were still getting good press, with *Sounds* enthusing, 'Rock'n'roll the Heartbreakers are through and through . . . They cross barriers other new wavers wouldn't dare for fear of losing face. The Heartbreakers are great, hot and anybody's.'

On 20 October, the Heartbreakers headlined at the Rainbow Theatre, Finsbury Park, north London. A bill-topping appearance at the beautiful former cinema was always a sign that a band had moved several rungs up the ladder. They were supported by Siouxsie and the Banshees and Marco Pirroni's Models. It was strange seeing the band on such a big stage but they pulled it off spectacularly, coming on to a riotous intro tape of sirens, explosions and street noise and smashing through a sheet of carefully positioned glass with a brick. As the Heartbreakers tore through their familiar set with breakneck dexterity and stage-spilling attitude, it really looked like they were on the rise.

Sadly, the momentum and the following that the Heartbreakers had built up through 1977 was not capitalised on. After the UK tour ended in Croydon on 6 November, they played what turned out to be farewell gigs at the Vortex on 21 and 22 of that month. By then, Jerry had returned to New York, unable to endure his reduced status in the band. This time, Terry Chimes stepped in at short notice for the two concerts.

As ever, the Heartbreakers put on a good show, with new songs like 'Too Much Junkie Business', which emerged from Walter fusing Chuck Berry's 'Too Much Monkey Business' with a re-keyed version of the Dolls take on 'Pills'. 'John loved the song so much that I think he couldn't bear to see it published it without his name on it since he had lived it so much – we all had – so I guess he thought all our names deserved to be on it,' explained Walter. 'It didn't really bother me at the time since nobody was making millions off of it so I just let it go. Jerry wasn't in the band at the time so he wasn't included.'

The Heartbreakers' problems were compounded when Track Records ran out of money and ceased operating, before subsequently going into voluntary liquidation. 'One day I came to my office at Track Records on Carnaby Street to find the front doors chained and padlocked, accompanied by a "No Entry" sign from some law office or another,' recalls Leee. 'I called Peter Gerber. He had wisely worded our contract to state that all tapes were owned by the Heartbreakers and only leased to Track Records. So, I legally owned them.

'Among the constantly changing houseguests at Cross Street staying with us then was Mrs. Simpson, a friend of mine from high school, along with her twelve-year-old son, Rocky, and [another teenage boy named] Chris . . . So, owing to their youth, vigour, and small stature I enlisted their help. There in front of hundreds of gaping tourists Rocky scaled up the front of the building, retrieved the *LAMF* tapes and threw them down to me. Right next to them on the shelf were The Who, etc, but we stayed legal and only stole what was ours. We spirited the tapes away and hid them under the bed at Linda Clark's literally for years, until the coast was clear.'

Although this meant that the band was without a label, there had been some interest from CBS. On 15 December, the Heartbreakers checked into Riverside Studios to demo 'Too Much Junkie Business' and a stinging retort to the Sex Pistols' Dolls-baiting 'New York', called 'London Boys' (which Johnny would later use on *So Alone*). However, the label were slow in following up their initial attention and without a deal, or Jerry, Johnny found himself losing interest in the band and at odds with Walter and Billy who were keen to carry on.

Shortly after the Vortex gigs Johnny announced he was quitting, which effectively dissolved the band. 'I quit the Heartbreakers 'cos there was a whole fucking problem getting on with Walter and getting along with Billy,' explained Johnny. 'I just lost interest in working with them.' Lure and Rath went back to New York and formed the Heroes. Only a year had passed since the Heartbreakers landed in London to commence the Anarchy tour. Now the Heartbreakers had gone the way of the Dolls and Johnny, David, Syl, Arthur and Jerry were left to plot their next moves as very separate musical entities.

Missing In Action

'New York's really a drag. It's nothing like it used to be. All the kids who I used to hang out with are either dead or in jail.' – *Johnny Thunders*

As 1978 was ushered in by the Sex Pistols imploding photogenically before the American media, Johnny hung around in London hoping to get his solo career up and running. During the first three months of the New Year, the immediacy of his habit proved a far stronger motivating force than any creative aspirations. As a means of raising cash quickly, Johnny set about organising a series of one-off gigs at the Speakeasy, backed by anyone who was willing to be pushed onto the stage behind him.

Appropriately named the Living Dead, on any given night this loose ensemble could include various combinations of singers and players drawn from former Pistols Cook, Jones and Vicious, Snatch mainstay Patti Palladin, teenage French guitarist Henri Paul from the Maniacs, Eddie and the Hot Rods rhythm section Paul Gray and Steve Nicol, Only Ones frontman Peter Perrett and drummer Mike Kellie. 'It was a good period,' Johnny recalled. 'I like playing with different musicians. Actually, I got in a rut playing with the Heartbreakers for so long.'

In February, Johnny encountered Dave Hill, who had recently set up his own record label, Real, and also managed Chrissie Hynde's Pretenders. Dave had caught the Living Dead at the Speakeasy and believed that Johnny had sufficient potential to risk making him the first act on his new label. Johnny signed up for a single and an album, which were to be distributed through Warner Brothers.

Within a few weeks Johnny was driving Dave to distraction, living next to a Soho 'sauna' in D'Arblay Street and up to his usual tricks – scouring the locale for anyone willing to sub him some cash for a hit, becoming embroiled in hassles with dealers and getting wasted. At the time, Johnny was the most obvious drug casualty in town. Despite this, he managed to drag himself into Island Studios to record two tracks for a single, 'Dead Or Alive' and 'Downtown' – which was set for release on 26 May. It was co-produced by the up and coming Steve Lillywhite, who would later go on to work with the Rolling Stones.

For this session, Johnny again called upon Steve Nicol and Paul Gray to provide him with backing and the trio duly produced the goods; 'Dead Or Alive' is an effective slice of twelve-bar desperation, while 'Downtown' is a sleazy blues rumble that was notable for being the last song that Johnny wrote for the red patent Dolls.

'I put out "Dead Or Alive", then the Heartbreakers were supposed to get back together again because we'd broke up, but we never got back together,' explained Johnny. 'I had an option to do an album with the single, so I did the album. I had nothing else to do.'

After the break up of the Heartbreakers, Johnny had approached former Led Zeppelin and Marc Bolan publicist B.P. Fallon to be his manager when they met at a party given for Patti Smith. Like Leee Childers, Fallon was short on funds but rich in compassion and enthusiasm. He'd been around the music scene since 1964 and had plenty of friends and associates he could call upon whenever additional personnel for gigs or studio sessions were necessary. When Johnny returned to Island to record his debut solo album in June, his new manager's contact book proved invaluable. 'Musicians who lent their support came from the Sex Pistols, the Only Ones, the Heartbreakers, even Traffic. Chrissie Hynde sang backing vocals,' recalled Fallon. 'On the storming version of Derek Martin's R&B classic "Daddy Rolling Stone", first Johnny, then Phil Lynott, then Steve Marriott sing a verse. Phil, he was concerned at Johnny's health. "He's too out of it, knowarramean?"'

Of all the post-Dolls solo projects, *So Alone* would emerge as the most complete album. Of course, it would have been even better if Johnny hadn't been so utterly wasted during the sessions. This served to irritate Dave Hill further, as he felt that the album was Thunders' last chance to make a minor dent on the big time.

The first indication that Johnny was making some effort to live up to Hill's expectations came with the recording of 'You Can't Put Your Arms Around A Memory', which Fallon described as 'Johnny's most beautiful, sensitive, tragic song.'

This track would ultimately be released as a single in advance of the album on 29 September. For Johnny, putting out a sensitive ballad as a single was a bold move. This was the side of him that had inspired Dave Hill – pouring his heart out over a castanet-topped groove, which could have come off a Drifters song. Effectively utilising the backing of Perrett, Gray, and Kellie, the song bears comparison with anybody from Gram Parsons to James Carr as a timeless, beautiful cry from the heart. 'It doesn't pay to try, all the smart boys know why,' laments Johnny while his guitar gently bleeds.

The flip side of the single would be 'Hurtin'', an up-tempo rocker more in-keeping with what Johnny's audience was likely to expect. Here Henri Paul handled lead guitar alongside long-time Fallon buddy Phil Lynott, who supplied a typical Thin Lizzy-style bassline. Mike Kellie again handled drum duty.

The remainder of the album tracks were recorded and mixed during June and July. Among these was a searing rendition of the Chantays' instrumental 'Pipeline' – which would be Johnny's set opener for the rest of his career. Other covers included a version of 'Give Him A Great Big Kiss', which saw Johnny duetting with Patti Palladin, a slightly duff pub-rock re-working of 'Daddy Was A Rolling Stone', featuring former Small Faces frontman Steve Marriott, and a version of 'Subway Train' that is closer to the original 'That's Poison' and prompted Johnny to pronounce, 'I always wanted to sing it.'

The recording of 'Give Him A Great Big Kiss' represented the realisation of Johnny's girl-group dream that first coalesced in front of Mariann's Dansette fifteen years earlier. For many Dolls fans it had been a huge disappointment when the song had been omitted from the band's studio albums. Johnny's version does the Shangri-Las' classic full justice, utilising a riotous sax-driven backing courtesy of John 'Irish' Earle, on loan from pub rockers Graham Parker and the Rumour. More significantly, the track features Walter Lure and Billy Rath who were in town and demonstrating that there was little in the way of hard feelings over the Heartbreakers break up – readily agreed to Johnny's invitation to take part in the sessions.

Four additional original songs were selected to make up the album's ten tracks: 'Ask Me No Questions', a reflective ballad, 'Leave Me Alone', which is essentially 'Chatterbox' revisited, the melodic, moody sax 'n' guitar duel of '(She's So) Untouchable', and 'London Boys', which had first been recorded by the Heartbreakers as part of their demo for CBS.

Given that the song was conceived as a riposte to the Pistols' 'New York' (itself a scathing attack on the New York scene in general and the Dolls in particular, complete with such lines as 'Four years on you still look the same. / I think it's 'bout time you changed your brain'), it was ironic that Steve Jones and Paul Cook supplied their customarily beefy guitar and drums for the version included on *So Alone*. Johnny's lyrics decry the Pistols as 'mama's boys' and concludes with the sneering 'you poor little puppet', sung in the same cadence that Rotten had applied to his 'poor little faggot' jibe. 'They're Malcolm McLaren's puppets. He pulls the strings and they do what he says,' blustered Johnny. 'I still think McLaren's a genius. I think he's great. You can't take credit from him. I think he's a great manager but, y'know, them guys, he pulls the strings and they do it.'

Johnny also recorded a decidedly lo-fi version of Marc Bolan's 'The Wizard', which was omitted from the original LP, but subsequently surfaced on the 1992 CD reissue – 'I heard Tyrannosaurus Rex doing that back in '69,' recalled Johnny. 'But I just couldn't capture the right feeling.'

The *So Alone* sessions were Johnny's first experience of having sole command in the studio, a situation that he found very much to his liking. 'It's the only album that I've ever done that I'm proud of – production-wise – 'cos I did it myself . . . . Anything else I did there was someone in the band that wanted something this way. This time I had complete control. It's produced by me, Peter Perrett and Steve Lillywhite. I called all the shots. I used to write tons of ballads and I just could never do them with the Dolls or the Heartbreakers because they didn't like playing ballads and they didn't like slow songs. That's the main reason why I did the *So Alone* album – so I could get my favourite ballads out.'

Shortly after the album was finished, Johnny was deported back to New York for the second time. 'They escorted me on the plane and made me go back. I had a manager who never took care of all my business – my passport, getting extensions and stuff. It got worse and worse and they threw me out.'

While Johnny had spent more than half a year getting *So Alone* from the conceptual to finished stages, David Johansen had made far quicker time in getting his debut album recorded and into the stores. By recruiting guitarists Tommy Trask and Johnny Rao – who he knew from the bar circuit in his old Staten Island neighbourhood – he'd rounded out the roster of his Staten Island Boys. 'We practiced for about eight months playing in the provinces around New York, Connecticut, Long Island and Jersey, as well as practicing in a garage in Staten Island, all this. When I decided it was a good band I went and got the deal with Blue Sky because I was ready to get back on the road again.'

After signing with Steve Paul's label, a subsidiary of Epic, the new group recorded some demos with producer Jack Douglas. Originally, Douglas was going to co-produce the first album with Joe Perry, but the Aerosmith guitarist spent eight months recording his own solo album, so David asked Richard Robinson –who had previously recorded Lou Reed, and later gave up music to become a full-time illusionist – to take over.

The ten-track *David Johansen* was recorded during February and March and released in May 1978. The album was designed to be more accessible to the mainstream than his Dolls material, but included 'Funky But Chic' and 'Girls', both of which had survived from the Dollettes period. More significantly, David demonstrated he knew his way around a ballad better than most. Both 'Donna' and 'Pain In My Heart' show him summoning up convincing displays of emotion that may have had some creative assistance from his recent break up with Cyrinda Foxe.

The album also benefited from Syl Sylvain's guitar assistance and songwriting contributions, which added to the overall catchy pop aesthetic. 'Frenchette' proved that Johansen and Sylvain could still raise a roof without any great effort, and David's choice of cover version was typically astute – Irma Franklin's 'Pain In My Heart', which had been a massive hit for Otis Redding as well as a track on the first Rolling Stones EP.

Each week, Robert Christgau of *The Village Voice* produced his essential guide to new albums. He reckoned, 'This is in many ways a better record than either Dolls albums. Conceptually, though, this singer-with-backup in a post-garage mode, packing no distinctive structural or sonic kick, is pretty conventional for the pied piper of outrageousness.'

In addition to working with the former Dolls frontman on *David Johansen* and guesting with the Staten Island Boys on the road, Syl had found time to record a debut single with the Criminals, which emerged in June 1978. Issued on his own Sing Sing label, 'The Kids Are Back' was an energetic slice of power pop and had a lively reworking of Henry Mancini's 'Peter Gunn' (titled 'The Cops Are Coming'), as its flip. With next to zero publicity, the single sold out of its initial pressing of 5,000 – a significant number of which arrived in the UK as imports.

For his part, Arthur had been equally active. The Corpse Grinders had made their live debut at Great Gildersleeves in New York, the previous Halloween. In addition to the established line-up of Kane, Rivets, Wylder and Criss, the Grinders had attracted a wannabe member named Billy Ballz. 'Ballz was a very weird piano player,' explains Stu Wylder 'He put guitar strings on his piano and had Arthur put piano strings on his bass to get a really nutty and annoying sound.' The unconventional pianist was also keen to encourage the band to shave their heads like his, a suggestion that earned him short shrift from Rivets and Wylder. He was cautioned not to hit his ass on the door on his way out.

Undaunted by such rejection, Ballz turned up for the Corpse Grinders' first gig with his girlfriend in tow. 'She was wearing an overcoat with nothing under it and when she took it off the bouncers tried to throw them out, but Billy had her put it back on so he could see the show,' recalls Rick. 'Stu was really high that night and when we hit the stage he was nowhere to be found, so we started playing an instrumental and he came up during the end of the song – falling over everybody. We started to do our set but he was too far gone and tackled Arthur, knocking him over his amp. Then he came at me. He got me down, but when I got up we started having this fist fight, while all the time the drummer was keeping a beat and the guitars were feeding back and the audience didn't know what to make of it. When things calmed down, the crowd started screaming and going crazy for more. We had played all the songs we knew, so we just got off and they all thought that this was part of the act. The place was crowded and Ballz came up to us after the show and was praising us at how great it was.'

In addition to delighting the crowd with their pugilistic prowess, the Corpse Grinders' performance alarmed their manager, Debbie Cohen, so much that she fled the gig. Cohen overcame her trauma sufficiently to organise a cable TV appearance for the group, thanks to her connections with a short-lived Manhattan public broadcast show that she hosted. In addition to having the Corpse Grinders lip-synch to their demos of 'Take What I Can' and 'Bulldog' (which had been recorded with pianist Bob Casper, bassist Mike Pollot and drummer Stix Nicholson two months earlier), the band's manager agreed to let Billy Ballz prance around on roller skates while the Grinders mimed. This spectacle was followed by a brief interview, during which research took a back seat as Arthur was asked what his mother thought of his green hair. With customary vacant brevity he replied, 'Like, wow.'

Arthur's tenure in the Corpse Grinders proved to be equally brief. By July 1978, he'd left the band, where he was replaced by Bill Spence. 'His wife, Babs, was very controlling,' explained Stu. 'She advised Arthur that the name of the band should be changed to "Kane's Corpses". Then something happened outside CBGB's one night, when the whole band was hanging out front. Johnny Thunders came walking by and stopped to chat with Arthur. Then Arthur just walked away with Johnny and that was the last we saw of him for quite some while. A couple of months later we hear that Arthur is playing with Sid Vicious at Max's.'

The Corpse Grinders' debut single, 'Rites, 4 Whites'/'Mental Moron' had already been recorded before Arthur left and was released on Whiplash Records in July. The band continued playing at Max's and around Connecticut and New Haven until November, when they called it a day. Rick Rivets subsequently joined the Slugs, a Long Island quartet that combined Thunders-style guitar chops with the breakneck sonic velocity of the Ramones.

Once back on his home turf, Johnny continued his practice of playing one-off concerts to raise quick cash. Between the end of July and September he hooked up with Walter and Billy for a series of Heartbreakers reunion gigs at Max's. Although Lure and Rath had previously claimed that the band would never reform on account of Johnny's unreliability, relations had been restored during the *So Alone* sessions. Jerry's place was taken by Ty Styx, who was a regular face on the CBGB's/Max's scene. Ty was a more than competent drummer, and, while he may not have had Jerry's prodigious strength, he assimilated the Heartbreakers set with little practice and was beat perfect during these shows. Johnny also played a pair of shows at Max's with the Senders, led by French rocker Philippe Marcade who would subsequently go on to team up with Thunders in Gang War.

On 7 September, Sid Vicious – who had left London to spend more time with his addiction – was given a 'Welcome To New York' gig at Max's, and played a twenty-minute set with a pick-up band comprised of Jerry Nolan, Arthur Kane, Steve Dior and a slightly bemused Mick Jones, who was in town finishing the second Clash album. They played five ramshackle songs but it obviously wasn't happening. Mick was stunned at the state of the participants. 'It was a serious drug thing,' he acknowledged afterward. 'The people there were as out of it as you can be without actually being dead.' When asked about the possibility of forming a band with Sid, Johnny shrugged. 'There was talk of it. We got it together a few times but it wouldn't have worked out.'

After the gig, Jerry, Arthur and Steve Dior formed the Idols with guitarist Barry Jones – another axe man who took many of his cues from Johnny. The quartet quickly became regulars on the CBGB's/Max's circuit and released their only single, 'You'/'Girl That I Love', in 1979.

Back in the UK, reaction to 'You Can't Put Your Arms Around A Memory' had been encouraging – at one point, sales were strong enough to raise hopes that the single would reach the Top 40. However, demand for the coloured vinyl pressings of the twelve inch were quickly exhausted, catching Real by surprise, and the disc failed to chart.

So Alone followed on 6 October, and was enthusiastically welcomed by *Sounds*' Giovanni Dadomo: 'The first surprising thing to a lot of people will, I'm sure, be the overall excellence of this here recording. Mr Thunders is, of course, one of rock'n'roll's more erratic luminaries – one night's Jet Boy, the next night's snailman. It's a part of his magic, to be sure – like the Stones, his mistakes make him more lovably human.'

Johnny admitted to a degree of ambivalence in respect of *So Alone*'s reviews. 'I wasn't knocked out by them. The papers over here are really bad. French rock mags are better, they have colour pictures. I find it very hard to talk to most writers. They use really big words. I have to ask them what that means. I hate most of the writers. I dunno how to explain it but they're really tacky.'

One of the most obvious ways in which the album differed from Johnny's Dolls/Heartbreakers backlist was the inclusion of slower numbers such as 'You Can't Put Your Arms Round A Memory', 'Untouchable' and 'Ask Me No Questions'. These songs developed elements of Thunders' widening creative palette previously only partially revealed on 'Lonely Planet Boy' and 'It's Not Enough'. For those who viewed Johnny as a one-trick songwriter, such sensitivity could come as a surprise.

'I always had a lot of slow songs,' he explained. 'They didn't wanna do 'em in the Heartbreakers. I always wanted to do 'em, but we never used to do "It's Not Enough" on stage. Jerry doesn't like playing slow songs. I got my chance to do it now. That's why I'm doing it.'

Dave Hill showed further belief in Johnny's talent by giving the album as much of a promotional push as his fledgling label could provide. In addition to persuading parent company Warners to feature Thunders on the front of their monthly in-house magazine, he secured funding for full-page ads in most of the major British music publications. Additionally, Hill overcame the customary personnel and visa hassles to set up a major promotional showcase for the album with a gig at London's Lyceum on 12 October.

Billed as the Johnny Thunders All Stars, the band was scheduled to include many of the luminaries who contributed to the album, with rehearsals set to commence on 5 October at the Harlesden Roxy. With typical disregard for his public profile and relationship with Real, Johnny materialised, via an Air India flight, four days late.

To exacerbate matters, Cook and Jones dropped out two days before the gig. McLaren issued a disclaimer – Jones was in LA producing the Avengers, while Cook was allegedly busy with the *Rock'n'Roll Swindle* movie. 'I doubt if I'll work with them again,' Johnny told *Melody Maker*'s Harry Doherty. 'I wouldn't mind working with Paul. He's great. Jones is just a Thunders-imitator. Success that went to somebody's head. A classic example. He's got a gold album and shit . . . so many of the Pistols' songs were Dolls' songs. "Liar" was "Puss 'N' Boots". They've got "Personality Crisis" in the middle of something.'

The absence of the ex-Pistols – whose appearances had been advertised on tickets and posters – meant that Paul Gray and Mike Kellie had to be brought in at short notice. Equally disruptive was Johnny's physical condition. 'All that everybody told me (warned me) about Johnny Thunders is true,' wrote Doherty. 'He actually does look wasted.' Pete Frame said that he'd seen Johnny in a Soho second-hand record shop, selling a box of his own albums.

On the night, the Lyceum was packed with a pick 'n' mix selection of punks, rockers and every Thunders impersonator in town – all hopeful of catching their man on top form. Instead, Johnny sauntered on, launched into 'Pipeline' – and promptly blew his amp. This heralded a cavalcade of sound problems that plagued the rest of the set. Hardly surprisingly, the band was under-rehearsed and Johnny was unsteady and aggressive. Despite this, he managed the odd moment of magic, such as when Patti Palladin came on to join him for a tour-de-force rendition of 'Give Her A Great Big Kiss', aching versions of the ballads 'You Can't Put Your Arms Around A Memory' and 'She's So Untouchable', and roof-raising treatments of 'Chinese Rocks', 'Born To Lose' and 'London Boys'. There were also some new cover versions, including Nancy Sinatra's 'These Boots Are Made For Walking' and the Senders' recent single 'Living End'.

On the evening of the gig, the news of Nancy Spungen's murder and Sid Vicious's subsequent arrest was just breaking. Johnny had caught a radio report just before going on stage. 'It's incredible. I can't believe it. Sid . . . you never know what to expect from him . . . What'll be next? If he goes to jail I bet he kills himself in jail . . . the poor guy, man. I feel worse for him than her. It's the worse thing that could ever happen to him anyway. He'll be in the Tombs now.

'You get arrested. They take you to the precinct first, right? Then, uh, they take you to 100 Centre Street, right? And that's the tombs. There's like, 75 guys in one cell and like 95 per cent of them are black and they're all heavies, right? Heavy, heavy. If they get Sid in there I'm sure he's gonna say something. He's gonna mouth off to 'em and they'll beat his head in. He'll need all the help he can get.' Sid survived jail and would o.d. at a Greenwich Village party the following February, inspiring Johnny to write 'Sad Vacation'.

In his *Sounds* review of the All Stars show, Andy Courtney identified the way in which Thunders' gigs had become 'a sicko zone' populated by vicarious onlookers who'd turned up to gawp at the junkie. As Syl later observed, 'There's a certain charisma about a guy that everybody thinks is about to drop dead. It's like when Daffy Duck blows up on stage and then you see him as an angel in heaven saying, "Yeah folks, it's a great show, but you can only do it once!"'

The muted response from the Lyceum crowd suggested some sections of the audience may have been disappointed that Johnny got through the set without keeling over. 'It's kind of reassuring to know that one guy is capable of digesting all this shit and managing to survive,' wrote Courtney.

Johnny left the UK without making any further attempts to promote *So Alone*. He had become accustomed to having pick-up bands put together for him by B.P. Fallon or Dave Hill. And he'd failed to capitalise on the faith shown in him by the Real Records chief through his inability to put together a touring band and gig behind the album in Britain and Europe, where it was selling respectably well for an independent release. When asked about his future plans by *Zigzag*, it seemed that he was looking to make another fresh start.

Kris Needs: *Friday the thirteenth – the day after the Lyceum. Johnny Thunders has to do one of the things he hates most – press interviews. Luckily, I've been hanging out with him regularly for nearly two years, which makes the going easier. Johnny's slumped forward at the end of a huge table in the Warner Brothers Records boardroom, sporting a yellow New York t-shirt and crumpled brown leather jacket. A speaking Mickey Mouse doll sits on the table in front of him, next to bottles of vodka and whisky. His flickering eyelids betray the fact that he hasn't slept and is chem-*

ically altered. He says he's suffering from laryngitis, but is still friendly and funny. Fuelled by chain-rolled spliffs of Jamaican weed, with Johnny on vodka and me on whisky, the 'interview' is more like a lethargically pleasant chat – respite from the stream of stock questions he's been getting all day.

We start with the previous night's gig where he encored with Gene Vincent's 'Be-Bop-A-Lula', which I've never heard him do before.

'It was the anniversary of his death. I love Gene Vincent . . . but I love Eddie Cochran more! D'you see The Buddy Holly Story? *It's alright, but you just know everything that's gonna happen!' he laughs. When he announced the Vincent song he was sarcastic, in the manner of 'Here's one by someone you don't know.' Like they didn't appreciate him.*

'Ah, most of them knew who he was. I was talking to the punks. I didn't appreciate them very much either.'

I gush for about five minutes about So Alone. *Johnny smiles sleepily.*

'I'm pretty happy with the album . . . well, 99 per cent of it anyway.'

What's the one per cent?

'I don't wanna get into that,' he says mysteriously. 'Might offend some people.'

So Alone *took three weeks to record. Was it easy?*

'Much easier than before because I was in complete control of everything. I had nobody to argue with.'

The one time Johnny becomes animated is when he announces his plans to visit New Orleans in search of new musical collaborators.

'Yeah, what I'm planning to do is go to New Orleans and try to find some old 40-to-50-year-old black musicians. It's my dream and I've got someone to finance it. They have the greatest musicians there. We'll play rhythm and blues, rock'n'roll – those guys can play anything. Bourbon Street's got maybe 150 clubs. They got the greatest old blues players. I'd like to find the right guys and make 'em some money, get on the road and get out.

'I wanna play the States 'cos my album's gonna come out there. I miss touring the States . . . but I'll always come back here.'

Do you feel an affinity with London?

'Starting to feel that way, never used to. I've been here for a long time . . . New York's really a drag. It's nothing like it used to be. All the kids who I used to hang out with are either dead or in jail.'

However, New Orleans proved to be a pipe dream that Johnny would wait more than a decade to try to fulfil. Instead, he returned to New York to spend time with Julie – who was shortly to give birth to another son, Dino. Once back in town, he hung out with the likes of Jerry and Sid Vicious – who was now on parole – and made a handful of live appearances, such as a couple of shows with Blondie and a Max's Rolling Stones tribute night, where he performed 'Cocksucker Blues'.

Shortly after Johnny had left London, David and Sylvain arrived in town for an eight gig UK tour to promote *David Johansen*, which was part of an extensive European trek. Although Syl would have preferred to make progress with his Criminals, he saw the tour with David as a means of acquiring funds to enable the group to record a decent demo, in the hope of securing a record deal. David's management paid Syl $2,000 and the Criminals duly laid down a set that would emerge in 1985 as the *78 Criminals* bootleg.

Jerry was welcomed back into the Heartbreakers fold when the band reformed once more in March 1979. His return was no great surprise, as any ill-feeling between him and Johnny over the break-up of the band the previous year had been set aside, and the two drug buddies resumed their symbiotic relationship. The Idols were making little progress and would subsequently dissolve, so Jerry had plenty of time to appear with his old band, which played sporadically throughout the spring and summer, usually at Max's.

On 6 July, UK label Beggars Banquet released an album recorded the previous autumn that showcased the band in full flow at their venue of choice, *The Heartbreakers – Live At Max's Kansas City*. Interestingly, the set started with 'Milk Me', which was followed by most of *LAMF*, plus 'London Boys'. Robert Christgau awarded the album an A minus in his *Village Voice Guide*, enthusing, 'captures the boys in all their rowdy, rabble-rousing abandon, and I know that when I feel like hearing them I'll be pulling it off the shelf.'

On the other hand, *NME*'s Nick Kent was less than complimentary, calling the album 'a piece of shit'. *Sounds*' Pete Makowski placed himself between these two extremes of opinion: 'as people these guys are odious creeps [too real for their own good] but plugged in they are magic.'

Their profile raised by the release of the live disc, the Heartbreakers embarked upon some out-of-town gigs. During a show at Bookies in Detroit on Midsummer's Eve they were joined on stage by Wayne Kramer – Johnny's guitar hero from the MC5. Kramer had recently completed two years of a four-year stretch in a Kentucky jail for dealing cocaine. The experience had scared Wayne onto the straight and narrow. Now he just wanted to play rock-'n'roll and had already re-recorded the Five's 'Ramblin' Rose' as a single.

Excited by the possibilities of hooking up with the Motor City axe strangler, Johnny made the decision to relocate to Detroit to form a new band with Kramer. Using the ex-MC5 man's rhythm section of drummer John Morgan and bassist Ron Cooke, who had played in Mitch Rhyder's Detroit and Sonic Rendezvous Band, they started rehearsing under the name Gang War.

This effectively dissolved the Heartbreakers once again. In 1980, Billy and Walter would form the Heroes with Walter's brother Ritchie and drummer Billy Rodgers, who had previously stood in for Jerry in the Heartbreakers. The Heroes recorded an unreleased single, 'Crazy Kids', which was produced by former Stones associate Jimmy Miller. They continued until late 1981, when Billy fell ill and Walter gave up being a full-time musician in favour of the far more lucrative option of becoming a stockbroker.

In 1983, Skydog Records released a posthumous Heroes single, 'Seven Day Weekend', backed with 'Too Much Junkie Business', which had originally been recorded for Island during the *So Alone* sessions and also featured Henri Paul and Steve Nicol.

Perhaps influenced by earlier missed opportunities, Johnny's decision to uproot his young family indicated his commitment to his latest band. Certainly he would have much preferred to remain in New York, or go to London where he was an established part of an embedded music scene. Although the Dolls and the Heartbreakers had both been popular in Detroit, the city was experi-

encing significant economic and social decline caused by a slump in the auto-
motive industry that employed a large proportion of the local workforce. The
city centre was well on the way to becoming a burned out no-go area and, by
moving to the suburb of Dexter, Johnny was hardly positioning himself where
it was at. Worse still, unable to face the move, Julie left.

'Julie ran off with the kids and effectively disappeared off the face of the
earth,' recalls Mariann. 'I think this was on the eve of Johnny moving to
Detroit. Johnny's biggest problem was that he missed his kids, what he had
with both boys. Julie took the boys and disappeared. He never did find
them, right up to his death . . . She changed both their names. It was never
done legally. I don't know how she got away with it. She enrolled them in a
different school and travelled around.'

Kris Needs: *One night my phone went in the early hours of the morning –
it was Johnny phoning from Detroit. He sounded gushing and enthusiastic,
'I got a new band, and it's with Wayne Kramer!' That woke me up. He went
on to explain how he was now living in Detroit, split from the
Heartbreakers – 'I put 'em out of their misery' – and writing a bunch of
new songs. After rattling off a few of the group's song titles, he became
downcast as he explained how the attempt to move his family to Detroit
with him had failed to the extent that Julie had taken the kids and left him.*

*This would turn out to be a turning point for Johnny. He was missing his
sons and had been throwing himself into writing and rehearsing new
material as a means of staving off depression.*

*But why was he calling me? 'Ah, you guys [Zigzag] have always treated
me good and wrote about the music, and I gotta tell you about this. It's hot!'*

*Johnny had already written a song about Julie's defection, 'M.I.A.' –
Missing In Action – which would become a pivotal, compelling addition to
the Thunders canon for the rest of his life. The tune resonated with haunt-
ed rockabilly soaked in Thunders' sardonic six-string raunch, undercut
with wounded emotion. Live, he would sometimes end the song by shouting, 'Bitch!' Its likely that these feelings of bitterness prompted the addition
of Nancy Sinatra's 'These Boots Are Made For Walking' and the Stones' 'I'd
Much Rather Be With The Boys' to his live set. 'Here I am, I'm all alone, I'm
all dressed up to kill,' he sighed in his most plaintive tones, 'But I'd much
rather be with the boys, than be with you.'*

*But on the phone, Johnny sounded positive and excited. He claimed
that Gang War's set would contain 'no Heartbreakers or Dolls songs. I got
plenty of other material so I don't need to fall back on that. I wrote all new
songs and we did a few oldies that I liked.'*

*Before Johnny hung up he promised we'd meet when he came to London
again. 'We wanna do a big tour of Europe . . . in fact, everywhere!'*

True to his word, Gang War's live set was comprised of new material such
as 'Just Because I'm White' and 'M.I.A.', interspersed with covers and selec-
tions from the So Alone era. However, they also included the odd crowd-
pleasing oldie such as 'Ramblin' Rose' and the 'Courageous Cat Theme'.

In the hope of securing a record deal, Gang War laid down some demos at an Ann Arbor studio in June 1979. These included the raw, Bo Diddley-esque 'Who Do Voodoo', Fats Domino's 'I'm Gonna Be A Wheel', 'M.I.A.' delivered at escape velocity, and the inflammatory twelve-bar of 'Just Because I'm White'. Johnny asked Sylvain if he'd produce, but the lack of any kind of budget made this impractical. Eventually the sessions would surface as part of the *Crime Of The Century* and *These Boots Are Made For Fighting* bootlegs.

In February 1980, *New York Rocker* gave Gang War a half-page feature, which declared that Johnny's ambition was to release 'a string of perfect three-minute singles'. Thunders was numbered as a traditionalist, citing Richard Hell, the Senders and Mink DeVille as his favourite bands, along with the Stones. He said his philosophy was, 'Everything's been done already.'

While Kramer expounded on the way in which rehabilitation had dragged him out of 'the depths of depression, depravity and mental weakness' because 'being a dope fiend is a full time job', Johnny was succinct as ever, describing his ongoing non-rehabilitation as 'walking the tightrope'. This incurred Kramer's disapproval. It didn't bode well for the band when he insisted, 'Johnny's got one foot in the gutter and the other poised to slip on a banana peel.'

Gang War continued to play club gigs during the first half of 1980, including My Father's Place on Long Island – which Johnny had played with the Dolls eight years earlier. Matters came to a head in July when two nights were booked at Max's. Kramer only played the first, but the second saw the Dolls' original front-line reunited on a stage for the first time since the split.

'Wayne Kramer didn't wanna play the second night 'cos I wasn't paying him enough money,' recalled Johnny. 'So it ended up with me and Peter Perrett and he only knew a limited number of songs that we both could do and David and Sylvain came up and helped me. The real friends and the real boys came through.'

RCA had certainly come through for Sylvain, offering him a solo album deal at the start of 1979. At this point, he reduced his involvement with David's Staten Island Boys to the occasional guest appearance and focused on his own career. The result was *Sylvain Sylvain*, which spelled the end for the Criminals as the group were effectively reduced to Syl's backing band. Michael Page and Tony Machine departed, while Bobby Blain remained. Johnny Rao and Buzz Verno were borrowed from the Staten Island boys and the line up was completed with the recruitment of a new drummer, Lee Crystal, and saxophonist Jon Gerber. This line-up would coalesce into a tight gigging unit, which took the name Teenage News, after Syl's album opener.

Sylvain Sylvain included many of the tracks that the Criminals had demoed eighteen months earlier, with production duties shared between Tony Bongiovi and Lance Quinn – who had hit pay dirt in 1977 when they produced Meco's disco reworking of the '*Star Wars* Theme' and would subsequently go on to produce Bon Jovi's eponymous debut in 1984. Although he was also involved in the production process, Syl felt that he had been compelled to complete the album too quickly and subsequently insisted that he preferred the original demo versions.

'My first meeting with RCA, I was sitting outside the President's office and who comes walking in but Perry Como,' recalled Syl. 'I'm proud of my first RCA album, but they cleaned it up too much. They took away all my danger, the things that I was known for, the things that I'd loved recording.'

The interchangeable nature of the Staten Island Boys and Teenage News was further underlined with the release of David's second album for Blue Sky, *In Style*, which arrived in October 1979. In addition to featuring the communal duo of Rao and Verno, the Motown-influenced disc included four songs that were co-written by Syl, who also provided some guitar and vocal embellishments. The album was produced by former Bowie sideman Mick Ronson, who had guested with the Dollettes in July 1976. Ronson brought along his long-time collaborator, former Mott the Hoople frontman Ian Hunter, who added some piano to the album's final track, 'Flamingo Road'. *In Style* featured a host of additional musicians and pointed the way toward the cabaret sound that Johansen would later embrace as Buster Poindexter.

Although neither *Sylvain Sylvain* nor *In Style* would trouble the chart compilers, both albums shifted enough units to ensure that both David and Syl were offered the opportunity to record further albums for their respective labels.

With Wayne Kramer increasingly disgruntled by Johnny's lack of interest in cleaning up, and Johnny's dislike of sharing the stage with another frontman resurfacing, Gang War reached the end of its brief campaign in July 1980. 'Music is important to me and I value the honour, the opportunity, to be an important musician,' proclaimed Wayne. 'Johnny, on the other hand, didn't consider himself to be a musician. He considered himself an entertainer.'

'It was a great idea, but that's not enough,' reflected Johnny.

Although Johnny stayed in Michigan for eight months, Gang War failed to score a record deal or break out of the Detroit club circuit. This was entirely predictable – Johnny hadn't had a US deal since he had been in the Dolls, and both his and Wayne's reputations scarcely encouraged labels to take a chance on the group.

This was a huge disappointment, as Kramer and Thunders had formed something of a mutual admiration society. 'I thought if I played with Johnny, using my rhythm section, we could control the music and he could knock shit over, be dangerous on stage and it could be a great rock'n'roll band,' explained Wayne.

'I always wanted to play with Wayne Kramer,' declared Johnny after the band's break up during the spring of 1980. 'He was a teenage idol of mine when I was a kid . . . But it was like from two really different generations so it didn't gel on a personal kind of magic thing on stage. Musically it was great. I learned a lot from playing with Wayne. MC5 were a really good band. When they were bad they were bad, when they were good they were fucking great. I saw them in London a bunch of times and in America twenty, 25 times. They were my only teenage idols.'

A further setback came courtesy of Sire, who passed up the opportunity to exercise the US option they had acquired for *So Alone*. Additionally,

Johnny's lack of enthusiasm for promoting the album and his permanent return to the USA had scuppered any chance of continuing the relationship with Real Records. Denied the opportunity to make any progress musically, Johnny found that he was unable to dull the pain of Julie's departure through non-chemical means and returned to New York to sink deeper into the mire of addiction.

One of the most intimate interviews with Johnny appeared in the December 1980 *Zigzag*, after Nikki Sudden – best known as a member of quirky lo-fi punks the Swell Maps – tracked him down in New York City. Whereas many journalists would play safe, cloaking overt references to any narcotic proclivities, Nikki laid his cards on the table. After some discussion concerning the problem caused by the abundance of police on the normally safe scoring grounds of East Houston and Suffolk Street, the pair dug into Johnny's stash at his temporary apartment on Third Avenue and Fourth Street.

'The New York drug scene? Yes, it's so full of shit. Every place you turn now . . . All these kids who used to put me down for taking heroin, they're all doing it themselves. It's become a really trendy thing. I mean, everybody thinks it's really cool to do. They don't know how it destroys one's fucking life. Yeah, speaking from personal experience but knowing when to get out of it . . . It's something that I have no regrets about but it's not something that I'll do forever. I mean, every fucking place you go now you run into it, from thirteen-year-old girls to 50-year-old men.

'All the kids think they gotta shoot heroin and play guitar and they're accepted and they're cool and they're, "I'm a pop star, man." They're so fucking lame. They have no conception of what rock'n'roll is about. They just – y'know – shoot up and think they're a pop star. Then they get straight and they realise they're just the pieces of shit they were before they got high. These kids get high and they live in this fantasy world.'

Alone and without a band, Johnny was aware of how his life was unravelling and made an effort to kick his habit. 'I went to acupuncture treatment for a couple of months – the same place Keith [Richards] went to. It just got a little too embarrassing at one time. They put staples in my ears and I had this little box – it's supposed to take away the sickness but it's a bunch of bullshit . . . sit down in like a dentists chair and they put this buzzing thing on you. I didn't really give it a fair enough chance. I don't think it would've worked.

'I'm gonna try to be cured. I've never tried before in my life. I've been on heroin eight years and I just want to try a different style of life. It made me split up from my wife. It ruined a lot of things for me, a lot of chances. A lot of people don't think they can count on me, but I've never missed a gig in my life. It doesn't affect my musical life at all. All these people think I'm gonna die in the next week and I'll outlive all those fucking assholes, man, 'cos I want to live.

'A lot of people want to die for a lot of reasons. I take smack because I enjoy it. I enjoy all it makes me feel. I don't do it to be in with the in-crowd or shit like that. I do it because I enjoy it. If I didn't enjoy it I would never do it, and if it interfered with my music I would never do it. I can rock out with it. It doesn't affect my performance at all. It hasn't hurt my music, it hurt my credibility in the industry, but what does the industry understand? What they read? And how much of what you read is true? Many people love me, many people hate me – there's nobody in between. That's the way I prefer it. I mean, no one really knows me. People think they know me. People write all this shit like I'm a big heavy drug scene – fuck all that. Too many people assume too many things. They'll never know the real me – except my wife. We're separated at the moment but we'll be back together real soon.'

In comparison to the trail of wasted rock'n'roll pyrotechnics blazed by Johnny, David Johansen's post-Dolls career so far had been somewhat tame. There had been nothing wrong with the first solo album. It was a good, well-produced rock set. 1979's *In Style* was pretty average, despite Johansen's attempt at a new, sophisticated sound and image. Robert Christgau, who reckoned that the song 'Big City' boasted 'the most banal lyric he's ever written', concluded that, 'the problem isn't how often you think but how often you don't think "that's great."' This was a damning criticism of a man who once fronted one of the most outrageously notorious groups in pre-punk history. Johansen now seemed to be trying desperately to crack the US mainstream, but falling to bridge the schism between his own interests and influences and what was currently popular.

But there was still plenty of life in the old Doll. He had been collaborating with Blondie Chaplin, who'd made his name with the Beach Boys (and later went on to work with the Stones). During the first three months of 1981 they'd written and recorded an album called *Here Comes The Night*, then taken the songs on the road ahead of the album's October release.

Zigzag's Marts described the new disc as 'a return to basics after the disappointing albeit pleasant mainstream pap of *In Style* . . . *Here Comes The Night* shows an older perhaps wiser Johansen with material that is nothing particularly fresh, but signals a return to the old school of Johansen rockers . . . this is a rock album and it is meant as such. It's not subtle, it's not sweet or tasteful. It's Johansen at his crude, nasty best.'

Marts was a lovable Thunders impersonator who also happened to be a junkie. He would give up smack years later, but sadly died after a trip to the gym. Blue Sky invited him to New York to interview Johansen for *Zigzag*, with the meeting taking place at his apartment on East Seventeenth Street, off Sixth Avenue. Marts describes how, on arrival, David sprinted to the liquor store for a bottle of vodka, leaving him in the 'carnage' of his bedroom – 'cassettes, a Telecaster, empty bottles, mags, the wardrobe'.

'I always try to do the best I can, y'know, I don't really intellectualise too much,' began Johansen. 'The album's something you gotta do, so I do it. I try to do the best I can but what the fuck do I know? I do more rockers on this one. The reviewers thought I was spreading myself a bit thin on the last one. I should pay more attention to what I'm doing, I guess I'm the sort of person who signs to make an album and makes an album. It's not like I do demographic research or anything . . . .

'It's like my third album – I don't know if it compares or anything. I think this album is the most accessible one. I don't know if that's good, bad or indifferent or what. I get compared to the Dolls still, but it doesn't bother me, it bothers the critics. I mean, I don't really pay that much attention to writers. Sometimes you can learn something from their critique, but most of the time they've got their head up their ass and don't know what they're talking about. It's like that guy from *The Village Voice* [Robert Christgau]. I couldn't believe a word he was saying. He was just saying, "I love him, I hate him, I need him, I don't need him, I love him." What am I supposed to think? It's rock'n'roll, not the Dead Sea Scrolls or something. Kids here don't go along with the press anyway. That's the way I was when I was a kid too, if I read a review and it said something sucks, I generally assumed it was good . . . .

'[Critics don't have] any idea of what the fuck I do. They wonder why I stopped wearing a dress. "What happened to that great dress, David, where is it?" Y'know, the whole costume thing is a late teen/early twenties kind of a trip. If you do that for the rest of your life they're gonna be calling you Quentin [Crisp]. It's okay for kids but it kinda bores you after a while.'

David said Johnny checked him out at the Ritz, and that he hadn't seen Jerry in six months. He added that he was closest to Sylvain. They still wrote together – usually when there was a record due: 'Help! Come over right away, bring your guitar.'

In an interview for *Musician* magazine, Roy Trakin asked David if his previous life as a New York Doll had proven a help or a hindrance in getting his solo career up and running. 'Well, I consider the Dolls like my college days, my old alma mater,' he replied. 'The make-up and costumes was the Dolls' thing, their *shtick*. That's how we used to dress when we were kids. We used to pick clothes out of the garbage can. We never sat down and planned it. It was just something you had to get out of your system, like an exorcism. I have no desire to wear high-heeled shoes anymore . . . except in my most private moments.'

Sylvain's sole involvement with *In Style* was a co-credit for 'Bohemian Love Pad', which he wrote with David. This was hardly surprising as the guitarist had been busy recording and producing his second album, *Syl Sylvain And The Teardrops*, which came out on RCA in May 1981.

Syl's latest band was a stripped down trio that included his girlfriend Rosie Rex on drums and bassist Danny 'Tubby' Reed. The album again provided a showcase for Syl's trademark shimmering pop/rock and was described by Trakin as 'a straight-ahead album of subtle pleasures, with New Orleans honky-tonk keyboards, scattered Latin reggae rhythms, blaring Stax sax and a non-stop urban rockabilly beat.'

Unfortunately, the LP flopped and the Teardrops were reduced to touring the West Coast in a borrowed van. Despite these setbacks, Syl remained enthusiastic about the future of the group, 'We're making a lot of new fans, but the record company insists on stressing my past accomplishments instead of the present. They see me as an East Coast regional performer, not a potential international artist. All I have going for me out there is my name. You begin to realise how tied to New York you are when you get out into the country.' Irrespective of Syl's potential, RCA dropped him once the album's poor sales became apparent.

'You've got to be a real *shnook*-face to get bitten twice,' observes Syl. 'It's not like love, it's business. And I'm a fairly business-oriented cat. It's just not enough to have people who like you. Even with a good manager, a good agent and good press, I get lost at a company the size of RCA. You've got to have love *and* business.'

Even if the business front wasn't holding up too well, Syl was doing alright in regard to love; during this period he married Rosie and celebrated the birth of his son, Odell.

1981 saw Johnny at rock bottom. He spent most of the year in New York doing drug money club gigs. He was in serious danger of becoming a self parody – when he travelled to LA for a show at the Whisky on 15 May, Thunders was so wrecked that he kept forgetting which song he was playing and had two roadies behind his amps to prevent him from knocking them over. *Trouser Press* magazine's Rock Predictions had mischievously declared that Johnny was 'legally dead', although still playing in a group – this assertion was accompanied by a cartoon of a syringe-embedded Thunders. *New York Rocker*'s Roy Trakin – a big fan of Johnny's – wrote, 'He has at once profited, and been made victim to, the rock dream as nightmare . . . There's no reason Johnny Thunders has to prove he's an artist by dropping dead for our amusement.'

Wayne Kramer's ex-wife, photographer and actress Marcia Resnick – who captured the legendary image of Johnny that graced the cover of Nina Antonia's *In Cold Blood* – asked the guitarist to be in a film about a rock star. Johnny ended up moving into her apartment, as he was wont to do. The projected movie's producer, East German-born underground filmmaker Christopher Giercke – who'd recently produced *Cocaine Cowboys* with Andy Warhol and Jack Palance – became the latest in a long line to take on the unique challenge of becoming Johnny's manager.

Believing that his new charge simply required some personal stability to begin cleaning up his act and capitalising on his enduring popularity in Europe, Giercke installed Johnny in the Paris apartment beneath his own. He then put into practice the theory that trust and friendship could save Johnny from himself. Many thought the man was mad. Johnny couldn't believe his luck at the new piggy bank that was living upstairs.

'When Christopher met Johnny he had sold his guitar and wasn't playing music any more,' explained Alan Hauser. 'He'd never heard of him before, but he knew everyone like Marcia [Resnick] and Wayne Kramer. Just the crowd that he hung out with in New York. They all said what a wonderful person and musician this was. He thought of it as a huge challenge to try and to get this guy back to being a musician again. And probably Johnny made him feel sorry for him and all that, because he was very good at doing that! Make a wide big-eyed face at him when he was going, "Hey, can you gimme 50 bucks?"

'One of the things Christopher did for him when he brought him over to London was get to him see a Harley Street doctor, which was, for some reason, a psychiatrist who prescribed him methadone. Being a heroin addict is partly psychological so I think that's the reason for that. Christopher really sorted him out because he was really a mess in 1982 and '83. Christopher basically did a management deal that was 50-50 of income, which sounds an incredibly high percentage. But he looked after him. He would live in the same apartment as him. He was a saint . . . I think he thought it was a very interesting thing to do. He had a very intellectual approach. Johnny was a very endearing guy. He'd make you feel sorry for him, like a kid brother. He was brought up by his mum and his sister and spoilt rotten. He'd just whine. Both me and Christopher had real problems keeping him onside or whatever. He could be very difficult, but he could also be very charming and very nice.'

In 1982, Jungle Records released a live Heartbreakers single, recorded in 1977, of 'Chinese Rocks' and 'All By Myself'. This was followed by a whole album, *DTK – Live At The Speakeasy*, which Johnny initially regarded as a glorified bootleg as he had no contractual relationship with the label. 'Christopher brought Johnny with wraparound shades and the leathers on to say "How come you've released this record?" I said, "Well this is our company and Leee's given me this and that paper,"' explained Hauser. 'They weren't happy about it because they weren't getting money but Leee wanted to come to a good arrangement. We all had a big meeting and arranged that we should re-release *LAMF* with the Heartbreakers involved.' Shortly afterwards, Jungle also released the *Vintage '77* EP on twelve-inch, which lashed together the first three *LAMF* demos cut at Essex Studios.

The deal with Jungle and Giercke's attentive management enabled Johnny to overcome some of the feelings of depression he had been experiencing in the wake of his break up with Julie. A run of Swedish gigs were booked for the end of March and a band was assembled that featured Jerry, ex-Bo Diddley guitarist Luigi Sciorcci and Tony James from Generation X on bass.

Johnny and the band were booked to play the long-running TV music showcase *Mandagsborsen*. It was an important opportunity for Johnny to get himself before a mass audience right at the start of the tour – and he fucked it up.

The band had turned up late after spending some time in a local studio, recording a new version of 'Too Much Junkie Business'. Johnny and Jerry were clearly the worse for wear as they lurched through shambolic renditions of Booker T and the MG's' 'Green Onions' and 'Just Another Girl'. Then Johnny fell off the stage, bringing their performance to an abrupt end. 'He fell over about ten times,' claimed English performance artist John Hollingsworth, who witnessed the debacle. 'He was generally fucking things up and kept shouting insults at people. The funny thing was, the TV prompters still tried to get people to cheer.'

Not much happens in Sweden, and the drug laws were notoriously severe, so the local press went overboard, describing Johnny as a 'Drugged Human Wreck' and installing him as the Swedish national substance abuse poster boy. Stockholm had a very serious heroin problem, and Johnny became a convenient figure to demonise as a warning to any potential users. The papers carried a story saying that the Salvation Army wanted to kidnap the hapless chemical dustbin, in order to 'save his soul'.

Two days later, Johnny was arrested when he broke into a medical kit during a flight taking the band back to Stockholm, following an appearance at an anti-heroin show in a provincial town – foisted on him through pressure from the local authorities – during which he had collapsed into the crowd.

'I was in Sweden for ten days and they put me on the front page of the daily papers eight days in a row,' marvelled Johnny a few months later. 'I actually did nothing to warrant any of the attention. It was ridiculous. It started off, we did a TV show and they thought I was too messed up and wouldn't show it. That started the ball rolling with the Press. They started following me . . .We were on an aeroplane coming into Sweden and someone stole a medical kit to try and get some morphine or something. They had the army there, searched us, but it wasn't any of us . . . at least it wasn't me,' he claimed.

After the Swedish debacle, Jerry, Johnny and Tony James, travelled to England where they recruited former Rich Kids guitarist Steve New for a series of London gigs, which included the Hope & Anchor, Kensington Ad Lib, Dingwalls and the Venue in Victoria.

On the night of the Venue concert, Johnny's reputation again gave rise to a whirling pre-gig rumour mill that included reports of him being carried unconscious into the soundcheck and downing a whole bottle of Jack Daniel's. Irrespective of the veracity of such tales, Johnny succeeded in remaining vertical for the duration of the well-attended show. Sylvain, who was by then fronting the Roman Sandals, jumped up for the encore of 'Chinese Rocks', pointing at Johnny and singing, 'He's living on Chinese rocks.'

Syl's latest band, the Roman Sandals, were simply the Teardrops under a new name. After being dropped by RCA he'd relocated to London and brought Rosie, Odell and bassist Danny Reid with him. In an interview with *NME*'s Barney Hoskyns, Syl insisted they wanted to make it in Britain as a singles band. 'I wanna make hit records, and I think the records we've made *should* have been hit records . . . In the states we coulda just toured and toured and toured, but that way you get to hate everything, however much you love to perform. We don't wanna make it just for the sake of making it, but I think we can make it.' Unfortunately, Syl's optimism was misplaced and the band recorded just one single, 'This Is It', which emerged on the Body Rock label in 1983 and promptly sunk without trace.

Johnny and his band continued gigging around the UK until the beginning of June. While in London, the group went into Croydon's Wickham Studios and recorded backing tracks for 'Ten Commandments Of Love' – which Johnny had been doing with Gang War – 'Sad Vacation' and 'Give Me More'.

After a final UK gig at the Marquee on 3 June, the band returned to Sweden for a show in Gothenburg on the following night. After the brouhaha that followed his wasted performances earlier in the year, the concert was set up to ascertain whether he was straight enough to play the rest of the country.

Johnny walked on stage, fell right off again, insulted the Swedish girls and then wandered off halfway through the first song, which instigated a minor riot. The Swedish promoters now had empirical proof that Johnny was too wasted to tour, and abandoned any idea of sending the band on the road. As a consequence of their withdrawal there was no money to pay hotel bills and the group were out on the street.

On his return to Heathrow, Johnny was busted with a small amount of smack, detained at Pentonville prison for a few days and fined £50 for possession. As soon as he was released, Johnny flew back to New York and played the Peppermint Lounge with backup from Walter, Billy Rodgers, bassist Luigi Sciorcia and Steve Jones – who by then was reduced to selling *Great Rock'n'Roll Swindle* videos to support his own habit. Minus Jones, the same band played Irving Plaza on 15 July – Johnny's thirtieth birthday.

He started by dedicating 'In Cold Blood' to John Belushi, who had died of an overdose on 5 March, and promptly lost the strap on the black Gibson he'd managed to acquire for the show. Johnny arrived dressed to kill, in red drape jacket, distressed white silk shirt, pale vest and red bandana. However, he'd been celebrating heavily and was clearly wasted – his eyes were permanently hooded, and when they did open they rolled back into his head. Despite spending extended periods shambling around the stage or lying on the floor, Johnny somehow managed to coax the necessary spirit to drive his ravaged frame through the set – which climaxed amidst the triumphant sonic napalm drops of 'Born To Lose'.

As an example of just what made New York rockers regard going to see their favourite son as some kind of gladiatorial sport, this couldn't be beat. The music spilling out of this chaotic, shambling figure provides clear evidence of the burning spirit of rock'n'roll that propelled Johnny through his opiated haze.

Meanwhile, Jerry Nolan had remained in Sweden, where he'd found a new girlfriend and joined the Teneriffa Cowboys, a Stockholm band fronted by former Bitch Boys guitarist Mike Thimrén – who had supported Johnny earlier in the year when Finnish rockers Hanoi Rocks were forced to withdraw at the last minute. The band released a single, 'Take A Chance With Me'/'Pretty Baby', which emerged on the Tandan label credited solely to Jerry and featured Syl on keyboards.

After a handful of gigs at the start of 1983, Johnny left New York for London in April, where he stayed at Tony James' flat in Pindock Mews, Maida Vale. The flat had seen its fair share of action when Sid and Nancy were staying there, infamously creating Jackson Pollock-style murals on the bathroom walls with their syringes. As Pat Gilbert pointed out in his Clash biography, 'The house at Pindock Mews was filled with bad junkie ju-ju.'

Kris Needs: *One day in May, I got a call from Tony James, saying that Johnny wanted to see me for a chat at the flat. I think he wanted to put the record straight that he wasn't – contrary to popular rumour at the time – dead.*

Tony had the look of a man at the end of his tether. He's usually a quiet, pleasant sort of chap whose only over-indulgence might have come from lethal Jellybean cocktails (white bar spirits, blackcurrant, lemonade). In the two weeks that he'd had Johnny on board, Tony's usually tidy flat had been given the Lower East Side junk den makeover courtesy of Johnny. Aside from his good nature, Tony was reluctant to eject his fetid houseguest, as he was Johnny's biggest fan. Johnny had been his hero from the first Dolls album and the band he formed with Mick Jones – London SS – took the group as its template. Tony was always going on about rock'n'roll and now Mr Rock'n'Roll himself had moved right in with all the trimmings he was notorious for. When I turned up, he smiled and shrugged with the air of a man between rock'n'roll and a hard place.

At the time, rumours were rife that Johnny Thunders was dead. He'd replaced Keef as the Man Most Likely Not To Make It, and the weeklies were full of stories about his demise. Not yet. There was Johnny, crouched on Tony's sofa, one eye on a video of Performance *and chuckling at the absurdity of it all. In the next room was Christopher Giercke, keeping an eye on his investment.*

'It went out in Paris that I died three times,' *he said with some incredulity.* 'It was in all the papers. Your guess is as good as mine where it came from. Everybody thought I was dead. Jerry Nolan phoned up from Sweden, friends phoned up from London. I thought it was really funny actually.*

'Everybody makes more out of it than it is. It's so blown out of proportion, it's ridiculous.'

Not even a close scrape with the Reaper then?

'No, I handle it alright. As well as anyone can handle it. I mean, it's not easy for anyone to handle it. A lot of people take it seriously because of the things they read about me. The things they write about me are so incredible and ridiculous it's just kinda hard to take it serious. Maybe they wanted to sell more records – that's my guess.'

The thing about junkies is that they don't think people notice when, in their mind, they're just 'maintaining'. That is, feeling relatively normal, having fended off the dreaded smack withdrawals. It takes one to know one, and I could see that Johnny that day had definitely partaken of the opiate with his hooded, pinpoint eyes – and his were pretty dark, so it was often difficult to make out – the slightly slurred, croaky voice, that general aura of junkdom. I say this because, at that time, I was on the stuff myself. Maybe that's why we got on.

Having exhausted Tony James' hospitality, Johnny departed for a series of gigs in France at the end of April. This time around he was backed by a semi-permanent band that featured Jerry, Billy Rath and Henri Paul, which – with a nod in the direction of his Italian heritage – he dubbed Cosa Nostra. The band performed a selection of songs encompassing Johnny and Jerry's entire career: old Dolls numbers such as 'Personality Crisis', the Heartbreakers' 'Born To Lose' and 'Chinese Rocks' and the crowd-pleasing 'Too Much Junkie Business' and 'Pipeline' – which opened (and often closed) the set.

After a trio of French dates in mid-May, a series of shows in Sweden were arranged for the following month. Henri Paul had opted to stay home and was to be replaced by Mike Thimrén at Jerry's recommendation. Typically, the band had left their departure to the last minute, ensuring that there was no time for rehearsal before the opening show at the Sky High Club, in the Southern city of Malmo on 15 June.

In the disorganised rush to catch their plane, Johnny's guitar had been packed with the regular luggage and had consequently been smashed to pieces in transit, compelling him to borrow a curious looking mini-flying V from a local guitarist named Claes Yngström. Although the guitar looked stupid, it at least had the advantage of functioning – unlike Johnny's amp, which blew the moment he struck the opening chord to 'Pipeline'. 'He just dropped the Mickey Mouse guitar and walked off,' recalled Thimrén. 'Me,

Tony and Jerry carried on with a twenty minute version of "Waiting For The Man" – and we certainly were.'

The trip improved for Johnny when he met a hairdresser called Susanne Blomqvist. The couple hit it off immediately and became an item. Johnny's enthusiasm for the relationship was such that, during one of the Swedish shows he dragged Susanne on stage to introduce her to the bemused audience. As well as providing him with someone to embarrass in public, Susanne's arrival had an immediate beneficial effect on Johnny's state of mind and – perhaps as a consequence – the tour passed without any of the gouched-out chaos that had undermined his previous visits.

July saw Cosa Nostra play a short run of dates in Holland, before heading back to the UK for a one off appearance at the Marquee on 23 August. Further gigs were lined up in France for the following month, with Richard Hell guesting at the band's Le Palace showcase on 19 September. Five days later, the group travelled to Rennes, which was experiencing an autumnal heatwave. During the gig – which took place in sweltering conditions – Johnny wandered to the edge of the stage and opened a fire door, hoping to cool down. 'Ten dogs ran in nearly knocking him over,' recalled Mike Thimrén. 'Johnny began to play around with them on stage and even found a ball that they hunted back and forth . . . The band smiled and played away in the background. And it ended with what must be the ultimate version of "Walking The Dog". Johnny sitting in the middle surrounded by his new found friends, all howling along in the chorus.'

A sold-out gig at the Lyceum on 9 October was a resounding success, with Johnny playing for over two hours, bringing on Peter Perrett and Patti Palladin – who he introduced as 'Patti Muppet from Snatch'. That night, he seemed to effortlessly undo any damage caused by his previous appearance. Sure, Johnny insulted the audience, but he also backed it up by being on top form. During his acoustic section, the whole crowd joined in on 'Memory'.

Back in France, Johnny recorded his next studio album in Paris – alone. *Hurt Me* came as something of a surprise considering the rock'n'roll firestorms on which he had built his reputation. It was an acoustic album that emerged as a fascinating and often poignant attempt to strip his creativity to its barest bones. Opening with his Sid Vicious eulogy, 'Sad Vacation', the album features the surprising selection of a couple of old standards that would formerly have been considered far too folky to fit Johnny's rock fundamentalist *oeuvre* – Barry McGuire's 'Eve Of Destruction' and Dylan's 'It Ain't Me Babe'. He also revisits his own past on acoustic renderings of 'Diary of A Lover', 'Memory', 'She's So Untouchable', 'Ask Me No Questions' and even 'Lonely Planet Boy'. The title track dates from the original Heartbreakers line-up with Richard Hell. Some of the Gang War repertoire gets nailed down ('I'd Much Rather Be With The Boys', 'M.I.A.') and there's also new songs, including 'I'm A Boy, I'm A Girl', 'I Like To Play Games', 'She's So Strange' and one called 'Cosa Nostra'. He also tackled Dylan's 'Joey', making it sound like it was written for him.

The album was released in November – on French label New Rose, much to Alan Hauser's dismay. 'When we did the deal for *LAMF*, we found we were supporting the [Heartbreakers] tour. Then we found out that Christopher had done another deal with New Rose to do the acoustic album at the same time. There were always these other deals that were going on.'

Johnny supported the album with a couple of solo club dates in Brighton and London in early December. The Dingwalls gig sounded good – or what you could hear above the general bar-room hubbub. At least the top of Johnny's hat poking over the sea of craning necks proved it wasn't his record playing. Later that night he played another set at the Pipeline, a sub-Batcave bastion of Thunders impersonators.

After spending the start of 1984 in Sweden with Susanne, Johnny – accompanied by Tony James – spent three nights at London's Greenhouse Studios, attempting to re-remix *LAMF* into what it should have sounded like in the first place. They worked from sunset to sunrise clearing away the production stodge, and the results were released as *LAMF Revisited* later that year. Johnny was also filmed playing an acoustic set, including Dylan's 'Like A Rollin' Stone'.

To coincide with the album, the Heartbreakers reformed, starting with a warm-up at the Gibus in Paris on 19 March and continuing with dates in Nottingham and Manchester, before returning to the Lyceum, where they were supported by their old friend Jayne County. Reforming the band presented no great problem as Billy was keen and available, and, although Walter had to be dragged away from his job on the stock market and his 'hobby' band the Waldos, he was enthusiastic about the short tour.

The Heartbreakers took the stage to Elmer Bernstein's ominous, jazzy theme to *The Man With The Golden Arm*, Otto Preminger's harrowing 1955 film of Nelson Algren's novel about an aspiring jazz drummer fighting heroin addiction in the Chicago ghetto.

It seemed like every time Johnny did a gig during the 1980s, those who had been in the dressing room had to give a report on the state he was in. It was now part of following his career, and especially rife in New York where, around the same time, there had been stories of him playing entire sets on his back. This evening's reports alleged that his dealer hadn't shown up, so Johnny had downed a whole bottle of vodka before going on.

After the intro, it was straight into 'Pipeline', through an incredible version of 'Personality Crisis' and into the perfect follow-through of One Track Mind'. It was mayhem, further stoked by 'Too Much Junkie Business', 'Do You Love Me', 'Just Because I'm White', 'Copycat', 'Baby Talk', 'Born To Lose', 'All By Myself', 'In Cold Blood', 'Seven Day Weekend', 'So Alone' and a volcanic 'Chinese Rocks'. Despite the backstage rumours, Johnny was on fine, crowd-baiting form – 'Hey, any of you kids in the audience old enough to get a hard-on yet?' 'Can't Keep My Eyes On You' became 'Can't Keep My Cock In Your Face'.

In early April, Johnny returned to Sweden, where he told the press that he'd stopped using smack and was cutting down the methadone. For the next two months, he made another concerted effort to get his shit together; he continued his methadone programme, spent time building his relationship with Susanne, organised proper work permits for a Swedish tour and reunited with Sylvain.

(But it was not a good time for Syl, who had broken up the Roman Sandals due to their inability to secure either a following or a record deal, and was in the process of separating from his wife Rosie.)

After a trio of dates in Madrid and an appearance on Spanish TV, Johnny, Jerry, Billy and Sylvain set off around Sweden for what they called the Revenge '84 tour. In addition to his extensive back catalogue and new songs such as 'Have Faith', 'Size Ten Shoes' and 'Who Needs Girls', Johnny shared the lime-light with his former Dolls brethren. Jerry did 'Countdown Love', while Syl sang 'Teenage News'. The Stones dominated the covers, which included 'Under Assistant West Coast Promotion Man', 'The Spider And The Fly', 'Wild Horses' and 'Play With Fire'. They also got to do their favourite 'Courageous Cat Theme', and attacked 'Personality Crisis' and 'Great Big Kiss'.

However, the reunion with Syl was not to last, as Johnny's claims about cleaning up turned out to be typical junkie lies. 'They were trying to pro-mote Johnny like he was cleaned up . . . and he wasn't,' insists Syl. 'He had me doing all his interviews and I said, "Hey man, I'm not digging lying about your situation." He had me saying, "Oh, Johnny's off the stuff." At first he was, but later he wasn't. I confronted him with that. He said, "Syl, I don't give a shit. I shoot up every day." So I just said, "I'll see you later, I have to go. Bye." He was booked in at the Marquee . . . but I didn't show up for that.'

Between 20-24 August, Johnny – still with Jerry and Billy – played a stint at the Marquee Club and sold out every night. Supporting was Neon Leon, for-merly of Pure Hell, who'd supported the Dolls at the Little Hippodrome in '75.

During what was billed as 'Johnny Thunders Week', many punters estab-lished a pattern of getting wasted in The Ship next door then staggering into the small Wardour Street venue to catch Thunders on top form. It was great seeing him in control, taunting the crowd and delivering the music with an assured knockout punch – with the classic Heartbreakers rhythm section too.

After the Marquee shows, Billy and Jerry returned to Sweden. Johnny embarked on a run of sporadic gigs in London, Belfast, Rotterdam and Paris ahead of a ten-date UK tour with Hanoi Rocks in October. Johnny's backing musicians tended to fluctuate and change with every gig. Sometimes there were familiar partners-in-crime, often he recruited a last-minute, Chuck Berry-style, pick-up group. Between mid-November and the end of the year Johnny undertook an extensive European schedule, which took him through Italy, France, Austria, Switzerland, Germany and finally Belgium.

By the end of 1984 David Johansen had embarked upon a process of creative reassessment that would see him re-emerge in his Buster Poindexter persona.

Although his 1982 live album, *Live It Up*, had been well received and the disc's version of the Animals 'We Gotta Get Out Of This Place' had been a minor hit on MTV, David's fourth studio album – the synth-driven, dance-ori-entated *Sweet Revenge* – had failed to capitalise on that success.

'I woke up in the early eighties and I was with six guys in a van driving across America opening for heavy metal acts,' David told *Uncut*'s Nigel Williamson in 2000. 'It was like performing at Hitler Youth rallies. The uni-verse is expanding and we should be expanding with it, not dumbing down. So all the time in the van I was listening to old jump blues and all this old music and it just seemed so much more real.'

David started hanging out at Tramps, his neighbourhood bar.

'It was a really groovy place. They'd book people like Big Joe Turner and Charles Brown for a month's residency. But they didn't have a show on a Monday night – so I started doing it, playing in the back room. I called myself Buster Poindexter to throw people off the scent. Soon, I was making as much money as I was killing myself on the road and it was just two blocks walk from where I lived.'

Kris Needs: *One evening in January 1984, some mates in New York said, 'You've gotta see what Johansen's doing now.' We made our way over to Tramps and walked into a full bar. For the next two hours, with a short break, David and some obviously seasoned blues musicians joyously worked their way through old blues, lascivious Andre Williams tunes, swinging jump blues and smoky ballads. As a soundtrack to a boozy evening, it couldn't be beat.*

To someone who'd seen the Dolls at their peak ten years earlier it was a major shock. Johansen and the band all wore black tuxedos, David with his customary bangs slicked straight back. He was obviously entering into the spirit of the occasion and, afterwards, our party joined him at his table. He was friendly, loquacious and hilarious drunken company, swigging Martinis and firing out one-liners and anecdotes. He only lived round the corner and was having the time of his life. 'And I'm getting paid!' he grinned. The general impression was that he liked this life better now those 'crazy days' of the Dolls were over.

While David was busy re-inventing himself, Syl and Arthur were faring less well. After his marriage had broken up, Syl chose to bring up Odell on his own and had been compelled to work as a cab driver in order to make ends meet. Arthur had dropped from sight almost completely and, although he made some very occasional appearances with his former Dolls pals, hadn't recorded anything since the Idols' single six years earlier.

In January 1985, Johnny assembled another band. He reinstalled Henri Paul and recruited the black rhythm section of bassist Keith Yon and drummer Tony St Helene from the Tribesmen. The group – which Johnny named the Black Cats – made their debut at low-key gig in Geneva, which was designed as a warm up ahead of a nine-date tour of Japan.

The Black Cats set offered little in the way of new material, but still drew an enthusiastic reception from Japanese audiences delighted to hear such old favourites as 'Personality Crisis' and 'Born To Lose'. The tour was Johnny's first visit to the country, and he was delighted by his popularity there.

In the first week of April, Johnny was booked for a three-night run at New York's intimate Irving Plaza. Although he was suffering from a throat infection, the shows proved particularly memorable, as they featured a series of reunions with old bandmates including Sylvain, David, Walter, and even the hermitic Arthur.

Almost inevitably, Johnny's ongoing clean-up mission suffered another setback. He'd continued shooting up once back in New York, and dealt himself an even bigger blow when he returned to Stockholm to meet Susanne's family by necking a fistful of Valium tens on the plane. With Johnny in a less than coherent state, he hardly made a sparkling impression and promptly flew back to London alone and depressed.

Following some emotional and residential support from Patti Palladin and former Dead Boy Stiv Bators, Johnny reconstituted Cosa Nostra for a handful of gigs, beginning with a show at the Croydon Underground on 27 June. On 5 July, they played the seedy Clarendon Ballroom in Hammersmith, where a power failure interrupted his shambolic momentum. Johnny played the Marquee the day before his birthday and also an 'Alternative Live Aid' at Dingwalls on 13 July.

Despite the live action – which included a brief Canadian tour – Johnny remained in the doldrums. His relationship with Susanne was at a low point and, without a record deal, cohesive touring strategy or much in the way of fresh material, his 'career' was little more than a means of making a bare living. 'Johnny was needing somewhere to live, had run out of money and run out of gigs,' recalled Alan Hauser. 'Christopher had said, "You can stand on your own two feet for a while." Susanne said the same thing. He got into trouble with this that and the other, so we said, "We can give you some more money but you need to do some more recording." So we did the *Que Sera Sera* album, which I think Johnny was a bit disappointed by because I think he wanted a big major label deal.

'When we did our arrangement with the Heartbreakers we did it on a five year deal . . . Johnny was always ready to deal with us, but getting him to sit and commit to anything was difficult. Partly, he was too out of it and you'd feel that isn't the right time to talk about something like that. Partly, he was distrusting of anybody and didn't want to commit himself to anybody.

'One of the things I realise is, having been in the New York Dolls and being in this glamorous situation where they were the next big thing and people were getting them limos, they were just going out and doing whatever they wanted to do and had girls all over them, management all over them and magazines all over them. You get used to that lifestyle! Nice things to have and then when it's a different reality it's always difficult for anybody to adjust. There is a bit of vanity in being a rock star, an arrogance and all of those things. It's very difficult for a person, particularly when they wanted that attention, when that gets diminished and they have a much smaller level. It's difficult for any artist to get through that stage. They know they're only as big as their last hit record.'

Imperfect Lives

'The love between Johnny and Jerry was the most tragic love affair I have ever had to stand by helplessly and witness.' – *Leee Black Childers*

As a performer who'd had two separate heydays but no hits, Johnny recognised his album deal with Jungle was an opportunity to break out of the circle of playing concerts simply to fund his habit. His pharmaceutically-based lifestyle guaranteed a hand-to-mouth existence, while those who took their cues direct from his musical legacy were enjoying the lavish lives that had briefly seemed attainable by the Dolls over a decade before.

Bands such as Motley Crue, Hanoi Rocks, Kiss, Poison and WASP (featuring the re-tooled Blackie Lawless) had turned the big hair and glitzy cross-dressing into a heavy metal *Rocky Horror Show* in spandex trousers and stencilled-on makeup. Most notably, Aerosmith had gone this same safe, cliché-ridden route and been rewarded with mega-sales, stadium gigs and a fantasy sex 'n' coke lifestyle that nearly killed them. There was precious little of the flash, aplomb and humour that epitomised the Dolls – the mid 1980s hair metal boom was lowest common denominator rock, without style, or substance and lacking in wit. Perfect for the materialistic and vapid Reagan generation.

Johnny couldn't be anything he wasn't already; his music was an inherent part of him – so there was little possibility of his adapting to catch any commercial swell. However, he had a loyal following, had influenced at least one generation and could ignite a stage any time it took his fancy. There was no reason why he couldn't enjoy a moderate level of success and live less squalidly. He simply needed to play these sessions straight – to be himself and demonstrate his formidable abilities in the most effective way possible, not to shoot himself in the foot with his behaviour or sloppy playing. From his live sets since *So Alone*, and the reductive acoustic outings on *Hurt Me*, it was obvious that he had the songs.

Johnny's brief to himself, and the label that was putting itself on the line, was to turn in a killer representation of his talent and then get out on the road and capitalise on it.

To this end, Johnny, Keith Yon and Tony St Helene entered London's West 3 studios on 8 August 1985 to commence work on what would become *Que Sera Sera*. Initial sessions were hampered by Johnny's stoned inertia and rock star demands. At one point he ordered Alan Hauser to travel to Paris and pick up a special custom-made guitar – otherwise the album wouldn't happen. While Hauser, who had already hired a collection of the best guitars in the world, made the two-day trip, expensive studio time was ticking away. In the end, the guitar was barely used and Johnny had bitten another chunk from one of the last hands willing to feed him.

Recording finally started to gain momentum with the trio putting down basic tracks. On the 22nd, guests started arriving including Patti Palladin, Stiv Bators, guitarist and keyboard player John Perry, formerly of the Only Ones, former Dr Feelgood guitar strangler Wilko Johnson and Mike Monroe from Hanoi Rocks. Recording wound up by the end of the month.

Alan suppresses a laugh as he gives his version of events. 'We booked the studio for three weeks and he went in and recorded it. He went home and Patti mixed it, then he went back to sleep and that was it.'

The end result was a good album, but not the all-time Thunders classic it might have been. This is largely down to the restrained mix, while the lack of Johnny's trademark guitar heroics also leaves a big hole. Many of the solos are left to Monroe, whereas Perry and Johnson contribute most of the album's bedrock axe work. Johnny appeared content to concentrate on his vocals.

The disc kicks off with 'Short Lives', a prescient mid-tempo analysis of the mortality rate among rock'n'roll stars. Then, at last, 'M.I.A.', gets a storming studio showing. The album's sensitive ballad is 'I Only Wrote This Song For You', Johnny's comeback plea to Susanne. It almost feels too personal to listen in as he pleads, begs and declares his faults. By the end, he's desperately wailing, 'I'm sorry.' Like 'Sad Vacation', when Johnny broke away from his usual rock'n'roll blueprint he was capable of moments of heart-melting poignancy. This was the most important track for Johnny. He wanted Susanne to hear it and give him one more chance.

'"I Only Wrote This Song For You" was for Susanne, because he had to,' revealed Alan. 'He wanted to take it back to her, so all he wanted was that song to be mixed. That was sweet. He was very romantic. A lot of his songs were love songs, actually. He always said it was Jerry who insisted that the Heartbreakers should do just hard rock'n'roll.'

Just in case he might be labelled a softie, the next cut – 'Little Bit Of Whore' – insists that 'there's a little bit of whore in every little girl'. Although unlikely to win plaudits from the politically correct, the song was not quite as sweeping a generalisation as the title suggests. The (pelvic) thrust of Johnny's lyrics contends that even high-society figures like Jackie Onassis get down and dirty when the opportunity arises. 'Cool Operator' is a swaggering declaration of independence in which Johnny installs himself as the god of hip allure, invoking Elvis's sassy persona in 'Trouble' with the line, 'I was born standing up and talking back.' The song also juxtaposes lines about receiving head from Godzilla with descriptions of getting his sister to do his washing.

'Blame It On Mom' is another ragged rocker, recorded earlier in the year at Tin Pan Alley studios, with ex-Dead Boy Stiv Bators credited with drums and 'tea and biscuits'. After 'Tie Me Up', there's a rocker called 'Alone in A Crowd' which also features Patti on vocals. 'Billy Boy' is interesting. It's a heated instrumental topped by Johnny's only truly notable guitar contribution. According to Nina Antonia, the song was originally going to feature Johnny's eulogy to Billy Murcia, but he dried up halfway through writing them. This is a shame – the existing lines are printed in the CD booklet and read like another instalment of Johnny's open-heart surgery. 'Billy boy you made everything fit, with you gone everything wasn't quite it. / Why did he take you away, and make our lives that way, I'm crying.'

Johnny also resurrected 'Endless Party' (which he'd written with Johansen in the latter days of the Dolls) to close the original vinyl version of the album.

Once the sessions were completed, Johnny went to Sweden to make up with Susanne, armed with 'I Only Wrote This Song For You'. The gesture worked and the couple spent the late summer rebuilding their relationship.

After his romantic reconciliation, Johnny returned to Paris where he started work on a film with award-winning director Patrick Grandperret. He was typecast as Johnny Valentine, a heroin-addicted rock star prone to collapsing onstage and struggling unsuccessfully to get his shit together. The movie would premiere in Paris as *Mona et moi* nearly five years later.

However, despite this positive development and the impeding release of *Que Sera Sera* – which Patti Palladin had been mixing during the autumn – Johnny remained at a low ebb. Inevitably, more than a decade of sustained heroin use was starting to take its physical toll on the guitarist. He looked far older than his 33 years and was increasingly using cocaine as a 'cure' and an accompaniment to his smack habit.

'He'd come over to England every three months to see a doctor, whether he was living in Sweden or Paris or New York or wherever,' explained Alan Hauser. 'Christopher had sorted him out with a Harley Street doctor and he'd always come back to London to get his methadone. So we'd see him every three months at least.'

Why here?

'Christopher explained that in New York you had to queue up for it amongst all the junkies. He wanted to keep Johnny out of that. I really believe that Johnny was trying to give it up . . . He was always trying to get back with Susanne a lot of the time. And maintain that relationship. I think Christopher managed to convince him that he had to look after himself to get ahead.'

Despite his positive influence on Johnny, Giercke's tenure as his manager reached its end during the autumn. Giercke felt that Thunders was unlikely to change his lifestyle, and any type of commercial success remained a distant prospect. His departure appeared to make little impression on the guitarist, who simply carried on eking out a living through playing live.

After *Que Sera Sera* was released on 25 November to little fanfare and moderate sales, Johnny just got on with it – taking the Black Cats back on the road in December for short tours of Sweden and Finland.

Another New Year began with Johnny once again putting together a new band. His latest backing group consisted of Jerry Nolan, Glen Matlock and

Barry Jones from the Idols, all of whom had been playing occasional small venue gigs with Steve Dior under the guise of the London Cowboys. This ensemble toured the US between February and April 1986, including a visit to Jimmy's, New Orleans on 12 March. Johnny returned to Japan in July, followed by several shows in Italy, Australia for the first time, and Spain.

'In 1985, we did *Que Sera Sera*,' recalls Alan, 'then he supposedly made a partnership with Jerry, then he broke up with Jerry. At the beginning of 1986, they did some gigs with Jerry. He was gonna make an album with Jerry. It was gonna be 50-50 but he decided not to do it with Jerry and do it with Patti Palladin instead. That's when we did the *Copycats* album. That was recorded through 1987 and eventually released in 1988. It's far more a Patti Palladin album than a Johnny album. She got in all session musicians. She wanted to make it as authentic to the originals as possible and did it so well it has to be said that some of them may be better than the originals. That meant that Johnny Thunders' guitar didn't fit on those sort of records.

'*Copycats* was a financial disaster. It took six months with 28 musicians. Patti was a complete perfectionist over it, mixing, mixing and mixing it. That was a problem, but Johnny was also a problem because every time he came over he would get out of his head and I didn't have much to do with him.'

Kris Needs: *When I lived in New York in the eighties, I would see Johnny around quite frequently, at his gigs and on the street. In '87, I was working in a West Village record store called Bleecker Bob's, often with ex-Dolls roadie Peter Jordan. It was the Friday night graveyard shift. Johnny came running in, immaculately decked out in purple drape jacket but with an edgy, panicky look on his face. He was looking for Peter, who wasn't working that night, but was relieved to see me. He needed $20, so I sorted him out. Shouting, 'Thanks!', he then bolted out the door to God knows where. I never got the twenty bucks back, as that would be the last time I'd see Johnny alive. Even then he managed his sweet, lost puppy-dog smile, and it would haunt me.*

While Johnny had been struggling to break out of his downward spiral, David's career was ascending in an unexpected manner. His transition from street corner harpy to louche sophisticate was complete. As Buster Poindexter, he'd put together a backing band called the Banshees in Blue and set about building a significant following in and around New York.

Poindexter's profile snowballed after he and the Banshees were installed as the house band on *Saturday Night Live*, and reached something approaching meltdown when they scored a huge hit with a cover version of Arrow's 1984 soca floor filler, 'Hot, Hot, Hot'. Although the song had charted in the UK on its original release, it had largely slipped under the radar of US audiences. Once Poindexter got hold of it, it quickly became so inescapably ubiquitous that David later described it as 'the bane of my existence'.

Unlike Johnny, who had consistently failed to capitalise on any opportunities that came his way, David moved fast to record an album, *Buster Poindexter*, which was released on RCA in 1987. The record combined old standards such as the Animals' 'House Of The Rising Sun' and Leiber and

Stoller's 'Whadaya Want' with his own material that evoked the golden age of 1950s R&B big bands. 'We do a couple of Leiber and Stoller songs,' explained David. 'They wrote "Bad Detective", which we also did in the Dolls. I open up the Poindexter show with "Bad Detective" usually because it's like a link between the Dolls and Poindexter – it puts the thing in perspective. We do "Smokey Joe's Café". I think they wrote that one. And we do "Shoppin' for Clothes" which they wrote.'

In an interview with Glenn O'Brie for *Other* magazine, David explored the schizophrenic duality of his Poindexter persona. 'Buster Poindexter is the cafe incarnation of David Johansen. More than a pseudonym: a happily split personality, an alternate ego, Buster is sometimes surprisingly real . . . He shares an apartment with David Johansen, not to mention a body. The Poindexter-Johansen relationship is not the best kept of secrets. But Poindexter remains something of a mystery. He's not a songwriter, although he sings numerous Johansen songs. He's an interpreter. He puts the Poindexter stamp on everything he performs. When not working he can be found lurking in out-of-print record shops.'

A by-product of David's televisual exposure as Buster was the resumption of his acting career, which had been on permanent hiatus since the start of the 1970s. After a cameo appearance as a lounge singer in the mid-eighties style-over-content cop show *Miami Vice*, Johansen transferred to the big screen. He appeared alongside crusty boho and reformed barfly Tom Waits in Robert Frank's *Candy Mountain*, popped up as a priest in the feather-weight comedy *Married to the Mob* and a malevolent taxi driver in *Scrooged* – which starred Bill Murray, himself a huge Poindexter fan.

By November 1987, there had been little variation in Johnny's apparently endless cycle of cash-in-hand gigs, nightly line-up changes, attempts to kick junk and splits or reconciliations with Susanne. His health was continuing to deteriorate, he was beginning to look fragile, and his behaviour on the road was becoming increasingly erratic and fractious. He had become increasingly paranoid – on one occasion dragging Alan Hauser from his bed, convinced that Darth Vader was outside his window – and was experiencing regular problems with his voice.

With the release of the long-delayed *Copycats* imminent, Alan Hauser made a final concerted attempt to relaunch Johnny's moribund career. After installing him in a central London flat and arranging a series of press interviews, a six-date UK tour was set up in the hope of ensuring the new album didn't encounter the same lack of interest that greeted *Que Sera Sera*. The tour's major showcase was to be a show at the Town & Country Club in Kentish Town, north London, on 2 December.

On the night, it initially appeared as if Hauser's efforts were bearing fruit – the venue was pretty full and there were a good number of press in attendance. After support band the Quireboys had finished their set, Alan realised that Johnny and his group were nowhere to be found. 'They were still at the hotel in Paddington, twenty minutes drive away,' he recalled. 'I rush there, they're casually hanging around, Johnny "isn't quite ready", he's actually still in his room taking drugs with John Perry, says he has laryngitis and is feeling lousy. Eventually at the venue, the promoter Jim Robertson has called a doctor who supplies a syringe with a dose of Vitamin B. Jim administers the shot and pushes him onstage, 90 minutes late, meanwhile people are queuing up to get their money back.'

Since his earliest days in the Dolls, Johnny had usually managed to get through gigs – regardless of what was floating around his system – with sufficient gusto to at least satisfy, if not delight, his audience. This time it was different. Whether it was his mental state, his health or simply the smack, Johnny appeared to shut down once he was pushed out onto the stage. What's more, he seemed past caring.

Longtime Thunders fan Carol Clerk made little attempt to hide her disgust and disappointment when she reviewed the gig for *Melody Maker*. 'It was the night that Johnny finally blew it, the night that the joke, if ever there was one, died a pitiful death and began to stink. Even the diehards, the Thunders clones who will usually accept anything from their hero so long as he's legendary (i.e. out of his head), found this apathetic performance quite unacceptable, saw the legend revealed as a lazy little man who was prepared to take the money and not even run, just stumble sadly, through a mere handful of songs with all the enthusiasm of a stuffed goat.'

After completing the final three dates of the tour without further incident, Johnny returned to New York for Christmas. At the end of January 1988, he embarked on a lengthy series of dates in Japan, which was quickly reconstituted as a solo acoustic showcase when his band deserted him after the second show – citing lack of payment, poor organisation and Johnny's vacant state as reasons for their departure.

Although these Japanese gigs had been relatively lucrative, the manner in which his band had quit represented the latest in a lengthening litany of setbacks, all of which were largely self-inflicted. Again, the patterns that defined Johnny's life repeated themselves. In a reprise of the time in New York when he'd attempted to settle down with Julie when Dino was born, he attempted to achieve some sort of domestic stability with Susanne, who had recently given birth to a baby girl the couple called Jamie.

'Then he made some strong efforts to get clean,' recalls Alan. 'After *Copycats*, he set up with the Oddballs and they did a lot of touring together, and kept him going in a good way. I'm sure he did some [smack] but it was all manageable.'

The Oddballs included drummer Chris Musto, singer Alison Gordy, guitarist Steve Klasson and bassist Stuart Kennedy. These musicians represented the latest in a procession of itinerant minstrels that hopped aboard the Thunders charabanc during the 1980s. According to Alan Hauser, this group were genuinely nice people who made real efforts to care for and help their ailing frontman.

While Johnny was getting his latest band together, Syl invited him and Jerry to take part in a pair of benefit shows he was putting together for Arthur who'd shattered his kneecaps in a drunken fall and needed help with his medical bills. However, when Syl hooked up with Johnny to finalise details for the gigs, Johnny couldn't remember anything about agreeing to appear and the project collapsed.

Jerry and Syl subsequently teamed up to form the Ugly Americans with former Vipers bassist Graham May. However, as with Johnny, the years of heroin use and associated health problems had reduced Jerry to a weakened husk. The beat powerhouse that had propelled the Dolls and Heartbreakers songs onward with intense pneumatic salvos was no more, and after a few low key gigs in New York and Connecticut – during which he struggled to maintain a beat – Jerry threw down his sticks in disgust and quit.

Conversely, David continued to go from strength to strength. His 1989 album *Buster Goes Berserk*, which featured former Dollettes drummer Tony Machine – maintained the buzz established by the success of his debut LP and the 'Hot, Hot, Hot' single. To promote *Berserk* and his latest single, the cod-calypso 'All Night Party', Johansen appeared on the vacuous *Live with Regis and Kathie Lee* morning chat show. Asked about the whereabouts of his former Dolls *compadres*, David asserted 'they're turning a buck, they're working, they're vital,' before paying tribute to Arthur as 'the heart and soul of the New York Dolls . . . a big Swede of a guy.'

Johansen's movie career continued to blossom, as he co-starred with Richard Dreyfuss in the gambling comedy *Let It Ride* and delivered an effective performance as the cat-killing Halston in the portmanteau horror movie *Tales from the Darkside*, which also featured Debbie Harry. Additionally, he appeared on *Late Night with David Letterman* and performed at the grand opening of the Disney-MGM Theme Park alongside George Burns, Jane Fonda and Walter Cronkite.

While David was enjoying a taste of the high life, Johnny, as ever, needed some fast cash. So, in 1990, he and Jungle put together *Bootlegging The Bootleggers*, a collection of bootlegged live material linked by Johnny's unmistakable introductions. He explains that the idea for the album came from seeing the glut of Thunders bootlegs doing the rounds, 'dudes making all this money,' so, 'I had this idea of taking songs off the bootlegs. You assholes thought you'd put one over on me.'

Johnny opens the album by drawling, 'Hello, children of a lesser god, [he slips into a dodgy Louis Armstrong impersonation] hello Dolly. This is me, Dolly, it's so nice to have me back where I belong.' He goes on to introduce 'M.I.A.' as coming from 'a very educational place experienced in my life. It's the roots of music, my music.' This referred to New Orleans, where this tight, storming rendition was recorded.

'In Cold Blood' – recorded in New Jersey – segues into the Monkees' 'I'm Not Your Steppin' Stone', which in turn takes a slice from Ray Charles' 'Hit The Road Jack'. Subtlety is abandoned as Johnny adopts a stereotypical Oriental accent to introduce a blistering 'Personality Crisis', recorded in

Japan. After Dylan's 'Joey' from the acoustic gigs, Johnny announces, 'This one I writ up about a friend of mine called Sid – and God bless him wherever he may be,' before easing into a stripped-bare version of 'Sad Vacation'. Side one roars out with a riotous take on Chuck Berry's 'Little Queenie'.

Side two commences with Johnny introducing the Surfaris' 'Wipeout', before confusingly going into 'Pipeline'. An enthusiastically received 'Just Another Girl'- introduced as 'Just Another Bitch' – gives way to an acoustic version of 'You Can't Put Your Arms Around A Memory'. This set's Stones' cover is a fragile 'As Tears Go By' recorded in Paris, before Bo Diddley gets revisited again on 'I Can Tell', which sounds more like 'Shakin' All Over'.

'Johnny was a very endearing guy,' says Alan Hauser, pointing out the little studio in Jungle's basement where some of the album was recorded. 'You'd feel sorry for him, like a kid brother. He was brought up by his mum and his sister and spoilt rotten. He was a spoilt kid! [whines] "I need some money."'

In February 1990, Johnny travelled back to Paris to link up with Stiv Bators and play some dates at the Gibus club. Bators was in the process of recording some demos for a new album with Vom Ritchie from pantomime goths Dr and the Medics, guitarist Kris Dollimore, who had just left the Godfathers, and Neil X, of Tony James' techno-punks Sigue Sigue Sputnik, as sound engineer. The former Dead Boy had also hoped to assemble a junkie-punk supergroup, which he had invited Dee Dee Ramone and Johnny to join.

Since his departure from the Ramones a year earlier, Dee Dee's often fragile grip on reality had become progressively more tenuous. 'He went to the psychoanalyst everyday, but then he quit his recovery program, he thought that everyone else was crazy and he didn't listen to anyone because he thought that they were enemies trying to harm him,' revealed Joey Ramone. Having made an ill-conceived and fruitless attempt to become a rap star, Dee Dee had separated from his first wife and was looking for a new outlet for his talents.

Stiv's new band should have presented a reasonable opportunity for Dee Dee to rebuild his career. However, the bassist had developed an aversion to Johnny that bordered on phobia. The roots of Dee Dee's complex could be found in three separate incidents: an occasion during the mid-1970s when Johnny had refused to show him some guitar chops; a row that had developed between the two about ten years later, over which of them should go to score some smack from a potentially hazardous source; and a more recent occurrence, when Johnny had visited Dee Dee in New York and bent several of the ex-Ramone's spoons while cooking up his fix.

On arriving at Stiv Bators' Paris flat, Dee Dee was horrified to discover Johnny present – especially as he had agreed to hook up with Bators on the explicit proviso that Thunders wouldn't be involved. 'He's sitting there, all depressed,' recalled Dee Dee. 'My heart went out to him – I didn't realise how bad you could get.' Although Dee Dee's brain had been fried by many years of dedicated substance abuse, he was generally kind-hearted. Johnny's physical deterioration shocked the bassist to the extent that he overcame his misgivings and – with little alternative option – agreed to give the project a chance.

With predictable inevitability, things started to unravel almost immediately. Dee Dee was highly paranoid and became convinced that Bators' flat was the nexus of some type of demonic activity. He then became convinced that Johnny was stealing from him and, after discovering his coat and watch in Johnny's suitcase, he freaked out, pouring bleach all over Thunders' clothes and smashing the guitarist's Les Paul Junior. After pulling a knife on Johnny, Dee Dee was dragged away. 'Talking about John really pisses me off,' he carped in a subsequent interview with Lech Kowalski. 'John and I never got in a real fight . . . but I guess your blood is always bad if you're doin' dope.'

Unsurprisingly, the 'supergroup' project quickly collapsed. Dee Dee returned to New York and the demos were recorded with Neil X filling in for him. Johnny guested on two tracks, 'Ain't Got Nobody' and 'Two Hearts' (the latter of which surfaced on Bators' *Last Race* LP). Sadly, these sessions were to be Stiv's last – on 5 June he was on the way to meet his girlfriend, Caroline Warren, when he was hit by a car while crossing the road. He refused to go to the hospital to have his injuries checked over and returned home to his Paris flat. At about 3 a.m. that night, Caroline realised that Stiv was having difficulty breathing, and called an ambulance immediately – but, by the time it arrived, Bators had died from internal bleeding and a blood clot that formed near his heart. He had recently turned 40.

Nearly penniless and short on clothing, Johnny played several shows at the Gibus to raise funds. In April, he took his acoustic set on the road, playing extensively in Ireland (where he arrived after being delayed in immigration during a transfer at Heathrow), Greece and Germany, as well as a couple of dates in Spain. Unfortunately, Johnny's return visit to Ireland did not echo that of '84, which had been a storming triumph. The Belfast gig was repeatedly on-off and poorly publicised. Johnny didn't get paid. 'It must have been disheartening to turn up to play for fifteen people after the success of his previous visit in 1984, when he tore the place apart,' says local radio presenter Brian Young. Johnny ended up getting drunk and the PA was terrible. Next night in Dublin, he decided to do an electric set with local band the Golden Horde but got pissed again, and threw up during the second song, curtailing the show.

Brian interviewed Johnny for the local BBC radio station on the day of the Belfast gig on 27 April. He recalls, 'Johnny was pretty lucid, if dispirited.' It was one of the rare occasions when Thunders commented on the legions of impersonators who proliferated throughout the eighties. 'I don't see the bands nowadays copying the Dolls – every stud on their pants is in the perfect place. You can't tell one band or one lead singer from another without a scorecard. There's no roots to their music. It's just wank music, I call it. There's no tenderness, no compassion. It's just, "Look at me." I find it quite depressing. I haven't listened to music in over ten years.'

But Johnny was enthusiastic about the Oddballs. 'This is the band that I'm going to remember when I'm 80 years old for having a good time. This band gives me the incentive to keep myself together and not get fucked up or make a jerk of myself in front of them because they're all so professional and they play so well. I have a lot of new material but I don't want to go with an independent label.'

He cited two new songs, 'Children Are People Too' and 'Help The Homeless', which concerned the police operation to clear the tent community from Tompkins Square Park in the East Village. 'They went in with garbage trucks and rolled them all out. I was really infuriated. I've never believed in no causes really but this is one cause I really believed [in]. I did a Thanksgiving benefit in LA, raised a thousand dollars to help fund some turkey dinners. Then I went down to the mission and there were twenty church pews and a pulpit and I sang three songs for them. It was the scariest time of my life!'

Maybe living on Chinese rocks and other people's charity had left Johnny with the realisation he was only a step from the gutter himself.

Brian asked Johnny what he might have done differently in his life. 'There's a lot of things I'd change but I wouldn't change anything I've done musically.' And how did he want to be remembered? '[As] Somebody that you could dance to.'

Following two nights at the Marquee at the end of June and an appearance on short-lived UK TV show *The Power Station* – where he performed 'Lydia' and 'Nine Lives' with Oddballs guitarist Stevie Klasson and sax-player Jamie Heath – Johnny returned to New York. On previous occasions when he had returned to his home turf, Johnny had often gravitated towards the clusters of junkies and dealers that orbit New York's rock scene. This time around, motivated by the possibility of reconciliation with Susanne, Johnny made yet another attempt to get clean. Unlike many of his previous half-assed stabs at straightening out – which entailed talking about kicking his habit rather than actually doing so – this particular effort seemed genuine. With the help of a cash windfall that had come his way through the re-sale of the rights to the 1984 *Live At The Lyceum* album, he acquired an apartment and booked himself into rehab.

Johnny spent the next six weeks at Hazelden, a non-profit drug treatment organisation with six facilities in Minnesota and four others dotted around the US. When he returned to New York he gave every impression of being a changed man – for the first time in sixteen years he didn't need his methadone, and, according to Alan Hauser, was 'calm, quiet and thoughtful, without the constant feeling of stress, panic and paranoia that the chemical dependency had previously induced'.

Although he found it necessary to move apartments to avoid junkie pals who kept showing up, Johnny initially maintained his resolve to stay clean. He began writing a far wider range of material than his previous junk-centric worldview had explored, about homelessness and terrorism rather than copping and shooting up and its disastrous affects upon his love life.

Some of the last music Johnny recorded blessed a low-budget black and white movie called *What About Me*, by East Village filmmaker Rachel Amodeo – who plays herself in a slightly surreal look at homelessness in New York. Johnny plays her brother Vito Napolitano, who is only seen phoning his doomed sister from New Orleans, while Richard Hell is the Good Samaritan who pulls her out of the gutter. There are also cameo appearances by Jerry Nolan (who gets shot) and Dee Dee Ramone. Johnny played new instrumentals 'Bird Song' and 'In God's Name' on acoustic guitar, accompanied by Jamie Heath's sax. New versions of 'So Alone' and 'Joey' also appear, while 'You Can't Put Your Arms Around A Memory' provides a suitably moving backdrop for Rachel's death scene. By the time the film was released, Johnny himself would be dead.

(More recently, the evocative power of 'You Can't Put Your Arms Around A Memory' gave the track a new life as a soundtrack standard – the song was featured in Martin Scorsese's *Bringing Out the Dead* [1999], and again the same year in episode 24 of smash TV Mafia series *The Sopranos*. The series stars former Springsteen sideman Steven van Zandt as stoic *consigliere* Silvio Dante. In August 2004, van Zandt would perform the song at his annual Underground Garage Festival, accompanied by Sylvain and Johansen.)

'He wanted to record a new album and I got a bit overruled at Jungle – Debts and the other things,' recalls Alan. 'For a number of reasons it was just too risky with some of the things going on like Rough Trade going bust . . . I wanted to see if he could prove himself over a longer period. One deal he did was selling a tape of a live album to another company. The money he got from that he spent checking into some clinic or some equivalent where he did get himself completely clean off the methadone. That lasted from August through to the New Year. Meeting him in that period he was a very changed person. It was like all the nervousness and panic that had been there, coupled with a bit of aggression and edginess, had all been taken off. It was great.'

Given that the rehabilitation of a long-term addict often depends on a fragile mix of willpower, support and avoidance of temptation, it was probably not the most sensible idea to arrange a Heartbreakers reunion at the Marquee on 30 November. As Dee Dee Ramone observed, 'a typical Heartbreakers show definitely didn't revolve around the soundcheck. It involved them going to cop in the afternoon and setting it up so that when they got paid after the show you had your dealer there and you could get high all night.' For Johnny, Christmas started early as the likes of Anita Pallenberg, Brix Smith of The Fall, Gun Club's Romi Mory, Peter Perrett, and an army of old pals turned out to party backstage. Johnny returned to play a solo set at the same venue on 21 December before returning to Paris to spend Christmas with Susanne.

'He came to London to do a couple of gigs at the Marquee near Christmas, and he went out partying,' recalled Alan. 'I dunno what he done . . . but my impression was he just drank and smoked quite a lot, probably fixing other things as well. Then he went to Paris to do the Gibus for a week – acoustic gigs. The next time I spoke to him was about February and he said, "Ah, I got to come and see my doctor." I said, "I thought you didn't need to do that anymore." He said, "Ah, well . . ."'

'He wouldn't stop,' remembers Mariann. 'He was always asked about being on drugs. He knew how wrong it was. But he only went into rehab the one time – to Hazelden . . . He was good when he came out, but he was always afraid. It was always private to him. I mean, you'd know when he's stoned and everything else and everybody would, but it was really like this inner thing with him. He never wanted anybody else to do it. He never wanted anybody else to start on that. He wanted them to enjoy his music and it was a fact that he was a drug addict too. It was that kind of thing. He wasn't proud of it. Not at all.'

Johnny spent the New Year partying in Paris. However, with every drug hustler in the city seemingly intent on homing in upon him, he beat a hasty retreat to New York, where he attempted to reduce the temptation to shoot up by taking large amounts of tranquilisers. Again short of funds, he played a handful of local bar gigs in late February and early March. On 3 March he appeared at the Continental Divide, a long, cramped bar on the corner of St Mark's Place and Third Avenue – a block West from Gem Spa. Six days later Johnny made what would be his last US appearance, at Milestones in Rochester, NY, with an hour-long set backed by local garage revivalists the Chesterfield Kings.

Although he had become something of a forgotten boy in his home country, Johnny had built up a sizeable following in Japan. 'For the kids, for the critics, for the Japanese people, Johnny Thunders is a cult hero,' explained rock critic and record producer Gaku Torii. Through Torii, Johnny had managed to set up a deal for the Oddballs to tour the country in April, and spent the remainder of March preparing for the trip. Toward the end of the month he phoned Alan Hauser, insisting that he desperately needed to see his Harley Street doctor. 'I thought you didn't need anything anymore,' repeated Hauser. 'I'm just the same old jerk, I guess,' Johnny replied.

Realising that it could prove problematic to obtain either heroin or methadone in Japan, Johnny arranged to travel to London on 26 March in order to lay on a supply ahead of the Oddballs tour. However, he missed his flight and was forced to make his own *ad hoc* pharmaceutical arrangements in New York. Four days later, he and the band left for Japan.

Before he departed, he ran into Sylvain for what was to be the final encounter between the two old friends. 'I was playing this club called the Spiral. It was just one of these kind of crazy nights where they had like a gypsy kind of a band, people playing drums and all this kind of stuff. He came up to me and said, "Hey Syl man, you wanna smoke a joint?" And then we smoked a joint. He was saying to me, "Goodbye." He was like really sick, poor thing. This was just before he went to Japan, like the week that he went to Japan. That was the last time I saw him. He was staying with this girl called Jill, I think, and he gave me this card with the number where he was staying. It was 21st Street. I still have that.'

Johnny's last tour kicked off on 2 April at the Tokiwaza venue in Tokyo. Despite his haggard fragility, he still scrubbed up nicely, sporting a knee-length, blue, Edwardian-style coat over tight red trousers and vest, a white, wing-collared shirt and long, polka-dot bow tie. This ensemble was topped of by a sailor's cap, complete with red bow, which he replaced during the encore with a wreath of red roses.

During the tour, Johnny debuted a reflective ballad called 'Your Society Makes Me Sad', which Syl subsequently recorded for his 1997 album *(Sleep) Baby Doll*. Featuring elegiac lines such as, 'Do I feel guilty about an imperfect life, you ask. / Now's the time to take what's mine,' the song prompted Syl to pay full tribute to his former guitar partner. 'He never had a fuckin' American deal, but he had anthems – and he was the best writer.'

Following a show at the 1500-capacity Club Citta in Kawasaki – a sweaty hall where the unseated crowd moshed enthusiastically – the Oddballs visited Osaka and Nagoya before returning to Tokyo. After the rest of the band returned to the US, Johnny stayed on to play a pair of acoustic shows backed by Klasson and Heath.

The success of the Oddballs' brief tour prompted the Meldac Corporation to offer Johnny a lucrative Japanese record deal, which included an advance payment believed to be in the region of $50,000. Flush with cash, but only able to obtain small amounts of cocaine in Tokyo, Johnny left for a 'holiday' in Bangkok on 9 April, claiming that he was hoping to stock up on silk suits.

After getting some tattoos at a less than antiseptic-looking Bangkok parlour, Johnny made an unsuccessful attempt to score some methadone at a local hospital. Having failed to maintain his habit through legitimate means, Thunders resorted to scoring on the street.

Bangkok has long been established as a hub of the international heroin smuggling trade. In 1988, the largest ever seizure of the drug – 2,400 lbs destined for New York – was made in the city. It's hardly surprising that, the moment Johnny started making discreet enquiries around town, he attracted a significant amount of local interest. Before long, Johnny's hotel suite resembled a junk warehouse. 'The whole room was just full of heroin,' recalled his startled tour manager Mick Webster, 'the hotel staff were definitely getting sussed to what was going on . . . We paid the hotel for an extra day and we left one by one.'

Johnny arrived back in New York on 15 April, where he hung out with a long-time acquaintance, John Spacely – who enjoyed a squalid fifteen minutes of fame when he appeared as Gringo, the protagonist of Lech Kowalski's 1984 movie *Story of a Junkie*. Spacely, who was also featured in Kowalski's *Born to Lose* and briefly published *Punk* magazine, claimed to have spent much of Johnny's visit shooting speedballs with his guest. According to the *Montreal Mirror*'s Matthew Hays, Spacely was 'widely hated on the scene'. He died of AIDS, contracted, inevitably, through sharing needles, in March 1994. Kowalski was on hand to interview his former leading man as he lay dying in hospital.

Three days later, Johnny was back in London to obtain some methadone to see him through a recording session in Germany, scheduled for the following day. After laying down a version of 'Born To Lose' with German punks Die Toten Hosen and collecting his fee, he played what was to be his final concert – a low-key acoustic set in Berlin on 19 April 1991.

On 22 April, Johnny finally went to New Orleans to realise his ambition of forming his own blues band. He had a fair amount of cash left over from the Japanese tour and his German excursion and enough white to maintain his habit for some time. Johnny planned to stroll around the bars and streets and recruit musicians, who he planned to incorporate into the loose framework provided by the Oddballs.

He checked into the St Peter's Guest House, at 1005 St Peter Street, in the French Quarter. That evening he phoned Mariann and Steve Klasson, who was due to join Johnny as soon as the new band started to take shape. In an attempt to stave off jetlag, he dropped in at the hotel bar, which was bustling with guests, local hustlers and assorted lowlifes. Johnny fell into conversation with a group of fellow drinkers and headed off with his new acquaintances for a night on the town. He returned to the hotel some time after midnight.

When the maid arrived to clean up Johnny's room at 1p.m. the following day, she was horrified to discover that he was lying dead on the floor, with his head under the dresser and his meagre possessions scattered all around his twisted corpse.

By a strange twist of fate, Willy DeVille happened to be living next door to the hotel and was familiar with many of the staff. Neither Willy nor Johnny had been aware of their proximity to one another. 'I didn't see him at all, other than the time he came out in a plastic bag,' recalled DeVille. 'That guy must have died a terrible death – he was all bent up like a pretzel. It was real sad.'

Willy then found himself on the end of an unwarranted harangue from the hotel manager, who wrongly believed he had recommended the hotel to his former CBGB's buddy. Once this misunderstanding had been straightened out, the maid who had discovered Johnny's body enlisted DeVille's help in clearing the room. 'She was afraid to go in there herself,' he explained. 'She said, "Willy, I know you knew that guy – would you go in with me 'cos I'm kind of afraid?" . . . we went in and she was packing up the bags and by that time he was down at the coroner's office and I just kinda helped her pick up the bags . . . there was clothes all over the place and there was some change on the floor.'

The coroner's report stated that Johnny's death 'may have been drug-related', as empty packages of methadone were found along with a syringe in the toilet. An autopsy failed to confirm a cause of death. Traces of methadone were found but – curiously, considering that he had spent the evening drinking – no booze. Police were investigating the disappearances of his passport, $2,000, his new silk suits and a three-month supply of prescribed medicines.

Mariann has always maintained that her brother was murdered. 'I spoke to him that evening and he sounded fantastic. I believe there was foul play. I've been to New Orleans and nobody wants to talk to me. I went to the police department and the coroner's office and when I mentioned Johnny's name, everybody shut up. Nothing corresponds – the time on the death certificate, the time the police were called.' When Mariann got to New Orleans and asked to look at the police report, they couldn't seem to find half of it. Mick Webster subsequently told Nina Antonia, 'The coroner was apparently later sacked for falsifying a report in another case.'

Steve Klasson told *Melody Maker* that he believed that Johnny had been spiked with LSD and robbed. 'Klasson further suggests that Thunders died from shock, a heart attack, or homicide,' stated the article. This hypothesis was supported by Mick Webster, 'Johnny hated LSD. If they spiked him with that, he would have had a terrible time. The body was all curled up, sort of like a ball, and I understand that's often a sign of strychnine poisoning.'

Although to some extent Klasson and Webster's assertions are compelling, their theory is undermined by several ambiguities. While it's commonly believed that strychnine is routinely used in the illicit manufacture of blotter and windowpane acid as a bonding agent, there is little actual evidence to suggest this. As noted pharmacologist Alexander Shulgin – who has written four books and over 200 papers on psychoactive chemicals – explained, 'I have personally looked at a large number of illicit street offerings and have never detected the presence of strychnine.' However, this would not necessarily discount the possibility of strychnine being used as a poison. Shulgin adds, 'The few times that I have indeed found it present, have been in legal exhibits where it usually occurred in admixture with brucine (also from the plant *Strychnos nux-vomica*) in criminal cases involving attempted or successful poisoning.'

The lack of any information as to the tests on Johnny's corpse is a huge barrier to determining the exact cause of death. It's not clear whether any tests aimed at discovering anything other than methadone or alcohol were carried out. Additionally, the lethal dosage of LSD would be equivalent to something in excess of 1,000 regular-strength trips, and would be a phenomenally expensive and uncertain means of poisoning.

Furthermore, the failure of the toxicology report to find any alcohol present in Johnny's bloodstream is, at the very least, incongruous – it would have been entirely out of character for Johnny to spend the evening touring New Orleans bars without having a drink. It is possible, if unlikely, that the time that elapsed between Johnny's final drink and his death was sufficient for much of the alcohol to have been metabolised. But again, the toxicology report's findings could have resulted from a less than rigorous examination.

Even in death, Johnny's reputation as one of the all-time heavyweight rock'n'roll junkies worked against him. So far as the police and the coroner's department were concerned, this was just another dead addict, and therefore any investigation of the circumstances surrounding his death was a low priority. Although several of those who were in and around the St Peter's Guest House were questioned, there was never any indication that the police viewed Johnny's death as anything other than an accidental overdose.

Like many popular tourist destinations, New Orleans attracts plenty of petty criminals and hustlers looking to take advantage of fresh arrivals in the city. Although Johnny was hardly a wide-eyed innocent, his addiction made him vulnerable and the city has its own unique dangers. 'Things can happen down here that don't even happen in New York,' explained Willy DeVille. 'You can wind up dead 'cos there's so many slimy street hustlers, you have homosexual hustlers, you got prostitutes, you got drug dealers – this is New Orleans.'

Several witnesses claimed that Johnny's room showed definite signs of a struggle, with a chair and a table tipped over and his possessions scattered around the floor and bed. 'We keep asking the New Orleans Police to re-investigate, but they haven't been particularly friendly,' explained Mick Webster. 'They seemed to think this was just another junkie who had wandered into town and died . . . They said nothing about the missing money or the theft of Johnny's passport and some of his clothes. The state of the hotel room was also ignored. It was totally wrecked.'

It's extremely unlikely that the exact cause of Johnny's death will ever be confirmed. The New Orleans Police Department seemingly has little interest in re-opening what it believes to be a simple case of junkie misadventure. (Certainly, following the devastation caused by Hurricane Katrina in 2005 and the civil unrest that followed in its wake, the city's authorities had more pressing matters to deal with.) 'To them, Johnny Thunders was just another junkie John Doe,' lamented Nina Antonia.

However, bearing in mind Johnny's experience with narcotics; the fact that there was absolutely no indication that he wished to end his life; and that he was a lightning rod to every hustler in town, it is very possible that he was – as Mariann and others believe – robbed and murdered. 'The circumstances surrounding Johnny's demise are pretty suspect,' affirmed Nina. 'He was in a weakened state, exhausted and ill, easy prey for any passing opportunist. Thunders' arrival in New Orleans triggered a surge of activity in the drug dealing community.'

Certainly, Johnny was in an extremely vulnerable position. It's uncertain how much of the money he'd accumulated in Japan and Germany remained in his possession, but if he was in any way flush it would merely have served to expose him as an even more attractive target for anyone looking for an easy mark. Also, although he appeared to be using only methadone at the time of his death, if he had managed to retain any of the large amount of heroin that he is believed to have scored in Bangkok, he would have represented a lucrative hit indeed. Admittedly, the logistics of a known junkie being able to transport a sizeable quantity of heroin through a series of international airports seem at best tricky, but not impossible.

The grim, but most likely scenario for the unnecessary way in which Johnny met his end was that he was picked out by his assailant(s) while he was touring the local bars, followed back to the hotel and attacked and robbed in his room. Given the horribly contorted state in which he was discovered, it's possible that he may have been murdered by his killer shooting him up with an overdose of methadone. Sadly, it seems that alone and sick in a strange town, Johnny had proven irresistible to the local hustlers.

'He had a constant load of people that would look after him,' says Alan Hauser. 'That's what people did. He was looked after so much – so many liked him or loved him or whatever. One of the things Patti Palladin said was, "Oh it's terrible, no one was looking after him that night he died."'

Johnny was buried on Monday 29 April 1991 at St Anastasia Church in Queens, after a two-day wake.

'Until he died I didn't realise what he was doing or who he was doing it with,' says Mariann. 'I really didn't realise how popular he was – not at all until I read about it when he died. He had a lot of friends. He always brought his friends home. Steve Tyler was one. There were so many people at Johnny's funeral. I had no idea who Steve Tyler was. He came up to me and my daughter said to me, "Do you know who that was?"'

Melody Maker devoted two pages to an obituary written by Richard Hell: 'There was something perfect about Johnny . . . But he always surprised me when I talked to him. The surprising thing was how smart he was. Smart the same way Elvis Presley was. It was almost spiritual, a kind of grace, a kind of innate ruling of the world. That's what you wanted and Johnny had it. And he knew it; to him, the highest compliment was to be "as good as Frank Sinatra and Elvis" . . . He was perfect because he made no apologies. He was just graceful. He instinctively knew how to make do with what he had.'

'I don't think that anybody really knew Johnny,' asserts Mariann. 'Not the wanna-be's. There's always people coming up to me, saying, "Oh, I knew your brother," and I'm like, "Oh yeah, okay, you did." They go, "He was like this and he was like that," but you really didn't know my brother! You may have met him on the street one day and said, "Hi" to him, but that was about the extent of it. But if you talk to Nina or Patti – people like that were really good friends, they really knew Johnny – I think they have a different opinion. That he was caring, that he loved kids. Like I said, he hated drugs. He did them but they were like a crutch. It was a different side to him. Nina told me stories about how he used to play with her daughter. I was so surprised. I mean, he would go on tour and he would come back with presents for every one of my kids. Never when he went out on tour did he never come back with something. He was crazy about Jamie. His daughter Jamie was the light of his life. He loved Jamie so much. She's grown up to be such a beautiful young lady.'

Does she know who her dad is?

'Oh, definitely! Susanne, Johnny's girlfriend, the mother of Jamie, she's wonderful. She took care of her daughter. She brought her daughter up beautifully and I can't say enough about her to say how wonderful she is. Jamie knows about Johnny. All about him. The good, the bad and the ugly. She knows everything about him.'

Despite the way in which his life was undermined by junk, to the extent that Johnny is often identified as the consummate doomed addict, his true legacy is that of a unique and highly individual musical innovator and style icon. He epitomised the energetic cool of his influences and will be remembered as the genuine embodiment of smart, sassy, rock'n'roll rebellion. 'Music was everything to Johnny,' asserts Mariann. 'He wouldn't compromise his music in any way. If somebody wanted to do something else with it and he didn't feel it was right, he wouldn't do it.'

'He lived it,' sums up Alan Hauser. 'He wasn't an accountant and then took a different personality on stage. It wasn't an act.'

'Johnny always felt that the guitar playing was much more important than anything else that he did,' insists Syl. 'Johnny was a great guitar player, of course. His style was basically what you would stumble on if you were just learning how to play guitar. You know that stuff. It's like the beginning. That's why the whole punk generation took a hold of that, 'cos it was so simple. Johnny himself felt that he really wanted to be more like a Jeff Beck. He wasn't, but how can you make him feel like that? Really he was a great songwriter. An *incredible* songwriter. On one of her last albums, Ronnie Spector covered "You Can't Put Your Arms Around A Memory". Keith Richards helped her on that album and when she played live in New York he came up and performed "You Can't Put Your Arms Around A Memory" with her. Keith Richards played and Ronnie Spector sang. Johnny would have loved that! They were two of his favourite people. That would've been *it* for him.'

Mariann took the responsibility for maintaining her little brother's estate. 'When Johnny died I made a promise – to him and myself. Johnny had a manager called Mick Webster. When Johnny died, Mick came over here for the funeral. Then I started to talk to him and he said he'd still represent Johnny, because I knew nothing about the music business. I'm executor of the estate so I had to have help, so Mick has been a godsend to me because he's done everything.

'I made a promise. I told Mick that anybody who had screwed my brother throughout the years in music, I would get them back. And I accomplished that. I stopped them all, through lawyers . . . Now everybody has to account to me. There's no Johnny around who doesn't remember who accounted to him and who didn't. Now every three, four months – whatever the contract says – they've got to send me a statement and a cheque if it's due. The only one I have to chase up all the time is Alan [Hauser], but he senses when he's supposed to get one out. But that's one promise I made that I was gonna do and with Mick's help we were able to do it. At least it went to the right people. It went to his kids.'

Erudite rocker-stockbroker Walter Lure – Johnny's most regular onstage sparring partner between 1975 and his death – paid tribute in Nina Antonia's sleevenotes to Jungle's *Down To Kill* Heartbreakers set.

'John was unique. He was a primal force. He wasn't like anyone else and there won't be anyone else like him. He modelled himself after Keith Richards and the fifties guys. He wasn't an accomplished musician but he had something that no one else could play like him . . . . There was something magical, mystical about it where you had this unique sound . . .

'He was a great guy when he wasn't screwed up on drugs, then he was shy and nice. He'd laugh and giggle. Not the loudmouth you'd see on stage sometimes. As soon as he'd take a few pills or get high, everything would change. He'd turn into this bull in a china shop. But other times he'd have that little boy face on him. It was amazing how he could be two different people; almost a Jekyll and Hyde thing.'

Jerry Nolan also wrote a piece in *The Village Voice* about losing his old friend. 'I have a rough time getting through the days. I get real lonely, and I miss Johnny terribly. I don't like the idea of living without him . . . He never had a father. I was like a father to him, a brother to him. It's just not fair.'

Jerry recalled how, early one morning a few weeks later, he spotted Keith Richards leaning against a wall a few blocks up Broadway from his apartment on Fourth Street. Keith was reading and having a cigarette, but spotted Jerry. 'He'd seen me first. He made a motion showing we knew each other. There was no one out – it was me and him . . . he says, "Look, Jerry, I'm sorry. I know what it's like. I don't know what to say. I wish I had a poetic answer. But I will say one thing: somehow, I don't know how, but somehow, hang in there. Stick to it. Don't give up." Keith really picked up my spirits.'

Despite this consolation and encouragement from Johnny's all-time hero, Jerry was finding the loss of his 'brother' difficult to bear and became subject to bouts of depression. His health was also continuing to fail, leaving him prone to infections such as bacterial meningitis and pneumonia, which he contracted toward the end of the year. He was admitted to hospital for treatment, where he suffered a stroke and lapsed into a coma from which he never awakened. After spending several weeks on life support, Jerry died on 14 January 1992. He was buried in the same cemetery as Johnny.

'Jerry lived that life and he died for it as well,' surmised Nina Antonia. 'They were great heroes, Johnny and Jerry. They were what they were. It wasn't a guise.'

Post Millennial Mystery Girls

'Everybody gets what they deserve in the end.'
– Johnny Thunders

During the 1990s, it seemed as if all trace of the New York Dolls had passed into history with Johnny and Jerry. Indeed, the surviving members of the classic Dolls line-up were almost reduced to a duo, when, during the 1991 Los Angeles riots, Arthur was attacked from behind and severely beaten with a baseball bat. His injuries necessitated the insertion of a metal plate to reinforce his shattered skull, but after a year in hospital it was the blond bass behemoth's spirit that seemed to be most in need of repair.

The previous decade had been a washout for Arthur. Countless attempts to get bands together had foundered and, although he harboured ambitions for an acting career, his biggest credit was as an extra in Joe Dante's 1987 comedy *Innerspace*. To make matters worse he'd become estranged from his wife, Babs. Always an immoderate drinker, Arthur had sought to numb the sting of creative and personal disasters and the painful legacy of the fall from a third-floor window through drinking binges that would often leave the quietest ex-Doll immobilised. Indeed, although it was treated as an accident it was highly possible that Arthur had thrown himself through the window in an attempt to end it all. As ever, Arthur was no trouble to anyone except himself.

The time spent convalescing from his head injures afforded him the opportunity to assess his life. Looking for some means of arresting the downward spiral, Arthur sent away for the *Book of Mormon*, which had floated across his consciousness by courtesy of a TV advertisement. When Joseph Smith's testament arrived it was accompanied by two blonde missionaries, who appealed to Arthur's libido as much as they did his spirit. 'They don't send it,' explained the Killer to filmmaker Greg Whiteley, 'they bring it.'

Aided by the duo of sexy zealots, Arthur underwent a spiritual epiphany he later described as 'an LSD trip from God', and duly joined The Church of

Jesus Christ of Latter-day Saints. Like all religions, the Mormons had established a hierarchy founded on mythology and the personal search for spirituality. However, on an individual level, observance of their tenets and adherence to their lifestyle could provide stability and routine to a life running out of control.

This seemed to be the case for Arthur. 'This was nothing new for him as he was brought up on religion and it was just a new religion for him when he joined the Mormons. I believe they saved his life and he always said that they saved his life,' asserts Rick Rivets. 'I think he hit bottom and they were there to pick him up, so being a man of honour, he followed their rules in order to be part of their organisation . . . People think he was brainwashed, but that is far from the truth. There were times when he left the church only to come back on his own when the void that the church filled in his life was empty, and he realised he needed the sense of family that the Dolls and then the church gave him.

'He found a place with people that cared about him for himself and not because he was in the Dolls. He finally found a place where he could spend the holidays sharing with decent people instead of spending them alone. You have to remember that he had been on his own since his mom died when he was sixteen, and it can be very lonely out there without family or people who cared. I guess the Mormons did show him they cared about him in a genuine way and not for who he was and what they could get out of him.'

During the years that Arthur was rebuilding his life, his former bandmates continued to follow their own paths. Syl had moved to Los Angeles in 1992, where he occupied himself with a series of small production jobs and low-key live appearances, before relocating to Atlanta two years later. To a large extent Syl was pleased to be away from his hometown. 'When I was living in New York, Johnny died, my parents passed away and everything was really bad. I was a single parent, I had to take care of business . . . and New York was just too expensive.'

David was still riding high as Buster Poindexter. In 1994 he released *Buster's Happy Hour* – an album of jump-blues influenced drinking songs – as well as furthering his film career with appearances in such movies as *Freejack* (alongside a wooden Mick Jagger) and *Mr. Nanny* (a comedy vehicle for ex-wrestler 'Hulk' Hogan), and starring in a remake of *Sgt. Bilko* creator Nat Hiken's *Car 54, Where Are You?*

In the mid-1990s, aside from the odd live European bootleg LP, or Morrissey performing 'Trash' in tribute to his teenage favourites, there was little Dolls-related product for nostalgic fans to enjoy. Periodically there would be rumours of some kind of reunion between the three remaining members, but, with David's time fully occupied by the demands of his acting and Bustering careers, these came to nothing. 'Every year there's offers,' explained Syl. 'Real, real offers. I don't like to tell them to Arthur anymore because sometimes it upsets him. He gets really excited and then there's a let down.'

The 1997 release of the *Buster's Spanish Rocketship* album marked the beginning of the end for David's goodtime gadfly. The album sold poorly and failed to garner many critical plaudits. In his *NY Rock* review of a Poindexter gig in April 1998, journalist Otto Luck observed, 'Buster and company closed the evening with the obligatory "Hot, Hot, Hot" . . . Half the band formed a rumba line for the song and marched through the crowd. There was something inherently sad about seeing Poindexter at the head of the line, parading through the audience and smiling at his customers like a suit salesman. I mean, the man is history. In my mind, he's accomplished incredible feats . . . All that just to Bossa Nova his tiny fanny through a crowd of tired office workers on a Saturday night.' Aided by *Spanish Rocket Ship* producer Brian Koonin, David hung up his tuxedo and embarked upon a period of creative re-evaluation that would occupy him for much of the next two years.

In 1998, Syl released his first new album in well over a decade, after he secured a deal with the recently formed Fishhead label to issue *Sleep Baby Doll*. Although Syl had been preoccupied with bringing up his son and keeping a roof over their heads, he'd continued recording and had even constructed a studio in the basement of his Atlanta home. 'I kept on writing songs because that's my passion . . . I used to go to the record bins in New York with my own little bootleg cassettes in day-glo colours. I'd put my tag on the back of them, $6.99, and if you want some more just call me up.'

Described by Syl as 'really a homemade thing', *Sleep Baby Doll* was recorded quickly and cheaply with help from producer Brian Keats on drums and some guitar assistance courtesy of Frank Infante (ex-Blondie) and Derwood Andrews (formerly of Generation X). The album's title track was Syl's tribute to Billy, Johnny and Jerry, reminiscent of Eddie Cochran's 'Three Stars' – a eulogy to Buddy Holly, Ritchie Valens and the Big Bopper. 'That song started off as a lullaby when I was trying to get my son O'Dell to go to sleep,' revealed Syl. 'Everyone kept asking me, "Why don't you write one of those Eddie Cochran-style numbers that pay tribute to the guys that have passed away."'

'Sleep Baby Doll' sounds very much like an urban lullaby, its simple structure enhanced by Syl's fifties doo-wop stylings. '[It] was my way of saying goodbye, my parting words to Johnny, Jerry and Billy. That was really my concept – it's got to come up naturally and be for a reason.' The album also contained new versions of 'Trash', 'Frenchette' and Johnny's valedictory 'Your Society Makes Me Sad', which had originally been destined for inclusion on an abandoned Thunders tribute disc alongside Arthur's Syl-produced cover of 'In Cold Blood'.

Along with Brian Keats, Syl took the album on the road, rounding out his touring line-up with bassist Joe Carlucci and Oliver LeBaron on guitar. Although *Sleep Baby Doll* was never likely to be a significant commercial success, it received several good reviews in the small press and on the 'net and generated sufficient interest to ensure the album's reissue in 2000 and 2004.

Inevitably, many of the interviews that Syl did in support of his solo project urged the guitarist to revisit his seventies heyday, enquiring about the possibility of a Dolls reunion.

Speaking to Canadian website *The Eye* in 2000, Syl insisted, 'I'd do it at the drop of a hat! I'd welcome the money – I'm not going to be stupid and say I'd give it to charity. But I don't think it's going to happen . . . I said "yes" years ago, and Arthur Kane said "yes" years ago, and even when Johnny Thunders was alive and well, he said "yes". The only one standing in the way of the end of our rainbow is Mr. David.'

Having moved on from the Dolls by establishing himself as a solo artist, then re-invented himself as Buster Poindexter, David established a pattern of leaving his earlier musical incarnations behind. In 2000 he emerged from his latest creative larval stage to release *David Johansen And The Harry Smiths,* an album that drew heavily on *The Anthology Of American Folk Music*, edited by Harry Smith – a massively influential set which fuelled the work of Bob Dylan and the folk movement of the early sixties. The *Anthology* was released as a six CD set in 1997, which may have re-ignited David's interest and prompted him to fully realise a lifelong dream.

'Allan Pepper from the Bottom Line called me up to see if I wanted to do a gig for his 25th-anniversary show. I said I'd been working out this string-band thing, playing these old songs. "Okay," he said, "what's your name?" "Shit," I said, "call us the Harry Smiths,"' David told *NY Metro*'s Mark Jacobson. The Harry Smiths came together as a one-off, but a good review in the *New York Times* persuaded David to take things further, roping in guitarist Brian Koonin, Larry Saltzman on dobro, Kermit Driscoll on bass, and drummer Keith Carlock on a permanent basis.

After a DAT of the band's rehearsals came into Bob Dylan's possession, he expressed an interest in releasing the set on his vanity label, Egyptian. 'Apparently Dylan went insane,' David told rock journalist Barney Hoskyns. 'He said this was the shit and made his band learn our arrangement of "Delia" . . . And I'm thinkin', like, that's really flattering, y'know? To be on Egyptian, with Dylan's imprimatur or somethin'. So they bring it to Sony, who distribute Egyptian, and Sony goes, "What are you, nuts? We knew you were nuts, but now its official!" So they just said, "No, we're not gonna put it out."'

New York producers David and Norman Chesky swooped in and set about recording the Harry Smiths as a live ensemble at St. Peter's Episcopal Church (described by Johansen as 'a big spooky old church that smelled of myrrh') over four days in late 1999. The result was *David Johansen And The Harry Smiths*. Recorded with no overdubs, the ensemble tackled songs such as 'Oh Death' and 'Old Dog Blue' from the *Anthology*. There are also covers of Lightnin' Hopkins, Mississippi John Hurt and Muddy Waters.

Uncut's Nigel Williamson gave the album a four-star review, calling it, 'an unexpected delight . . . Johansen's voice sounds totally authentic (you might imagine it was Taj Mahal on a blind hearing) and his natural empathy for country blues is as enjoyable as it is unexpected.'

'You can crank out generic versions of old blues songs,' David told Williamson. 'But I wanted to do something different. Take the songs apart. Give them a jazz feel.'

After a string of dates in the US, David brought the Harry Smiths to the UK in January 2001, playing London's Forum, Leicester, Belfast and Dublin. 'Tell all the New York Dolls fans not to come,' Johansen told *Mojo*. 'They must be

60 years old and not half as self-destructive as they like to think they are. I don't do New York Dolls covers, just new stuff all the way.' Despite his tongue-in-cheek bluster, David and the band performed acoustic versions of 'Pills' and 'Looking For A Kiss' alongside their classic blues standards.

In addition to getting the Harry Smiths up and running, David continued to make regular film and television appearances; he once again found himself cast as a cabbie in the 1997 comedy *The Deli*, as well as branching out into voice work – such as his role as a bus driver in kids' cartoon comedy *Cats Don't Dance* (1997).

Surprisingly, Arthur made an unexpected contribution to the straight-to-video film *oeuvre* when he turned up in *Hustler's Jail Babes #5*. Despite his conversion to Mormonism, Arthur had retained his appreciation of the female form. When the opportunity to appear as an extra in a *Hustler* photo shoot presented itself, the Killer had cheerfully signed up. Once it was realised that the magazine had a New York Doll on the set, Arthur was promoted to a more prominent role and asked to appear in the video. 'This will hopefully let rock and roll fans know that I am alive and well and that I am looking for [a] fabulous new and inspirational rock and roll girlfriend – I am considering having a "Win a Wild Weekend with New York Doll Arthur Killer Kane Kontest,"' he told Dolls fan site supremo Chris Ridpath in July 1999.

During the first years of the new millennium, rock became fashionable again. Suddenly, it seemed as if a whole slew of bands taking their cues from punk rock, proto-punk and garage had beamed down from the 1970s. Groups such as the Strokes, the Libertines, the Black Rebel Motorcycle Club and the Hives tapped into the mainline of stripped-down rock'n'roll and made it hip again. Additionally, the silver anniversaries of punk's *age d'or* in 2001 and 2002 prompted many media re-evaluations of the genre and its influences. As the new groups namechecked the Dolls, the Heartbreakers, the MC5 and the Stooges, t-shirts bearing their likenesses began appearing in boutiques aimed at this season's rock chicks. 'I see all these fifteen-year-old kids in Dolls t-shirts – I don't know where the fuck they get them,' harrumphed Syl. 'I wish somebody would send me two per cent, because to this day I don't get paid anything for merchandise.' Catching the way that the commercial wind was blowing, Jungle released *Manhattan Mayhem – A History Of The New York Dolls*, a double CD retrospective that featured early sessions and demos alongside a live set from 1974.

Former Dolls superfan Morrissey was also enjoying a renaissance. By 2004 he'd released his first studio album in six years, broken his long media silence, patched up his differences with the *NME* and put together a new touring band. Now establishing himself as a godfather-of-indie figure to a new generation of fans, confirmation of Morrissey's return came in the form of his being invited to curate the Royal Festival Hall's annual Meltdown Festival. Each year, the festival provides a respected musical heavyweight with the opportunity to host a fortnight-long series of events reflecting their personal taste and influences. Previous curators have included Nick Cave,

Lee 'Scratch' Perry and David Byrne, while the 2005 festival would be guided by Patti Smith.

In addition to performing new material from his critically acclaimed comeback album, *You Are The Quarry*, Morrissey employed his Wildean charm to good effect by persuading a number of his favourite artists to appear. The line-up reflected the breadth of Mozzer's influences, featuring Nancy Sinatra, Sparks, former Slit Ari-Up, Jane Birkin, Alan Bennett and – for reasons that defy rational comprehension – East London's most violent musical export, the Cockney Rejects. He also convinced the remaining members of the Dolls to reform.

Kris Needs: *As a teenager, young Steve Morrissey from Stretford, Manchester, was one of the Dolls' earliest champions. His membership of my Mott the Hoople Seadivers fan club sparked a barrage of correspondence where he would report on the latest developments in his obsession. Morrissey wrote to me regularly between 1972 and '74. Always about his passion for Mott, the shitty nature of his existence, how he lived for the music and so forth. If a group came along that had Mott's seal of approval then he would check them out, and that's really how his Dolls fixation came about. He was very sweet and I think he appreciated the fact that I bothered to write back to him.*

When Morrissey performed 'Trash' as an encore at Santa Monica Civic Centre in 1991, Sylvain and Arthur were backstage visitors. 'He invited me down to a show,' recalled Syl. 'I saw the set list with "Trash" on it, so I took it and got him to sign it. I asked him how he started liking the Dolls. He said he saw us on the BBC while he was sitting there with his mom. He used to walk to school holding the first album – just the cover, no record inside – just to show people where he was at.'

Morrissey got in touch with David Johansen and 'begged and pleaded' with the frontman to reform the Dolls for Meltdown. Although he hadn't spoken to Syl or Arthur for more than a decade, such was Morrissey's enthusiasm that David agreed to give the project a go. He duly approached Syl – who readily agreed – while Arthur heard about the reunion from a third party. 'I was just checking my email . . . and I got an email from a friend I hadn't heard of in 30 years, and he says, "Oh Arthur, I understand you'll be in town playing Morrissey's Meltdown Festival this summer."' Shocked, Arthur overcame the considerable hurdle of tracking down Morrissey by telephone. 'I said, "Please tell me what's going on." He said, "I've spoken to David Johansen and I've talked him into doing a Dolls reunion."' Arthur was overjoyed at the prospect of appearing with David and Syl as the Dolls. '[It was] So far fetched, I couldn't ever have imagined it,' he told Greg Whiteley.

Alarmingly, a month before the Meltdown gigs the whole project was almost derailed when Syl suffered a mild heart attack. 'The doctors said, "Have you ever heard of exercise?" I'm like, "I jump up on stage and run around every chance I get,"' he told *The Times*' Peter Shapiro. 'Rock'n'Roll's great for you. I think aside from James Brown I'm the hardest working. I'm the hardest working, white, Jewish boy in show business.' Fortunately, Syl's years of hard, white, Jewish work paid off and he was passed as fit to travel. For the two Meltdown shows, the trio of surviving Dolls would be augmented by David's righthand man Brian Koonin on keyboards, guitarist Steve Conte and Libertines drummer Gary Powell. 'David Johansen was looking for a drummer, I got a call from our booking agent and was asked if I'd like to perform with the New York Dolls,' Powell told the *NME*. 'What sort of question is that? Of course I'd like to do it!' While Powell had grown up as a fan of the Dolls, Conte – who was charged with the nigh-impossible task of filling Johnny Thunders' white platform boots – had been introduced to the group by Alphonse Murcia. 'I met Alphonse, Billy Murcia's older brother in the late 1970s in Matawan, NJ – where I went to high school,' Steve explains. 'I saw this cat (who looked way older than me) with long curly hair, platform shoes and elephant bells walking down the highway by himself and I wondered, what is this guy's story? When I approached him we got into a conversation and he said, "Hey man . . . you look like Johnny Thunders!" I didn't know who Thunders was at that time. Al told me that he was the guitarist in his brother's band, the New York Dolls. I had heard of the Dolls but didn't know the depth of the music so Al would come to my house and bring over vinyl by the Dolls, Heartbreakers and Criminals.

'As a cocky young guitarist in the 'burbs I had aspirations of being a "virtuoso" player like Jeff Beck or Jimi Hendrix – I hadn't yet been exposed to the blossoming punk scene in New York City. On first listen, I didn't fall in love with the Dolls sound but it's logical that I would eventually come around to it. During those high school years I was in a basement band playing a mix of Stones, Bowie, Mott, T. Rex, Black Oak Arkansas, J. Geils and Chuck Berry. I was into both the Brit and American – glam and blues. I'd always get dressed and made-up for gigs, that's why being a Doll feels like home for me.

'I discovered *Rock Scene* magazine where I'd see photos of David, Syl and Johnny, the Dead Boys, Aerosmith and the Ramones guys all hanging out at Max's Kansas City and CBGB's. Then I knew that I had to start an original band and get my ass to New York. But I was still too young to get into bars so I had to be content just drooling over the photos.

'When I finally moved to New York City I saw Sylvain play at the Cat Club once but I never ran into Thunders anywhere. (I had an ex-girlfriend who worshipped JT so I never listened to him on principle.) I still have the single of Sylvain's song "Every Boy, Every Girl" on RCA that Alphonse brought me. I heard David Jo's early solo records on the radio and liked them . . . little did I know that my favourites of those songs were co-written by Syl. In the late 1980s my blues band, the Hudson River Rats, had a weekly gig in Manhattan where David came to sit in with us doing his jump-blues thing as "Buster". He told an amusing story about being thrown in jail back in the Dolls days ("I was dressed like Liza Minelli at the time") and that sort of rekindled my interest in his past. I had no knowledge of Arthur or Nolan's post-Dolls activities (except that Jerry was a Heartbreaker) until recently when I met the Killer.'

Like Gary, when the call came to hook up with the Dolls, Steve didn't need to be asked twice. 'David got a call from Morrissey to put the Dolls back together with the remaining members. He asked a few respected guitar players in NYC to recommend someone. Both Jimmy Vivino (from the Conan O'Brien show who also plays with David in Hubert Sumlin's band) and Larry

Saltzman from David's band the Harry Smiths told him, "There's only one name I'm gonna give you – Steve Conte – don't call anyone else!" So he called me, we met for lunch and talked about many things, including music. At the end of our meeting he gave me a package of CDs and lyrics saying, "I took the liberty of making this package for you – so whaddaya think – you wanna do this?" To which I replied, "Hell yeah!"'

After a reunion between David, Syl and Arthur in New York, a small number of rehearsals were organised, which also included Koonin and drummer Brian Delaney. The band travelled to London a week before the first Meltdown show. Arthur had taken leave from his job at the Mormon Family History Centre on Santa Monica Boulevard and was accompanied in London by filmmaker Greg Whiteley, who was capturing the reunion for his documentary on Arthur, *New York Doll*, which was released in 2005.

On 16 June 2004 the New York Dolls reunited for the first time in nearly 30 years. Although the band could never be as they were – Johnny and Jerry being irreplaceable – the gig enabled the remaining trio to receive what can only be described as waves of sheer love from their adoring audience, many of whom had grown up during punk and were too young to see the Dolls during their British tours.

It was an emotional night. It seemed – though hindsight may be romanticising the recollection – to be Arthur's night. Syl and David repeatedly walked over to his customary position toward the back of the stage and hugged and kissed the Killer. Arthur seemed almost beatifically happy, not grinning wildly but simply standing there in a halo of light reflecting off of his white shirt, doing what he was born to do – holding down a rock-steady bass rumble while the Dolls worked through a surprisingly tight rendition of their greatest (shoulda been) hits. Throughout it all, Arthur exuded a quiet dignity and gentle satisfaction. 'Arthur – his whole life – when you see that movie [*New York Doll*] his whole life he was waiting for the New York Dolls to get back together,' observes Syl. 'Meltdown was almost like a miracle because for Arthur it was mind over matter. The guy was so sick, but he was still happy and wanting to do this.'

Throughout the gig, Syl and David paid tribute to Arthur, Johnny and Jerry, their English fans and Roy Hollingworth. Despite the impossibility of covering for Jerry and Johnny, Gary Powell and Steve Conte made seamlessly unobtrusive contributions to the set, never becoming noticeable enough to shift the focus of attention from Sylvain, David and Arthur.

The set was double the length of any seventies Dolls show, covering both albums minus *Too Much Too Soon*'s covers and 'Chatterbox'. They also laid into 'Piece Of My Heart', the Irma Franklin song which David had made a personal tour de force during his solo career, an old blues called 'In My Girlish Days' and a sumptuous rendition of the Shangri-Las' 'Out In The Street', where the line, 'He don't hang around with the gang no more,' took on an extra poignancy.

With any reunion gig, there is always likely to be a split in opinion between those who feel that the band can't be true to their legacy unless the original (or classic) line-up appears complete, and others who are simply happy to see their heroes in whatever form possible. Stepping into a reformed band as a replacement is never easy. Attempting to cover for Johnny Thunders in the New York Dolls would cause many to break out in a sweat. Conte made a far better job of the Thunders role than many would have imagined possible. Without attempting to ape Johnny, he somehow succeeded in making an immense void less noticeable. 'If you distil the Thunders style down to its essence it's like, "Chuck meets Keith on speed through a high gain amp." Fortunately, I come from those roots so there wasn't any learning to do,' explains Steve. 'I did what I would do in any situation where I had to replace someone – I played the main guitar themes and the most memorable hooks . . . things that make the song identifiable. I also looked for places where I might inject some of my own personality into the music. Playing live, you can't over-think it though. If I played a riff that Thunders wouldn't have or couldn't have played I didn't stop myself. I just went for it in the spirit of the moment.

'I just couldn't get over how much fun it was to play in this band. It's a classic rock'n'roll band set-up: a star front man, his rhythm guitar partner-in-crime and the flashier lead guitarist, with killer bass and drums. I've learned that for a player like me, there are no mistakes when you're a Doll – only notes and chords of "tension" to be resolved.

'When we were setting up the stage I was on stage right with Arthur while Syl was on stage left with Brian Koonin. David asked me if I'd mind moving to the other side because he thought I was making Arthur nervous (it was me who had been reminding Arthur of his parts and the song arrangements). Whether it was true that I was intimidating him or not, I was happy to move to the other side for Arthur but also because it created a better visual with him, Syl and David all close to each other instead of spread out.

'Although Koonin (who has played with David for the past twenty years) was appointed as "musical director", and I was supposed to lead some songs, Sylvain had his own ideas of where songs should end or go longer which just added to that Dolls-chaos. If you watch the DVD you can see it. I love Syl, he's a total natural – a great showman and songwriter – the real deal.'

One of the gig's most emotional moments came when Sylvain altered the words of 'You Can't Put Your Arms Around A Memory' before it segued into 'Lonely Planet Boy', shouting emotionally during the chorus, 'I can't put my arm around Johnny.'

'Being with the Dolls and the excitement that surrounded the reunion was a real rush,' continued Steve. 'The audiences and the luminaries that came out to witness it proved to me how important this band was. Backstage I talked with Sex Pistols and Clash, Pretenders and Generation X, Boomtown Rats and Pogues – all who professed their love for the band.'

Two nights later, they returned to the Royal Festival Hall and did it all again. 'The second show however was different though,' recalls Steve. 'We had a day off in between the two shows and we opted not to do a soundcheck that day. On that gig, everything we'd rehearsed went out the window and there were some train wrecks onstage. After the show I was a bit bummed because I heard that it had been filmed and recorded for a live DVD. David said, "Nah, it's cool – it's what people expect from the Dolls". Later at the after-party I met Chrissie Hynde, Mick Jones, Bob Geldof and

Morrissey who all raved to me about how great the show was and what a fantastic job they thought I did filling Thunders' shoes.'

Despite the second show's 'train wrecks', the press reacted with surprise that a band so renowned for being sloppy in their prime could reconstitute so effectively after so long. Pete Clark's *Evening Standard* review carried the headline, 'Battered Old Dolls Come Out To Play The Best Rock'n'Roll'. Clark admitted pre-gig 'feelings of trepidation' as he'd seen the Dolls in their prime and felt a bit 'queasy' about revisiting the experience as a 50-year-old. 'After an opening burst of "Looking For A Kiss", it was clear that instead of a ruin, I had stumbled on the remains of a great band.' Filmmaker and former Roxy DJ Don Letts observed, 'I was worried that the reality would destroy the myth, but that wasn't the case – the guys delivered – 100 per cent.'

Mariann Bracken was among those who were less than enthusiastic about the reunion. This was understandable. From her perspective, there was another guy up there trying to be her brother and she felt marginalised by the lack of any invitations or courtesy calls from the band. 'They didn't invite me to any of the concerts. There was a concert in New York but they never called and invited me. When they first started to do it, the manager called me to tell me they were going to do it, but after that I never heard anything. They played in New York and they never said, "Why don't you come and see us?" or anything, which I think would have been the right thing to do.

'The Dolls are Johnny, Arthur, Syl, David and Jerry. Those are the New York Dolls. Those two guys up there right now are singing with another band, so they're not the Dolls. I really don't think they should call themselves that. I didn't think it was right but there was nothing I could do about it.'

For longstanding fans with a less personal stake in the reformation, the joy at any kind of Dolls reunion was always likely to be tempered by Johnny and Jerry's absence. Certainly, Nina Antonia found herself torn by ambivalence. '[I had] very mixed feelings. I just couldn't bear that there was some guy who looked a bit like Johnny, just a substitute. It did not sit well with me.'

Any controversy about the Dolls' reformed line-up was overshadowed on 15 July 2004, when Arthur Kane died. While Syl and David had stayed in England for an 11 July appearance at the Move Festival in Manchester, Arthur felt exhausted from the Festival Hall dates and returned home to Los Angeles. Feeling unwell, he arranged a medical check-up and was diagnosed with leukaemia. Two hours later he was dead.

Less than a month after he had stood onstage in London, in his rightful place at the heart of the New York Dolls, Arthur was gone, making his evident joy on those nights seem all the more poignant. 'I have to thank Morrissey for bringing us back together and giving Arthur his best last moments on earth,' declares Syl. 'He was never as lucky as any of us. He always wanted the New York Dolls to get back together. If the Dolls didn't get together, Johnny, David and me could always find some kind of musical gig somewhere. We could keep on calling ourselves musicians, but Arthur had it tough, poor fellah. When we got back together, he only just made it through the Meltdown thing. He was so sick. It was like mind over matter, like witnessing a miracle. It was great. It was love, man. It was how I would have liked to have gone.'

A DVD of the Festival Hall gig appeared towards the end of 2004. David Johansen contributes an eloquent, heartfelt eulogy, writing about Arthur's unique view of the world – 'Arthur's perceptions were not those of mortal men' – and describing him as 'the glue that held all the disparate iconoclastic elements together [in] our band of miscreants.'

David also wrote about the reunion: 'delightfully I found Arthur to be more mesmerising a personality than ever . . . he had emerged to my eyes as a mystical almost translucent being . . . He was non-judgemental, bawdy and holy.' He went on to say how disappointed he was that the rekindled friendship had no further chance to develop. In conclusion David noted, 'The passing of Thunders and Nolan is somehow comprehensible to us, but in the instance of Arthur "Killer" Kane I'm afraid it will take some time.'

The release of Greg Whiteley's *New York Doll* also provided a fitting memorial to Arthur's life. In the movie he talks about, 'living a life that most people don't get to live on Earth . . . because of our bad behaviour and the use of drugs we lost the New York Dolls. We were so young and too stoned to appreciate what we had.' Arthur seems totally surprised and bowled over by the reunion, which came after '30 years living in obscurity and being told I'm a loser.'

It's a poignant film, especially the scene where this gentle giant of a man announces in his strange, other-worldly voice that he wants to play something on the harmonica for the Family Centre called 'Love One Another'. ('He was blowing me a few of those right there during our rehearsals in New York,' declares Syl.) Arthur then expresses his unparalleled joy at being offered a job in the Centre's library. In some ways it's the clichéd story of a life ruined by the bottle, then the discovery of redemption and peace through religion, but Arthur's story was so much more than that. It was a story of a sweet, quiet man who combined outrageous style with gentle behaviour and was always different and special. In his own private world.

Unsurprisingly, Greg Whiteley's film proved universally popular with all who saw it. 'It's an Arthur movie,' confirms Syl. 'It's really about a guy and what happened in his life and how he found faith in his last years . . . It's so fucking great. They did such a great job. The soundtrack is amazing, it's really fucking cool . . . It was great, because you couldn't write a story like that.'

'I'd see Artie every time I was on the west coast and all he would talk about was the Dolls,' Rick Rivets recalls. 'That was his whole life and I'm really glad that he had the chance to relive his glory days one more time before he passed. He will be missed.'

Initially, it seemed as if Arthur's death would, logically, signal the end of the Dolls in any form. However, Sylvain and David opted to keep going, and, with a line-up rounded off by former Hanoi Rocks bassist Sam Yaffa, they set out on a series of intermittent, but well-received, US dates throughout 2004 and 2005. 'These days it's a whole new band. The show has come a long way since the Royal Festival Hall DVD,' enthuses Steve Conte. 'Of course, I miss Arthur and his spirit but Sami is doing a great job in his place. Drummer Brian Delaney is playing his ass off too and I am totally at home with the music now. I hadn't even embodied those songs yet when we did the DVD – I was still reading cheat sheets on the floor for "Frankenstein!"

'The shows have been *fantastique*,' adds Steve. 'We just got back from the Voodoo Music Festival in Memphis and New Orleans to benefit Hurricane Katrina victims. It was pretty heavy seeing the devastation with our own eyes. We played between Queens of the Stone Age and Nine Inch Nails. Some of the touring highlights for me have been Little Steven's Underground Garage Festival with Iggy and the Stooges and Bo Diddley, Los Angeles Sunset Junction Street Festival, Seattle's Bumbershoot festival with Garbage, the HFS festival with Coldplay and the Foo Fighters. For club shows the most memorable was our three-night stand at NYC's Irving Plaza and gigs in other big cities like Detroit, Chicago and LA.'

By May 2005, Syl and David were harbouring ambitions of scoring a record deal for their new Dolls, 'We're always looking for a record deal,' David told *Gasoline* magazine's Cameron Carpenter. 'I wanna play hardball. I wanna play with the big boys, I fuckin' wanna play against Britney Spears and those other bands whose names I don't know . . . I wanna make records for all of the people. I wanna make records that everyone in the world knows.' 'We wanna keep everything that was great except for the part where we didn't sell many records,' added Syl.

The band struck a deal with Roadrunner Records, setting some kind of record for the length of time elapsed between a band's second and third albums when they went into a New York studio with producer Jack Douglas in January 2006. Steve Conte was enthusiastic about the new material, declaring, 'We haven't had a whole lot of time to sit down as a band so we're doing it kind of whenever we can get at least two or three of us in a room together. There are lots of new Sylvain/Johansen tunes, some Conte/Johansen songs and Yaffa/Johansen songs that are strong contenders. It's a cross between the girl group sound that Sylvain is so good at, with some bluesy/punky rockers by myself, Sami and Syl too!' David was equally keen. 'Everything feels right, we're delighted to get back in the studio to record what we feel are the strongest tracks of our careers.'

Regardless of any impact that the new New York Dolls may make, the band already hold a unique place in the history of rock'n'roll. The band started by Johnny, Billy, Rick, Syl and Arthur, and made famous during David and Jerry's tenure, has already come to symbolise the city that the group were named after at a unique period in time.

In 1980, Marty Thau – the man who did everything inhumanly possible to try to break this wonderful ragbag of glamour, excess and rock'n'roll to the world – said, 'If the Dolls had stayed together, and made certain personal concessions I think they could have had all that they ever would've hoped for. They'd be around today and playing Madison Square Gardens, no doubt about it. They were one of the greatest groups of their time.'

In 2005, Sylvain Sylvain – described in 1973 by David Johansen as 'the soul of the New York Dolls' – could reflect on how the band he'd christened all those years ago was on the rise again. 'I've learned over the years that it wasn't fake. It was for real. We didn't go home and take it off and hang it up in the closet and become something else. That was us and still it's us.'

Epilogue

by Kris Needs

After seeing the Dolls that one and only time at Biba's, it transpired that my next opportunity – 33 years later – happened to be at another department store – Selfridges, on Oxford Street. The very place that Malcolm McLaren voiced a desire to loot during his junior anarchist days at the turn of the seventies. Two days after the new Dolls blitzed the place on 9 March 2006, McLaren would take the same stage and, in true Barnum style, explain how he invented punk rock.

The idea of a Selfridges' Future Punk festival was surreal and incongruous. Reportedly a vanity project for a boss's daughter, it featured punk groups old and new in the basement amidst 'punk workshops' and stalls selling records and punkwear.

At least the organisers had the nous to book the New York Dolls for their opening party, even if only a select few punk 'faces' and diary columnists could get in. 'It's like a youth club for old people,' laughed Glen Matlock, the only ex-Pistol present, as Don Letts spun a sublime reggae set similar to his Roxy days.

After Don's heartfelt and rabble-rousing introduction, the New York Dolls sauntered on appropriately behind schedule. David Johansen wore black leather, rested a battered book of lyrics on a music stand and, without further ado, pouted out the 'When-ah-say-ahm-in-love, you-best-believe-ahm-in-love, L-U-V' intro to 'Looking For A Kiss'. Sylvain, sporting his trademark denim cap and black White Falcon vintage guitar, hopped and pointed in the air like a demented cheerleader. It was cacophonously loud to the point of feedback squalls, but spectacularly energised and jaw-dropping.

The nearest thing to the buzz-sparking lunacy and cavorting in front of the stage was the previous summer's re-enactment of *Fun House* by the Stooges at Hammersmith Apollo. The disbelief and delight were tangible among the members of the audience who weren't still propping up the free bar. Unfortunately, the exclusivity of the event and mishandled guest list (the Dolls' passes even went missing) robbed the event of that complete Dolls party experience. But they did kick up a furious, glorious racket.

Johansen and Sylvain are now supported by four new musicians who have an unenviable task in replacing the departed. Steve Conte makes no attempt to grandstand a place as the new Thunders. He's simply a great blues-based guitarist with the right attitude. Sami Yaffa does a solid job, becoming particularly lethal when rhythm section partner Brian Delaney begins impersonating a ton of sonic bricks. Keyboard embroidery is provided by Johansen's long-time collaborator Brian Koonin.

The presence of founding fathers David and Sylvain imbues the group with the unquenchable spirit of the Dolls. By any standards, it's a shit-hot rock'n'roll band. There are sparks flying here, you can tell by the smiles being exchanged on stage. The set is short and to the point. A wired 'Puss 'N' Boots', a clonking 'Private World', then Sylvain hollers, 'I wanna do this for Johnny Thunders!' and the biggest cheer goes up as they strike up 'You Can't Put Your Arms Around A Memory', which segues effortlessly into 'Lonely Planet Boy'.

'How come they don't have a glam rock revival?' asks David.

Bo Diddley's 'Pills' takes it back to the Mercer Arts Centre in '72, while the anthemic 'Trash' is delivered at breakneck double-time. Raging versions of 'Personality Crisis' and 'Jet Boy' bring the set to a boiling close, complete with stage invasion from former Aloof drummer Wildcat Will, who plants a smacker on David before springing back into the pit. There's no encore, because another punter revives one of '76's more obnoxious customs by throwing a glass.

Removing preconceptions and prejudices, this was a ferociously great live onslaught of the kind you rarely get nowadays. Despite the shortcomings of the setting, the Dolls underlined their continuing importance with a display of suitably vulgar power and panache.

As I was winding up my part in this book, *Mojo* asked me to do a major Dolls story. This meant hooking up with David and Sylvain – and going to New York to hear the new album! The first interview took place the day after the Selfridges event. The incorrigible pair kicked back in the bar of the Commodore Hotel, a modest, comfortable establishment on Lancaster Gate. There were no groupies, liggers or any associated hassles to contend with.

David Johansen is nothing like the camp primadonna or gruff blues veteran you might expect. He's tall, still dressed in black, wearing shades, which coolly double as reading glasses, and sporting bling in both quantity and quality. He chain smokes Camels with a vengeance, drinks tea and devours rolls splattered in jam. His voice is deep and resonant, conversation slow, deliberate and often peppered with a rich, riotous laugh. After years of stage patter and delivering devastating one-liners, David knows how to fire off his anecdotes.

Sylvain is still the ball of enthusiasm that carried the Dolls through their most troubled times. The pair are like two old soldiers who've survived the war and lived to tell their memories. They laugh a lot and, after a few minutes, are battling to get the next word in. It puts me in mind of a rock'n'roll Odd Couple, their banter showing an obvious underlying affection. They are wonderful company.

David is disparaging about the previous night's event. 'Last night was kind of ridiculous because the promotion was some kind of bogus, faux fashion shtick or something. Parties are different than concerts because in a concert you're playing for people who actually want to see you. At a party you're just kind of like a vase of flowers or something. It's difficult to get any ideas or any kind of pulse from that. But we just go in and play a few songs.'

The duo can't stop enthusing about the new group and the album they're just finishing up, which has all come about as a result of the 2004 Meltdown reunion.

'We were just gonna do one show at that point,' says David. 'We weren't gonna have a band or anything. Then that one show turned into two shows. Then we started getting calls from the mudbaths so we did that. Then we were having so much fun that Syl and I had a talk and said, "Let's keep doing this, as long as we're having fun." It happened very organically.'

'We're natural beasts in having to play live,' adds Syl. 'We could've lived on and on without even making a new record but David insisted. He said, "Sylvain go back, try and write a couple of new songs." At first there were growing pains, which is a natural thing with twenty new songs, y'know?'

'It's a great fucking band,' stresses Johansen. 'Not just the fact that they are great players, but the way everybody fits together, and does their part and knows instinctively what their part is. We were in the Dolls first, which was essentially like a democracy where everybody had an equal say. Syl and I then went on to have bands where we said, "Well, here's what you're gonna play." That's all different now. I mean, it's a Band and you have camaraderie and all that kind of stuff. In this band, it's more like everybody's bringing something to the table. Then you have like a real soup because there's a lot of ingredients in it. You never know what's gonna happen. It's exciting like that. We've carried that right into the studio on our new album.'

I remember Sylvain saying he felt like 'a second class citizen' during the recording of the previous Dolls album (32 years earlier), because his songs were ignored. In the Dolls' final year, they had almost come to a creative standstill as communications worsened between David and Johnny. This time, there's no stopping them. Sylvain has written a whole bunch while Yaffa and Conte have also contributed songs. David wrote all the words which, it has to be said, are absolutely captivating and up there with his very best.

Basic tracks were recorded live and Sylvain was particularly surprised when producer Jack Douglas insisted on using first takes. ('When we were playing I was looking at my nekkid chick book!')

The production, historically the Dolls' main bugbear, is spot on this time. David's explanation is simple: 'We made the first record in six days but we spent like a month or something on this record. It was funny when we made the first album, because we didn't even know what we were doing. We were barely conscious. Like, "We've got to wrap this record up 'cos we've got to go to a gig in Long Island!"

'I would say it's a big, important record,' he says with a proud smile. 'I knew it when Syl sent me the demos of the riffs and stuff we made the songs out of. The other guys bought into it as well. The way it works is Syl gives me a bunch of stuff to see what I can get behind and concentrate on. Out of that batch there were so many tunes that I dug that I could write words to. I knew then that we had some really good stuff.

'When we were doing the record, I would come into the studio and go, "I know this song." It's like they were in the collective subconscious. It was really interesting to me how familiar they were. It's almost like I'd heard them on the radio or something. I think people have the impression that a band like us, they can tell from experience that, "Oh, they'll make some quick knockoff record so they can tour," or something. We actually sat down and made a real record.'

Talk inevitably turned to the media-led furore building around punk's 30th anniversary, in particular, the Dolls' old 'haberdasher' Malcolm McLaren and his group who, if history had taken a different course, would have included Sylvain. Although quite aware that McLaren used the Dolls as a dry run for his adventures with the Pistols, Johansen is philosophical. 'The fact that he came back and did this whole thing and we didn't . . . more power to him. That's the way rock'n'roll works, especially if you haven't got . . . it's hard to express . . . '

'Originality!' chimes in Syl.

'No, but that's true though,' adds David. 'Because what I'm talking about is really spontaneity. Most of the stuff that we do, it comes up and we just do it. It's not like we go [strokes chin], "What if we put on a dress?" It's not like a plan, it's just like, "Hey, this'll be a laugh, let's do this!" and it happens instantaneously. But then I think other people look for cues and grab ideas from people who are spontaneous. The majority of people are very self-conscious and don't really have that much spontaneity.

'That whole thing about boredom and "I'm so bored" and all that kind of stuff – I never really got that. I gotta feel sorry for people who had that. I've never really been bored. I mean, we were bored with what we were listening to.'

'That's why we formed the group!' declares Syl. 'Some people are great at creating, some people are great at marketing. That's all I have to say about that,' he adds.

'Usually by the time we're ready to market something we're on to something else,' David observes.

Whereas McLaren seemed to use the Pistols' all-boys-together rowdiness and penchant for making a mess in public to garner punk-horror headlines, Johansen sees the Dolls' behavioural slips as just a part of life.

'When things like that used to happen, like when somebody would throw up at the airport it wasn't like a publicity stunt. It was because they were sick [laughs]! I remember one time when we played in Newcastle. We were all sick, like fluey, let's put it that way. We were with Billy. Everybody said, "You guys have got to check the Newcastle Brown." We were like, "We'll drink anything, it doesn't matter what it does or what it is." And so, we start drinking this Newcastle Brown Ale. We're playing at some college and Billy threw up on his snare drum. 'Course he'd just eaten stuff which was, y'know, chunky. Every time he hits the drum, globs of it are flying. I don't really remember the pecking order, but Arthur got hit in the face and just spontaneously threw up. And then he did it again. Somebody else would get hit and they were puking and in the end the whole band was like puking. It wasn't like, "This is cool, do this," it was because we were sick. Then it became puking onstage is like the thing, which wasn't exactly the intention of the exercise!'

During the Dolls' short life, they were usually referred to as a glam or glitter band. Then punk rock came to town and they were credited with starting that.

'Somebody's always trying to make something out of something,' says David. 'Really, it's just bands playing music. When things become like movements and whatnot, then you're just setting yourself up for the club to come down on you. We were a rock'n'roll band. Somebody says you're a glam band. Who is gonna be the arbiter of what you do? Some punter says, "Oh well, that's brown." It's not brown, it's red. "Well, kind of brown." You know what I mean? Somebody says something and everybody goes, "Yeah, that's what it is." But really it's just rock'n'roll.'

'We were quite aware of how the business works and, as they say down South, y'all need to name it so you can sell it,' declares Syl. 'But we don't need it. To us, in the case of the New York Dolls, especially in my case, take away my lipstick and the frilly-loomed nylon tights and it's really the blues under there. It's three-chord progressions. Two, three-minute songs, maybe five minutes, whatever, they're catchy, they're smart and the lyrics . . . we do like intellect in our songs. It's not just, "One-two-three, let's go, and I wanna dance and party all night long." You've got to say something. It's gotta take you somewhere. I think, in our case, we have one step in the past and one step in the future.'

'This way you can totally avoid the present!' laughs David, with perfect timing, adding, 'What's the present? It's regret of the past and fear of the future.'

'But you gotta live it,' adds Syl. 'Right here and right now and not later. Don't forget what you did though.'

'That's why I forget everything and you remember everything,' concludes David, who then starts talking about Howlin' For Hubert, the occasional group he's started with Hubert Sumlin, Howlin' Wolf's legendary guitarist. 'Hubert is such an unbelievable guy, he's one of the inventors of rock'n'roll.'

While Syl visits the bathroom and I'm preparing to leave, David leans forward and talks about the man he described as 'the soul of the new York Dolls' in 1973. 'We really just picked up where we left off. I love that guy. When we were in the Dolls we were like roommates on the road. This guy is like my brother. I love this guy so much, y'know? When we were kids we were inseparable. We'd do everything together so it's really just kind of picking up where we left off, like you haven't seen your brother in ten years but then you see him.'

David and Sylvain don't want to talk about the new album in detail until I've heard it. To this end, I'm flown to New York City the following week. It's the first time I've been there since the initiation of the 'zero tolerance' cleanup campaign which has been going on since the late nineties. Whole neighbourhoods have changed and former no-go areas have been cleansed of the poor and unsightly. There are flower gardens on Avenue D. Andy Warhol's old haunt, the Dom, is a fast food joint. Rents are astronomical and, it has to be said, the electric energy that coursed through the city seems to have dulled. New cabs, new street lights and subway passes. Tourist-friendly sanitisation everywhere. 'It might look the same but look a bit closer and everything's different,' says my old friend Parker DuLany.

The original New York Dolls could never have been spawned here. There is still the odd homeless person trying to catch some sleep in a doorway, but the streets seem to have been swept clean of junkies, dealers and hookers. A hopeful stroll around the Dolls' old East Village-Lower East Side stamping ground yields few landmarks. The Mercer is a car park, Max's houses a gym complex and Chrystie Street is upmarket residencies which Syl says sell for around a million dollars. Only Gem Spa, the St Mark's Place candy store pictured on the back of the first album, survives, along with the soon-to-be-closed CBGB's.

The seamy underbelly which inspired David Johansen 30 years ago has been scrubbed clean. His inspiration for the complex lyrical adventures he calls 'screeds' has switched from the massage parlours and heroin dens of yore into the modern world, but with dutiful homage to the beat poets, bluesmen and soulsters who have peppered his work from the very start. 'What's that, "My pencil starts moving and I can't stop it?"' he explains.

Roadrunner Records' office on lower Broadway is more used to the kind of cranium-cracking heavy metal proffered by the likes of Slipknot and Soulfly, but there is a tangible buzz about the Dolls album, which is still being tweaked in the studio. A&R man David Bason, who joined the company from RCA four years ago to run publishing, was responsible for signing the Dolls. 'I'm not a metal guy,' he stresses, describing how he's been brought in to broaden the label's horizons.

Bason is clutching a work-in-progress CD of album tracks and b-sides. He looks like the cat that got the cream. 'These guys have still got it,' he declares. And he's right too. The new Dolls album is a rip-roaring *tour de force*. After the chaos and unfulfilled potential of the two studio LPs recorded in 1973-4, Johansen and Sylvain have finally cracked it. Jack Douglas's production is spot-on, bringing out the dynamics on a bunch of songs which live, breathe and banish nostalgia to the sidelines.

Johansen's brilliant lyrics and Sylvain's feel for sixties girl-pop rock'n'roll imbued the group with raw panache – both out front and in its very heart. This is still so, but with an added maturity and sensitivity drawn in equal parts from bitter experience and their unique mutual rapport. It's a bonus that the two survivors now find their Technicolor talents augmented by sympathetic new recruits, who retain the Dolls spirit without attempting to ape the irreplaceable trio of Kane, Thunders and Nolan. Most importantly, the new songs are fantastic. 'Syl's just a hook machine,' enthuses David Bason. 'He just can't stop turning them out.'

Sylvain and Johansen turn up. The former arrives in head-to-toe black, while Johansen sports tight faded denim, motorcycle boots and long brown fur-collared coat. These guys know how to accessorise and could walk onto any stage just as they are. The gags start immediately. Nowadays, laughter is the Dolls' drug of choice, with frequent danger of overdose. 'It's the best thing for you, mentally,' says Syl later. 'Sometimes we're like two grumpy old women. We can get like that too. Then we get started.'

The duo decide they want to hear their album for the first time outside the studio. The boardroom is commandeered. Sylvain brings his wine, while David sets up his tea and muffins. The music starts blasting out of the huge speakers. David alternates between listening intently with his feet on the table and gyrating around the room. To the horror of the office, he lights the first of a steady chain of Camels, using the teapot as an ashtray. In post-millennial New York, such behaviour is considered worse than shooting up. 'We all have our addictions,' smiles David.

Sylvain can barely conceal his joy at the primal Dolls rock'n'roll coursing through the room, conducting and pointing at highlights. The rockers are pungent and brazen but suffused with killer dynamics. Sylvain's incandescent backing vocals shine soaringly on his 'Dance Like A Monkey' – which tackles the evolution of man, while recalling 'Stranded In The Jungle' in the ape-call intro and Bo Diddley tribal drums. The killer guitar solo is Syl too.

Sam Yaffa co-wrote the music on the widescreen 'We're All In Love', whose mood evokes the epic soundscape of 'Frankenstein' while the chorus recalls mid-period Alice Cooper. David dashes out the striking lead melody on harmonica. Good line: 'the light shines in the darkness, where else could it shine?'

'Gimme Love And Turn On The Light' bangs together UK R&B and Detroit high-energy with rampant harmonica. Here, Johansen manages to rhyme 'fight' with 'troglodyte', concluding, 'Our shortcomings may be human after all.' While it's playing, he leans over and points out, 'I'm a uniter not a divider.'

'Fishnets And Cigarettes' contains another classic slice of blues-infused Johansen imagery: 'I was listening to a blues song and smoking like a mental patient.'

Syl and Steve's 'Runnin' Around' recalls the twelve bar good-time blues *a la* Mott the Hoople. 'Who cares what the neighbours say, they're gonna talk about us anyway,' caterwauls Johansen over a raunchy bar-room piano vamp. The lyrics are not so much straightforward rock'n'roll though, and slip in a reference to Esmeralda and the hunchback of Notre Dame before concluding, 'I love you baby, you're so warped.'

The Dolls' timeless fixation with the sixties girl groups surfaces on the uplifting, melodic 'Plenty Of Music' and its Spector-style castanet canter. The melody recalls Spector's 'I Can Hear Music', while the words deal with music being the answer in a world Johansen likens to 'an ashtray'. 'Loving tributes. That's what I like to call them,' explains David.

'Rainbow Store' concerns a teenage girls' budget clothing chain while 'Beauty School' takes a trip to the 'exquisite agony' of cosmetics training, but ultimately hasn't made the album. (Maybe a B-side?) These are the two most quintessentially 'classic Dolls' trash anthems. The former cheekily revisits the Shangri-Las' 'Give Him A Great Big Kiss', while the latter camps it up with a surf chorus, Eddie Cochran bass and lines about having a 'brain shampoo at Beauty School'.

Johansen reaches back into his Staten Island adolescence on the balls-out 'Gotta Get Away From Tommy', which concerns a weird childhood friend. Two minutes twenty seconds of raw power-surge with big chords reminiscent of The Clash's *Give 'Em Enough Rope*. 'Punishing World' belts and shouts like 'Puss 'N' Boots'. Steve Conte's composition demonstrates that the new recruits are perfectly adept at slipping into the Dolls' style of rock'n'roll.

The absence of cover versions is due to the re-born Dolls' ability to generate new material which, after the initial creative supernova of '72-'73, quickly dried up. There are also some distinguished guests. Michael Stipe joins the chorus of 'Dancing On The Edge Of A Volcano', because he struck up his friendship with REM guitarist Peter Buck after selling him a New York Dolls album in the Atlanta record shop where he worked. (Sylvain: 'That's a beautiful thing. Now that we didn't make any money in the Dolls, we spawned people that made gazillions and gazillions.') Iggy Pop is simply another old soldier. Bo Diddley makes a sumptuous cameo on the steamy voodoo shimmy of 'Seventeen', which the group want to be a hidden track on the CD. Diddley had been playing at the city's B. B. King's club and didn't mind supplying liquid 'Superfly' wah-wah over the most out-there track on the album.

The biggest but most poignant departure from the good-time template comes with two impassioned soul ballads. Syl's 'Maimed Happiness' thrusts Johansen's upfront vocals against a piano-dominated backdrop which recalls the Bad Seeds at their most elegiac. As the track climbs to its strings 'n' sax driven vertex, the emotion wells like a Tom Waits tearjerker. It's the Dolls reflecting on the past, and it's the most tender they've ever been.

'I Ain't Got Nothing' is Johansen in the gutter, with only Jack Douglas's out-of-tune saloon bar piano and mournful harmonica to keep him warm. 'Good times and all the fun that I had/Seems so odd, it makes me wonder if there is a god.' He concludes, 'the party's over, I'm all alone.'

Maybe the most typically Johansen *a la* Harry Smiths tune is the arcane country blues 'He Won't Marry Me'. That elusive hit single could even be nestling in the yearning, heart-soaring 'Take A Good Look At My Good Looks, Baby'. The girl is walking out the door with the payoff, 'close your eyes, take a picture in your mind, I'll be gone.' It's classic Brill Building girl-group melancholy with luxurious backing vocals and a swelling, soaring climax. It's always a good sign if a song embeds itself instantly; this one, like several other tracks, sticks after two plays.

Both Dolls seem delighted and exhilarated at hearing the fruits of their past weeks' labours in near-complete form. 'Compared to that shit they put out these days, that record wasn't so bad after all,' decides David.

'I think they're gonna be surprised right now in 2006,' adds Sylvain. 'It's really up to the public though.' Both are painfully aware how things can go wrong. In 1973, the New York Dolls were tipped for the highest peaks. The rest was history, but for all the wrong reasons. Certainly it had nothing to do with sales.

'The public?' roars Johansen. 'Well I have an uncle who's in the railroad business and he could buy a million tomorrow!' Then he reflects. 'At this stage of the game we're good, y'know? Every time you make a record you think, "Ah great! This is the one!" Put it out and people are like, "Pee-ooh." But we together and decided to do this. We made the best record we could possibly make, or close to it. And then it's not really up to us any more what happens. We've done our work, is what I'm saying.'

That point is brought home by a DVD I coincidentally picked up on St Mark's Place: *You Can't Put Your Arms Around A Memory* was filmed at a one-off reunion gig by Johnny Thunders, Arthur Kane and Jerry Nolan in Los Angeles in 1987. It was the last time these three would play together, but years of excess has dissipated their muscle, especially the mighty Jerry, who struggles while Johnny does his patent strung-out solo cruise, Arthur skulks in the background and 'Personality Crisis' is the only track they try off of the Dolls' albums. Although historic and interesting, it is ultimately quite sad, which makes David and Sylvain's on-the-money revitalisation nearly twenty years later all the more remarkable. But then, on the Richter scale of excess, they were always the sensible ones.

Right now, the album still doesn't have a title. Sylvain is considering *Brain Shampoo*. Both agree that *27th Street* might be suitable as that's where the album was rehearsed and recorded. 'We had a lot of fun making this record,' says Johansen.

'We had a couple of cute little apartments where we recorded it. That shed was really nice with those arched ceilings. The whole record was made on 27th Street. We rehearsed on West 27th street, then we went over to East 27th Street and did tracks, and then we came back to another place on West 27th street. Hey, we could call the record *27th Street*!

'It was purely coincidental but everything was on 27th Street. The street doesn't really have a lot to say for itself, but now you can see that there's actually a cosmic significance. 27th Street may actually be the centre of the universe. It's possible! We used to think it was in front of the Hotel Diplomat, but it may have shifted. The universe is expanding somewhere. It's expanding as we speak.' But David is hellbent on *One Day It Will Please Us To Remember Even This*, after he scribbles the title in my notebook.

His mention of the place where the Dolls played their earliest gigs triggers Johansen into a lengthy stream-of-consciousness rant, delivered like Staten Island's answer to Captain Beefheart. He struts around like he's onstage, gets on the table and continues to light up Camels. When a police siren is heard outside, Syl cracks, 'They're coming to get ya, David.'

He's off. 'Do you remember the best thing about the Hotel Diplomat was the Christmas Bar? That's what made me feel that we were at the centre of the universe. I remember one time when we were playing at the Diplomat, I think I had a couple of hits of LSD in my system, but I went down to the Christmas Bar, had a couple of pops, sung a few carols. That put me in a nice mood and I went out on to 43rd and Sixth and I was just standing there and I had this overwhelming feeling that I was in the centre of the universe. You could feel it. That was it temporarily. When I left it was still the centre of the universe, but I was no longer in it.

'But I was caught and drawn back to the Christmas Bar. Every day was Christmas at the Christmas Bar. Bing Crosby was Number One every day. All the drunks thought it was Christmas every day! It could be the middle of July but you'd go in there and say, "Happy Christmas everybody," and they'd go "Happy Christmas! Ya cocksuckers!"'

There's no stopping him now. David Johansen doesn't just idly reminisce. He savours his tales, draws the rich sap of times past from every line and acts them out with extravagant gestures. The strongest thing he's drunk for years is tea, but he's quickly on to the subject of Times Square's old bars, to make a point about the castration of Manhattan.

'Do you remember Grant's on 42nd Street between Seventh and Eighth? It was like a supermarket, it was so bright, with fluorescent lights. There were bars on each side and there would be a thousand people in there, everybody getting drunk. Everybody was like cashing their cheques and all the guys from *The [New York] Times* drank there, all the cops drank there, all the pimps drank there, all the hookers drank there. It was the grandest mixture of people, the most vivacious and lively, life-loving people that could ever be within one place. And we would shoot down those 30 cent Wilsons and life was grand. Life was grand! Not that life isn't grand today, but at that moment it was! Grant's . . . what a bar. On a Friday night a thousand people would be in there, carrying on. It was so great. That big sign saying Grant's in neon lights. It was gigantic. Like half a block.'

Then comes the punchline. 'Now look at Times Square, it's like Disneyland!'

'The one thing about David is how fucking funny he is,' says Syl later. 'As you saw, when we start cutting up we can have such a good time. I missed that through the years when we didn't work together. I lost my best friend and my funniest friend. There's more than just music between me and him. It's much more than that.

'I'm so fucking happy. That's all we really want to do, make something that's important. I don't want to be forgotten or just remembered as that old band that didn't make it. If we did anything wrong now, we made a rock'n'roll album. Something that's timeless. Who makes that today?'

That question lingers, especially after I bid farewell to a subway-hopping Johansen and CBGB's-bound Sylvain. 'Arthur was one in a million,' David calls back, suddenly stripped of all his bambast, 'the *only* one.' There's a queue outside Webster Hall, where carefully-marketed balladeer James Blunt will be performing to gaggles of immaculately groomed young professionals and excited secretaries. A depressing contrast to the brash, mutoid gaggle who would greet the Dolls around the corner at Max's in 1972.

The New York Dolls could never have been spawned in today's New York City, but they can certainly be reborn there. On 28 March 2006, they announced their return at CBGB's – the club McLaren wouldn't let them play. The place was packed with a mixture of current scenesters and original faces like Deborah Harry and Bob Gruen. The Dolls played the classics and around six new songs. Nobody was left in any doubt that the real lords of misrule are back. And they mean business.

Discography

Singles
Trash/Personality Crisis (Mercury 43414)
Jet Boy/Vietnamese Baby (Mercury 6052
402, 1973)
Stranded In The Jungle/Who Are The
Mystery Girls? (Mercury 73478 2-51259,
1974)

Studio Albums
New York Dolls (Mercury SRM 1-675, 1973)
Personality Crisis/Looking For A
Kiss/Vietnamese Baby/Lonely Planet
Boy/Frankenstein/Trash/Bad Girl/Subway
Train/Pills/Private World/Jet Boy

Too Much Too Soon (Mercury SRM 1-
1001, 1974)
Babylon/Stranded In The Jungle/Who
Are The Mystery Girls?/(There's Gonna
Be A Showdown)/It's Too Late/Puss 'N'
Boots/Chatterbox/Bad Detective/Don't
Start Me Talking/Human Being

*One Day It Will Please Us To Remember
Even This* (Roadrunner, 2006)
We're All In Love/Runnin' Around/Plenty
Of Music/Dance Like A Monkey/Punishing
World/Maimed Happiness/Fishnets &
Cigarettes/Gotta Get Away From Tommy/
Dancing On The Lip Of A Volcano/I Ain't
Got Nothin'/Rainbow Store/Gimme Love
And Turn On The Light/Take A Good Look
At My Good Looks/Seventeen (hidden track)

Live Albums
Red Patent Leather (Fan Club FC007/
NR340, 1984)
Red Patent Leather/On Fire/Something
Else/Daddy Rolling Stone/Girls Girls
Girls/Ain't Got No Home/Dizzy Miss
Lizzy/Down Down Downtown/Pirate
Love/Pills/Teenage News/Personality
Crisis/Looking For A Kiss

*Morrissey Presents: Return Of The New
York Dolls Live From Royal Festival
Hall* (Attack ATKCD009, 2004)
Looking For A Kiss/Puss 'N'
Boots/Subway Train/Bad Girl/Lonely
Planet Boy/Private World/Vietnamese
Baby/Frankenstein/Babylon/Trash/Jet
Boy/Personality Crisis/Human Being

Demos
Actress – Birth Of The New York Dolls
(PIDM 598392, 2000)
That's Poison/I Am Confronted/It's Too
Late/Oh, Dot/I'm A Boy, I'm A
Girl/Coconut Grove/Take Me To Your
Party/Oh, Dot (take 2)/It's Too Late
(take 2)/We Have Been Through This
Before/Why Am I Alone

THE HEARTBREAKERS
Singles
Chinese Rocks/Born To Lose (Track
2094-135, 1977)
One Track Mind/Can't Keep My Eyes Off
You/Do You Love Me (Track 2094-137, 1977)
It's Not Enough/Let Go (Track 2094-142, 1978)
All By Myself (live)/Milk Me (live) (Max's
Kansas City CTK 213-45, 1979)
Get Off The Phone (live)/I Wanna Be
Loved (live) (Beggars Banquet BEG21, 1979)

Studio Albums
LAMF (Track 2409 218, 1977)
Born To Lose/Baby Talk/All By Myself/I
Wanna Be Loved/It's Not
Enough/Chinese Rocks/Get Off The
Phone/Pirate Love/One Track Mind/I
Love You/Goin' Steady/Let Go

JOHNNY THUNDERS
Singles
Dead Or Alive/Downtown (Real ARE1, 1978)
You Can't Put Your Arms Around A

Memory/Hurtin' (Real ARE3, 1978)
In Cold Blood/In Cold Blood (live)
(New Rose NEW 14, 1983)
Hurt Me/It's Not Enough/Like A Rolling
Stone (New Rose NEW 27, 1984)
Crawfish/Tie Me Up (Jungle JUNG23,
1985)*
Que Sera Sera/Short Lives (Jungle
JUNG33, 1987)
She Wants To Mambo/Uptown/Love Is
Strange (Jungle JUNG 38, 1988)*
Born To Cry/Teach Her Right (Jungle
JUNG 43, 1988)*
    * with Patti Palladin

Studio Albums
So Alone (Real RAL1, 1978)
Diary Of A Lover (Jem PVC5907, 1983)
Hurt Me (New Rose ROSE26, 1983)
Que Sera Sera (Jungle FREUD9, 1985)
Copy Cats (Jungle FREUD20, 1988) with
Patti Palladin

DAVID JOHANSEN
Singles
Funky But Chic/The Rope (The Leg Go
Song) (Blue Sky BS 6663, 1978)
Melody/Reckless Crazy (Blue Sky
BS7827)
Swaheto Woman/She Knew She Was
Falling In Love (Blue Sky BS 8125, 1979)

Studio Albums
David Johansen (Blue Sky
JZ34926,1978)
In Style (Blue Sky JZ 36802, 1979)
Here Comes The Night (Blue Sky
FZ36589, 1981)
Sweet Revenge (Passport PB6043, 1984)
David Johansen & The Harry Smiths
(Chesky JD196, 2000)
Shaker (Chesky JD236, 2002)

Albums as Buster Poindexter
Buster Poindexter (RCA R32P-1146,
1987)
Buster Goes Berserk (RCA 9665-2-R,
1989)
Buster's Happy Hour (Rhino/WEA
71680, 1994)
Buster's Spanish Rocketship (Polygram
524414, 1997)

SYLVAIN SYLVAIN
Singles
The Kids Are Back/The Cops Are
Coming (Sing Sing S1001, 1978)*
Every Boy And Every Girl/Deeper And
Deeper (RC, 1980)
Out With The Wrong Woman/A Little
Pussy (Sing Sing SSS501, 1983)
    * as The Criminals

Albums
Sylvain Sylvain (RCA AFL1-3475, 1979)
Syl Sylvain & The Teardrops (RCA AFL1-
3913, 1981)
Sleep Baby Doll (Fishead FCD 02142, 1998)

ARTHUR KANE
Singles
Mr Cool/Don't Need You/Longhaired
Woman (Whiplash EP200, 1977)
You/Girl That I Love (Ork NYC2, 1979)*
    * as The Idols with Jerry Nolan

JERRY NOLAN
Singles
Take A Chance With Me/Pretty Baby
(Tandan TAN SIN 006, 1982)

RICK RIVETS
Singles
Keep Doin' (What You're Doin')/If You
Can't Rock (You Can Roll) (Whiplash 45-
100, 1976)*
Be A Man/Quaalude Queen (Whiplash
45-101, 1977)*
Rites 4, Whites/Mental Moron (Whiplash
45-102, 1979)**
Problem Child/Suspicion (Whiplash 45-
104, 1979)***
I'm In Love With You (Again)/Never
Should Have Told You (Whiplash 45-
105, 1980)***
    * as The Brats
    ** as The Slugs
    *** as The Corpse Grinders

Studio Albums
Legend Of The Corpse Grinders (Fan
Club FC004, 1983)
Valley Of Fear (New Rose ROSE 39, 1984)

Bibliography/Credits

The following books have proven useful in the writing of Trash!: Adams, Peter The Bowery Bhoys: Street Corner Radicals and the Politics of Rebellion (Praeger, 2005); Antonia, Nina Too Much Too Soon (Omnibus, 1988); Antonia, Nina Johnny Thunders – In Cold Blood (Cherry Red Books, 2000); Asbury, Herbert The Gangs of New York: An Informal History of the Underworld (Thunder's Mouth, 2001); Bangs, Lester Blondie (Omnibus, 1979); Bangs, Lester Psychotic Reactions and Carburetor Dung (Serpent's Tail, 2001); Bangs, Lester Mainlines, Blood Feasts and Bad Taste: A Lester Bangs Reader (Serpent's Tail, 2003); Bromberg, Craig The Wicked Ways of Malcolm McLaren (Harper Collins, 1989); Colegrave, Stephan and Sullivan, Chris Punk (Cassell, 2001); Gibbs, Alvin Neighbourhood Threat – On Tour with Iggy Pop (Britannia 1995); Gilbert, Pat Passion Is a Fashion (Aurum, 2004); Gimarc, George Punk Diary: The Ultimate Trainspotter's Guide to Underground Rock 1970-82 (Backbeat UK, 2005); Harry, Deborah, Stein, Chris and Bockris, Victor Making Tracks: The Rise of Blondie (Elm Tree Books, 1982); Haylin, Clinton From The Velvets to the Voidoids – A Pre-Punk History for the Post-Punk World (Penguin, 1993); Hell, Richard Hot and Cold (Powerhouse, 2001); Hirshey, Gerri Nowhere to Run: The Story of Soul Music (Pan, 1984); Kent, Nick The Dark Stuff: Selected Writings on Rock Music 1972-1995 (Da Capo Press, 1995); Lydon, John Rotten – No Irish No Blacks No Dogs (Plexus, 2003); Marcus, Greil In the Fascist Bathroom: Punk in Pop Music, 1977-92 (Penguin, 1994); McNeil, Legs and McCain, Gillian Please Kill Me: The Uncensored Oral History of Punk (Penguin, 1997) Morley, Paul 77: A Story of Punk (Hodder & Stoughton, 1997); Pop, Iggy and Wehrer, Anne I Need More: The Stooges and Other Stories (2.13.61., 1997); Porter, Dick Ramones – The Complete Twisted History (Plexus, 2003); Price, Richard The Wanderers (Chatto & Windus, 1974); Pye, Michael Maximum City: The Biography of New York (Picador, 1993); Ramone, Dee Dee Chelsea Horror Hotel (Thunder's Mouth Press, 2000); Ramone, Dee Dee and Kaufman, Veronica Lobotomy – Surviving the Ramones (Thunder's Mouth Press, 2000); Savage, Jon England's Dreaming: The Sex Pistols and Punk Rock (Saint Martin's Press, 1992); Spungen, Deborah And I Don't Want to Live This Life (Fawcett Books, 1994); Vale, V. (editor) Search & Destroy: Authoritative Guide to Punk Culture Vols. 1 & 2 V/Search Publications, 1997); Valentine, Gary New York Rocker – My Life in the Blank Generation, with Blondie, Iggy Pop, and Others 1975-81 (Sidgwick & Jackson, 2002).

A number of magazines and music papers were consulted during the writing of this book. These include: Circus, Creem, Disc & Music Echo, Interview, Melody Maker, Mojo, More On, New Musical Express, Sounds, New York Rocker, Punk, Q, Record Mirror, Rolling Stone, Uncut, and Zigzag.

We would like to thank the following picture agencies and individuals for providing photographs: Leee Black Childers; P.Felix/ Stringer/Getty Images; Chris Ridpath for Michael Geary's photographs of the Dolls at the Mercer Arts Centre; Gems /Redferns; Golly; G.Hankeroot/Sunshine/Retna; Dennis Recla; Michael Ochs Archive /Redferns; Ian Dickson/Redferns; Alain Dister /Redferns; Mick Hutson/Redferns; Dave Hogan/Getty Images.

There are many websites devoted to the Dolls that provide excellent information on the band and their members, chief among these is Chris Ridpath's excellent Johnny Thunders Cyber Lounge at www.thunders.ca. The LAMF – A Tribute To Johnny Thunders site at www.bunbun.ne.jp is an invaluable source of facts and figures. Other useful and interesting sites include; www.newyorkdollsonline.com, www.rickrivets.com, www.new-york-dolls.com and www.thecontes.com.